PC Hardware and A+ Handbook Obj

W9-CQZ-392

A+ Core Hardware Objectives 2003

Domain 1 - Installation, Configuration, and Upgrading	
Identify the names, purpose, and characteristics of system modules. Recognize these modules by sight or definition.	4, 5
Identify basic procedures for adding and removing field replaceable modules for desktop systems.	6-15, 17-20, 23
Identify basic procedures for adding and removing field replaceable modules for portable systems.	22
Identify typical IRQs, DMAs, and I/O addresses and procedures for altering these settings when installing and configuring devices.	2, 4, 12, 14, 16, 20
Identify the names, purposes, and performance characteristics of standardized/common peripheral ports, associated cabling, and their connectors. Recognize ports, cabling, and connectors by sight.	4, 9
Identify proper procedures for installing and configuring common IDE devices.	15, 16, 23
Identify proper procedures for installing and configuring common SCSI devices.	15, 16, 23
Identify proper procedures for installing and configuring common peripheral devices.	9-13, 15, 18-23
Identify procedures to optimize PC operations in specific situations	7, 8, 9, 13-17, 23
Determine the issues that must be considered when upgrading a PC.	5-13, 15-19, 21, 22

Domain 2 - Diagnosing and Troubleshooting	
Recognize common problems associated with each module and their symptoms. Identify steps to isolate and troubleshoot the problems.	5, 6, 7, 8, 9, 10, 11, 12, 14-16, 18, 19, 21, 22
Identify basic troubleshooting procedures and tools and how to elicit problem symptoms from customers.	3, 17

Domain 3 - Preventive Maintenance, Safety, and Environmental Issues	
Identify the various types of preventive maintenance measures, products, and procedures, and when/how to use them.	5-9, 12, 14-22
Identify various safety measures and procedures, and when/how to use them.	3
Identify environmental protection measures and procedures, and when/how to use them.	1

Domain 4 - Motherboards, Processors, and Memory	
Distinguish between the popular CPU chips in terms of their basic characteristics.	6
Identify the types for RAM, form factors, and operational characteristics.	7, 22
Identify the most popular types of motherboards, their components, and their architecture (bus structures).	4, 5, 6, 22
Identify the purpose of CMOS memory, what it contains, and how/when to change its parameters.	5*

Domain 5 - Printers	
Identify printer technologies, interfaces, and options/upgrades.	4
Recognize common printer problems and techniques used to resolve them.	21

Domain 6 - Basic Networking	
Identify the common types of network cables, their characteristics, and connectors.	8*
Identify basic networking concepts including how a network works.	12, 18
Identify common technologies available for establishing Internet connectivity and their characteristics.	6

* Additional information about both hardware and operating system related subjects, including CMOS, network cables, commands, and installation can be accessed at http://www.kchase.com/aplus.htm.

Microsoft

A+ Operating System Technologies Objectives 2003   Chapters

Domain 1 - OS Fundamentals

Identify the major desktop components and interfaces and their functions. Differentiate the characteristics of Windows 98/Me, Windows NT 4.0 Workstation, Windows 2000 Professional, and Windows XP.	2
Identify the names, locations, purposes, and contents of major system files.	2
Demonstrate the ability to use command-line functions and utilities to manage the operating system, including the proper syntax and switches.	3, 14*
Identify basic concepts and procedures for creating, viewing, and managing disks, directories, and files.	14*
Identify the major OS utilities, their purpose, location, and available switches.	3, 14

Domain 2 - Installation, Configuration, and Upgrading

Identify the procedures for installing Windows 98/Me, Windows NT 4.0 Workstation, Windows 2000 Professional, and Windows XP, and bringing the OS to a basic operational level.	2*
Identify the steps to perform an OS upgrade from Windows 98/Me, Windows NT 4.0 Workstation, Windows 2000 Professional, and Windows XP.	2
Identify the basic system boot sequences and boot methods, including the steps to create an emergency boot disk with utilities installed for Windows 98/Me, Windows NT 4.0 Workstation, Windows 2000 Professional, and Windows XP.	2, 3
Identify procedures for installing/adding a device, including loading, adding, and configuring device drivers, and required software.	7, 9, 12-22
Identify procedures necessary to optimize the OS and major OS subsystems.	2, 3

Domain 3 - Diagnosing and Troubleshooting

Recognize and interpret the meaning of common error codes and startup messages from the boot sequence, and identify steps to correct the problems.	2, 3, 18*
Recognize when to use common diagnostic utilities and tools.	8
Recognize common operational and usability problems and determine how to resolve them.	2, 7, 9, 14-18, 20-22

Domain 4 - Networks

Identify the networking capabilities of Windows.	12*
Identify the basic Internet protocols and terminologies. Identify procedures for establishing Internet connectivity.	12*

* Additional information about both hardware and operating system related subjects, including CMOS, network cables, commands, and installation can be accessed at http://www.kchase.com/aplus.htm.

Microsoft®

PC Hardware and A+ Handbook

Kate J. Chase

PUBLISHED BY
Microsoft Press
A Division of Microsoft Corporation
One Microsoft Way
Redmond, Washington 98052-6399

Library of Congress Cataloging-in-Publication Data
PC Hardware and A+ Handbook / Kate J. Chase.
        p. cm.
    Includes index.
    ISBN 0-7356-2049-0
    1. Electronic data processing personnel--Certification.   2. Computer technicians--Certification--Study guides.   3. Programming languages (Electronic computers)--Examinations--Study guides.   4. Operating systems (Computers)   5. IBM Personal Computer.   I. Title.

    QA76.3.C427   2004
    004'.076--dc22   2004049953

Printed and bound in the United States of America.

1 2 3 4 5 6 7 8 9   QWT   9 8 7 6 5 4

Distributed in Canada by H.B. Fenn and Company Ltd.

A CIP catalogue record for this book is available from the British Library.

Microsoft Press books are available through booksellers and distributors worldwide. For further information about international editions, contact your local Microsoft Corporation office or contact Microsoft Press International directly at fax (425) 936-7329. Visit our Web site at www.microsoft.com/learning/. Send comments to *mspinput@microsoft.com*.

Acquisitions Editor: Andy Ruth
Project Editor: Valerie Woolley
Technical Editor: James Robertson
Development Editor: Maureen Zimmerman
Production Services: nSight, Inc.

Body Part No. X10-53127

This book is dedicated to my late parents,
as well as to all of those who
ask questions and try
to learn more.

Table of Contents

Part II   Internal Essentials

What do you think of this book?
We want to hear from you!

Microsoft is interested in hearing your feedback about this publication so we can continually improve our books and learning resources for you. To partcipate in a brief online survey, please visit: *www.microsoft.com/learning/booksurvey/*

Acknowledgments

In some respects, this book was born a few years ago, but it breathed real life when Microsoft Press came to me with the idea of reprising an earlier project we had worked on together. The time was both right and ripe. Too many books of this nature exist that are either rather vague in presentation or go into so much detail it's difficult to sort out current specifications from those of 20 years ago.

Now, some authors really sweat the editorial process during which their great works are turned over into the hands of editors. That certainly was not the case with this book.

While I've had the honor to work with a number of talented editorial teams over the years, I couldn't ask for a better crew than I was gifted with by Microsoft Press, starting with product planner Kathy Harding. With initial assistance offered by developmental editor Maureen Zimmerman, project editor Valerie Woolley was exceptional at coordinating the efforts of a number of different people in a tight time-frame, and her encouragement and professionalism made this book a joy. I have nothing but praise for project manager Sue McClung, of nSight Publishing Services, and copyeditor Roger LeBlanc, who handled my tortured sentences with aplomb and skill, while technical editor Jim Robertson contributed so many strong suggestions drawn from his breadth of expertise. I've rarely had the pleasure of working with a team that was so knowledgeable about the material being presented, and it shows in the final product.

Also, I sincerely wish to thank Jane Holcombe, a talented woman and technical author who served as the peer reviewer of this text. I came to know Jane before on some earlier collaborative works, and was delighted when she joined this project. Jane brings a very practical and helpful approach to everything she does and this book is better for her assistance.

My appreciation goes to my family as well. Their support is always most needed when I work on any major project. My significant other—who helped me learn much of what I know—makes certain large doses of caffeine are always at hand, while my dog is ever at the ready to provide me with an exercise break.

My agent, David Fugate of Waterside Productions, was instrumental in seeing the project through. Thanks, David!

Finally, believe it or not, much of this book was started while I was an ICU patient at a central Vermont hospital hooked up to an incredible number of wires and tubes, so credit goes also to the men and women, including Dr. Mark Yorra, who helped me recover from a nasty respiratory illness. They were kind enough to realize that I don't go anywhere—including a bed in the ICU—without my laptop and an available Internet connection. I suspect I need to get a TabletPC, however, if I get ill again; the ergonomics just work better.

Introduction

Don't let anyone tell you that the personal computer is dead. It's not, and the platform on which it is based is not likely to disappear anytime soon. This means many things; in particular, it means that talented people will be needed to keep these systems operational.

In fact, with the increasing convergence of consumer electronics and the personal computer, you can expect to see more technology that works across both platforms. Today's digital camcorders connect easily to many PC video adapters, for example, and home or portable audio units often feature a universal serial bus (USB) port and cable to allow you to transfer popular MP3 audio files from your PC to your audio setup. Remember, too, that Internet-ready refrigerators have actually been on the market for a few years now. While this type of convergence still seems a bit odd to us, homes are rapidly becoming far more computerized, just as our cars are. For example, did you know that most modern-day cars actually ship with a basic input/output system (BIOS) similar to that of a PC motherboard?

Whether you've opened this book to study for a certification exam or to otherwise expand your available knowledge about today's Microsoft Windows–based PC technology, this book was crafted to give you the essential information you need to know for working with the PCs of today. Consider it a book written by one no-nonsense professional for others.

This book also largely draws on my experience working with tens, if not hundreds, of thousands of customers seeking help with hardware and operating-system issues through the technical support online communities I've managed on America Online and MSN. This experience is coupled with the knowledge gleaned from the time I've spent talking with customer-support professionals, IT administrators, and students training in various fields of technology about what good technicians most need to know to work effectively. Added to my expertise is the body of knowledge brought to this project by the gifted support team who helped review and prepare this book for publication.

Where possible, we've tried to correct the model used by many other extensive PC hardware books that dig too deeply into PC history. Most of the PCs in service today around the world were built within the last few years, so spending exhaustive amounts of time on technology from 1990 and before isn't smart. However, you can expect to see some older systems around—some people are as reticent to give up their 486-class PC as they are to relinquish that classic 1972 VW Beetle.

In working with this book, you will see that each chapter includes a lab for hands-on practice. Each lab has its own specific recommendations. For example, I typically recommend that you have a recent-vintage computer available to work with, preferably one using a current version of Windows (Windows XP, for example). Where possible, this should not be the system you depend on to do your work. If you have only one system, however, make sure you perform full backups of the entire system before you do the labs so that you reduce your risk of losing data should a problem arise.

Different chapters focus on specific issues or components. Chapter 1, "Computer Evolution," gives you an overview of how we got to where we are today in PC technology, while Chapter 2, "The Operating System's Role in Hardware," zeroes in on the connection and interdependencies between your operating system and your hardware.

In Chapter 3, "Defining Your Tech Toolkit," the requirements for a highly useful PC repair kit are spelled out for you. Read this material carefully and assemble your kit wisely. It's important, too, that you keep this kit easily accessible and in good shape. The last thing you want in an emergency is to lose precious time looking for a disk or other needed object. Chapter 4, "The Workings and Connections of the PC," gives you an architectural-level overview of the PC and its inner workings and connections.

From there, each chapter focuses on a major component or subsystem, as follows:

- Motherboards in Chapter 5

- Central processor units (CPUs) in Chapter 6

- Memory in Chapter 7

- Power supplies and cooling in Chapter 8

- Video in Chapter 9

- Audio in Chapter 10

- Modems, both analog and broadband, in Chapter 11

- Network cards and networking hardware in Chapter 12

- Small Computer System Interface (SCSI), high speed Advanced Technology Attachment (ATA), and other controllers in Chapter 13

- Drive interfaces and hard drives in Chapter 14

- CD and DVD drives in Chapter 15

- Floppies, removable, and backup drives in Chapter 16

- Monitors in Chapter 17

- Going wireless in Chapter 18

- Audio externals in Chapter 19

- Input devices and gaming hardware in Chapter 20

- Printers in Chapter 21

- Laptop and mobile hardware in Chapter 22

All this leads up to Chapter 23, "Building Your PC," where you learn how to build a computer from the empty case up through final connections.

Also, please follow the precautions offered throughout the book. For example, removing power from the PC and grounding yourself before you touch the components within a PC case is not just a smart idea—it's the only safe way to handle PC troubleshooting and upgrades. Far too much damage to both PC equipment and the humans handling that equipment occurs because such precautions are not followed.

Finally, before we begin, let me say congratulations to you on your decision to learn more about the very hardware that helps us be so productive. Once you remove some of the mystery and begin to appreciate the details, you will become a far better PC-and-peripheral shopper; you will be far more able to make intelligent decisions about what you add and how you can configure it for best results; and you'll likely shave considerable time off the tasks that make up diagnosing and resolving a problem on a system.

> **Note** Additional information about both hardware-related and operating system–related subjects, including complementary metal-oxide semiconductor (CMOS), network cables, commands, and installation, can be accessed at *http://www.kchase.com/aplus.htm.*

Part I

PC Need to Know

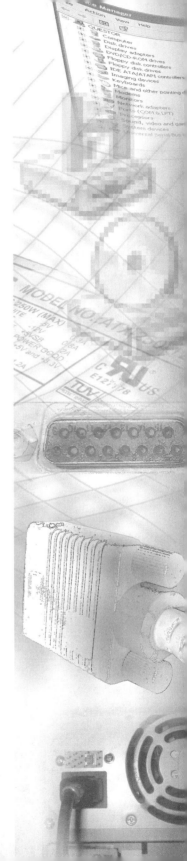

1

Computer Evolution

Why devote an entire comprehensive handbook to a machine that some say isn't long for this electronic world? Contrary to opinions stated far and wide for the last few years, the desktop personal computer, or PC, isn't dead yet. It probably won't be for some time to come. Gartner DataQuest, a technology research company based in Stamford, Connecticut, has estimated that PC unit shipments are forecast to grow 11.4 percent in 2004. Although that's considerably lower than the more than 20 percent growth the industry experienced each year for several years from about 1985 until the late 1990s, those numbers hardly suggest it's time to call the electronics mortuary.

Lack of interest in the PC hasn't really been the problem. After all, the PC has not been a luxury for some time; it's considered a basic appliance in both homes and offices. Despite industry pundits insisting that a replacement for the PC was right around the corner, statistics tell us that most users aren't so much replacing their PCs with something else as having their PCs *and* something else—with the something else being a laptop or a TabletPC, Personal Digital Assistant (PDA), Web-access phone, and so on.

Instead, the issues surrounding the PC industry slump of recent years were manyfold: the technology bubble bust of the late 1990s after companies and consumers had engaged in massive spending in constant upgrades, and the overall decline in the global economy that was worsened by the terrorist attacks in the United States in September 2001, to name just a couple. People began to demand a compelling reason to move beyond the machines they already had. The promise of an ever-speedier processor just wasn't enough anymore.

But times are changing again. Technical equipment spending is projected to take a serious jump in 2004 because of both an (albeit slow) economic recovery and the signs of wear that so many PCs purchased in 1999 and 2000 are beginning to show. The hardware is evolving, too. Recently, conventional cathode-ray PC monitors were outpaced by liquid crystal displays (LCD), which now account for more than 50 percent of monitor sales. Many PCs now ship with 1 gigabyte (GB) of very fast memory and hard drives that exceed 100 GB.

Throughout this book, you're going to learn about the hardware: what is currently available, what you need to look for, and how to work with it successfully. First things first: rather than follow the track of many PC hardware books that become mired in history in each chapter they address—and which often don't give serious attention to server environments and networked PCs when those are a fact of everyday life today—you're going to get most of the swift evolution of PC history in this chapter alone. Then you'll move quickly on to current trends and issues.

A Brief History of a Revolution

We have moved quickly up from a processor running a whopping 4.77 MHz to the current pinnacle of one operating beyond 4 GHz. And we've gone from having very few extra pieces of equipment added to our systems to packing in every device that can fit.

Yet footprints of architecture first sketched 20 and 25 years ago remain. For instance, there is a limited array of physical system resources like interrupt requests (IRQs) and direct memory access (DMA) channels (discussed in Chapter 2, "The Operating System's Role in Hardware"), which is a problem because they are used by devices to be recognized and used by the system. We've also kept around versions or standards that permit us to use some older hardware and software we have used for years. To a large degree, users have chosen some older hardware bus architectures for backward compatibility over the evolution to all faster buses that forces users to upgrade their devices.

As you read through this first chapter on history and get into other chapters that focus on a specific current issue or component in the PC or high-tech arena, you are bound to see both the blessings and the printed-circuit bondage we experience at the helm of this hardware and that we keep pushing this hardware forward even as we also hold it back.

How It Began

The personal computer landscape before the introduction of the IBM PC in 1981 lacked a lot of discernible standards. Sharing files between various types of personal computers was usually frustrating. Some PCs used cassette tape for storage, while others used 8-inch or smaller floppies. An assortment of microprocessors abounded, including the famed Z80. Many of the microprocessors used different, very basic operating systems, so programs that worked on the popular Radio Shack TRS-80 Model 4P wouldn't run on a Commodore PET or a Timex Sinclair. Data had to be saved to ASCII format, which eliminated all of the data's specialized formatting, so that it could be read by a different type of personal computer.

For hobbyists of the time, this was more an annoyance than anything traumatic. Hobbyists tended to either use their personal systems for independent work that they didn't need to share with others or band together in enclaves that were divided by the type of system used. The result was that there were Osborne user groups, Altair IV user groups, groups who preferred Commodore over Amiga, and so forth.

But for business use, a lack of standardization is a very tough problem. Two computers in the same office should be able to communicate, either directly through some type of common network or indirectly by trading files using common media, such as floppies. They should be able to do this without having to strip files of any unique application characteristics—such as the styles and settings from a word processor. So computers in the same office needed to be able to run the same software.

In office situations prior to the introduction of the IBM PC, computers, if they existed at all, were usually just large, blocky terminals running off a minicomputer or a mainframe large enough to require its own large room and special cooling conditions. Each terminal ran only the programs or functions the mainframe designated and, for most of its users, this amounted simply to data entry and record lookup screens. When the big computer needed to perform a backup or went down in an emergency, the terminals blinked unresponsively. All computer work halted. Companies didn't employ these expensive machines to do anything as mundane as typing letters, so the IBM Selectric and other commercial-grade typewriters usually had to vie for space on the desktop next to the computer terminal.

How We Wrote Papers, Reports, and Documents

What was the world like before the introduction of word processing programs for the personal computer? Our clerical past was surprisingly hardware-intensive (as well as hard labor–intensive). Before the introduction of the IBM PC in 1980, which helped set the standard for the industry and introduced word processing to many, all printed materials were typed on either manual or electric typewriters. Computer terminals, where they existed, mostly provided a means of entering and checking records in a database.

If you were lucky, you had an electric typewriter with a not-too-complex self-correction feature. If not, a major mistake forced you to restart a page from scratch. If you needed to make more than one copy of that printed matter, you either used a messy carbon sheet or a copy machine, or you typed the document on a cumbersome, thick, and very fragile stencil and cranked it through a mimeograph machine. This was a time- and strength-intensive exercise, and it too was potentially very messy. Any modifications that needed to be made to a document usually required a full retyping.

What if the documents typed had to be sent to someone in another city? Fax machines were rare and were usually used only by news and wire services and law enforcement agencies. Because of this, you had to type the document, make copies, and send it by special courier or wait for the postal system to deliver it. (Overnight services were few and far between—and prohibitively expensive to boot.)

Because computerized storage was not yet commonplace, all that paper had to be filed (and large companies employed large numbers of clerks specifically for this task). Those files then amassed month by month and year by year until they were, in some cases, copied onto microfiche (requiring more bulky equipment). If the company was very advanced, it *also* stored some information on big tape reels filled with data backed up from the mainframe. Think of the full-sized filing cabinet of documents that can now be stored (in text or document format) on a single CD.

While the *paperless office* concept generated much discussion and many news articles in the 1980s and 1990s, even today we're far from having realized that concept. Don't expect the printer—or the need for a file cabinet—to go away anytime soon.

> **Fact** For 1982, *Time* magazine suspended its usual practice of naming the "Man of the Year" on its cover to honor the computer as the "Machine of the Year," noting the major advancements it brought forth. Rumor has it, however, that the copy for the printed article in that issue of *Time* was prepared initially on a typewriter and then passed along to a typesetter.

The IBM PC Debuts

The IBM PC is a product rushed to market by a crew of IBM engineers in Boca Raton, Florida, under orders from the executives in Armonk, New York, and its release foretold little of the phenomenal success it would boast and the architectural legacy it would create—a legacy that remains with us today.

It is said that IBM hoped sales would meet their expectations of about 50,000 units each year during the first five years from its introduction. But instead of moving the 250,000 or so units in five years, IBM was selling close to that number every four to five weeks. The IBM PC had many things going for it:

- **Brand stability** The IBM name was synonymous with standardized business equipment (because the company's mainframes and minicomputers drove data processing technology) at a time when business people were beginning to want a system less transient than the various standards consumer hobbyists were using.

- **A 16-bit CPU** Most microcomputers were 8-bit, although the 8088, the first chip used in PCs, communicated on an 8-bit bus to keep the design costs lower.

- **Upgradability** Because there was no true add-on market yet, IBM provided a good deal of room inside the case so that you could add components you wanted when and if they were developed.

- **Price** While the price tag certainly seems high (for what it was) by today's standards, it was within the higher end of what other microcomputers were going for and was a true bargain compared to paying for a mainframe or minicomputer.

- **Good documentation** While today, our PCs often include only a small amount of printed documentation (in favor of providing users with online resources), the IBM PC came with wire-bound, notebook-encased bundles of documentation. (To be fair, many other microcomputers, including Tandy's TRS-80, also were packed with heavy documentation, including highly detailed schematics.)

- **Aesthetics**   Compared to the massive cathode-ray tubes (CRTs) and clunky keyboards many companies were using to provide terminal access to the main system for most employees, the IBM PC (a boxy, horizontally set case and a monitor that could sit atop it) fit more easily on most desktops and in most workstations (when the word *workstation* meant a physical work area and not a type of system design).

The IBM PC was certainly not created in a vacuum. Its designers, while under incredible pressure to get the product completed and released, were certainly aware of what was already out there in the microcomputer realm in terms of hardware connections and setups. Plus, because they intended PCs to be used primarily as business machines, and IBM was one of the most recognizable names in office machinery, they brought to the design board an experienced view of what business users needed in a personal computer even before users knew they needed a PC at all.

The Xerox Alto/Star

If there is a single computer from the last two decades that might be the most accurate forerunner of today's systems—in concept if not actual hardware implementation—it's a workstation Xerox created at its Palo Alto Research Center (PARC) in California. Originally named the *Alto*, it was finally called the *Xerox Star.*

Introduced the very same year as the IBM PC and created by a stellar design team that included Alan Key, who had created the SmallTalk computer language, the Xerox Star was notably different from what was available at the time.

For one, it was a fully graphics-capable system, using a What You See Is What You Get (WYSIWYG) interface, a mouse to help the user navigate around the bitmapped-display desktop, and pull-down menus to perform key functions. It used graphical representations of raw commands or program launches—in other words, icons. Laser printers were developed specifically with the Xerox Star in mind because users needed to reproduce the graphical screen properly in printed form and to do so without it taking hours to process.

Such features made the Xerox Star far more preferable to the casual user—often an employee sitting at a workstation creating and printing documents—to perform his duties without a vast knowledge of commands and functions. This was the user the Xerox PARC had in mind when creating the Xerox Star. This was an extraordinary insight because few early systems were created with normal mortals in mind. Despite the capacity many older machines—from microcomputers to minicomputers to mainframes—were built with, they were not generally easy for an inexperienced person to use without training or self-education. Instead, they were often the domain of electronics junkies, academics and their students, scientists, the military, and those working deep in the artificially cooled computer rooms of major corporations. Easy user interface wasn't a key concept.

But if computers were ever going to jump the barrier between the elite and the common user, they had to be designed so that they weren't so difficult to learn. The PARC team had addressed this in its design and implementation.

From a performance standpoint, however, the Xerox Star also stood above the crowd with its windowed environment and the ability to have multiple windows or functions open on the desktop at the same time.

These features, when compiled, should sound familiar. They form the basis of what you use now if you're running Microsoft Windows, the graphical component of Linux, or the Macintosh operating system. The Xerox PARC team, you see, invited other designers and developers in to see their work. Among the first to visit were the two Steves of Apple Computer: Wozniak and Jobs.

By 1983, both Microsoft and Apple were at work on a graphical operating system, with the Xerox Star probably very much in mind. To achieve this, both companies would need the support of hardware manufacturers willing to create the necessary equipment—such as monitors with advances in video display handling and color graphics as well as computers with faster and more memory—to make this a reality. Fortunately, both companies would come to have the power to largely write the standards that others followed.

> **Fact**   The Xerox Star's interface was written not in SmallTalk, as many have assumed because of Alan Key's presence on the project. Instead, it was written in a Pascal language variant called MESA.

The Rise of Bill Gates and Microsoft

Long before there was an MS-DOS per se, there was a PC-DOS, brought to fruition through the efforts of a small software company based in Bellevue, Washington (whose former claim to fame was creating a BASIC compiler for the

Altair computer that also compiled traffic data under the name Traf-o-Data). PC-DOS changed the fates of men like Bill Gates, Paul Allen, and Steve Ballmer.

Exactly how Microsoft became forever linked to the PC depends on which version of the legendary story you hear. IBM was in talks with Gary Kildall of Digital Research (known ultimately for products like the GEM operating system and DR-DOS, an MS-DOS competitor) to develop an operating system that would run on its PC. Digital Research already had CP/M, popular at the time among microcomputer users for its command-line and basic command set and for how well it ran on 8-bit microcomputers. It represented as much of a standard as existed at the time. IBM apparently wanted CP/M for its new product, but that meant modifying CP/M code to make it run on the new 16-bit Intel chipset.

Here is where story versions diverge. In some accounts, Kildall balked at the very detailed and limiting nondisclosure agreement (NDA) IBM wanted him to sign, so he instead went flying (still other versions say hang-gliding). In this version, IBM gets miffed, calls Bill Gates instead, and many billions of dollars later, the moment became etched in history. In other accounts, Kildall remained in active negotiations with IBM, but Microsoft maneuvered around him and got the deal.

The DOS and the Microsoft operating system would actually be in part a product bought from others and adapted. Close to Microsoft headquarters, as they existed at the time, was a small company named Seattle Computer. There, an enterprising fellow, Tim Paterson, had coded his own CP/M-similar operating system. He originally called it *86-DOS* because it was designed to run on the Intel 8086. Quickly, however, it became better known as *QDOS* for its nickname, the "quick and dirty operating system."

QDOS booted to a command line and required users to know a set of commands and their available switches or parameters—both usually signs of an environment better suited to more advanced users. However, QDOS wasn't really any more capacious or effective than anything else currently available. What QDOS did do was run on the 16-bit CPU, and that's what Microsoft had agreed to deliver to Big Blue, as IBM is often called. After quickly arranging to acquire the license for QDOS from Tim Paterson and Seattle Computer (Microsoft later purchased full rights), Microsoft renamed it the Personal Computer Disk Operating System (PC-DOS) and then licensed the product to IBM in what would prove to be a very lucrative and fairly long-lived deal.

Beyond PC-DOS to Programs

The IBM PC actually supported three different operating systems:

- CP/M, the same operating system that ran on so many other types of microcomputers

- USCD p-system by Softech

- PC-DOS

Unlike PC-DOS, the other two operating systems in the list were well established and fairly well documented (for that time period). Both also had something PC-DOS did not: a body of applications that would run on them. Naturally, Microsoft was already looking ahead to application development to have a roster of useful programs to run on the systems that used PC-DOS. Within a few years, several of the programs still in active use and development today—including Microsoft Word (originally called Multi-Tool Word and released in 1984)—were already being worked up. A developer named Mitch Kapor was elsewhere, working away at the product that would become Lotus 1-2-3 (introduced in 1982). While many software companies struggled to learn the new operating system and hardware design well enough to write programs to run on it, IBM looked to others to license products such as Spellbinder—an early and successful word processor for CP/M machines—to adapt to their platform. Without software to run on it and specifically without software for the business customers who could afford it, PC-DOS would be fairly useless. However, the IBM name was *the* standard, and programmers from companies both in the U.S. and around the world hopped onboard what looked to be a very promising train. Almost everyone, it seemed, was ready to develop products for the IBM PC.

While code was being written to bring document creation and financial calculations to the PC, PC-DOS was already somewhat more popular among users than the other two operating systems for a simple reason: it was cheaper. Adding PC-DOS to a system cost about $40, while CP/M went for about $450 and USCD p-system cost more than $500.

> **Fact**   The Ctrl+Alt+Del (also known as "C-A-D" or "the 3-fingered salute") keyboard functionality was programmed in from the start because the original IBM PC had a tendency to hang up, and engineers wanted a way to quickly restart the system.

> **Fact**   Moore's Law—credited to Gordon Moore, one of the cofounders of Intel—states that computer processor performance and disk-storage capability roughly double every 18 to 24 months. Recently, Intel and Moore said that this law still seems to apply.

Homegrown Applications

While the first year of the IBM PC might have seemed a bit lean software-wise for those used to the multitude of company-designed and home-coded programs that ran on other microcomputers, the success of the first "true" PC had developers scrambling to fill the void. It is credited with being a time that began to attract more people to software development because the landscape ahead seemed long and lush.

IBM was selling so many units each month that it appeared a major standard was evolving. The market was extending beyond hobbyists, past those with prior experience using mainframes and minicomputers, to whole new audiences—companies and people who might have the money to actually pay for software rather than just people trading code with each other. "There could be money in this!" was the prevailing thought.

But not everyone's immediate thought was financial gain. The early 1980s was a time when there were at least as many "free" contributions—in the form of software that users could share and use and other developers could borrow ideas from—as there were commercial offerings.

People were interested in writing their own programs, and they often taught themselves programming languages such as Assembly and BASIC to do so. This was no small feat because resources then weren't what they are today. Computer publishing had not yet been fully launched, although there were many small magazines, some books, and lots of tips being posted on bulletin board systems (a dial-up hobbyist network of Internet-like communications).

Fact   The birth of online services and modem communications for microcomputers occurred in 1978, when Ward Christensen is credited with getting communications software to answer the first incoming call from a remote user through a modulator-demodulator (also known as a modem). The technology spread rapidly, particularly among hobbyists, in the few years before the debut of the IBM PC, which did not ship with a modem as standard equipment.

Modems were not typically offered in a PC setup until the very early 1990s. In the first decade of the IBM PC and its clones, you bought a modem separately (and a fast one of that day's hastening standard often cost a minimum of $400) and struggled to install it. Then you would struggle further to configure your communications software to work with the modem.

The Online of the Early 1980s

Although Arpanet, the U.S. Department of Defense (DoD) forerunner of today's Internet, was already available in a rudimentary state in the early 1980s, most of us didn't even know it existed. For early computer hobbyists who had acquired an asynchronous modem (where the telephone handset was placed in the cradle of the external device to allow for communications between systems), there were an abundant number of freely available bulletin board systems (BBSes) in the U.S. and abroad where people came to virtually meet, exchange messages, share files, and sometimes type-chat via a whiteboard window interface. If you've ever used HyperTerminal in Windows for dialup communications, you have an idea of how raw it looked.

For the more serious user, there were subscription-based online services such as CompuServe (the grandfather of them all), which had started in 1979, and BIX, a service run by *Byte* magazine. Both of these were targeted at a serious technical audience where novice users were the exception rather than the norm. For usually an hourly connection fee, you could rub elbows with the still-growing giants of the personal computer industry who could be found online, posting messages about new products and technology. Microsoft would later run communications for its beta testing programs through CompuServe technical forum channels, and CompuServe was *the* place to go for PC users to gain in-depth knowledge about all types of current and future products, hardware, troubleshooting, and operating system design.

The online world wasn't graphical then, either. While "shell" environments were later created to make it easier for new users to find and execute functions, services such as CompuServe ran from a command line. This meant you navigated by struggling with syntax and switches rather than by clicking an icon or a button.

The Burgeoning PC Application Market

Despite the limited resources available for learning more than the IBM PC documentation told you about the operating system, applications sprang up quickly. A former Boeing summer intern named Peter Norton bought his first IBM PC soon after its release and began to adapt a set of tools he had already developed for the Boeing mainframe to this new system. These tools would later become known as Norton Utilities.

In this same time period, Ashton-Tate would develop a product that would become the de facto standard in PC-based database management, dBase. Mitch Kapor would finish work on a financial program written to make special use of the PC's video system for superior operation. This begot the meteoric rise of the PC spreadsheet, sparked by Kapor's Lotus 1-2-3.

And perhaps even before the first IBM PC booted up to PC-DOS, Microsoft programmers were already hard at work looking for a way to make the operating system graphical for easier use. After all, Apple had already seen the light on this matter when Steve Jobs and Steve Wosniak visited Xerox and discovered the power of a good interface. Microsoft watched whatever Apple did because the two companies were in competition for some of the same market.

You'll learn more about the history of the PC operating system in Chapter 2.

The Cloning of the IBM PC

With every success usually comes a horde of onlookers looking to copy the formula that worked so well. IBM was racing to try to fulfill the demand for its first personal computer, both on the bare-bones model that shipped without monitor and video, keyboard, floppy drives, or operating system for a bargain price of just under $1300 and the full-blown setup with printer going for nearly three times the price. Already, there were growing rumbles among the following groups:

- Core computer hobbyists, who felt that IBM was charging exorbitant prices for products that weren't compatible with almost everything else out there in the microcomputer world. This group also felt that IBM made it more difficult for them to build their own systems, which was a major issue when you consider microcomputer history is rich with those who built their own systems from separately purchased components or in kits like those offered by HeathKit.

- IBM PC novices, who often resented the high prices they paid for software through IBM (especially when software for other platforms often seemed to be free, was treated as free even when it was not, or was sold at lower prices).

- Other microcomputer manufacturers, who found a growing market that wanted true IBM compatibility (with *true* meaning software written specifically to check for IBM-like markers, which reported "yes, this is genuine IBM or IBM-compatible" before it would run) but without IBM prices and who found themselves wanting a slice of IBM's phenomenal success.

- Other hardware manufacturers, who also wanted a share of the IBM PC market but whose products weren't being used in IBM's PC. IBM hardware was proprietary—you were only supposed to replace parts on an IBM with other IBM or IBM-licensed parts.

- Developers of software not likely to be licensed by IBM or one of its major software supporters (for example, most games and applications without a specific office-use function), who wanted a PC platform that people would want to buy and run their wares on.

It was into this environment that the IBM PC clone was born within a year after the original was made available. Re-creating the PC for other companies was simple in some respects. The IBM PC had been very well documented by this time, and the basic architecture was copied. Copying other components was more difficult, like duplicating the full aspects of the boot process and the system's handling of hardware. To some degree, this required reverse engineering, which companies like Phoenix stepped in to perform. Reverse engineering refers to a process by which you go back through the history of how something was designed to learn how it was put together and to make improvements and other modifications to it.

The first company out of the gate was a small one, Columbia Data Products, which released its system in 1982. But a different company, one that released its first clone the following year, grabbed the industry's attention. This company, Compaq, had released non-IBM systems, including its first portable and the first-ever color portable in 1982. It was the first and most successful at re-creating the IBM phenomenon when it offered its first clones in 1983. In its first year of operations, the company recorded $111 million in sales, which at that time was the most ever reported by a U.S. business in a single fiscal year.

Like IBM's design, Compaq's design was mostly proprietary and required Compaq or Compaq-licensed replacement parts. Compaq's DeskPro series became a strong competitor against the true PC in the business office market. It was also more expensive than many clones that would follow, but it was competitive with IBM's prices. Compaq would lead sales for years to come.

IBM Is Cut Out, Then Rebounds

By the mid-1980s, CPUs advanced to the 80286 and then to the 80386, the 16-bit CPU was finally working on a 16-bit bus, and new hardware debuted (including the CD-ROM drive, the musical instrument digital interface—or MIDI—and the first laser printer). IBM had all but lost its market to manufacturers who were making clones that were cheaper, sometimes faster, and often not quite fully compatible with IBM's design.

However, IBM was a large corporation with the resources to make new inroads. It wasn't ready to give up. It took a few years, and in the meantime IBM had to watch Compaq become the first PC manufacturer to release Intel's hot new 80386 CPU that boasted a 32-bit (16 MHz) data bus with more than a quarter of a million transistors (275,000, to be exact). The Intel CPU brought the power of a minicomputer—or a low-end mainframe—to the desktop.

In 1987 IBM made its move by introducing a new line of microcomputers called the PS/2 (PS for *personal system*, rather than *personal computer*, implying something of a next-generation design) that had a different architecture than before. The PS/2 MicroChannel Architecture (MCA) was revolutionary rather than evolutionary, meaning that it was not backwardly compatible with the existing PC architecture called Industry Standard Architecture (ISA). As a result, the hardware you plugged into your IBM PC or PC clone was usually not the same hardware you installed on your PS/2. The impetus behind this was clear: IBM was looking to regain exclusive and potentially very lucrative rights to future PC design by reinventing its original implementation and locking its specifications into legal licensing. IBM declared it would not fall prey to the clone wars again. If anyone else wanted to use MCA in their designs, they had to pay IBM a fee.

While the PS/2 line did very well in the corporate environment for several years, becoming standard issue in every cubicle of huge companies such as Pepsi and Avon, its price and proprietary hardware kept it from achieving popular success in the slowly growing consumer and small-office market. Only as PC prices finally fell below $2000 and $1500 for lower-end systems did this market begin to emerge. Later, IBM would go after this market again with a more personal line of systems called the PS/1, which tried to make the desktop foolproof from user-initiated changes or corruptions. The PS/1 also had its own dedicated member-only online service for support run by the same company (Quantum Computer) that would later become America Online (AOL)–Time Warner.

Other PC manufacturers also balked at implementing the MCA design changes in their systems because they didn't want to pay a licensing fee to IBM. So they developed their own PC bus architecture, which extended the ISA bus.

The Slide of the Non-IBMs

Other microcomputer designs came and went during the early 1980s. The Commodore-64 and –128 were reasonably inexpensive, packed with a sound chip, and had 16 colors in the video composite graphics output (while the IBM and IBM clones were still monochromatic). They sold well among young adults and teenagers, who would keep buying them used for many years after the Commodore design was dropped.

The same year the first clone came out, Digital Equipment Corporation (DEC) announced its dual processor, Rainbow 100. Its debut was exciting because the Rainbow 100 paired the popular alternative platform of the Zilog Z80 CPU with an Intel 8088. It, too, had the color that IBMs and clones lacked, although IBM boosted the monochromatic display's resolution to 720x348 with the introduction of the Hercules Graphics Card (a bargain at $499). And this was the same year that Timex debuted its Timex Sinclair 1000.

By 1983, Apple was looking at clones of its own. Franklin had released a computer that was compatible with an Apple, ran most of the software, and cost less. But Apple was already looking ahead to the launch of its Macintosh line in 1984, which took some of the most critically acclaimed features of the LISA (the first personal computer with a graphical interface) they had introduced two years before. The Mac was destined to do better, at least in part because it cost 25 percent of LISA's prohibitive $10,000 price tag.

However, by the mid-1980s, personal computers were largely being oriented to one of two specific lines: Intel-based IBM compatibles, and Apple and its compatibles using a Motorola chip. Many of the other microcomputer companies were either struggling to stay viable in any market or they were folding. Osborne Computer, which was started by Adam Osborne and manufactured with the Zilog Z80A microprocessor, at one time had sales of 10,000 units a month and was one of the great names in early personal microsystems. Yet it declared bankruptcy and shut down in 1984. Other companies that were in a situation similar to Osborne's rolled their products into the inventory of other manufacturers.

Across the U.S. and the world, the various types of PCs—the Osbornes, the Tandy/TRS systems and the CoCos (the color Tandy), the old Timex Sinclairs, the DEC Rainbows, and the Commodores (PET, 64/128, and the VIC-20)—began to be turned off, accumulate dust, and be forgotten until they were sold at garage sales or electronics swap-meets. As these machines were retired, their owners often felt as if they had only two choices for replacements. And the choices were not so different from what we have today: Wintel or Macintosh.

For those who preferred the PC platform, only one chip company made the processor they needed: Intel. As the 1980s developed, only one PC operating system company dominated the operating system market and (increasingly) the application market: Microsoft. Standards the two corporations didn't forge themselves were forged by others largely under their direction. This would remain the case for years—even after Intel lost the fight to keep competitor PC processor-makers like Advanced Micro Devices (AMD) and Cyrix (later bought by VIA) from selling Intel work-alikes, and even as Microsoft faced competition from companies such as Digital Research, IBM, and Quarterdeck, who offered windowed desktop environments of their own. When DEC introduced its Alpha processor in 1994 (a professional-level processor meant for servers and powerful work-stations and later transfigured into Compaq servers), it drew a great deal of excitement for its speed and performance, but its sales were a disap-pointment. One rule has stood the test of time: it's expensive to adopt innovation as a corporate strategy in the hope that it will pay off.

PC State of the Art

PC state of the art is often called by some cynics the "state of the minute" because that seems about how long a technology remains the "hot new thing." While this was more true in the aggressive upgrade environment of the later 1990s, it still rings true today. As this book goes to press, LCD screens, DVD recorders, Tablet PCs, and the next generation of Windows (Windows Server 2003 and Longhorn, which is still in development at Microsoft) are the hot top-ics; but by the time you read this, some of these new or improved technologies might have been set aside in favor of even more recent advances.

But just take a look at Table 1-1, and you'll see that in the past 20 years or more our systems have taken a mighty jump in capacity and processing ability. In 1981, if you were like me, you might have paid as much as $4000 for an IBM PC with a printer. Today, with the configuration shown in Table 1-1, you should expect to pay $1600.

Table 1-1   Typical PC Configurations Over a 20-Year Span

Components	1981	1991	2003
CPU	8088 4.77 MHz	486/33 MHz	PIV 2.5 GHz
RAM	256K	4 MB	256-512 MB
Video	Hercules Mono	SVGA 1 MB	GE Force FX with 128 MB
Disk Storage	160K floppy	80 MB	60 GB
CD	None	Sometimes	Standard (or coupled with DVD)
Mouse	None	Usually	Standard
Sound	None	SoundBlaster 16-bit	Advanced 24-bit

The PC of today is a dazzling appliance, capable of producing incredible audio and video, connecting us through high-speed connections (256 to 700 KBps on average) to the rest of the world, and capable of handling almost any application we toss at it—from complex graphical rendering to digital editing to the most sophisticated math.

The "Build-Your-Own Vs. Buy" Debate

The word around the virtual street has always been that it is cheaper to build your own system than it is to buy one. Historically, this was almost always true. Today, however, this view is often relegated to the urban myth category, although it isn't always complete fiction.

For several years now, the PC hardware industry, faced with massive competition and razor-thin price margins, has grown leaner and meaner. Many manufacturers who were big names in the 1980s and 1990s no longer exist or have been gobbled up by competitors. Ironically, perhaps, today there are a number of so-called hardware manufacturers who no longer make any of their own hardware. Instead, they buy products from cheap, mostly non-U.S. outlets (very little PC hardware is produced in the U.S. anymore) and brand them with their own label.

But when it comes down to the "buy vs. build" debate, you have to think of how a major PC manufacturer such as Dell buys components. (Here, I use Dell simply as an example.) When you go out to buy a high-end consumer-gamer graphics adapter, you can expect to pay anywhere from $150 to $300. Should Dell decide to include such an adapter in one of its systems, Dell is going to pay only a fraction of that cost. Think bulk sales. More than likely, in fact, Dell will license the chip technology to install it on an integrated mother-board, further driving down the cost. It's going to be very difficult (although not impossible for the most aggressive of shoppers) for you to compete dollar for dollar against what a PC manufacturer can put together.

Where the "buy vs. build" debate still has some integrity is in unit customi-zation. Depending on the manufacturer, it can be difficult to find a system that's made to your exact specifications. You might have to build it yourself. The man-ufacturer is likely going to depend on integrated components (modem, plus audio, video, and network adapter), while you might opt for individual add-in boards to preserve the ability to mix and match components as you desire.

Of course, for some, the satisfaction of building their own computer mea-sures far and above what any preconfigured box will offer them. That will likely continue to be the case for some years to come.

Evolutions in PC Design

The key word in PC design has been *evolution* rather than *revolution*. Look at a motherboard (as you will in Chapter 4, "The Workings and Connections of the PC" and again in Chapter 6, "Central Processing Units") and you see some of the same architecture that was present in 1986.

Oh, many components are smaller now, more streamlined. But several of the connections hardware devices must make—including serial and parallel connections—can seem eerily the same. As you read through this book and work with PCs, you might ask yourself, "Are we ever going to fully dispense with the architectural standards developed back in the 1980s?"

The answer is yes, but slowly. When Intel and other manufacturers began discussing a major PC redesign effort, code-named Arapahoe (also called 3GIO), in 2001, many expected the PC to be completely rethought and recon-structed from the inside out. As it is adopted, the reality is more that we'll see the Peripheral Component Interconnect (PCI) bus replaced by a much faster serial bus–based standard.

We still want backward compatibility, and we continue to pay a price for it by not going as far forward as we might like. This is evidenced when you understand that the interim jump between PCI and Arapahoe, called PCI-X, started rolling into wide distribution only in 2002, although it had been on the drawing board since the late 1990s.

It's not just backward compatibility, however. A concept called total cost of ownership (TCO), which refers to the real dollar figure a PC costs you to pur-chase and run, is something the PC industry has had to keep as low as possible in the face of businesses less and less willing to spend a bundle on the machines they buy. The theory is that the lower the TCO, the more competitive a PC model will be and the more likely both businesses and consumers will be to purchase it. A low TCO, however, doesn't scream for innovation.

Where costs often get cut with PCs, besides in the areas of dramatic new design development and strong customer support, is through the increasing integration of components into the motherboard that were formerly offered as standalone add-in boards. These components include modems, network cards, and both video and audio boards. This integration can make a PC cost far less than it would otherwise. It can also cause some hardware headaches, as you will see once we begin looking at the components type by type.

The Easy PC Initiative

One of the major initiatives pushed through both by Microsoft and major hardware manufacturers in recent years is called the *Easy PC Initiative*, an effort designed to make PCs easier for users to operate and modify without superior technical knowledge.

We've already seen modifications in PC hardware connectivity as part of this approach. For example, more and more PC hardware—including digital video cameras, external hard drives, DVD players and recorders, and more—connect through external ports and are *hot-swappable*, meaning that the PC is up and running when you install or change devices. The add-on boards that can be installed inside the case are almost exclusively Plug-and-Play (PnP) now. All a user needs to do is insert the board in the correct slot and, when the machine boots, the PC and Windows automatically recognize the new device and go through the procedures to install it for use.

We saw it, too, with the introduction of Windows XP, the first Microsoft operating system to recognize a new hard drive and let you easily prepare it for work. Windows XP also takes over more of the role traditionally assigned to the PC BIOS (discussed in Chapter 2 and Chapter 6) in terms of hardware recognition.

The Easy PC Initiative is also striving to get PCs to reach a point where they are never turned off. Instead, a PC will always be on, albeit in a low power state when not in use, and the time involved in booting up will be eliminated.

However, *easy* can be a relative term. While externally connecting hardware that is hot-swappable is an incredible boon over older alternatives and the speed of external hard drives based on second-generation universal serial bus (USB) and IEEE 1394) makes them highly attractive, we still face issues inside the PC itself that aren't so easy to resolve, either for consumers or PC professionals.

As this book is being written, we still fight with hardware resources assigned to the motherboard in an overall design architecture still based on one concocted in the 1980s. Today, we can continue to exhaust those resources as we add more equipment to our PCs. Such hardware resources still confuse consumers and aren't very easy for them to cope with. In other words, work remains to be done to make the PC so easy that technicians for it are no longer needed.

Major Changes Ahead?

It's difficult to make major predictions about where the PC industry is going because so many earlier forecasts have been wrong. As already stated, Arapahoe does not appear to be the massive redesign first envisioned and reports of the PC's demise have been exaggerated. Indicators seem to tell us that the desktop PC will continue to be the major workhorse, while other devices—laptops, Tablet PCs, and handhelds—will offer processing power apart from the desktop itself, especially as easy access to wireless connections becomes more prevalent.

However, a smaller desktop certainly seems to be in the cards. People sometimes like a big display but don't always appreciate a large bulky box. At the same time, many aren't willing to replace a full desktop unit with a notebook computer; the latter can cost more initially, is more difficult to repair, and is more prone to theft and accidental damage.

One alternative that companies such as the UK-based Pelham Sloane are hoping people will adopt is the all-in-one PC, where a flat-panel display, processor, memory, and all other components are rolled into a single sleek unit. It's not new. Early, pre-IBM PCs often employed this approach. Recently, IBM had one of the best-known entries in this market with a NetVista system that it discontinued selling in early 2002; Apple's iMac is based on the same sort of design. Gateway has the Profile PC, which fits this scheme although it has not been a major seller.

The relatively near future might also bring us magnetic memory, in development from IBM, which might be the first form of widely used memory that won't lose its data the moment the PC is shut down. IBM also expects to bring us the first hand-held half-pound PC, called the MetaPad, in 2006. The MetaPad is a unit the size of a PDA that offers the full processing power of a desktop unit. I can't wait to see the size of the keyboard for that.

The 10 GHz CPU and Beyond

With PC CPUs now typically running at 2 to 3 GHz or more, it should come as no shock that designers have been at work for a few years planning for a 10 GHz chipset in the not too distant future. By 2007, Intel is expected to introduce a 20 GHz chip containing a whopping 1 billion transistors.

But what are the possible applications of a 10 or 20 GHz (or greater) system in an environment where many attest that even their aged Pentium IIs running at 350 or 450 MHz still run the applications they need to use? We were once enchanted with each new processor speed jump, but we're not anymore.

note ⎰ Analysts predict that as we approach this higher and higher range of chipset capacity, our focus might shift to parallel processing. They suggest we will also be looking for ways to have some of the new performance finally bridge the gap between human interaction and PC functionality. Because of the load that a robust approach would place on a normal PC of yesterday and today, we don't have much in place yet for humans to communicate directly with their PCs without the use of an intervening device such as the standard keyboard and mouse. When we do "communicate" with them, it's not in real time. For example, if I speak a sentence to a voice recognition application in the same way I would to my officemate, my entire system slows down while the application tries to handle the "transaction" and process the request by swiftly and accurately typing what I just spoke. The software has come a long way, but it's still not there yet.

Virtual reality (VR) software and hardware ignited great interest since their first big splash at SIGGraph in Boston in 1989. A healthy percentage of users, and not all of them under the age of 20, would love to see VR truly behave like the extension of computer games to our sensory selves. But it's certainly not going to do that successfully while a PII-350 or even a PIV 3 GHz PC is also processing e-mail, downloading some work files, and running a network communicator in the background. Or, at least it won't do this right now outside of a Hollywood movie.

That's a big component of why VR has never fully taken off in the personal computer realm. You can buy accessories such as VR gloves and glasses, but they are not widely supported in games and applications, and the effect the user experiences is often the gritty reality of a system chugging under the hardware calls rather than virtually enjoyable reality.

Likewise, voice and handwriting recognition are still in their infancy. Digital voice recorders got a lot of attention for a time, but it was really hard to take your recorded speech and have it recognized as more than a sound file when your preference was to turn the recording into a memorandum or letter that the PC would accurately transcribe and print. Similarly, dictation programs with accessory hardware let the curious users test the waters of being able to tell word processors what to type. But dictation programs suffered—and still suffer—from the long lead time it takes the software to train itself to recognize the user's voice as well as from a disappointing end-product, such as a document that requires much editing because of what the software could not discern.

Parallel processing used with a chipset running anywhere close to the 10 GHz mark could change all of that. This truly could spell a PC revolution.

Smart Upgrading

A major subject in this book will be performing system upgrades intelligently. As part of this, you will be encouraged to do more than buy a piece of hardware and hope it works.

Successful and satisfying upgrades are the result of a number of well-calculated steps, including:

- Intelligent evaluation of current and future needs and the base unit being upgraded
- Product research
- Making sure there is driver support for the version of Windows being used
- Attention to detail
- Performing modifications one at a time, systematically

When you read about each major type of component within the major categories such as video and audio, you're going to learn the basics you need to know before installation, along with the troubleshooting methods you should undertake if the device is not detected, does not appear to work, or causes some other issue with the system as a whole.

Smart Disposal

Because this book is about PCs, upgrading them, and servicing them, the subject of smart PC equipment disposal cannot be ignored. One of the biggest issues with electronics today, including PCs and their associated peripherals, is the waste they generate. It even has a name of its own now: *e-waste*.

After all, we have a tendency—driven both by low initial pricing and difficulty or expense of repair—to replace our equipment rather than fix a problem with it. For example, some consumers and professionals have noticed that there are situations where it is less expensive to buy a replacement laser printer than it is to purchase replacement materials for the printer.

Many consumers and small offices have between one and three obsolete PCs on hand or in storage (a closet, garage, or warehouse) at any given time. Large companies can frequently fill a warehouse with their outdated equipment, even as many of them sell or give away PCs and peripherals they have replaced with newer models.

It's estimated that by 2005 one PC will become obsolete for each new PC placed on the market. A scarier estimate is that between two-thirds and three-quarters of all PCs sold in the past 20-plus years remain mostly intact somewhere, in storage, awaiting disposal. This means that they could soon find their way to a landfill, and most landfills are poorly suited to handle them.

Just in terms of space, future disposal of hardware is a massive concern throughout both the U.S. and the rest of the world. The U.S. now sends much of its e-waste to other countries, particularly China, for ultimate disposal. But there's far more to the story than just the physical space this equipment takes in a landfill. Just like that old saying that it's not the heat but the humidity that can affect you in the summer, it's not so much the space as the toxicity of electronic waste that can poison you and a host of others.

The Toxicity of PC Hardware

Electronic waste isn't just junk; much of it is considered toxic waste and should be treated as such. While you don't need a hazardous materials suit to handle it, you need to be mindful of what PC and other electronics components contain so that you can appreciate how bad the effects can be when they are disposed of improperly.

Take the case of cathode-ray tube monitors (and televisions). Each one can contain as much as 10 pounds of lead and other heavy metals (including things such as mercury and nickel-cadmium) that can leach into the ground and contaminate ground water until it eventually ends up in waterways and water storage facilities. That water filter you might currently have at home won't be any match for the potentially large volume of heavy metals coming through your kitchen tap, and that filter won't prevent them from being introduced into your body.

Over time lead can perpetrate serious damage to the human central nervous system, liver, kidney, and blood system. Children and the infirm are especially susceptible to its effects. Lead doesn't leave the body, either; it's stored there forever.

You've no doubt heard of dioxin and its harmful effects. But did you know that some plastics used in today's computers (which can account for up to 25 percent of a PC's total weight), when incinerated, produce a form of dioxin? Beyond what has already been mentioned, a PC can also contain aluminum, arsenic, cobalt, copper, germanium, titanium, and zinc, to name a few other culprits.

The subject has taken on crisis proportions, to the point that Europe implemented an aggressive plan in 2001 to force PC hardware manufacturers to take responsibility for the equipment they build now, with an eye towards phasing out the inclusion of hazardous materials in the future.

However, in the U.S., many states either don't regulate e-waste or don't enforce regulations they already have on the books. While many landfills regulate against the disposal of hazardous waste into them, little policing is done to keep this material out. Several organizations concerned with the issue have been formed in the United States, but widespread measures to reduce PC toxicity largely don't exist.

Proper Disposal and Recycling

You will find that a few manufacturers do take at least some responsibility for their equipment once it leaves their shipment centers, offering programs to accept the return of used or broken hardware for proper disposal. So far, however, these manufacturers are few and far between. Some started such programs in the 1990s only to abandon them when the economy weakened.

The reality, though, is that few consumers and professionals want to go to the trouble of boxing up a dead monitor or printer and shipping it back, usually at their own expense. They might discover that local electronics stores accept old equipment for disposal, but they might not know that those units go into the landfill rather than being broken down, decontaminated, and having their parts recycled.

It's important to look for programs that truly do handle this equipment adequately. Adequate disposal includes removing the toxic chemicals and components and harvesting recyclable parts and elements, such as copper and gold and other metals, that have at least some value. Sometimes, this is handled by state-level environmental departments. Other times, local initiatives have been created to accept such goods—sometimes as part of general hazardous waste removal programs.

There is often a cost involved in such handling, ranging anywhere from one dollar per piece of equipment to $30 or even $50 for a single monitor. Unfortunately, the higher the cost involved in adequate disposal, the less inclined people are to do the right thing.

Yet the more equipment disposal you need to perform, the more important it is for you to come up with an acceptable game plan—one that is responsible as well as effective in both time and cost. You might discover that programs exist to help PC professionals in your community properly dispose of such material at a bulk rate rather than at an individual rate as an incentive for you to handle this waste safely.

Those of you with hardware that still functions but is being replaced anyway: check to see whether your community offers any programs or foundations that accept hardware. Often these foundations donate used equipment to schools and sponsor special initiatives that help supply the underprivileged or the disabled with working PCs. Hospice groups, programs for the visually impaired, and job training centers are just a few agencies that sometimes process such used hardware. Some offer an invoice for tax deduction in return for an equipment donation.

Before you move on to Chapter 2, consider working through the following lab that is designed to help you identify resources in your area that can help you devise a disposal plan.

Lab 1: Disposing of Equipment Properly

This lab is intended to prepare you to properly recycle or dispose of old equipment rather than to simply push it into a closet or basement or send it to a landfill where it will contribute to local (and eventually) global pollution. It should also serve to alert you to organizations and facilities in your area that accept used but working equipment that can be serviced and passed along to those with special needs.

Objectives

When you complete this lab, you will be able to

1. Identify the harmful components or compounds found in PC equipment.

2. Determine the steps needed to prepare for disposal of PC equipment.

3. Locate the proper PC recycling options available in your immediate area.

4. Calculate the costs involved in proper disposal.

5. Identify resources to place used but still working equipment.

Necessary Equipment and Resources

The following equipment and resources are necessary for completing this lab:

1. A telephone or Internet access (preferably both)

2. A local directory

3. A disk utility

4. A screwdriver (The type depends on the screws and attachments for the equipment being removed.)

5. Equipment that is ready for disposal

6. Approximately 30 to 90 minutes to complete this lab

Before you begin, you might want to consult Chapter 3, "Defining Your Tech Toolkit," and Chapter 14, "Drive Interfaces and Hard Drives," for information about disk utility software designed to wipe a disk of data adequately before you dispose of it (by recycling, selling, or giving it away). All too often, it is relatively easy for someone to read the contents of even a reformatted drive and mine information from it.

Procedures to Follow

Complete the following steps to prepare old equipment for disposal:

1. Locate equipment that is no longer needed or wanted.

2. Identify which piece or pieces of the equipment remain in working condition and which appear to be "dead."

3. Remove the equipment from its current location. This might include uninstalling it from a working PC, which is discussed later in this book (the exact chapter varies depending on the component involved).

4. Use your local phone directory, use your Internet access to a Web search engine such as Google.com, or search through MSN.com (community and local government Web sites and state environmental Web sites can also be helpful), to locate the following:

    a. All general recycling programs in your area.

    b. All electronics-specific recycling programs in your area.

    c. If you cannot locate either a or b, locate the landfill authority in your area or your local government office to contact them for assistance.

    d. Any community organizations that accept used, working PC equipment for donation, with or without a tax deduction.

5. Ask appropriate programs and organizations the following questions, jotting information down into your notes:

    a. Where are they located and what days and hours do they operate?

    b. What types of equipment do they accept?

    c. How should the equipment be packaged for acceptance?

    d. What are the charges involved, if any? Get specifics.

    e. What is done with the equipment once you drop it off?

    f. How much, if any, harmful materials will ultimately be sent to a landfill?

g.   If the program or facility indicates the equipment will be sent overseas, ask for details. (Some simply send them to an Asian equivalent of a giant landfill.)

Your Lab Notes

Your lab notes should do the following:

1.   Specify the equipment (by unit, individual pieces, or both) being donated or disposed of.

_____

_____

_____

2.   Identify the programs and facilities contacted. (Be specific so that you can locate them again if needed.)

_____

_____

_____

3.   Provide specifics of their program and charges.

_____

_____

_____

4.   Discuss your disposition of the equipment and how you chose the route for disposal or recycling you ultimately took.

_____

_____

_____

5.   Discuss your observations of the process and which option you might prefer to exercise in the future for discarded equipment.

_____

_____

_____

2

The Operating System's Role in Hardware

Some people have a tendency to think of a PC as an amalgam of very different parts—the operating system, applications, and various hardware components—that just magically work together. Rather than magic, the workings have far more to do with careful analysis, planning and programming, rigorous standards implementation, and then testing by thousands of different users—many of whom have years of experience. The end result is that these different parts work in unison.

If you've ever participated in a Microsoft Windows operating system beta test, you know that a lot is typically required of you as a tester. (If you haven't participated in one and have the opportunity to do so, you definitely should so that you can appreciate what goes into developing an operating system.) As a beta tester, you aren't simply leisurely test-driving the operating system; you're expected to push it to the limits, try it against different software and hardware combinations, see what works well and what breaks under the stress, and then faithfully report your results to the beta team. You don't just test one version either; you get different evolutions of the operating system as it's tweaked and expanded to respond to design flaws and usability issues that need to be changed before the operating system is ready to RTM (or released to manufacturing, the first step in post-beta production).

The Windows operating system, almost regardless of version, is intrinsically tied to the hardware installed on the PC, and the hardware functions under the orchestration and management of Windows itself. In the past, this interaction has been accomplished largely in concert with the PC's Basic Input Output System (BIOS), where hardware installed to a PC is first detected and assigned resources. This design is less true of Windows today, as you'll see when you read about Windows XP later in this chapter, because Windows has started to assume more of the workload usually performed by the BIOS. (This also is true of Windows Server 2003.) You'll read more about BIOS in Chapter 5, "Motherboards," but understand now that it provides the primary interface between the core PC, the hardware attached to it, and the operating system.

However, because you might be working on PCs of varying vintages with different versions of Windows installed, you need to understand the basics of the operating system's roles and responsibilities and how the operating system interacts with the hardware you need to add, remove, diagnose, or repair. That interaction is the subject of this chapter.

A Background in Operating Systems in General and Windows in Particular

Before you dive into some of the intricacies of the operating system and hardware, let's look at a little history to see how we reached the stage of evolution in operating systems we now enjoy—and sometimes curse.

While this book will focus on hardware in a Windows operating environment, the same hardware is apt to be used with Linux-based and even Apple Macintosh operating systems, sometimes on the same machine. The question that needs to be answered is whether the hardware has what is needed to be recognized by and to work with the operating system being used.

The Evolution of the Operating System

For many people, the term *operating system* is inextricably associated with one company—Microsoft—because Microsoft operating system products dominate global sales and usage. But Microsoft didn't invent the PC operating system or the graphical user interface we see in Windows, as you read in the previous chapter. The company customized some initial code, and then it began development of its own system along with an aggressive marketing campaign that helped it capture more than 80 percent of most of the markets in which it offered goods.

It's not as if Microsoft had no competitors until the advent of the Linux operating system (discussed later in this chapter). Rather, its competitors were often companies with which Microsoft had a relationship—either one that was intricately tied to Microsoft (as is the case with IBM) or one that was a competitor from the start of Microsoft's appearance in the operating system market (as is the case with Digital Research).

Even though the IBM OS/2 operating system was seen as being in direct competition with Windows, the two systems had the same roots. Microsoft had developed the OS/2 user interface—Presentation Manager—for IBM, and Presentation Manager in turn had its own roots in the graphical shell for DOS that Microsoft started after the success of PC-DOS with the first IBM PC.

The evolution of the operating system from command-line to graphical user interface actually took longer than some had predicted. While Windows and other graphical interfaces were around in the 1980s after being introduced to the mass market by Apple Computer (which, as you remember from Chapter 1, "Computer Evolution," had viewed the Xerox PARC's graphical user interface), they weren't wildly popular with users at that time. From a typical PC veteran's perspective in the 1990s, around the time of the wide acceptance of Windows 3.1, a graphical shell or interface was something you placed on products to "dummify" them for less-experienced users.

A confluence of circumstances eventually helped the graphical user interface (GUI) finally succeed for the IBM clone market:

- Windows, after more than five years in use, was deemed a much better operating environment with the debut of Windows 3.0.

> **Note**   Windows, at this point, was an operating *environment* rather than an operating *system.* The difference is that an operating environment usually sits atop the foundation of an operating system. In those days, Windows required DOS as the operating system base, and then it installed as a graphical shell over the top of DOS.

- Slowly decreasing PC prices and the widespread use of PCs in the workplace brought more people into contact with computers. Many of these people weren't technically savvy and could benefit from an operating system where they only had to point and click rather than struggle through fussy commands that demanded perfect syntax to work.

- The evolution of Intel processors to the 386 and 486 generation in the late 1980s brought with it systems that could better support the graphical demands of a GUI and the hardware demands of a task-swapping (a less robust forerunner of multitasking) operating system.

Operating System Wars

Among enthusiasts, microcomputer operating systems have seemed to generate more competitive loyalist spirit among users than even among the companies developing them. After all, "my operating system is better than yours" wars have been with us almost longer than the floppy drive.

The basic rule has always been that if you're a Wintel platform user, you make fun of any computer and operating system offered by Apple; and if you're using a Macintosh or other Apple system, you denigrate Wintel users. Tossed into this mix now is the Linux line of operating systems originally created by Linus Torvald and now available in many forms and flavors.

DOS users told Apple users they were wimps for needing flying toasters and cute icons; Apple users replied that DOS people were Unix wannabes without the command set; Macintosh mavens charged that Windows users were GUI latecomers locked into a ridiculous PC architecture; Windows users claimed OS/2 users were shortsighted; and Linux users sometimes laugh at almost everyone else for paying to use an operating system.

For most of us, however, the operating system isn't a political statement and it isn't a side to take in an argument. It's the foundation on which our entire computer system and its installed applications must work. Thus, we make choices depending on our hardware and our personal or business needs for applications and functionality.

PROFILE: Which Comes First, the Operating System or the Hardware?

By their very design, operating systems are intricately tied to the PC systems they help operate. This is certainly true in a 32- or 64-bit operating system with built-in support for the detection, recognition, and administration or regulation of hardware as you see with Plug and Play (PnP) in recent versions of Windows. However, it's also true for command-line systems where components such as drivers can be loaded and unloaded by commands.

With the first microcomputers, the system often came first and then the operating system (or adjustments to an existing operating system) to make it run. That implies that the hardware, to some degree, determines how the operating system is constructed to manage the system's many different components.

Today, the relationship is more interdependent. The operating system manufacturers set standards for hardware and its drivers to follow (as we saw in the PC design specs discussion in the previous chapter), while the hardware designers have to take into account how the device will behave when installed to the target operating system (as well as when it is installed with the CPU and system chipset on the target motherboard). The hardware designers also might have input into how the next generation of an operating system is written to get the best use out of their products.

This change is probably driven in no small part by the dominance of Microsoft and its standards in the computing industry, along with the compelling profitability potential of products developed for use with Windows. PC manufacturers and those who supply components for them or for user upgrades often depend on the type of sales inherent with a new release of Windows to tide them over in slower times. For example, during fiscal year 2000 and 2001, Wall Street and high-tech analysts hypothesized that the PC sales slump would improve by the end of 2001. They believed this because Windows XP was due to be released to market. Unfortunately, their hypotheses were largely wrong.

Some of the same things are now happening with Linux, although the way it is marketed and distributed has many key differences.

About Linux

Various flavors of a desktop-style Unix operating system have appealed to those seeking something different, something hopefully more powerful and workable than Windows (or DOS or OS/2 before it). Old-time geeks remember a global computing community that was based on sharing and borrowing rather than on purchasing. They might also recall the outrage that some people felt when Bill Gates, founder of a fairly new company named Microsoft, announced that people had to actually pay for the operating systems and applications they used. Prior to this time, code was frequently an item one person wrote, another person borrowed and amended, and a third person developed still further. Not a lot of money changed hands in the process. But in this new commercial environment, code suddenly became something developers—private or corporate—owned as intellectual property. The owner controlled who used the code and how they used it.

Many manufacturers or retailers offer Linux as a choice or are considering doing so. Some systems are designed specifically with Linux in mind, and Linux tends to be more forgiving of less powerful machines than recent versions of Windows, which require users to replace their 486 and Pentium-class machines. Also, more and more applications and hardware drivers are written to support the Linux environment as well as Windows. This means there's a greater chance that the programs and devices you use with Windows might not be lost to you if you move to Linux.

Linux started with the same type of command-line environment that DOS had prior to 32-bit Windows (but with far more commands and functionality), but it was developed to include a GUI. Today, both through development of the product by a number of different individuals, companies, and organizations and by the sheer numbers of users who've ventured into Linux and shared their experience, a Linux install has probably never been easier or better supported. And bookstores are full of Linux help texts.

But Linux is still a domain for those with a good understanding of PC architecture and operating system functionality. As with Windows NT, Windows 2000, and now Windows Server 2003, the power is not in the GUI but in what you can make the operating system do when using a multiple-operating-system environment, running professional Web or network servers, setting strong security measures, or processing large chunks of data.

Rise of the Multiple-Operating-System PC

One growing trend is that more people are choosing to run more than one operating system each time the computer starts. Many factors account for this, including the following:

- More people wanting to try or test an alternative operating system

- More people choosing to run different versions of Windows (typically, in a dual-boot configuration) because they develop code for both versions, support both in their work, or enjoy the flexibility of services covered by having both

- Low hardware prices that make it more attractive for users to boost system requirements (such as RAM and physical/logical disk) that make running a second operating system more comfortable

- Operating system designers who realize people have an interest in running two or more operating systems and consciously attempt to make it easier for them to do so

What You Need to Run Two or More Operating Systems

Running more than one operating system brings with it special requirements, both concerning the PC itself and how you configure it. You need the following items:

- Two or more operating systems

- Either two physical hard disks or one physical hard disk divided logically into two (or more) partitions so that each operating system runs from its own drive partition

- A system that meets the minimum hardware requirements of each operating system

- Boot manager software

- Supported drivers for hardware for each operating system version

- Documentation from the operating system manufacturers that specifies in which order each operating system needs to be installed

Windows and Its Core System Components

All versions of Windows have the following three core system components at their foundation:

- **Kernel**   As its name implies, this component offers core Windows functionality and has several major responsibilities, including handling the input/output (I/O) services necessary for hardware to interface and operate properly, managing Windows disk-based virtual memory (VM) for smoother running, faster performance application use; and overseeing tasks scheduled on the system.

- **User**   This component is primarily in charge of taking input from the user—a mouse click, a key press, a digital pen click—and threading it through to the operating system so that the operating system understands that a menu item has been selected, a print choice has been made, or an icon has been selected and responds accordingly. Its job isn't restricted to standard input either. It also manages the operating system's interaction with features such as the serial communications ports, the system timer, and the system sound driver.

- **Graphical Device Interface (GDI)**   While its primary function is supervising the display you see represented on your monitor, GDI also oversees the entire graphics subsystem within Windows to manage and fulfill graphics support needs for I/O devices, including printers.

You'll find that many of the more serious types of errors and faults that appear in Windows will reference these components. Most often, the component at fault will be the kernel.

Fact   If you check your Windows installation, you should also see that each of these core components has a dynamic link library (DLL), a collection of executable functions or data used by Windows applications, in both 16-bit and 32-bit versions. Windows always tries to use only the 32-bit DLLs, and it should because 32-bit device drivers are loaded preferentially and both the I/O subsystem and memory management is 32-bit. The 16-bit DLLs are included, however, to load in place of the 32-bit DLLs in unusual circumstances (for example, to meet a backward-compatibility requirement or when 32-bit demands more memory than 16-bit).

DLL files do not always end in the .DLL file extension. They can also end in .DRV, .EXE, and .FON.

Some DLL files are installed along with Windows. Other DLL files might be installed by one application but ultimately shared with and used by many different applications—and as a result, removing something shared by other applications might cause problems when you try to use these other applications later. Yet others are copied to your system when you install a single application, and that single application is the only thing that uses it.

As a general rule, reinstalling an application will usually reinstall its necessary .DLL as well as other files.

Troubleshooting

Because we're knee deep in operating systems, hardware, and how they work together, now is a good time to visit a type of troubleshooting problem that can really test both patience and skill. It's one often reported to help desks, to technical message boards, and to support lines. Let's assume you're working with a group of PCs that otherwise work fine but for which some regular upgrading has occurred. In this example, let's say more RAM has been installed to different systems that were running fine before the upgrade.

Suddenly, however, users on these systems are deluged by KERNEL32.DLL and invalid page-fault errors and repeated system crashes. When rebooting their computers, they are faced with intermittent checksum errors. If you were the technician covering these systems, you probably would consider the RAM upgrades as the source of the problem. Yet, when you check online resources such as the Microsoft Knowledge Base, they might point you to a problem with the Windows installation or to new applications installed that might be affecting system stability. You would probably scratch your head because you're not certain how memory issues could be tied to Windows instability or why the instability would otherwise appear on systems that were running well before the RAM upgrade.

Let's break the issues down logically. If only systems where RAM was added are showing the problems, you would be wise to turn most of your attention to the added memory because it's the most likely suspect. In fact, the Checksum errors some users see on reboot is frequently linked to problematic memory (although I've seen a corrupted BIOS produce this, too). A good technician's first step after doing her research should be to remove only the memory installed on each of these troubled machines to see if the problems disappear. If they do, the answer might be that it was a bad batch of memory or memory incompatible with the machines it was installed on.

Now let's analyze the rest of the issue. The kernel is intimately involved in I/O handling for the operating system. Because hardware is part of the I/O, a problem with hardware can indeed be displayed in the form of kernel errors. Kernel errors appear when an application or program tries to access or use the area of protected mode memory in which the kernel is first loaded as the operating system is launched.

Problematic memory also tends to result in system lockups and crashes because it's not operating properly in the machine. In such a situation, you should completely rule out the issue of memory before you try anything else. However, if you've tried the absolute correct memory (and more than one stick of it) for the system and even restoring it to its former RAM does not help, you need to investigate the individual systems.

Look at which applications are running when the kernel and invalid page fault messages are seen. If the problem occurs only with one or two applications, you might want to uninstall these applications fully and then reinstall them. Doing this will rule out a corrupted program installation. But if the problem happens with many applications and programs, then it might be a corrupted Windows installation (in which case, installing Windows to a fresh folder or reformatting and completely reinstalling it should work).

> **Exam Tip**   Typically, insufficient RAM—or a lack of recognized RAM caused by the RAM being either defective, improperly seated, or of the wrong type—for system demands is often a factor, if not the chief cause, of many invalid page faults and general protection faults.

PROFILE: Windows Virtual Memory Management

An important underlying process intimately involved in determining how smoothly and quickly Windows (and other multitasking operating systems) is able to work with applications open on the desktop is referred to as *virtual memory (VM)*.

While main memory refers to the actual installed RAM on your system, VM management refers to a method Windows employs to have more "memory" available to it than is physically installed in the memory sockets. Interestingly enough, VM can actually contain twice as many addresses (or more) as main memory. (Address space refers to the amount of memory available to an application.)

In the course of loading and running applications and handling data files, Windows loads the main memory with as much data as it will accept. Once the main memory is fully occupied in an operating system that uses VM, the remaining data gets stored in a special area of the hard disk that is converted, using complex algorithms, into something the operating system can recognize as a form of memory. The disk space that is used is represented in the Windows swap file, a hidden file located in the root folder of the boot hard disk. The Windows swap file is dynamic in that it can expand or contract in size according to the immediate needs of the operating system.

The process by which virtual addresses are transitioned into real addresses (meaning ones in main memory) is called *mapping*. The process of copying virtual pages (a fixed number of bytes set by the operating system) from the disk-based virtual memory into main memory is called *swapping* or *paging*. However, paging is just one form swapping can take.

> **Exam Tip**   While earlier versions of Windows were reasonably amenable to user adjustments in the size of the swap file, Windows 98 and later usually function best when you allow Windows to handle this itself (which it does by default). If you opt to control this yourself and experience invalid page faults, kernel errors, protection errors, or other symptoms, reconfigure your system to allow Windows to manage it again.

Fact   VM and swapping are not concepts exclusive to Windows. Most multitasking operating systems—including OS/2, Unix, and some PC-based Unix variations—employ some type of these functions to help manage multiple applications open simultaneously on the desktop. However, under Unix, entire processes are moved in and out of virtual memory at one time rather than in segments such as data represented in pages.

Table 2-1   **Modern Windows Versions (Consumer)**

Windows Version	Release Year	Major Enhancements
Windows 95	1995	Full multitasking and full operating system
Windows 95A		Minor fixes
Windows 95B		Added FAT32 support, which allowed partitions over 2 GB
Windows 95C		Added USB support
Windows 98	1998	Added AGB support and full support for USB and FAT32
Windows 98SE	1999	Added Automatic Updates and better power
Windows Millennium Edition (Windows Me)	2000	Minimalized DOS, added System Restore and PC Health Initiative
Windows XP (Home Edition)	2001	Formed overall bridge between Windows consumer and professional editions; provided better support for newer hardware enhancements

Table 2-2 **Modern Windows Versions (Professional)**

Windows Version	Release	Major Enhancements
Windows NT 4.0 Server and Workstation	1996	Better hardware support
Windows 2000 Professional and Server	2000	FAT32 added with USB support; far greater hardware supported than earlier versions
Windows XP Professional	2001	Support for recent hardware initiatives, including better networking and mobile device interface; 64-bit version also available
Windows Server 2003	2003	Much enhanced security, support for Microsoft Office 2003 server procedures and extensions

Windows Files and the Root Folder

You should familiarize yourself with the files found in your root folder, including those that might be hidden and thus normally not in view. The root folder contains several files that are created or used during either the Windows Setup or normal loading process for versions of Windows 95 and Windows 98. Windows Me, Windows 2000, and Windows XP also create files in the root folders, although the most recent versions do not use the DOS-based files of its predecessors. Most importantly, some of the log files noted here can be very useful—or at least provide good clues—when troubleshooting a hardware, Windows installation, or Windows loading issue. With Windows 2000, Windows XP, and Windows Server 2003, it also becomes extremely important to have an idea of the files contained within your \Windows\System32 folder as well.

Depending on the age of your version of Windows, your root folder might contain the following files:

- **AUTOEXEC.BAT** One of the two DOS-based configuration files, containing command and environmental settings, that all Microsoft operating system–based machines prior to Windows Me processed upon booting.

- **AUTOEXEC.DOS** The AUTOEXEC.BAT (which was used only on Windows 98 and earlier machines) and the equivalent of the AUTOEXEC.BAT required on DOS-based systems. This optional file exists only in a dual-boot configuration.

- **BOOTLOG.PRV**   The BOOTLOG file used on operating systems prior to Windows 2000.

- **BOOTLOG.TXT**   The log that records the Windows boot (startup) process. It is created only under two conditions:

  ❑   If Windows determines the previous boot was unsuccessful

  ❑   If the log is requested by the user (by selecting the Logged option from the Windows Startup menu or specifying it in the MSDOS.SYS file)

  This file can be extremely useful in determining what devices and services might fail at startup.

- **COMMAND.COM**   The Windows command-line interpreter.

- **COMMAND.DOS**   The COMMAND.COM (which was used only on Windows 98 and earlier machines) and the equivalent of the AUTOEXEC.BAT required on DOS-based systems. This optional file exists only in a dual-boot configuration.. In Windows 2000 and Windows XP, this is located in the \Windows\System 32 folder rather than in the root.

- **CONFIG.DOS**   The CONFIG.SYS (which was used only on Windows 98 and earlier machines) and the equivalent of the CONFIG.SYS required on DOS-based systems. This optional file exists only in a dual-boot configuration.

- **CONFIG.SYS**   The second of two DOS-based configuration files run on boot (with the other being AUTOEXEC.BAT) in Windows 98 and earlier systems. This is a text-based file configurable by the user where you can configure DOS-based memory management and load real-mode (16-bit) DOS drivers for hardware (sound card, CD-ROM, and so on) that needs to be used in a DOS environment.

- **CVT.LOG**   This log is created when a drive is converted to FAT32. It can be useful for troubleshooting a failed conversion.

- **DETLOG.OLD**   The log of the previous successful Windows hardware detection process.

- **DETLOG.TXT**   The log of the last successful Windows hardware detection process. It's used by the system if the most recent hardware detection process hits a snag and needs to recover. It's also useful for troubleshooting issues.

- **IO.DOS**   The IO.SYS (which was used only on Windows 98 and earlier machines) and the equivalent of the IO.SYS required on DOS-based systems. This optional file exists only in a dual-boot configuration.

- **IO.SYS**   The input/output driver used to load Windows-based MS-DOS.

- **LOGO.SYS**   This file is used by Windows 95 to load the Microsoft Windows logo at startup.

- **MSDOS.DOS**   The MSDOS.SYS (which was used only on Windows 98 and earlier machines) and the equivalent of the MSDOS.SYS required on DOS-based systems. This optional file exists only in a dual-boot configuration.

- **MSDOS.SYS**   A file that contains configuration and boot parameters for the initial stages of the Windows loading process.

- **OEMLOG.TXT**   The log file created by an original equipment manufacturer's (OEM) Windows preinstallation routine.

- **SCANDISK.LOG**   The log of the most recent SCANDISK disk maintenance session.

- **SETUPLOG.TXT**   The log created by Windows Setup to capture the progress of installation.

- **SUHDLOG.DAT**   The data file created by Windows Setup that records a copy of both the Master Boot Record and Partition Boot Records both before and after Windows Setup runs. If you uninstall Windows, the previous Master Boot Record and Partition Boot Record are restored from this data.

- **SYSTEM.1ST**   The initial Windows Registry created during Windows Setup and used later, as necessary, if the permanent Registry becomes corrupted or damaged.

- **VIDEOROM.BIN**   A copy of the video adapter's ROM used to support the use of multiple monitors under Windows 98 and later. If it's missing, support for multiple monitors is removed until the user removes all other video devices except the primary (first) video adapter in Device Manager and then restarts Windows, which in turn re-creates this file.

Fact   AUTOEXEC.BAT and CONFIG.SYS are required only when booting to DOS. Windows 95 will use them, and Windows 98 will process them *only* if they exist. (You can operate without one or both if you want). Windows Me does not use them—if they are created, they will be wiped clean on the next boot.

Key Windows Configuration Files

Windows sets up your working desktop environment based on input provided from assigned settings in specific configuration files. Which files you will have depends on the version of Windows being used.

These files include

- **AUTOEXEC.BAT (root folder)**   A DOS-based configuration file that sets the environment and loads programs (used on older systems only).

- **CONFIG.SYS (root folder)**   A DOS-based configuration file that establishes basic memory management and loads DOS-based drivers (used on older systems only).

- **MSDOS.SYS (root folder)**   A file that contains PATH and boot options.

- **SYSTEM.DAT (Windows folder)**   One of two core Windows Registry data files. This one keeps computer and application settings and is required for Windows to load.

- **SYSTEM.INI (Windows folder)**   Note this file because it contains listings specific to installed hardware and data within it is used in loading certain drivers, including those for a sound adapter and a video adapter. This file is charged with loading 16-bit drivers for any attached hardware that does not use 32-bit drivers. Figure 2-1 shows the System Configuration Utility for the Windows XP Professional SYSTEM.INI file.

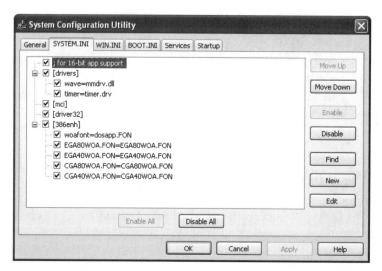

Figure 2-1   The System Configuration Utility for the Windows XP Professional SYSTEM.INI file

■ **USER.DAT (Windows folder)**   The second of the two core Windows Registry data files. It contains user-specific information and settings.

■ **WIN.INI (Windows folder)**   A settings initialization file containing information focusing on the overall Windows appearance. This file is automatically re-created in generic format if the existing WIN.INI is detected to be missing from the Windows folder.

■ **WINBOOT.INI (root folder)**   A temporary version of MSDOS.SYS that can override settings in the MSDOS.SYS in the event of a problem starting Windows.

■ **WININIT.INI (Windows folder)**   A configuration file for a utility that helps complete the installation of Windows components as well as third-party components. As changes are made with files, special instructions are noted in this file.

■ **WINSTART.BAT (if it exists, in the Windows folder)**   This file is used on a limited basis by those who need to run DOS-based programs with Windows functionality.

Understanding Windows Installation and Its Relation to Hardware

The three major phases to a Windows setup, regardless of the version of Windows being installed, are as follows:

1. Collection of data about the system on which Windows is to install. (This includes detailed information about the hardware attached.)

2. Physical copying of the new Windows files to the designated hard drive.

3. PC restarts and the configuration of the new operating system is complete from an installation perspective.

Logs Related to Windows Setup and Hardware

Windows consumer versions since Windows 95 have typically created three logs as part of the Setup install process. These logs, which report salient information regarding the success or failure of the steps, are as follows:

■ **Detcrash.log (root folder)**   This log keeps track of what hardware detection steps were successful, and it should be present only in the root folder of a system that failed Setup during the hardware detection process. (The log tells Setup which steps have already completed without problems so that these steps aren't repeated on the next try.)

■ **Detlog.txt (root folder)**   This logs the initialization of the hardware detection process and its final results.

■ **Setuplog.txt (root folder)**   Perhaps the most useful log of the three, this log records the steps of the Setup process and what problems, if any, were encountered. If Safe Recovery (used when Setup crashes or fails) must run to try to finish an install, it references this log to see where to pick up the job.

Hardware-Related Windows Setup Errors

Listed in Table 2-3 are some hardware-related error warnings that might appear during the installation (or Setup, which is the "SU" in these warnings) of Windows consumer versions.

Table 2-3   Windows SU Errors and Warnings

Error or Warning Number	Associated Problem
SU0010 (look for Microsoft Knowledge Base article Q129971 for information on actual message code syntax)	Detected a Boot Manager partition that a continued Windows install would overwrite, thus preventing the use of the original Boot Manager.
SU0011	Detected password-protected hard disk. The solution is usually to remove password protection and rerun Setup.
SU0012	Detected an OS/2 (HTFS) or Windows NT (NTFS) partition. Files on this partition will not be available when you use Windows 95 (or Windows 98).
SU0013	Can't install Windows to the specified drive because the drive might not be ready for use (that is, there's no active operating system partition and formatting or if you have HPFS or Windows NT file system, you must create an MS-DOS boot partition).
SU0014	Detected hardware device that won't respond.
SU0018	Similar to SU0013, but the error might be because of an excessive number (more than 255) of files in the root folder of the boot drive or because the particular drive has been remapped (either by networking or drive compression software).
SU0129	Can't determine a PC's hardware configuration.
SU0133	Can't determine system configuration.
SU0135	Setup was unable to properly identify all your hardware. To confirm your hardware settings, click Change Computer Settings to modify.
SU0142	Can't find enough capacity on the boot drive to copy all Setup files. The solution is to free up disk space.
SU0151	Can't determine whether PC has the minimum-required RAM installed.
SU0152	Detects RAM, but determines it's insufficient to install and run Windows.
SU0335	Can't determine hardware configuration, and there might not be enough memory to run this part of Setup. The best way to handle this is to restart the PC and retry.

Windows and Hardware

Now we'll explore a number of critical issues related to what goes on beneath the surface of a particular piece of hardware's relationship to the operating system it must work under. This exploration will include examining how new hardware gets recognized for use, how it communicates with the operating system when that device needs to perform work, how you can check the status of a device through Windows Device Manager, and the steps involved in a typical PC boot.

Hardware Recognition

When you install a new piece of hardware to your PC, you set off a chain reaction of events that are often fairly invisible to you as you restart your system. Here are the steps:

1. The device you installed passes information about itself to the PnP-compliant BIOS.

2. Windows retrieves that information from the BIOS.

3. Windows chooses the best match for driver information (that is, information within the .INF file) to install the hardware, and then locates the proper .INF file.

4. Windows checks the Registry to see whether the bus the hardware is installed to has an enumeration key, and then checks this against the new device's ID as supplied to the BIOS.

5. If the enumeration key is found, the device ID is used to choose and install the correct driver, or if no key is found, Windows writes one based on the device ID and the .INF file.

The first three steps in this process are known as *bus enumeration*. If you add drivers, which might happen if you update or otherwise change the current driver, Windows automatically writes additional entries to the Registry. However, as Microsoft notes in its Knowledge Base article Q275499:

> *"When drivers are updated or changed, a pointer in the Driver Information database or Hardware Information database is changed; however, there is no check to determine if mismatched files were installed during the driver installation. To work around this issue, you can rebuild the Driver Information database or Hardware Information database to eliminate any pointers that may cause mismatched files to be installed."*

We'll see more about this shortly when you learn about drivers and their role in the hardware-to-operating-system communication process.

Detection and Enumeration

Windows uses two processes to discover your newly installed hardware and configure it for initial use: *detection* and *enumeration*.

The detection process is charged with searching out and configuring older legacy and non-PnP devices. It runs at two specific times:

- When you run Windows Setup

- Whenever you run Add New Hardware, located in Control Panel, to look for and install a new device

> **Exam Tip** Check the root folder (C:\) of your boot drive for the presence of a text file named DETLOG.TXT. This file is created by your system during the Windows detection process and might give you clues to problems you need to troubleshoot.

The enumeration process, in contrast, is responsible for all PnP devices, including those on PnP-capable buses such as ISAPNP, Peripheral Component Interconnect (PCI), and PC Card (a mobile standard, formerly named PCMCIA). It also runs for two specific events:

- Whenever Windows is started

- Whenever the system detects a change in the hardware configuration (for example, when you've removed or added something)

About Hardware Resources

Beyond having proper installation and the right drivers, hardware depends on something known collectively as *system resources* or *hardware resources* to allow it to communicate with the PC. These hardware resources include the following items:

- Interrupt requests (IRQs), also known as interrupts, send a signal to the processor when a particular device needs attention or has work to perform.

- Direct memory access (DMA) channels help transfer data without being completely dependent on the processor's precious time to do it.

- The input/output (I/O) address represents a physical (hexadecimal or h) address at which a specific device can be found and used.

Some devices use all these resources, while others don't. A modem or mouse, for example, won't usually use a DMA channel. The toughest part about working with system resources is that they are very limited in nature. They have limitations partly because they are tied to the original IBM PC architecture that was engineered more than 20 years ago. At that time, our hardware needs were fairly finite. We didn't use sound cards (although there was a rudimentary sound chip that played through a simple internal speaker), let alone the fancy, multipurpose audio cards of today. Network cards weren't seen outside of business setups. Video was monochrome and a slow-blinking green. Hard drives weren't seen much before 1983. Modems were rare, and mice were nonexistent. Printers weren't even standard equipment.

But today's PC typically offers a cornucopia of hardware schemes. Many of us have at least one modem installed (if not two: one digital modem for broadband access and an analog one for backup dial-up communications), a mouse or trackball, a video card with more speed and video RAM installed than we used to see on a whole system, a multifunction and stereo-quality sound card, a network card to share an Internet connection between home or office PCs, multiple drives, plus perhaps adapters for special purposes (such as SCSI to add USB or Firewire ports to an older machine).

When the original PC debuted, we had just eight IRQs and four DMA channels to handle all our needs. And not all of these were available, because some of the resources were automatically snagged by the system itself to handle the system timer and system clock and to refresh memory.

With the advent of IBM's AT design, MicroChannel Architecture (MCA) by IBM, and Enhanced ISA (EISA) by a consortium led by Compaq and others, the number of IRQs has grown to 16 (with several still grabbed by the system) and the number of DMA Channels (some of which are also in use by the system) has grown to eight. This is the architecture we need to work around to get all our devices installed and working.

Tables 2-4, 2-5, and 2-6 give examples of common IRQ, DMA Channel, and I/O Address assignments seen in both past and present-day PCs.

Table 2-4 IRQs, Devices, and Availability

IRQ#	Devices	Availability
0	System timer	N/A to user
1	Keyboard controller	N/A to user
2	Used as a control for IRQs 8 through 15	Provides a bridge for IRQs 8 through 15, so N/A to user.
3	COM2, COM4	Normally used by COM2; also the default interrupt for COM4. Popular option for modems, sound cards, and other devices.
4	COM1, COM3	Normally used by COM1; also the default interrupt for COM3. Popular option for modems, sound cards, and other devices.
5	Sound card or LPT2 (if present)	Might be available unless it's being used for a sound card, a second printer, or another device.
6	Floppy drive	Generally N/A because it's reserved for the floppy drive controller.
7	LPT1	Available if no printer is connected, but it might cause a conflict if you install and configure an expansion adapter to this IRQ and a printer is installed.
8	Real-time clock	N/A
9	Available	You can't assign both IRQ#2 and #9 without conflict.
10	Available	May be used for another device to avoid conflict.
11	Available	May be used for another device to avoid conflict.
12	PS/2 mouse	Might be available if no PS/2 device is used.
13	Numeric Data	N/A
14	Primary Integrated Device Electronics (IDE) controller	For systems using IDE hard drive, this is used by the first (primary) IDE controller.
15	Secondary IDE controller	For systems using IDE hard drives on both IDE controllers, this is N/A; on SCSI systems or where the second IDE controller is not used, it should be available for device assignment jointly.

Table 2-5 DMA Assignment by Device and Bus

DMA Channel	Used For	Devices Using It
0	Memory refresh	Memory
1	Available if not used for another device	ECP parallel port, 8-bit and 16-bit adapters including network interface cards (NICs), SCSI host, sound cards, voice modems
2	Floppy drive	Usually just 8-bit and 16-bit floppy and tape controllers
3	Available	ECP parallel port, 8-bit and 16-bit NICS, SCSI host, sound cards, voice modems, old hard drive controllers
4	DMA	Bridge to add the controller, expanded DMA 4-7
5	Available	NICs, SCSI host, 16-bit bus
6	Available	NICs, SCSI host, 16-bit bus
7	Available	NICs, 16-bit bus

> **Note** In Table 2-4 and Table 2-5, *available* means there is no regular set device assignment for the DMA channel, and the channel should be available if no existing device on your system has grabbed it.

Table 2-6 Common I/O Address Assignments and Devices That Use Them

I/O Addresses	Device Using Them
000-00F	DMA controller, channels 0 to 3
010-01F	System use only
030-03F	System use
050-05F	System use
090-09F	System use
0B0-0BF	System use
0E0-0EF	System use
020-02F	Interrupt controller #1 for IRQs 0 to 7

Table 2-6   Common I/O Address Assignments and Devices That Use Them

040-04F	System timers
060-06F	Keyboard controller, PS/2 mouse, speaker
080-08F	DMA page registers 0 to 7
0A0-0A1	Interrupt controller #2 for IRQs 8 to 15
0A0-0AF	Nonmaskable interrupt (NMI) mask register
0C0-0CF	DMA controller, channels 4 to 7 (bytes 1 to 16)
0D0-0DF	DMA controller, channels 4 to 7 (bytes 17 to 32)
0F0-0FF	Math coprocessor/floating point unit (always reserved)
CF8-CFF	PCI bus I/O
120-14F	System use only
130-13Fh	SCSI host adapter (SCSI drives)
140-15F	SCSI host adapter (SCSI drives)
170-17F	Secondary drive controller
1F0-1FF	Primary drive controller
200-20F	Joystick controller
210-21F	Expansion chassis
220-22F	Sound cards, SCSI host adapters
240-24F	NICs, sound cards
260-26F	NICs, sound cards, PnP cards, LPT2, LPT3
270-27F	NICs, sound cards, PnP cards, LPT2, LPT3
280-28F	NICs, sound cards
2E0-2EF	Serial COM4
2F0-2FF	Serial COM2
300-30F	NICs, Musical Instrument Digital Interface (MIDI) ports
340-34F	NICs, SCSI host adapters
360-36F	NICs, printers, tape accelerator card (360h), secondary IDE slave drive
370-37F	NICs, printers, secondary IDE slave drive
3B0-3BF	Video Graphics Adapter (VGA) video
3C0-3DF	VGA video
3E0-3EF	Serial COM3
3F0-3FF	Primary IDE controller (slave drive) (3F6-3F7h) and Tape accelerator card (3F0h)
378-37F	LPT1 I/0 port

About Device Manager and Hardware Resources

Device Manager in Windows Control Panel serves as the user repository for information concerning which devices use precisely what hardware resources. Device Manager also lets you remove a device from Windows (without physically removing the device itself), disable a device, refresh or update its driver, and more. Let's take a look at it.

To access Device Manager, follow these steps:

1. Click Start, Settings, Control Panel (or in Windows XP, click Control Panel from Start).

2. Double-click the System icon.

3. Click the Device Manager tab (or in Windows XP, click the Hardware tab and select Device Manager). Device Manager is shown in Figure 2-2.

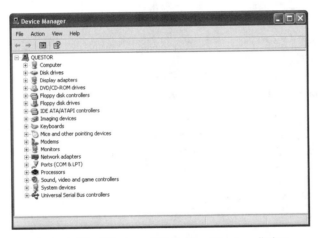

Figure 2-2   The Windows XP Device Manager listing

When you are in Device Manager, you can click the plus sign (+) next to any device category to expand that listing to show all devices contained within. Different devices will offer different tabs under its Device Manager properties, including the following tabs (as shown in Figure 2-3):

■   **General**   Provides general information about the status of a device and should normally report, "This device is working properly"

■   **Advanced**   Offers access to specific properties for certain devices such as network adapters and sound cards

■   **Driver**   Allows you to refresh, upgrade, and remove the driver for the specified device

- **Resources** Displays information about the hardware resources used for that device

- **Power Management** Permits you to make changes to any power management options for the device selected

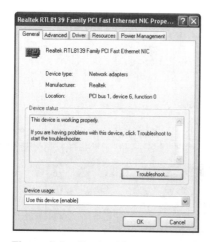

Figure 2-3   Device Manager tabs for specific device properties

Now let's look specifically at the hardware resources, found under the Resources tab, as shown in Figure 2-4. Particularly, you want to note anything listed under Conflicting Devices, because that can indicate the source of a problem if a device is not working properly.

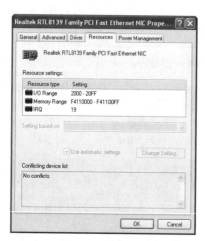

Figure 2-4   Hardware resource information for a RealTek network adapter in Device Manager's Resources tab

Take a moment to check the Driver tab under Device Manager as well, because you might use this resource frequently in working with hardware. As seen in Figure 2-5 for the Windows XP version, you can typically choose to perform any of the following actions:

- **View Driver Details**   Use this option to obtain information about the driver being used for a particular device.

- **Update Driver**   Use this option to apply a more recently released driver version.

- **Roll Back Driver**   Select this option when a newly upgraded driver misbehaves and you need to go back to the previous driver version for stability.

- **Uninstall**   Use this option to remove support for the device from Windows by uninstalling the driver.

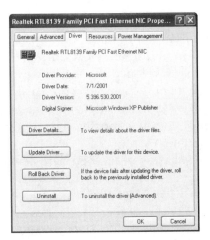

Figure 2-5   The Driver tab under Device Manager in Windows XP Professional Edition

Other versions of Windows will allow you to remove a driver right from the list or to select properties to let you view the various tabs.

> **Exam Tip**   Disabled or completely nonfunctioning devices will normally display in the Device Manager master listing with a red X, while devices whose hardware resources are in conflict or use a questionable driver might show up with a yellow exclamation mark (!).

About Legacy Hardware

Legacy is a nice way of saying *old hardware*. It can even refer to current-issue hardware designed to previous-generation standards and that continues to be used in modern PC setups. Often, this term is used to refer to older Industry Standard Architecture (ISA) hardware. Although ISA slots have not been included on Windows-compatible-rated systems since 2000, many Pentium IIs and earlier machines (as well as motherboards manufactured later that did not seek the Windows compatibility rating) have them.

When used, legacy devices often present particular challenges. As you read about the boot-up process, you'll see that all other hardware has to base its hardware resource assignments around legacy hardware, which might require very specific hardware IRQs. For example, legacy network adapters and sound cards love to argue over IRQ 5, and unlike their more flexible PCI versions, they aren't inclined to share that resource.

About PnP Hardware

PnP functionality isn't anything new, but it remains with us in an expanding form as we move into a world of instant-on devices and beyond to the ultimate convergence of the PC desktop and home electronics. Microsoft and companies such as Intel and Phoenix developed the technology to make PC devices easier to install and to have them recognized more easily by the system. PnP was around in a rudimentary form as early as the late 1980s, when MCA and EISA architecture reigned. PnP functionality has also appeared in the Apple Macintosh line for some time. By the mid-1990s, PnP functionality was standard in most PC hardware designs of motherboards, adapters, and even external devices.

PnP was a move away from the older form of ISA adapters that required you to change settings—usually in the form of rocker switches or jumpers on the adapter itself—to configure the device for use. Newer computer users found jumpers too much of a fuss to understand, and a lot of desired hardware never got fully installed. PnP was the start of a way to address this. Beyond this, PnP was designed to help the user juggle hardware resources, such as hardware IRQs, without having to understand the elements of hardware configuration in order to do so.

Soft menus were then developed to guide a user through a hardware install by using a software interface for configuration. Often enough, however, many technically savvy people complained that PnP just made adapters trickier to install (thus came PnP's nickname, "Plug and Pray"). These same folks often gave up and just configured the adapter using the legacy jumpers that were likely to still be on the adapter itself.

What Makes a Fully PnP Compliant System   To have a PC be fully PnP-compatible, you need the following three elements:

1.   A PnP-supporting operating system (as described in Table 2-7)

2.   A PnP-supporting motherboard and BIOS (which most computers manufactured since the mid 1990s have)

3.   Hardware additions that are PnP-capable

Table 2-7   PnP-Compatibility of Windows Versions

PnP-Supporting Versions	Windows Versions That Don't Support PnP
Windows 95	Windows 3.*x*
Windows 98	Windows NT 4.0
Windows 98 Second Edition	
Windows Me	
Windows 2000	
Windows XP	
Windows Server 2003	

How PnP Affects the PC Boot Process   During the boot process, a number of things have to happen for the system (the BIOS) to see all the hardware attached to the motherboard (directly or indirectly) and juggle resources to cover all of them for normal operation. (A description of the full boot process is detailed elsewhere in this chapter.)

These are the steps of the PnP component of the boot process that get the devices recognized and properly assign resources to them:

1.   BIOS compiles a list of all available hardware system resources (including free IRQs, DMA channels, I/O addresses, and so on). This list is known as the hardware resource table.

2.   BIOS checks for the presence of both PnP and non-PnP (legacy) adapters attached to the system buses.

3.   BIOS retrieves and loads the last successful hardware configuration from the Extended System Data Configuration (ESCD) stored in non-volatile memory.

4.   BIOS checks the last successful configuration against the configuration currently seen. If the two are identical, the boot process continues. Or, if it has changed, a new hardware configuration process commences.

5.   Resources for non-PnP devices are set aside (because they're less adjustable) in the resource table until the reconfiguration is complete.

6.   BIOS settings are consulted again. Here, BIOS looks specifically for any hardware resources reserved for non-PnP devices. If found, they're set aside, as in step 5.

7.   BIOS inventories known free resources from the hardware resource table and assigns them to PnP devices.

8.   BIOS verifies with the system that the resources have been reconfigured and reports changed assignments.

9.   The new configuration is written to the ESCD, and the boot process finishes.

Fact   ESCD is defined as a reserved area of complementary metal-oxide semiconductor (CMOS) memory, 32 KB or less, used as nonvolatile RAM (NVRAM). It is specifically used in PnP systems to store hardware resource configuration data that must be writeable at run time.

PnP Shortcomings   One essential fact you should understand is that PnP handling isn't wildly intuitive. It works its way around, dynamically juggling assignments for relatively simple configurations, but it might not make the best decisions when you have a trickier or less standard setup (and when you hit conflicts that display in Device Manager as red x's and yellow exclamation points).

One strong indicator of a trickier configuration includes using virtually any, and especially more than one, legacy adapter. PnP can't normally adjust anything related to legacy adapters' resources, so it has to move everything else that is PnP-capable around it. The more you have to "squeeze" in somewhere, the more likely you'll have a problem than PnP can't automatically resolve for you.

Beyond PnP: OnNow Technology and Immediate Installation   PnP now stands as the foundation of an evolving platform of changes to how we install our PC hardware. Part of that evolution includes designing for systems that are "always on" and where installation of new hardware can be immediately detected and available for use.

OnNow has several goals, as I'll discuss in a moment, and recognizes that users want a more sane, logical way to install hardware on a system without having to remove that system from service, even temporarily. This ease of installment is important because, compared to even a decade ago, we're apt to use far more hardware components in the course of a work day.

Hot-swapping refers to the ability to pop one device out, install another one without having to power down the machine or restart Windows, and still have the device change instantly recognized. HotPlugPCI refers to compact PCI cards, typically used in laptops and similar mobile devices, that can be swapped in and out this way.

Drive Bay, a separate technology, allows users to mount all drives and major devices (except for things such as RAM and CPU that must reside within the case) externally. Drive Bay maps what each device is and makes it quick to swap different devices without opening the case.

OnNow Goals   OnNow technology itself requires the cooperation of a number of entities: motherboard and BIOS manufacturers, operating system developers, hardware driver authors, and PC hardware manufactures. It requires these entities to create products that will work together and toward the initiative's ultimate goals. These goals include

- The PC is immediately available for use upon pressing the power button.

- All devices participate in the power management scheme for smooth transition between power operating modes.

- Newly installed devices are instantly available.

- The PC can go into an "off" mode that is still capable of responding to a wake-up call from a specific trigger—for example, an incoming fax or an otherwise ringing phone, mouse or keyboard activity, and so on.

- Applications running on the PC allow for a change in power operating mode and do not unnecessarily "wake up" the system to perform nonurgent functions—except for software that specifically schedules the system to wake up at a set time to perform a set task.

Yet several problems continue to thwart the full realization of OnNow. First, without some major engineering changes, PCs will go through a boot process of some duration (which gets shorter, but never seems fast enough) and won't be "instantly" available.

Second, power management on today's PC has come some distance over the designs of even 5 and 10 years ago, but too many factors must be *just right* in unison to have it work nearly flawlessly. Today's power management isn't just one overall mode of operation but several, from active and standby to virtually if not physically off. The operating system, the motherboard and BIOS, the hardware itself and the driver written for it, and the power source to which all of this connects all must work together to have a PC move effortlessly between these different states. Right now, power management in Windows and sometimes the BIOS needs to be disabled just to get an otherwise-fine PC to shut down from Windows 95, Windows 98, or Windows Me. (Power management seems a far cleaner proposition in Windows XP.)

Third, don't try hot-swapping your sound card or your video card anytime soon. You'll be happy if just the equipment is fried. And hardware of many kinds certainly isn't always easy to install, even now.

The list goes on.

Fact   Microsoft offers several white papers on the topic of OnNow technology in the Hardware Developers section of its Web site. A particularly good overview paper can be found at *http://www.microsoft.com/hhcd/hcdev/tech/onnow/onnow1.mspx* .

On-and-Off Chip Wear

According to information found at the OnNow site as well as through my experience and anecdotes I've heard, many users prefer to shut off their PCs after each work session rather than leave it on all the time, even with power management powering down energy to drives and the monitor.

Despite the potential effect on chip and component lifespan on systems that are very frequently turned on, users say they feel they'll save more power and prevent damage to their systems by turning it off. Whether to leave the system on all the time or not is another constantly resurfacing hardware debate, but the majority of frequent, experienced users prefer to leave their systems up except when away for a period of a few days or during special situations, such as electrical storms. Unfortunately, I've never seen many hard-and-fast figures I respect related to chip wear vs. number of times initialized, or even how much we save keeping our systems turned off sometimes vs. leaving them on all the time. Some users have tried to estimate this and report their findings, which suggested they saved less than $2 on a monthly power bill keeping a PC off most of the time but that the CPU and memory seemed to fail up to 20 percent faster when a unit is regularly powered on and off rather than kept on all the time. But there are really too many factors at work, I believe, to measure this with any wide statistical relevance.

The Windows Registry

In structure if not function, the Registry seems like a huge centralized database storing all the details of your Windows configuration, including the hardware, software, and customization applied to it. Some liken it to the old master card files in libraries, where the entire contents of the building can be summarized. In many respects, all the important details within your Windows installation can be found in the Windows Registry.

Understand that the Registry is an exhaustive topic in its own right, and no short section of a chapter can begin to do it justice because of the intricacies inherent in its design and detail. The *Microsoft Windows XP Registry Guide* (Microsoft Press, 2002) is a good source of information on Windows XP, and it can also be used to apply to Windows NT, Windows 2000, and Windows Server 2003 in many cases because the registry data of these versions is very similar.

Because it's one of the core elements of Windows and because it's not uncommon to be able to fix a problem with Windows—including problems related to hardware issues (for example, when an old device keeps being detected long after it's been removed because the Registry still contains an entry for it)—your mastery of hardware troubleshooting increases in proportion to your knowledge of the Registry. Thus, I recommend you familiarize yourself with it along with safe editing techniques with this caveat: the Registry is complex and does not tolerate foolhardy adjustments even if the issue is just a typographical error. Always back up your Windows setup, create a System Restore Point (for later versions of Windows), and otherwise be prepared in the event a mishap with the Registry leaves the system unable to work properly. Until you're prepared for that eventuality—and most of us hit it occasionally—leave the Registry intact.

Core Registry Information

Let's look at some basic facts that will help you to understand the Registry better:

- The core of the Registry is stored in two files—USER.DAT and SYS-TEM.DAT. Windows 98 and later versions automatically back up these files for you as the system starts, but you should always back them up yourself before editing the Registry.

- The syntax of the Registry is exact. Changes made to it must conform to the syntax. If they do not, the modification is ignored (at best) or Windows can fail on an unrecoverable Registry error, try to fix itself, and might or might not be able to do so (at worst).

- Much of the hardware, device drivers, and associated programs for your hardware are listed as entries, along with various services, options in the Windows printing subsystem, the Windows NT sub-system, and specific user preferences.

- SCANREG is a utility included with Windows to allow the scanning and repair of the Registry. To repair the Registry when you can, you work from the command-line and type the following:

  SCANREG /fix

- REGEDIT is the editor Windows includes to permit the viewing and editing of the Registry. (See Figure 2-6 for a view of the Registry Editor window).

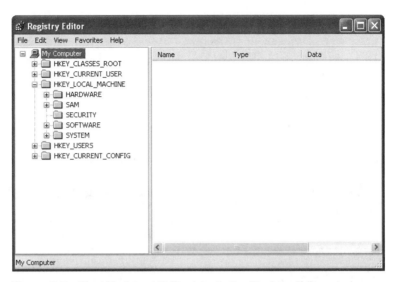

Figure 2-6   The Windows XP Registry in the Registry Editor window

- The Registry is organized into main or root keys that start with "Hkey_", branches out to subclassifications (such as CONFIG, ENUM, and HARDWARE), and branches down to individual listings referred to as keys, which can have both a subkey and value entries.

- HKEY_LOCAL_MACHINE is the primary key to which machine-type information, including the details of your hardware configuration, is recorded.

- HKEY_CURRENT_CONFIG looks to a section of HKEY_LOCAL_ MACHINE called CONFIG to see what the hardware inventory for that particular system looks like.

Changes you make to your system, including the installation and removal of hardware and its drivers, should be reflected in the Registry. Sometimes, however, a change fails to be registered or removed and the retention of out-of-date hardware entries can affect your ability to install new hardware or return resources for your use.

Familiarize yourself with the Registry, especially entries under the HKEY_LOCAL_MACHINE key, for a better understanding of your system as Windows sees it. Table 2-8 shows the kinds of entries stored specifically for PnP devices.

> **Note**   This table represents PnP component subkey entries under the following section of the Windows Registry: HKEY_LOCAL_ MACHINE\Enum\Bios.
>
> Registry subkey values are listed on the left, with the devices specified by the value listed on the right.

Table 2-8   PnP Registry Subkeys and Values for Windows 95, Windows 98, Windows Me, and Windows XP

Subkey Value	Device Specified
PNP0000-PNP0004	Interrupt controllers
PNP0100-PNP0102	System timers
PNP0200-PNP0202	DMA controllers
PNP0300-PNP0313	Keyboard controllers
PNP0400-PNP0401	Parallel/printer ports
PNP0500-PNP0501	Serial/communication (COM) ports
PNP0600-PNP0602	Hard disk controllers
PNP0700	Floppy disk controller
PNP0800	System speaker
PNP0900-PNP0915	Video display adapters
PNP0930-PNP0931	
PNP0940-PNP0941	
PNP0A00-PNP0A04	Expansion buses
PNP0B00	CMOS real-time clock
PNP0C01	System board extension for PNP BIOS
PNP0C02	Reserved
PNP0C04	Numeric data processor
PNP0E00-PNP0E02	PC Card/PCMCIA controllers
PNP0F01	Serial Microsoft mouse
PNP0F00-PNP0F13	Mouse ports
PNP8xxx	Network adapters
PNPA030	Mitsumi CD-ROM controller
PNPB0xx	Miscellaneous adapters

How a PC Boots

This step-by-step process assumes that the PC is being started by a *cold boot* (sometimes called a *hard boot*), meaning that the PC is cold or hasn't been running immediately prior to the boot. A *warm boot* (often referred to as a *soft boot*), in contrast, is one performed on a system that has already been started and initialized and will not repeat the first seven of the 12 steps listed here:

1. When you turn on your computer, the power supply engages and initializes. There is a time delay while the power supply begins to feed electricity to other components of the system. (Note the sounds you hear well before a display appears.)

2. Everything is on hold (in reset signal mode) until the system chipset gets a signal that the power supply's initialization is complete so that the process can proceed.

3. The CPU initializes and looks in the BIOS ROM to launch the BIOS startup routine.

4. The power-on self-test (POST) executes. If successful, the boot continues. If not, a series of beeps might be emitted to alert the user to a problem. Those beeps vary in number and signal, depending on what is wrong (such as a RAM failure or RAM not found, and so forth) and on which company developed the BIOS. (For more information see Chapter 7, "Memory.")

5. BIOS checks the video adapter to initiate the process of getting a display up and in place for user confirmation. If found, the video adapter is initialized and a display appears on the monitor.

6. Next, the BIOS looks for any other devices that have ROM that needs to be checked and initialized, including the IDE/ATA hard disk. If a problem is seen, an error message should display on the monitor because video was engaged in the previous step.

7. The BIOS then begins a virtual inventory of all hardware attached so that it understands what the system must acknowledge and work with in the course of preparing the operating system to load.

8. Then the BIOS looks for and configures all PnP devices for use, trying to fit resource demands around non-PnP elements.

9. BIOS information displays on the monitor, often giving you a basic picture of what hardware it has found and what resources are being used. (Depending on the speed of your system, it may display only for a few seconds.)

10. BIOS looks for a boot drive to initialize the final major stage of the boot process—loading the operating system. If BIOS is set to do so, it might look at the floppy drive first to determine whether a system boot diskette is inserted. If BIOS is not set to do this, it proceeds to look at the primary hard drive, searching for the Master Boot Record (MBR) to start the drive. (Note: Newer BIOSes can let you select a boot drive from a roster of hard drives available. Check your BIOS for details.) If no boot drive or disk can be found, it reports an error to the monitor display.

11. Once the MBR is successfully found, BIOS pushes the hard disk to boot and begin loading the installed operating system or, if you're using multiple operating systems, it presents you with a menu from your boot management tool to let you select the operating system to run during that session.

12. The operating system then works with the hardware information that BIOS has already gathered to bring these devices into operation and availability—including the loading of drivers and any necessary ancillary support for same—as the desktop loads (or as you reach a command-line interface, depending on which operating system you use).

About the Power-On Self-Test

The Power-On Self-Test (POST) is a critical component of the boot process because it's the first core test of hardware (once the power supply does its work). A PC that can't clear POST needs serious examination.

Remember the beeps discussed under the step-by-step boot-up process? You might ask why you get beeps only if something fails here. The beeps were designed to alert the user to a problem because, as you'll note in the boot process steps, video is not yet initialized and you can't count on the monitor to report the situation at hand. Besides, a good technician might occasionally be called upon to troubleshoot a problem system without a monitor attached.

Checking for Operating System

While this might seem like a no-brainer, even seasoned PC veterans find themselves working on a system only to discover they aren't fully certain which Windows version they are operating under. This can happen frequently in a busy office setting where people might work on a number of different PCs using different versions of Windows in the course of a single day.

A quick check of the Windows version can be performed at any time by following these steps:

1. From Windows Start, choose Settings and then Control Panel (or Start, Control Panel in Windows XP).

2. Double-click the System icon.

3. Select the General tab. The exact version is displayed there (as in Figure 2-7), along with the total amount of recognized memory installed.

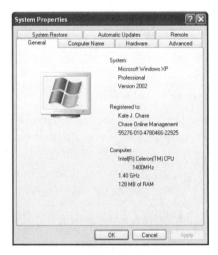

Figure 2-7   Checking the version of Windows in the General tab under System in Control Panel

The Role of Drivers as Go-Betweens

Drivers are often overlooked. If they install immediately and the device works right, we're thrilled and forget all about them. Yet they are key to how well a device will respond and perform under an operating system and its supported applications.

Drivers act as the intermediary between a device or service and the operating system, helping to translate communications between the two. A well-written driver is one that allows this communication to happen without exceptions, without undue delay, and with the full features of the device or service available for use in the operating system. A badly written driver (or a corrupted or outdated one) can be responsible for many symptoms, including

■ Temporary screen or full-system freezes

■ Erratic performance, slow performance, or both on the desktop

- Failure of the system to start up or shut down without errors or hangs

- Error messages that might indicate a device or service cannot be loaded or is otherwise unavailable

- Out-of-memory messages loading or frequent crashes in applications that typically interact with the device (a digital camera or scanner in Microsoft Word, for example)

However, be aware that these same symptoms can also appear when you have the following situations:

- A hardware conflict (that is, two devices trying to use the same hardware system resources at the same time, resulting in one or both being unavailable)

- Damage to the files that make up one of the Windows subsystems

- A situation where a bad driver for another device in use at the same time is misperforming and the effect is felt throughout the whole system

- A failing device—perhaps one that works sometimes but not always, making it harder to detect

- A corrupt Windows installation, Windows Registry, or both

- An improperly overclocked system or one that might be overheating

- A bad upgrade (application, operating system, or other)

- A computer virus infection

That's the challenge whenever you work with a nonworking or badly behaved system or device. Most symptoms can be traced back to more than one possible cause, and each possible cause needs to be ruled out until you can find the actual fault. The better you understand Windows or any other operating system and the hardware that runs under it, the more likely you are to develop a well-conceived list of possible suspects and the higher the possibility is that you can resolve the issue successfully. An experienced technician doesn't go into each situation knowing exactly what is wrong, but he or she brings to the situation a body of knowledge that helps reduce the variables and increases the speed and probability of a solution.

Driver Types

Since the release of Windows 98, Windows has supported the Win32 Driver Model (WDM) that standardizes driver design to ensure a common set of I/O services that can be read and recognized by Windows. This means that those who write device drivers need to create only one to apply to all WDM-supported versions of Windows, whether it's Windows 98 (consumer) or Windows 2000 and Windows XP (professional, Windows NT generation).

All major parts of Windows include universal driver and mini-driver support. The universal driver functions to provide general support for devices and services making up that Windows part or subsystem (for examples, the Printing Subsystem, Graphics Subsystem, and so on), while the mini-driver is for hardware-specific support. The universal driver is usually created at least in part by Microsoft, while the mini-driver is typically written by the hardware manufacturer.

A default or generic device driver usually provides just basic functionality for the device using it. For example, if you install a US Robotics voice-fax modem with many extra features and use a default or generic driver for it, you will (hopefully) be able to get basic commands and services from the modem. When prompted, it should dial and try to connect or disconnect. But because the default or generic driver was written to fit a general class of modems, it might not allow you to access the specific feature set of the actual modem you have. Thus, you might not be able to use the modem's prepackaged fax or telephony software. If you attempt to use other applications, such as Microsoft Net-Meeting conferencing software or WinFax fax software, you either won't be able to use the services or you won't be able to employ them as you normally would.

You might see this same sort of situation occur when you use an out-of-date manufacturer driver for the device. Or you might find that upgrading your operating system or browser makes the old manufacturer driver obsolete. Until you update to a manufacturer-released driver that supports your upgrade, extended features might be unavailable or less predictable in behavior.

Real-Mode Versus Protected-Mode Drivers

Real-mode drivers are 16-bit and used for backward compatibility and functionality for devices that cannot (or should not) use the 32-bit, protected-mode drivers that Windows would prefer to load for best stability and performance. In fact, by default, when Windows finds real-mode drivers loaded for anything for which protected-mode drivers exist, it automatically unloads the real-mode driver. An example of this is seen with the drivers for Microsoft's DoubleSpace/DriveSpace disk compression software that loads even when you are not using disk compression. (Note that you really should not use disk compression at all with the low cost of high-capacity hard drives because such compression can add layers of difficulty to troubleshooting system problems.) As the system boots in Windows 95 and Windows 98, the real-mode DBLSPACE.BIN driver is loaded invisibly, but then it is replaced by Windows with its protected-mode counterpart, DBLSPACE.VXD.

Some devices, particularly if they need to be supported from DOS (such as a sound card to play music for an old DOS-based game or something required by a DOS-based accounting or database program), will either load a real-mode driver or instruct you on adding one. If one is required, it must be written to either the CONFIG.SYS or AUTOEXEC.BAT DOS configuration files. (See the "Windows Files and the Root Folder" section.)

> **Fact**   Real-mode driver configuration information is stored in the DOS configuration files. Protected-mode driver configuration information is instead stored in the Windows Registry.

Virtualization Device Drivers

Often called just *virtual drivers*, virtualization device drivers (VxDs) are 32-bit protected-mode drivers that help supervise hardware system resources in such a way that multiple applications can use the same device simultaneously. Different VxDs have different file extension names that tie back to the I/O system and various subsystems with which they're designed to work. For example, drivers ending in VDD are virtualization display drivers, while VPD drivers are used in conjunction with the Windows printing subsystem.

Using the Windows Catalog/Hardware Compatibility List (HCL)

Do you want to greatly reduce the possibility that a device you purchase to add to a PC won't work properly right out of the box? If so, you need to know about and consult the Windows Catalog, formerly known (and still used for much older versions) as the Windows Hardware Compatibility List (HCL) before you buy. The HCL is an official compendium by Microsoft that lists all devices supported officially under different versions of Windows.

When accessing the list at *http://www.microsoft.com/whdc/hcl/search.mspx*, you can type in a specific device to search for or use device categories to look through various models available from different manufacturers to see whether the model you want is supported for the version of Windows being used. (See Figure 2-8.) Most major manufacturers—along with smaller ones—are listed with products they offer that have passed the Microsoft requirements for full Windows support.

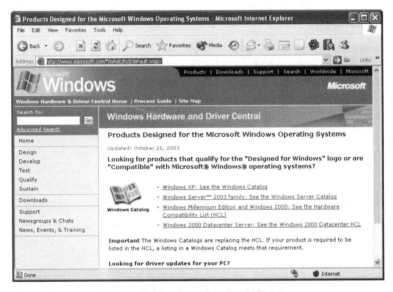

Figure 2-8   The Microsoft Windows Catalog/HCL site

Now, to be fair, you have to understand two things. First, just because a product is listed on the HCL as supported by your version of Windows does not mean you won't have trouble with installing or configuring the device on the operating system. The device could be defective, improperly configured at the factory, have shipped with the wrong driver version (it happens), and so on. Or your system might have special conditions that make the device's installation a challenge (overtaxed hardware resources, physical defects, or an unstable Windows installation). Also keep in mind that once Windows begins to experience problems in running, it might be more reluctant to accept new burdens or process requests properly.

The second issue to understand is the flipside of the first point: just because a device isn't listed on the HCL doesn't necessarily mean you won't be able to install and use that device. Some manufacturers submit only a limited number of products (and some submit none) to be considered for official

Windows internal support even though they have other products not on the HCL that have drivers that can be installed to support the device's detection and operation through Windows.

Still, you increase the chances for success when you regularly consult the HCL before you acquire new equipment, and you should find that it saves you the time involved in troubleshooting. Next, let's take a look at what you might need to do when you're working with unsupported hardware.

Problems with Unsupported Hardware

What happens when you have a piece of equipment you want to install but it "appears" to be unsupported because it's not rated for the version of Windows you're working with, because it shipped with a driver that is for a different operating system or Windows version, or because it doesn't provide express instructions for installing it to Windows?

The HCL would still be a good reference to check to see whether your make and model is listed. If you see it listed, you should be able to obtain the information and driver needed to install the device from the manufacturer's Web site (usually in their products or support area). Barring an available Web site (and the majority of major vendors have sites), which you can usually find listed on the device box or accompanying literature, you can call the manufacturer's support line. Other online sites, such as Drivers HQ at *http://www.drivershq.com*, can help you find a device driver as well.

Manufacturers' sites, by the way, often contain a wealth of additional information—including more detailed installation instructions and troubleshooting tips—greater than what you find in the literature packed with a device. So many of us toss the instructions and user manual as soon as we unpack a device because we know manufacturers aren't going to spend bundles on writing and printing massive volumes people won't read and that they instead place the information on their Web sites.

Don't be afraid to contact a manufacturer when you don't see a driver that supports your version of Windows. Some manufacturers pack drivers only for consumer versions of Windows with their consumer products, but they might have Windows NT, Windows 2000, and Windows XP drivers available on special request. Others might be willing to sign you up as a beta tester for a driver currently in development. If your PC comes from a known manufacturer, you also might want to check the PC manufacturer's site to see whether anyone else with your make and model of PC has reported similar issues in getting a device to work.

Beyond the manufacturer sites, you can often find additional technical sites—both professional and amateur—that offer information and assistance with problems you might encounter. Online hardware communities such as those found at *www.arstechnica.com*, *www.tomshardware.com*, and *www.extremetech.com* typically offer reviews and special information about products, and they feature message boards where you can post questions and get assistance. Such sites might discuss the problems with a particular model more honestly than a manufacturer's site, which might seek to minimize issues that could discourage other people from trying their product.

You should also make use of the Microsoft Knowledge Base, an online compendium of known issues with Microsoft products, such as the various Windows versions. It's available at *http://search.support.microsoft.com* and provides thousands of articles on different documented issues, including hardware problems.

Operating System Maintenance and Repair

A well-running PC operating system can go a long way toward the smooth performance of devices attached to it, while a badly behaved, seriously compromised operating system can manifest itself in many ways that might make you think your hardware is at fault.

In the course of your regular work with your PC, you should be performing regular backups of your data to protect it from loss in the event of a disk crash or corruption, and you should record disk images of your drive with its operating system and applications installed that can easily be loaded should you need to reformat your hard drive. Beyond this, you need to perform regular maintenance: clean up old, unneeded files (such as the tens of megabytes of temporary files you can accumulate in a single day) by using the Disk Cleanup utility under Start/Programs/Accessories/System Tools; defragment your hard drive using SCANDISK; and routinely uninstall drivers and programs you no longer use.

You should also do the following:

- Regularly check the Windows Update site at *http://windowsupdate.microsoft.com* to see what updates are available for your system and decide which to download and apply.

- Keep device drivers up-to-date, and closely monitor device and overall system performance following a driver upgrade.

- Be sure the applications and devices you install are designed for compatibility with your version of Windows. This is especially true for utilities such as disk management software, virus scanners, and crash prevention tools.

■   Promptly remove devices that are no longer needed or wanted. Be
    sure these devices are removed physically as well as through Device
    Manager (where disconnected hardware can sometimes continue to
    appear because the device remains in the Windows Registry).

■   Upgrade your PC BIOS as needed, and use only the proper BIOS for
    your motherboard.

■   Back up your Windows Registry before you make any manual adjust-
    ments to it.

■   If you install a device or even an application that does not perform
    properly, uninstall it until you can determine the source of the
    problem.

■   Regularly scan the system for computer viruses using an up-to-date
    scanning utility.

■   Use the MSCONFIG system configuration utility (shown in Figure 2-9)
    available in many Windows versions to familiarize yourself with the
    various Windows configuration files and what loads at system startup.
    (The rule of thumb is that the fewer programs and utilities running at
    startup, the better, especially when troubleshooting.)

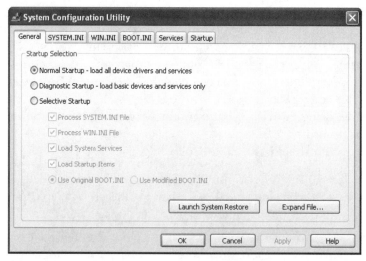

Figure 2-9   The MSConfig system configuration utility in Windows XP

■   Resolve stability issues with Windows before upgrading Windows
    itself or adding new devices or applications to it.

Lab 2: Determining Device and Windows Version Compatibility and Planning

This lab is intended to prepare you to do pre-installation research on relatively common hardware devices to reduce the chance that you might encounter unforeseen difficulty in adding each device to a PC with a specific version of Windows. While five real representative devices are given as part of the lab, the same research can be extremely helpful whenever you are planning to add a new piece of hardware of any type.

As you work, remember to note your results and the addresses of any additional Web sites you might visit as part of your research.

Objectives

When you complete this lab, you will be able to address the following:

1. How to use the Microsoft Hardware Compatibility List to check for device compatibility for a specific version of Windows.

2. How to use manufacturers' sites to obtain additional information about a device before installation or when troubleshooting a difficult installation, including identifying some of the common resources available on such sites.

3. Devising a plan for going ahead with an installation based on the additional information about the device and Windows version that you've been able to gather.

Necessary Equipment and Resources

The following equipment and resources are necessary for completing this lab:

1. Internet access with Web browser. A telephone line might be required as well to make inquiries to a technical support line.

2. A minimum of 20 to 30 minutes to research each device for compatibility and installation issues.

Procedures to Follow

For each device—and its specifically noted Windows version—in the following list, complete the steps, filling in your lab notes as you progress.

Device List

1. Asus TV FM Card (Philips SAA713x) to be installed under Windows 98

2. IO Gear 3.5 ION 120 GB combo USB/Firewire driver to be installed under Windows 2000

3. Creative Labs Modem Blaster V.92 PCI modem to be installed under Windows Me

4. LexMark x63 All-in-One Printer/Scanner/Copier to be installed under Windows 2000

5. FujiFilm Fine Pix A201 digital camera to be installed under Windows XP

Steps

1. Visit the Microsoft Hardware Compatibility List page, and check the device and its compatibility for the version of Windows listed.

2. Locate the Web address and visit the manufacturer's site for each product listed to obtain complete installation instructions, and note any special troubleshooting or installation tips.

3. Identify specific resources on each manufacturer site that are apt to be most useful in obtaining support and additional product information, including technical support Frequently Asked Question (FAQ) lists, support message boards, detailed instructions, support databases, and so on.

4. Identify the most recent driver version for the device and its associated Windows version, and locate the Web address it can be downloaded from.

5. Using a Web search engine such as Google or links at the manufacturer sites, identify at least three additional, nonmanufacturer Web sites that discuss each product from a technical or installation standpoint or that provide specific help regarding installation issues for the version of Windows cited.

6. Summarize what you learned for each device into a short recommendation note for how to proceed with the installation (or why such installation might not be successful).

Lab Notes

1. Is the device listed on the Microsoft HCL/Windows Catalog site? Does the Windows version cited support it?

   Asus _____

   IO Gear _____

   Creative Labs _____

   LexMark _____

   FujiFilm _____

2. Note the URLs and specific page references for each manufacturer site.

   Asus _____

   IO Gear _____

   Creative Labs _____

   LexMark _____

   FujiFilm _____

3. Note the most useful resources on each manufacturer site and why you found them helpful.

   Asus _____

   IO Gear _____

   Creative Labs _____

   LexMark _____

   FujiFilm _____

4. Identify the most recent driver version for each device and whether it's for the specific Windows version cited, along with the URL for downloading the driver.

   Asus _____

   IO Gear _____

   Creative Labs _____

   LexMark _____

   FujiFilm _____

5. Identify three other nonmanufacturer sites offering specific information or help with product installation and troubleshooting for each device. (Note the Web address for each.)

   Asus _____

   IO Gear _____

   Creative Labs _____

   LexMark _____

   FujiFilm _____

6. Summarize your recommendation for how to proceed with the installation (or your recommendation not to proceed) based on your research.

   Asus _____

   IO Gear _____

   Creative Labs _____

   LexMark _____

   FujiFilm _____

3

Defining Your Tech Toolkit

It's been said that good tools make for good repairs and a smart PC technician. That's true as long as you count knowledge and experience as tools in a good repair pack. Thankfully, you can obtain both knowledge and experience, although with quite a bit more effort than is required for you to acquire a good screwdriver. A good repair kit is composed of the following items:

- Hardware, including physical tools and common-sense items such as cotton swabs, rubbing alcohol, and a good knife

- Software, including boot disks, startup disks, and utilities

- Good reference materials, both print and online

- The means to restore work that might have been lost (through back-ups, drive images, and the like)

- A second Internet-accessible system you can use to check manufacturer sites, support databases, and the like (if possible)

In addition, there are the following "intangibles" that a technician should always be sure to have when working on a job:

- An adequate, well-lit work area

- An understanding of the normal working condition of the system, in addition to other knowledge and experience

- A calm and reasoned approach that follows a logical progression of troubleshooting techniques thoroughly and successfully

- The ability to use your senses, particularly sight, hearing, and some-times smell (as in knowing you should pay attention to a burning odor)

Let's explore many of these important points in greater depth, beginning with the tools you need to assemble.

Assembling Your Tools

Would you like to save time and frustration when you have a PC crisis on your hands? The best way to do that is to assemble the tools you'll need prior to entering a crisis situation, which is when you are best able to think logically and make reasoned choices. While not all these tools will fit easily into a small carrying case—although they would fit into a technician's briefcase or satchel—you should store them in readily accessible locations.

In addition to assembling the components you'll identify as necessary in the following sections, you should perform an occasional inventory check on them. Disks and tools often get misplaced or left behind, and instructions sometimes get mixed in with other papers. (How many times have you gone searching for your Microsoft Windows install CD?) Performing a regular inventory of your tools ensures you can respond quickly and effectively to all types of situations, without wasting time searching for basic tools.

Proper Hardware Kit Elements

When compiling a good hardware toolkit, you should acquire tools that you'll keep separate, fairly pristine, and easily accessible to you. You'll also want to ensure the tools are less accessible to a colleague or family member who is simply looking for a screwdriver to pry open a drawer. General household tools are subject to more abuse and pick up more grease and dirt than is acceptable for the tools you'll use on delicate electronics.

Good hardware kit accessories (such as the ones shown in Figure 3-1) are categorized by essential tools, wise-investment tools (items you should have), and smart extras. When assembling your kit, work through the lists in order of priority. Also, be prepared to augment these listings as you deem necessary from unique situations encountered in the course of your work.

Exam Tip   A screwdriver with a marred blade can ruin every screw it touches, making it more difficult to work with these screws later.

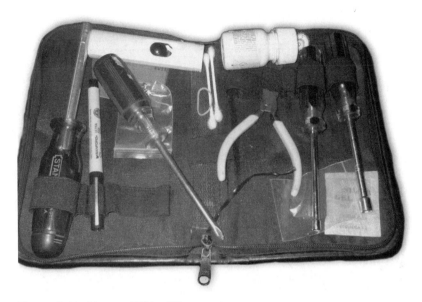

Figure 3-1   An open PC toolkit

Choosing Your Tools

A good hardware tool collection is typically separated into three categories: items you should always have with you, those that are great to have to extend your resources, and those you don't necessarily have to carry with you all the time. Table 3-1 prioritizes the tools you're most likely to need. You might need to adapt these lists to your particular working situation, however. Figure 3-2 shows two types of crimpers you may need, for example.

Figure 3-2   RJx crimper and cable crimper

Table 3-1 **Hardware Tool List**

Priority	List
Essentials	Two slotted screwdrivers of different sizes
	Two or three Phillips-head screwdrivers of different sizes
	Two nutdrivers, also of varying sizes
	Small, thin flashlight (such as a powerful penlight)
Wise-investment tools	Crimper/wire stripper
	Digital voltage meter
	Torx driver (a priority if your PC has Torx fasteners)
	Hemostat
	Long-nose pliers
Smart extras	Small container (preferably with dividers) for tiny parts
	Isopropyl (rubbing) alcohol in miniature bottle
	Good pocketknife or disposable-razor utility knife
	Compressed air (which comes in a can, for cleaning and removing dust)
	Dental mirror (which helps you check something closely with more success and less risk)
	Cotton swabs (preferably long-stick ones, which are best for deeper cleaning)
	Adhesive bandages (assorted), and minitube of antiseptic
	Cotton balls
	Set of small brushes
	Pair of disposable gloves (for dirtier jobs)
	Marker (for writing labels)
	Minipad of paper for jotting down information

Fact Not all tools fit all hands. Before you buy a tool, check the fit of it in your hand and imagine working with it for several minutes at a time.

Some PC chassis and lots of expansion boards come with razor-sharp edges. Don't underestimate the possibility of suffering a serious cut. Be careful when working! Adding a bandage or two to a technician toolkit is also a good idea, as it will help you avoid exposing the cut to metal, grease, or other debris in the PC.

Your Tool Case

Tool cases can be found in many places—general hardware stores, office supply stores, discount department stores, and consumer electronics shops, to name just a few. With the inexpensive nature of leather today, you can probably find a decent black leather tool case (black is good for hiding smudges) that offers years of wear for less than $20. For those opposed to leather, look for a quality vinyl, heavy-duty cloth, or microfiber case.

Fancy aluminum attaché-style tool cases with padding inside are available, but they often cost close to $100 and aren't as easy to carry as a simple zippered case. Use this option only if you have to carry a serious number of tools wherever you go.

Inspect the kit or case design. You want some degree of insulation for shock protection. Kits and cases get dropped, tossed around, and so on. You'll probably also want a way to secure individual tools within the case so that they don't bang against each other.

Also, check the closure on the case before you buy. You want to be able to close the kit or case reliably, and many models have a flimsy means of closure. If a zipper is the means of closing the case, it should be a heavy-duty zipper that won't break easily. A Velcro or heavy-duty tie closure works well, too.

> **Tip**   A good set of tools is an investment, and something you'll miss if you lose them or if they are stolen. Include some identifying information on the tools or inside the case, just as you might mark a bicycle or camera—but don't use your Social Security number, as an enterprising thief could steal that, too. Be sure to include a phone number so that someone can call you to return the case.

Prepackaged Kits

An obvious alternative to building your own customized PC toolkit is to purchase a preassembled package of tools. These packages range in price from under $10 to several hundred dollars, depending on the number and quality of the tools. The problem with such kits, however, is that you often see just a photo of the tools on the label. A photo isn't sufficient for assessing the quality of the equipment (which could be very poor) or for gauging the comfort and fit of the handles to your hand. These kits also have a tendency to include pieces you won't use.

In addition, some kits are packaged in cheap plastic or resin cases that have a tendency to crack, warp, or break. Because the case serves to protect your tools as well as organize them, you should evaluate the case as carefully as the tools within it.

> **Tip**   Do you know a technician with a particularly good set of tools? Ask where he got it, and check locally to see whether you can order something similar. If the technician assembled it himself, ask for recommendations.

Other Extras

It's smart to keep on hand extra power cords and other cables, such as USB, networking, printer, and video cables. Having working cables and cords on hand allows you to rule out the existing cord or cable as the source of a problem by swapping it with the reliable one you've brought with you. Even if you can't always carry these with you, having access to them can save you time and trouble.

It's also wise to keep extra standard video, network, modem, and other adapters on hand. Just like the extra power cords and cables, the extra adapters can help you provide faster, more effective troubleshooting.

Software

You might be able to fix a washing machine or clogged drain with an odd collection of hardware tools, but fixing a PC and its components is a far different matter. You need software, too, to cover all your bases. Remember: your goal is to design a kit that is useful for a variety of operations and repairs. The more essential tools you have at your immediate disposal, the better.

In this section, you'll learn about essential software you should have available. Some technicians combine all such disks (CDs, recorded DVDs, floppies, and so forth) in a single organized carrying case. Doing this makes it easy to take disks to remote repair jobs and to find the right disk.

> **Exam Tip**   Definitely avoid dumping CDs and disks unprotected by jackets or gem cases into your case. CDs and DVDs are easily scratched, and the metal edgings on plastic floppy disks can bend. And, if you accidentally toss your leaky lunch into the case, you've created a disaster.

Boot Disks

You should have a boot or startup disk for every version of Windows you work with. A *boot disk* is usually a floppy disk (and sometimes a CD or DVD) that has been formatted to include the essential files needed to start a system when the hard disk–based operating system can't. These disks should be precisely labeled and kept in a safe, readily accessible location. Where possible, keep multiple copies.

When you install a new Windows version—and this is true with most operating systems—you are prompted to create a startup or emergency disk to use for booting. If you don't already have one, you can create one through Windows. (Check online help for your Windows version.)

Check through your utilities, too. Several tool and diagnostic programs have you make a boot disk that is compatible with the product when you first use that program. They do this to ensure that you can get a new drive or a problem system going.

Windows CD/Recovery

Recent versions of Windows often allow you to use the Windows install CD as a sort of boot disk. Windows XP, for example, allows the CD to be used to boot the system as well as to run the Recovery Console.

If you're working with Windows XP systems, you need to familiarize yourself with the options, limitations, and commands available from the Recovery Console. For those familiar with old DOS-only systems, there are some apparent similarities for troubleshooting (such as being able to use CHKDSK—with limitations—to analyze and potentially fix certain disk problems, the Del or Delete key to remove a specific file, and Format to prepare a disk). For example, you can rewrite the system boot sector on a specified hard drive by issuing the following command in Recovery Console:

Fixboot [*drive letter*]

If you needed to rewrite the Master Boot Record (MBR) of your main hard drive, you might type this instead:

Fixmbr \device\HardDisk0

To start the Recovery Console from your Windows XP CD, follow these steps:

1. Shut down and restart the PC with the Windows XP CD inserted in the CD/DVD drive.

2. You might receive a prompt to load certain system-specific options. Choose any options you require.

3. Once the setup for Recovery Console loads, simply follow the onscreen prompts until you're given the option to select R for recovery.

4. If you have more than one operating system installed, you will be asked to select the Windows installation you want to recover.

5. The Recovery Console now loads. You can type commands or type **help** to produce a list of commands.

6. To quit Recovery Console, type **exit**.

Exam Tip   You can locate a list of Recovery Console Commands under Windows XP online help. To find this, use Start/Help and Support and type **Recovery Console** within the Search option.

Recovery Console can be installed directly to a hard drive as well, so there's no need to have the Windows XP CD available (although you should have it accessible). To do this, follow these steps:

1. With Windows XP loaded, insert your Windows XP install CD into your CD/DVD drive.

2. Click Start and point to Run.

3. When the Run dialog box opens, type **[drive letter:]:\ i386\winnt32.exe /cmdcons**.

4. Onscreen instructions guide you through the rest of the installation.

Utilities

A smart technician opts to keep copies of select utilities on hand that she finds particularly useful. These utilities should include the following:

■ Antivirus software, usually available with a copy that can be installed to a boot or startup disk

■ Diagnostic programs used to check for common and serious issues that might prevent the proper booting or operation of a system

■ Disk-checking software to check the integrity of a drive, to perform formatting or partitioning of a drive, or to copy or image a drive onto CD or DVD

A major issue you might encounter here is that some utilities can be version-specific, meaning that some might work with certain operating system versions or Windows-supported file systems (FAT32 vs. NTFS, for example) but not with all others. You must have available a version or versions that are specifically rated for the version of Windows (or other operating system) on which you are working. Using very old versions of such utilities can actually create problems—such as a disk-checking program that works fine with the FAT16 file system but that wreaks havoc on a FAT32 file system. Smart utilities check for compatibility before trying to run their processes, but some don't.

Also be aware of Windows-based utilities such as System Restore, available in Windows Millennium Edition (Windows Me) and all later versions of Windows with the exception of Windows 2000, that record specific system information, referred to as a *system restore point*, that you can later attempt to recover in the event of a problem. To use System Restore, you must have it enabled before you need to restore to a previous "time." This is true with most utilities that perform similar jobs. System Restore can be found by pointing to All Programs, Accessories, and then System Tools.

Drivers

You should have drivers on hand for all your essential hardware so that you can reload these drivers as needed in the event of an emergency with a system or in situations where you need to reformat and reinstall the operating system. Remember from Chapter 2, "The Operating System's Role in Hardware," that Windows doesn't automatically support every piece of hardware, nor can you download every possible driver needed through the Windows Update site or from your product manufacturer. This is especially true when you're dealing with an older device for which the manufacturer might have long since abandoned support and driver updating.

Backup Basics

If you think having a recent backup of your system isn't an essential part of an emergency repair and recovery kit, you're sadly mistaken. If you're routinely working on your own systems, you need to back them up, and if you're regularly working on client or employee systems, you need to be sure the people who use those systems are backing up their data regularly so that it can be restored in the event of an emergency.

With that said, some people would rather sit through a root canal than a backup procedure. Some studies suggest that even advanced users, who realize the bind they can be in if data is lost, will procrastinate on even considering the acquisition of appropriate backup equipment unless it's done as part of an automatic routine at the office.

Other studies suggest that in general, many users still rely on a backup medium that is older, slower, often more expensive (in dollars and time), and rarely has sufficient capacity. An incredible number of people still store off-load saves of a file to a floppy disk of less than 1.4 MB formatted, even though hard disks with over 20 GB are commonplace.

Over time, however, CD and DVD recording capabilities—along with external high-capacity and high-speed hard drives with USB 2.0 and IEEE 1394 connections—will change that, or at least reduce the difference between an inadequate backup and a selective one. CD recording appears to be the most-used medium today among personal and office systems, but there's considerable interest in DVDs as their recording standards and equipment continue to develop. DVDs offer far more storage capacity than CDs. Currently, DVDs hold 2.6 GB for each of its two sides (for a total of 5.2 GB; however, drives now in development should eventually write to as much as 17 GB). Unfortunately, DVD recording drives and the medium used to record upon them are still quite expensive compared to CD burning.

Major Backup Types

There are three major types of backups commonly used:

- **Full System**   This is a full copy of the drives.

- **Incremental**   Often used to back up all data files between full system backups or to place each day's work in storage.

- **Differential**   Used to back up only files that have changed since the last full or incremental backup.

- **Specific-Files (or spot)**   Specific important or critical files are chosen for backup.

Levels of Routine Backup Frequency

The following is a list of the various levels of routine backup frequency:

- **Level 1: Daily Full System Backup with or without Incremental Backups**   This level is used in commercial and enterprise situations and others, depending on specific need. It can be used in conjunction with incremental backups, specific file backups performed throughout the day, or both.

- **Level 2: Daily Incremental Backup with Weekly Full System Backup**   This level provides a good range of protection for almost everyone whose needs are less demanding than Level 1. Level 2 is ideal for those who generate several new or modified files each day but want the protection of a weekly full system copy.

■   **Level 3: Regular Incremental Backups or Specific File Backups, Bi-weekly or Monthly Full System Backup**   This is a minimum recommendation for those who regularly use their systems for personal and light professional use. Go with Level 2 if you frequently make modifications to your system.

In addition, there is a process called *drive imaging*, also known as *ghost imaging*, where software converts the contents of a hard disk, including configuration information and application settings, into an image. This image is then burned onto a CD or stored on a network drive or server. When you want to restore the image, the imaging software converts it back into its original format. Symantec Ghost and Powerquest Drive Image are two well-known, often-used commercial drive imaging packages. Consumers started using drive imaging more regularly within the last few years, as CD burners became standard equipment. Prior to that, the technology was used mostly by IT departments that wanted to install identical setups on a volume of systems.

Components of a Successful Backup Program

Let's spend a few moments looking at the components of a successful backup program, because the person called upon to repair systems is often the person who has to spearhead the efforts to begin a backup routine. There are five essential elements to setting up a successful backup program:

1.   Your understanding of the lost data's value (in terms of immediate need and time spent to re-create that which is lost)

2.   Your ability to make an informed decision about what data needs to be protected and your commitment to protect it

3.   A regular schedule of backups that you practice

4.   Backup software that is both fully featured and not too complicated to use

5.   A drive that has the following qualities:

❑   Adequate life expectancy and mean time between failures (MTBF)

❑   Adequate transfer rate for the capacity of the job

❑   Adequate size so that you do not have to be physically present to swap out media during a backup, which can take a long time

❑   Compatibility with the preferred backup software as well as compatibility with all features of the operating system being used, such as Active Directory for Windows and eDirectory/NDS for Novell NetWare

❑   A reasonable per-megabyte storage price for the job

❑   Compatibility with available connection methods (for example, if using IDE/ATA or SCSI, you have room to add it to your existing system)

Your Tech Journal

People often scoff at the idea of keeping a written record of either a single PC or all PCs they routinely work with. But it's a smart idea for a number of reasons. A journal—even if it's simply a sectioned notebook from the school supply section of a department store—can be used to record all the critical information about a system, including

■   Exactly what equipment and setup the system shipped with when it was first acquired

■   What changes have been made to the system over a period of time, including updates, upgrades, hardware failures, reinstallations of the operating system, and so on

■   Particular problems associated with the system and steps that have been useful in countering them

■   Special information, such as technical support numbers, unique IDs (such as the BIOS identifier string, which we'll cover in Chapter 6, "Central Processing Units"), Windows and other software product IDs, and so on

You can use a notebook with paper pockets for each section to store repair sheets, instructions, purchase slips, and whatever other paperwork you want to keep handy. Why use paper? You can store such a record on a PC as well, but this record could be lost—especially if you or your clients aren't diligent about backing up critical data—in the very emergency you need to troubleshoot.

You don't have to buy anything fancy—you just want something useful. A record can provide you with a blueprint of past problems, successful troubleshooting procedures, an understanding of what the system is equipped with, and an end to scouring your memory for how you fixed a particular problem the last time it came up (which can also help you avoid repeats of past disasters). For the investment of a few dollars and a few minutes each time you perform maintenance, an upgrade, or a repair, you'll have a valuable and tangible tool at your disposal. In fact, many Microsoft-provided utilities, such as System Information and others, allow you to make hard-copy printouts you can then add to your tech journal, either punched for a three-ring binder notebook or folded and tucked into sleeves.

Toolkit Intangibles: Knowledge and Experience

While not something you can physically put into a toolkit, knowledge and experience have to be present for success in most troubleshooting and analysis operations you'll perform. Most of these operations involve knowing the PC's operating environment, capabilities, and restrictions—along with the PC's onboard tools and information—before a crisis develops.

Let's take a few moments to cover some prerequisite knowledge for effective troubleshooting.

Know Your BIOS Before There's a Problem

Especially when working with drives, hardware resources, and the like, a common question in technical troubleshooting is, "Has anything changed in your BIOS/CMOS setup?" But if you don't know what those settings were before a difficulty arises, how can you respond accurately? Exact complementary metal-oxide semiconductor (CMOS) configuration and basic input/output system (BIOS) settings can differ widely between two machines, even two models from the same manufacturer produced around the same time. This difference arises because drive information, hardware resource assignment, power management options, on-motherboard integration, and specialty BIOS options (such as virus checking and thermal temperature checks) differ between motherboard and BIOS manufacturers and between motherboard versions.

You don't necessarily have to memorize (perish the thought) or jot down all the settings either. You can download special utilities from sources such as *www.download.com* and even from some system and motherboard manufacturer sites. These utilities are sometimes packaged as part of a BIOS updating tool, and they will document and save your CMOS settings so that they can be recovered later if necessary.

While this topic is covered in more detail in Chapter 5, "Motherboards," the following steps show what you need to do to access CMOS Setup, the user interface for the BIOS:

1. Start or restart your system.

2. As the system boots, follow on-screen prompts to enter Setup. (Often, this is a single keystroke such as Del or a combination of keys, which you also might find in your PC or motherboard documentation.)

3. Enter CMOS Setup, and begin moving through the various options.

4. When you are done, exit CMOS Setup without saving changes. The PC will restart.

Windows Startup Options: Safe Mode

Windows has long offered a number of ways to start a PC that will not load its operating system under normal conditions. One of these alternatives is a troubleshooting-only option called *Safe Mode*, which loads only the essential services and support for critically needed hardware so that the system can bypass problems that might be preventing Windows from loading as it should.

Operation of the PC in Safe Mode is limited, but it is useful for trying to troubleshoot an issue and is sometimes necessary to use when loading a recalcitrant driver, such as one for a video adapter. In the latter case, Safe Mode would allow you to set your system to use a default driver before you try to load the device-specific driver. You can also access special troubleshooting wizards built into Windows through Safe Mode.

A common operation in Safe Mode is to check Control Panel or access Windows online help. To do this in Windows XP, for example, you would follow these steps:

1. If the PC is off, start the system and press F8 when POST is complete. If the PC is on, choose Shut Down and Restart from the Windows Start menu.

2. The Windows Advanced Options Menu will load. When it displays, select Safe Mode.

3. Verify that Microsoft Windows XP Professional is highlighted, and then press Enter to choose.

4. Once the Windows desktop is loaded in this mode, go to Start, Control Panel or select Windows Help & Support.

Other options are available from the Windows Advanced Options Menu. Particularly helpful is the Using Last Known Good Configuration option, which allows you to restore the system to the last working configuration before your present one in the event that a change, such as a change to hardware or the installation of a problematic program, is affecting your ability to boot and load Windows. (This is not the same as a Driver Rollback.)

However, the Last Known Good Configuration is available to you only before you log on to Windows successfully; once you have, the previous working configuration is deleted and replaced with the configuration in use as the logon passed. For this reason, if you should receive a message "One or more services failed to start" as you start to log on, do not continue or you will lose the last known working configuration. Instead, reboot the system, press F8 to load the Windows Advanced Options Menu and choose the Last Known Good Configuration option.

Taking Proper Precautions

In this section, let's examine some precautions and preparations you should undertake before you get to work.

> **Caution**   Working with a PC, either inside the case or outside of it, requires special precautions both because of the overall frailty and minute size of certain components and because the PC usually has electricity flowing through it. No work should ever be performed inside the case with the PC connected to power. Don't underestimate these concerns. Everyone knows somebody who insists that he does all of his maintenance or repairs with the PC on or connected to power, just as everyone knows someone who either has harmed his system irreparably or has hurt himself while servicing a machine that wasn't disconnected from its power source.

Work Area Baseline Requirements

Almost all of us, at one time or another, will have to work on a PC in an environment that is less than ideal. Dim lighting causes mistakes. Unnecessary foot traffic in the area can contaminate or damage the machine or interrupt your concentration. Improperly placed cups of coffee or cans of soda often result in spills. Such situations should be the exception, not the rule. For best results, your work area should be:

■   Clean and dry

■   Well-lit

■   Spacious enough for you to move around in and to place needed materials close to you as you work

■   Free of children, pets, and other distractions

■   Free of any liquids that could easily spill

■   Supplied with adequate power outlets for devices you need to plug in

■   Equipped with a telephone, an Internet-ready second PC, or both, and easily accessible so that you can contact a technical support hot-line or online reference

Grounding

Static electricity is everywhere, particularly during colder months. By simply walking across a carpet wearing your partially acrylic sweater, you can create a great deal of it. If you introduce static electricity to delicate PC components, the effects can be powerful enough to damage the equipment and you might experience quite a zap yourself. Occasionally, you might hear of a PC motherboard that was "fried" from static electricity, or someone being sent to a hospital emergency room after receiving a sizable jolt. Such cases are no laughing matter.

Protect yourself and the equipment you work on through proper grounding techniques. You can, for example, obtain an antistatic grounding bracelet at many consumer electronics and hardware stores for under $10. When properly used, these bracelets can virtually eliminate the static electricity you bring to your work.

Grizzled veterans will tell you that another way to ground yourself is to touch your hands to the metal frame of the PC chassis before you place them inside. This usually works, but you might fail to do this every time you bring your hand out of the PC and reintroduce it again. Thus, an antistatic bracelet makes more sense.

Avoiding Dangerous Situations

The last thing you want to do when fixing a problem is create a wealth of new ones. But digging yourself into a deeper hole can be exactly what happens if you fail to observe proper precautions.

Several years ago, a friend of mine who was an IT specialist in Florida told me he was often called into storm-ravaged offices after a hurricane to try to salvage computer setups. The people working with him, unfortunately, had less experience than he did. More than a few of them sustained serious electrical shocks, while others further damaged already-compromised systems by failing to move the systems to a safe area before beginning to work. While this is an extreme situation, as a technician, you'll sometimes find yourself in such circumstances.

For your safety as well as the viability of the systems you work with, avoid working under the following conditions:

- There is either excess moisture or very low humidity present

- There are extremes of temperature (particularly temperature that is well below normal room temperature)

- There is fluctuating power (marked by lights dimming or power surging)

- You're too exhausted to think properly

The Process

Before you go inside the PC for troubleshooting, it's important to have a plan. Your plan could be to perform a physical inspection of the system, install or remove a component (or both), or just familiarize yourself with what's available. You can use BIOS (through CMOS Setup) and Windows Device Manager to give you a reasonable summary of many of the critical and working components without removing the case.

You've probably heard of Occam's razor. While some people easily translate this concept into the KISS (keep it simple, stupid) approach, it goes a bit beyond that. Occam's razor tells us that when presented with a number of possibilities to explain a particular phenomenon, the simplest and most common explanation is likely to be accurate. This concept applies to PC technical troubleshooting and is a good thing to keep in mind as you go to work.

When you are about to start a job, do the following:

1.   Choose a work site that fits the criteria previously mentioned in the "Work Area Baseline Requirements" section.

2. Prepare yourself in the following ways:

   ❑ Tie long hair back.

   ❑ Remove jewelry, including rings and long chains or necklaces.

   ❑ Roll up sleeves and anchor ties or scarves, and avoid wearing nylon or polyester clothing that can generate static electricity.

   ❑ Have a selection of tools, as described in Table 3-1, available to you.

3. Note the conditions of your work area. You should avoid working during electrical storms (that could detract from your ability to test) or other conditions that could affect clean, stable delivery of power.

Going Inside the Case, Step by Step

Remember to exercise care when working inside your system, as it takes little force to break wires, disconnect cables, stop a fan, unseat or badly seat devices, or fracture or otherwise damage a circuit board. The best way to exercise care is to follow these steps:

1. Disconnect the power cord from the PC. If you're using an uninterruptible power supply, disconnect the PC from it.

2. After noting all the connections and where they all attach, disconnect the video cable running between the PC and the monitor, as well as any cables running from the PC to other devices (particularly powered ones that might remain powered while you work on the disconnected system).

3. Check to see how the computer's case opens. (Often, this involves removing the cover, sliding the cover back, or sometimes pulling the contents of the case out using a special tray assembly.)

4. Begin removing screws while holding the cover in place. Place these in a container where they will not be lost. Set the loose cover aside.

5. Ground yourself.

6. With the flashlight, identify the components of your system (see Figure 3-3) and follow connections using information from Chapter 4, "The Workings and Connections of the PC," and Chapter 5. Make notes, as needed, in your tech notebook.

Figure 3-3   Exploring the inside of a PC chassis

7.   When done, be sure you have made no unwanted changes, and then replace the cover, replace the screws and fasteners that hold it in place, and reconnect power, video, and anything else you disconnected in the process.

Troubleshooting Essentials

A chapter on assembling a toolkit wouldn't be complete if it didn't go beyond assembling the kit to troubleshooting—the process that engages your brain, your senses, and your common sense.

Every good PC technician, whether professional or amateur, differs in the techniques, experience, and measures she will bring to bear on a problem. But good PC technicians tend to share certain knowledge and follow common guidelines. We'll look at some of those here.

Understanding Normal Conditions

The better you know the system in question, the better you'll be at evaluating which changes to the system might have caused the problem. Knowing the system includes knowing what is installed, how devices are connected, what problems have been experienced in the past, normal operating temperature range, and so on. The tech journal discussed earlier in this chapter and printouts from diagnostic or analysis programs, such as System Information, can be useful in this regard.

Early Intervention

While you can't always work on a problem the instant you experience it or get called in to repair it, you'll find that you can often achieve your most effective troubleshooting if you have the ability to address a problem as soon as possible after it first appears. There are several reasons for this, including the following:

- Continued operation of a PC or particular piece of hardware after a problem first develops might exacerbate or compound the original issue and eventually extend to other parts of the system.

- It might be difficult to gather all the salient information about "what happened when" if you don't explore these questions immediately. Memories fade, stories get embellished, or facts get confused with other incidents.

- Some issues will move quickly from malfunction to outright failure.

Developing Reference Resources

Competent technicians know that it's important to develop a good working reference library of print, disk-based, and online database collections (such as Microsoft TechNet), books, manuals, Web sites (such as the Microsoft Knowledge Base), and vendor product databases. It's also wise to organize this material by topic (such as hard drives, FireWire devices, bootup, CD drives, and so on) and keep a running index. Modify the list as soon as you discover something new or find that a listing has become obsolete or unavailable.

Where possible, you should also have access to the manuals and documentation related to the hardware and software installed on the system you're working on. Having these organized and available ahead of time further helps you to use your time efficiently. While you can often find this material duplicated (and even enhanced) through online sites provided by the manufacturer or publisher, it's still smart to have the hard copies around.

A Calm, Reasoned Approach

You can begin to arrive at a calm, reasoned approach to troubleshooting by adhering to the following guidelines:

- Start by examining what changed during the last session before the problem presented itself. Review and, if possible, restore the system state that existed prior to any modifications.

- Develop a hypothesis as to what is responsible for the behavior you're observing.

- Come up with at least a mental list of ways to determine the true source of the problem, and extend that list to ways to work around or resolve the problem.

- Prioritize that list from most likely culprit to least likely culprit, and investigate each item on the list sequentially.

Follow through on each idea on your list, record the system settings or conditions before you begin work, and then observe any changes in the behavior of the system or computer after you effect the modification. If the situation doesn't improve or it worsens, restore the system to the condition it was in prior to your modifications, and then proceed to the next list item. Avoid stopping halfway through one possibility and starting on another. Stopping halfway through a step makes it easier to lose track of what you have done and the order in which you have done things. Think of the process like a maze game of sorts: if you change course willy-nilly, you're more likely to go repeatedly down the same pathways than you are to find the finish line or exit.

Should you become overly tired or frustrated, find a good stopping place, note where you left off, and come back later. Proceeding when you're not in the optimal state of mind is unwise because you're more inclined to miss clues, perform incomplete steps, and forget to reverse settings. For that matter, statistically, you're also more likely to apply too much pressure to a circuit board, connect something incorrectly, and break something. Technical work should never be done while exhausted, under the influence of alcohol, or in other mental states in which both motor skills and cognitive processing are impaired.

And finally, if the final solution turns out to be something tricky or something you might need to repeat at a later date, jot it into your tech journal or notebook.

Using Your Senses

An experienced technician relies on much more than onscreen error messages and diagnostic software results when troubleshooting a tricky issue. In fact, several typical means of testing are done without a monitor attached to the system.

Error messages can be vague and sometimes even wrong (as when they report one situation when another situation is the actual cause). Diagnostic software often reports false positives and negatives, and typically just makes an estimated guess about the attached hardware (selecting the most likely option).

Once you become familiar with the layout of the system you're working on, as well as feel more grounded in PC architecture as a whole, it will become easier to rely on your senses, too, in diagnosing a problem. You can use your senses in the following ways:

- **Look**   You should seek out obvious signs of trouble, such as missing connections, frayed wires, subtle and not-so-subtle damage to a drive or adapter, and charring on a component surface. Also pay attention to what the system is able to report about the problem at hand.

- **Listen**   You can easily hear sounds such as the power supply fan, the powering up of the hard drive, the typical single beep as POST completes, as well as sounds indicating strain, excessive vibration, or grinding.

- **Feel**   You should use your hands as well as your eyes to be sure boards are seated properly, cables and connectors are attached firmly, and switches are engaged correctly.

- **Smell**   If you suspect overheating or even the "frying" of a particular component, determine whether you can smell a burning odor or that unique aroma of components running too hot.

- **Think**   Determine the most logical explanation for the conditions you're noting, and then check this out first.

Ten Most Common (and Easiest) Hardware Fixes

As much as 40 to 60 percent of all hardware problems boil down to uncomplicated issues with equally straightforward solutions. While the items in the following list might seem simplistic and easily managed by any fledging technician, the truth is that we all overlook the obvious from time to time. When we do, it costs us effort, time, and occasionally money. So here are questions you should ask that could lead to an easy fix:

- Is the PC or device plugged in?

    Countless consultants and technicians each day report that at least one of their service calls was resolved by simply plugging in the device or PC. It's also wise to test that electricity is working in the outlet, surge protector or suppressor, or other source the device is plugged into. Always check to see whether the power lights are on, and then move backward to the power source. If you can't confirm power, go all the way back to the circuit breaker.

■ Are the cables properly secured and in good shape?

Again, lots of service calls end up being for misconnected or disconnected cables. Triple-check these, both against your memory and any physical instructions you have. Also, always remember to check the condition of the cables. A frayed, compressed, or damaged cable might perform sporadically or not at all.

■ Have you rebooted?

It's not a joke—rebooting the system clears up a surprising number of problems. Printers that refused to print suddenly find their print jobs, errant scanners reset, desktop resources get refreshed. Rebooting can be useful if the difficulty was a misbehaving application or service, low system resources, or modems that wouldn't connect or disconnect. Perhaps before doing anything else, do a shutdown and restart on Windows or otherwise restart another operating system from warm boot.

■ Did you leave a floppy disk in the floppy drive?

Unless you changed it for performance reasons, your PC probably boots by first checking the floppy disk or CD drive to see whether there's a boot disk present, and then turns to your hard drive. If a non-bootable floppy disk is in the drive when it boots, you'll get a non-system disk error. Less commonly, you'll receive strange additional errors. If you leave a boot disk in the drive, however, you're going to boot to a DOS environment rather than to Windows. While you can get to Windows from DOS by invoking the WIN command at the DOS command prompt, the Windows that loads might appear slightly different than usual. Worse still, boot viruses that attach to floppies can be transmitted when a floppy disk is left engaged in the floppy drive and the system is restarted.

■ Did you install the device according to directions?

While the majority of us probably try to install a new device and read the directions only upon failure, always carefully recheck the directions and follow the diagrams (if included). The devil is certainly in the details here. Look for jumper or switch settings, if any, as well as the exact positioning of cables. Confirm that you have these set exactly right. If there's another person available to help you, have this person verify your configuration. A second pair of eyes can catch a lot that you might be missing.

Where possible, go to the manufacturer's Web site. More and more manufacturers are providing better online help than printed instructions. Plus, the online version might include revisions added since the printing of the manual or instruction sheet that reflect difficulties or questions people have had during installation.

■ Is the monitor turned on?

Don't snicker at this one either. Every day, someone arrives in an online support message base claiming that they just installed a new expansion card and now their display is dark. Before that person is even questioned about the seating and the resources of the newly inserted device (a common enough problem that can indeed prevent a display or even a full boot), someone will suggest the user do a quick check of the video cable. More often than not, the problem turns out to be a loose or disconnected video cable or a monitor power switch that was never turned back on. On some systems (although thankfully it's rare), if the monitor isn't on when the PC boots, the display can be slow to catch up or might just stay black until a reboot is done.

■ Is the cartridge or toner full?

Don't just eyeball a cartridge. It might be mostly empty but look OK because it is smudged with ink or toner. Take the cartridge out and check it *after* you've determined that the printer is indeed giving a "No Ink" display, signal, or error code. If you're still getting the error message with a newly inserted cartridge, check to see whether you need to clean the heads on your printer's software utility. Also verify that the tape commonly placed over the cartridge's printhead was fully removed.

■ What was the last thing you or the user did before the PC stopped working?

A large percentage of PC hardware problems come down to what the user did or changed in the session immediately prior to the development of the difficulty. Review any changes—however insignificant you believe them to be—and try to reset the system to its previous settings or installation to see if this resolves the issue.

■ If the equipment's new, did you completely prep it for install?

A leading cause of problems with new printers isn't hardware related, but a user's failure to remove the stays and immobilizers that typically ship with boxed printers. Most, not all, have brightly colored tags to help alert you to their presence and remind you to remove them. Also, again check the instructions or manual.

■   Is the phone line or high-speed connection working?

Probably the most common problem reported related to analog or digital modems isn't faulty hardware or configuration. Too often, the phone line isn't plugged into the proper jack, or no one has actually plugged a phone in to test the line for a dial tone. Another common problem is that no one has tested the connection to the high-speed provider or looked at the cable connecting the service to the modem or network adapter.

Lab 3: Assembling or Checking an Already Packed Tool Kit

This lab is intended to help you prepare in advance for your troubleshooting, installation, and repair work by showing you how to put together a comprehensive PC toolkit. While you do not need to have everything you've identified on your list at the time you perform this lab, you should obtain any additional items needed as soon as possible thereafter.

Objectives

When you complete this lab, you will be able to address the following issues:

1.   The essential components for your own toolkit (both hardware and software, plus important reference materials) based on the type of systems and work you are most apt to perform

2.   The specific need for each item chosen

3.   What items you need to obtain to complete your comprehensive toolkit

Necessary Equipment and Resources

The following equipment and resources are necessary for completing this lab:

1.   A repository (such as a tool bag or kit) to house the hardware you must carry; a shelf or storage area to store extra equipment such as cables, spare drives and adapters; and one or more boxes to house your software collection, manuals, documentation, and more.

2.   Internet access and a Web browser; a telephone line, which might be required so that you can contact a technical support line.

3.   Access to hardware tools, disks, and publications.

4.   At least an hour to organize and review these materials.

Procedures to Follow

First, review the toolkit components listed in this chapter and prepare your (empty) toolkit, storage area or shelf (as needed), and repository for your software (CDs, floppy disks) and documentation.

Next, pull your tools, disks, and reference sources into your working area. Perform an initial organization of them (hardware tools in one spot, disks and CDs in another, hard copy references in a third).

Then follow these steps:

1. Compare your hardware tools to the list offered earlier in this chapter. Assess them for durability, proper fit to your hand, and condition. (Badly marred screwdriver heads, for example, warrant a new tool.)

2. Clean any tools that have grease or dirt on them.

3. Divide these tools into groups according to their priority in your work. The first group should be tools you decide absolutely must be included in a carry-around toolkit; the second group should be tools that are good additions to have with you if possible; and the third group represents extra tools you would like to have available.

4. Note any tools missing from your collection that you need to obtain.

5. Examine your physical toolkit, satchel, or briefcase, and determine how your tools can best be organized and packed within it to limit the amount of rolling around and potential for damage. Then begin to pack your essential tools.

6. Review and organize extra equipment (for example, drives, cables, and spare adapters), and list any components you would like to have on hand but do not.

7. Organize your disk collection into categories, such as Windows and application install CDs, driver disks, diagnostic utilities, virus checkers, and so on.

8. Check these disks for dirt or dust; clean them with a soft cloth as needed.

9. Also check these for timeliness. Examine which tools need to be updated, and compile a list.

10. Note any missing software or drivers you need to obtain and add to your collection.

11. Organize these into a holder, box, or other repository, with each section clearly marked. (If you don't have section dividers, consider making cardboard or heavy-paper inserts that you can label and use accordingly.)

12. Organize your documentation and other reference materials accordingly. Note any material you think you should have on hand that you do not.

Lab Notes

This section contains three sections: hardware tools and equipment, disks and drivers, and reference materials.

Hardware Tools and Equipment

1. List by priority the hardware tools you have available.

   Essential: _____

   _____

   _____

   Wise Investment: _____

   _____

   _____

   Have Available: _____

   _____

   _____

2. List hardware tools you need to obtain to complete your kit, and give each a priority rank: 1) for Essential, 2) for Wise Investment, and 3) for Have Available.

   _____

   _____

   _____

3. Does your tool case, satchel, or briefcase accommodate your current needs? Can items you store there be properly organized and secured? How will you address this?

_____

_____

_____

4. List the spare equipment you have on hand. Be as detailed as you like, including describing where these items can be found.

_____

_____

_____

5. List any spare equipment you would like to have available that you currently do not have.

_____

_____

_____

Disks and Drivers

1. List your essential disk and driver collection. (Make special notes, such as "need to update," as needed.)

_____

_____

_____

2. Identify any disks or drivers you need but do not currently have.

_____

_____

_____

Reference Materials

1.   Identify your primary documentation.

———————————————————————————————

———————————————————————————————

———————————————————————————————

2.   List any documentation you feel you need but do not currently have.

———————————————————————————————

———————————————————————————————

———————————————————————————————

3.   List your major references.

———————————————————————————————

———————————————————————————————

———————————————————————————————

Enter the date you are performing this review (for later reference).

———————————————————————————————

4

The Workings and Connections of the PC

You will often hear the central processing unit (CPU) referred to as the brain of a computer. Carrying the analogy further, the motherboard—discussed in more detail in Chapter 5, "Motherboards"—is a combination of the central nervous system and circulatory system because communications between various components, to and from the CPU, occur through the motherboard architecture. In this chapter, you'll explore the essential hardware communications systems and some of the primary means of adding hardware to the computer. As you do this, you'll gain an understanding of the role of buses and caches and the actual geography of these components and connections within the PC.

How It All Works Together

Do you ever turn on the PC and find that the operating system loads as usual, you're quickly ready to work, and you simply appreciate the magic of electronics? Alas, however, it's not magic. Careful design and implementation get you from the point of pressing the power button to the moment you begin your work to the time you shut your PC down (assuming you don't leave it running continuously). Each nanosecond has been carefully planned and orchestrated by the people responsible for the development of the computer industry.

You learned about the PC boot-up process in Chapter 2, "The Operating System's Role in Hardware." Now let's look at what happens once the system clears its hardware checks and loads the operating system. Beneath the surface, out of your view, the operating system is very busy interacting with the PC hardware and your desktop as it manages a number of tasks, including:

- **Monitoring user interaction** The operating system constantly checks to see whether you've pressed a key, moved the mouse, or issued a command so that it can get your request processed without delay.

- **Handling CPU tasks** Before information gets sent to the CPU for processing, the operating system divides it into manageable bundles and then gives each bundle a priority rating.

- **Juggling memory** The operating system has to feed data in and out of your installed memory constantly and make flash decisions on whether virtual memory (that is, hard drive space used as memory) needs to be invoked to handle actions on the desktop.

- **Controlling devices** The operating system is responsible for controlling information relayed between itself, the CPU, other components, and the applications installed to the PC.

- **Storing data** The operating system is like the world's busiest switchboard operator as it directs necessary data to disk and memory storage.

- **Keeping track of itself** Microsoft Windows polls its processes and subsystems to determine whether everything is functioning as it should, whether all needed files are in place, whether you've plugged in a USB or IEEE 1394 device, and whether it can make available the resources you need as you need them. Windows will occasionally report a problem before you notice it yourself.

Meanwhile, on your desktop, you are loading and closing applications and files, downloading e-mail, performing a system check, printing a document in the background, checking a Web site. Yet, unless you're working on a very old system (like a Pentium 133 or older) or one compromised by having far too much running on too little memory, the system is keeping up with your demands, with rarely more than a split second or two's delay. This level of performance certainly was not always the norm. The evolution of PC architecture has brought it to us.

Wintel PC Design Specs

Almost every year, Microsoft, Intel, and select manufacturers put forth a set of criteria for new PC systems—including desktops, workstations, and mobile PCs—that want to be considered fully Windows-capable. This set of design specifications, part of the Windows Logo Program requirements, applies to all systems and the peripherals added to them that want to carry the "Designed for Microsoft Windows" logo. If a company's new line of desktops or workstations fails the minimum requirements, they don't get the logo sticker on the PC package that IT managers, purchasing agents, deployment administrators, and other consumers typically want as assurance that Windows will run properly.

An example that is still applicable for some is the PC99 design guidelines. In these guidelines, the death of the Industry Standard Architecture (ISA) bus (discussed later in this chapter) was spelled out. According to that now-historic specification, no motherboard could include an ISA bus as of January 1, 2000 and still retain its "Designed for Windows" certification. However, many of these motherboards were sold prior to that date and they typically had at least a shared PCI/ISA slot. These motherboards are still being used to run a vast number of PII and PIII CPUs, so ISA remains with us even today. While ISA devices are getting harder to find (and there's not a lot of reason to buy them) in the U.S., they're still widely used in countries where individual ownership of PCs is still a new concept or PCs are still reliant on older technology.

Of course, not all manufacturers seek or receive certification from Microsoft, which means they can still build systems using motherboards with at least one ISA slot or without meeting specific Windows requirements for power management. Most manufacturers, however, want Microsoft certification for the increased sales it can provide.

Color-Coded Connections

An example of the impact of the Microsoft-Intel PC recommended design standards (in this case, the PC99 specs) is that many types of PC connectors are now color-coded to help PC assemblers and consumers match cables, plugs, and other connectors to the appropriate jacks or ports. Not all connectors and connections are color-coded—including those for a network, telephone, or SCSI—and not every computer manufacturer follows this color convention. Some PC design standards are more hard-and-fast rules than others.

Table 4-1   Connection Color Codes

Connection Type	Color
Analog VGA	Blue
Audio (line-in)	Light blue
Audio (line-out)	Lime green
Digital monitor/flat	White
FireWire/IEEE 1394	Gray
Microphone	Pink
MIDI or game port	Gold
Parallel port	Burgundy
PS/2-type keyboard	Purple
PS/2-type mouse	Green
Serial port	Turquoise
Speaker out/sub-woofer	Orange
Speaker (right-to-left)	Brown
Universal serial bus (USB)	Black
Video out	Yellow

The PC Buses, Caches, and Essential Information

Once you tour the motherboard, as you will in the next chapter, you'll see the different ways various types of hardware connect to the PC, some of which you might already know from working with them. Buses are an important connection type because they provide the platform for add-on hardware, such as stand-alone adapters for modems, network interface cards (NICs), video and sound adapters, and special controllers. Beyond buses, you'll also learn about PC caches and the important role they play in making data accessible on demand.

PC Buses

A key part of PC architecture is the *bus*, such as the older ISA or current Peripheral Component Interface (PCI) bus. In fact, many systems used these days often have four or more buses included. *Bus* is a pretty accurate term here, too, because we're talking about binary traffic moving along that channel with the system chipset acting as the traffic controller. By definition, a bus refers to an information channel over which data flows back and forth between devices, and which allows an external device of the right type to be connected to it.

In the PC, the closer a bus is located to the CPU or processor, the faster it will be for communications. Thus, you want high-speed, high-demand components such as RAM and video or graphics to be closer to the CPU than slower types of hardware such as the mouse or printer. If you locate the Accelerated Graphics Port (AGP) on your motherboard, you'll see how closely it resides to the processor, which indicates its greater communications potential compared to a PCI or ISA video card, which plugs in farther away.

Depending on the age of your PC, you'll have the following buses on your system:

- **Processor bus**   This bus is for moving data back and forth to the processor. This is usually the fastest bus and has the highest priority. It might also be the same as the memory bus defined later in this list.

- **Cache bus**   The data here is restricted to information moving to and from the system cache.

- **Memory bus**   The data here flows between the PC chipset and processor and the memory subsystem.

- **Local I/O bus**   PCI is an example of this type of bus. It handles data from and to devices such as video adapters or other performance-specific devices. Communication flows through this bus to or from the chipset, processor, and memory.

- **Standard I/O bus**   Industry Standard Architecture (ISA), serial ports, and parallel ports are examples of this type of bus. This bus handles data from and to slower devices (such as a Web camera, mouse, or ISA modem) and the chipset and processor.

- **Accelerated Graphics Port**   Because of its limitations, there's some debate whether this is a port or a bus. This bus moves data back and forth between the video or graphics system and the chipset or processor.

In this section, installation information is combined with history to familiarize you with the technological evolution of expansion boards—such as video adapters—and to help you understand how they are connected to the overall architecture. If you don't currently understand why we can't just connect a few hundred devices to our PCs as cleanly as we add a few, you certainly should by the time you finish this chapter.

Industry Standard Architecture (ISA)

IISA has its roots in the very first IBM PC, but in many respects, the technology remains with us today. Even in systems without ISA slots for older expansion cards, the serial and parallel ports are still connected through ISA. (See Figure 4-1.)

Figure 4-1   An ISA bus expansion slot

Slow but steady, ISA has long served as the standard means of connection for lower speed devices such as simple video and sound cards, for SCSI host adapters that used slower SCSI drives, and for devices such as older scanners that required a SCSI adapter to be installed on an otherwise non-SCSI system. ISA originally ran at just 4.77 MHz, the speed of the original IBM PC processor (Intel 8088), and it had a data bus width of merely 8 bits. In 1984, when IBM expanded the architecture to become the AT (from the XT) bus based on the Intel 80286 CPU, the speed jumped to 8 MHz with a data bus width double its original size, or 16 bits. Today's systems, as you'll see, have expanded this quite a bit more.

Micro Channel Architecture (MCA)

As soon as cheaper IBM PC clones were recognized as a decent alternative to IBM PCs, many consumers opted not to pay a premium for the IBM name. IBM was slowly edged out of the very marketplace and technology it had initiated.

Micro Channel Architecture (MCA) was IBM's plan to recapture a proprietary PC market by introducing a revolutionary new bus design. Hardware resources were doubled. The data bus width was expanded to 32 bits while interrupt requests (IRQs) were doubled to 16 and direct memory access (DMA) channels doubled to 8. MCA became the foundation for IBM's PS/2 series, which was standard issue in most corporate office environments from 1987 through the early 1990s.

But the PS/2s were expensive machines, which prevented them from capturing the consumer and small business markets. Early models also had a tendency to overheat. Worse still, MCA architecture was completely proprietary. You couldn't mix in ISA devices, and you usually had to get parts from an IBM dealer or IBM itself. By this time, PC clone hardware pricing was very competitive. Although the real rush wouldn't come until the mid-1990s, many consumers and smaller businesses were shopping for their first systems around this time. People didn't want to pay a great deal more for their computer systems or parts just to have Big Blue's logo.

Enhanced Industry Standard Architecture (EISA)

When we talk about the ISA bus and devices these days, we're actually talking about original ISA influenced by Enhanced ISA (EISA). It was developed by a group of IBM competitors sometimes referred to as "the gang of nine." EISA was introduced in 1988 and was a major improvement over the original IBM PC ISA. It doubled two key resources: hardware interrupt requests (IRQs) and direct memory access (DMA) channels for non-IBM PCs. This increase in resources allowed more devices to be connected to PCs and reduced the potential for conflicts among those devices. The data bus width jumped to 32 bits. The intent was to provide a little more breathing room for adding devices until PC architecture evolved further.

EISA had one huge advantage over MCA. EISA-equipped systems could work with the older ISA cards just fine. MCA could not—and MCA was not compatible with EISA either. EISA also had rudimentary plug and play (PnP)–like functionality in that it tried to automatically configure installed expansion cards.

When Compaq, Hewlett-Packard, Epson, NEC, Olivetti, and the rest of the "gang of nine" joined together to develop and promote EISA, they probably never imagined how far PC technology would go while retaining EISA as part of the bus architecture. Their focus was to move away from depending on IBM architecture. There were a few reasons for this. To use the expanded ISA bus that IBM incorporated into the design of MCA in 1987, Compaq and other manufacturers would have had to pay a licensing fee. Also, many designers didn't want to be tied to the proprietary aspects of the MCA design, believing that it would limit the architecture's potential.

Microsoft and Intel, in the PC 99 Design Specs, sealed the fate of the ISA/EISA platform by specifying that no motherboard manufactured on or after January 1, 2000, that contained any ISA bus would qualify for the "Designed for

Microsoft Windows" logo endorsement. This turn of events was not a surprise. Having a single ISA device connected to an ISA bus in an otherwise fast PC degraded overall speed and performance, as the CPU had to interact with the slower bus. The ISA bus also occupied valuable motherboard real estate at a time when consumers were becoming interested in faster devices that also required a motherboard connection.

VESA Local Bus (VLB)

Also known as the VL bus, the VESA local bus (VLB) was mostly seen only in the early 1990s (peaking around 1993–1994) and largely disappeared as 80486-era machines were replaced with Pentiums. VESA stands for Video Electronics Standards Association, and that was the focus of this bus: to address video performance issues then common in other architectures.

Like MCA and EISA, VLB was a 32-bit bus. It was notable for its long connection slots and cards and the fact that it ran at 33 MHz (and sometimes faster). It was long because VLB was an extension of the 16-bit ISA bus (although ISA cards wouldn't install to a VLB), with third and fourth slot connectors added to the connection edge. At the time, a VLB video adapter in a VL bus system could seriously boost performance.

VL also had a built-in obsolescence, because it was also an extension of the 80486 processor and would be hard to fit to future machine designs. The VL bus allowed for only one or two VLB adapters because of its wiring peculiarities, and it offered no support for bus mastering (discussed later in this chapter). Ultimately, it was replaced by Peripheral Component Interconnect (PCI) technology, discussed next.

Peripheral Component Interconnect (PCI)

When Intel announced its planned implementation of PCI in 1993, the PCI bus ran at a maximum speed of 33 MHz, or about the same as the VLB. Macintosh systems were already using it then.

PCI, by design, is more configurable than ISA was, and it allowed users to determine tradeoffs based on individual needs, such as more throughput or a better response time. Also used on the Apple Macintosh line of systems, the PCI bus architecture was revolutionary because it allowed silicon chips to communicate directly, without building into the connection stream any hardware buffers. All PCI devices have a set of 256 registers, and each of these registers contains specific information. Some information is fixed, such as a device's ID, and some information can be reconfigured, such as address maps or interrupt types.

A big advantage of this approach is that with so much information stored on the PCI device itself, the PC should be able to detect, identify, and configure the device as soon as the PCI board is installed (as shown in Figure 4-2) and the

PC is booted up. Because of these registers, even early PCI devices supported PnP operations. With older ISA technology, it was often easier to kiss PnP goodbye and just jumper the device manually (meaning you moved shunts around specific jumper pins on the device itself).

Also, unlike the ISA bus that requires one unique IRQ per ISA device, PCI devices can—at least in theory—share an IRQ. This can be easier said than done, however, because the sharing of resources can lead to hardware conflicts. Certain types of devices share better than others, and device resource manipulation isn't for the faint of technical heart.

> **More Info**   In-depth information about PnP hardware and detection is included in Chapter 2, "The Operating System's Role in Hardware."

Figure 4-2   A PCI bus expansion slot

PCI allows for *bus mastering*, more expansion slots (typically, three or more), and ultimately, a greater variety of expansion devices than the VLB. It also lent itself reasonably well to the PnP technology that began to pervade the hardware industry by the mid-1990s.

The PCI bus and its devices are more user-configurable than other system buses. For example, the PCI bus has its own internal set of interrupts (often denoted as #A, #B, and so on) that can be configured through the Setup interface of BIOS to maneuver the exact operation of the PCI adapters installed to those slots. Understand, too, that the PCI chipset is well engineered to handle the identification of devices installed to it and will work with both the operating system and BIOS in the identification and resource assignment to cards installed to its bus.

One reason PCI is still with us is that its capabilities and speed have expanded over the years. This increase occurred partly because of the efforts of PC manufacturers, who wanted to extend the architecture but not abandon current standards in favor of faster interconnect technologies (such as FireWire/IEEE 1394) that were considered too expensive to implement. So the PCI design was pushed to 66 MHz, with a maximum data transfer rate of 264 MB per second. The current PCI specification is PCI 2.3, which was made available in 2002.

Exam Tip   You might see the phrase *PCI steering* either when reading about hardware configuration or checking through Windows Device Manager. PCI steering refers to the ability of the BIOS or operating system to direct or steer a PCI device to an available IRQ.

Where more than four PCI slots exist in a system, the first four PCI slots often each get their own IRQ, with additional slots then sharing one of these four.

CompactPCI (cPCI)

cPCI is an evolution or superset of the PCI bus architecture for industrial-level computers that offers a unique physical form factor called the *Eurocard*. (Form factors are discussed in more detail in Chapter 5.) One big advantage of cPCI is that it supports more PCI slots than regular PCI (eight vs. four) and this can be increased in increments of eight (for 16, 24, or 32 slots) using PCI-PCI bridge chips. Another advantage is that the cPCI connectors have 220 active pins that allow for enhanced grounding and more reliable PC operation in noisy, active industrial environments such as a factory floor or plant work area. Finally, some of the pins are there to support the development of hot-swappable cPCI cards in the future, meaning the system wouldn't need to be powered down to install a new cPCI device.

cPCI boards come in two versions: 3U and 6U. The 3U uses the original 220 pins, while the 6U boards allow for up to three additional connectors, totaling 315 pins, for more overall power and system control.

Bus Mastering (Two Types)

Bus mastering, in the context of the system bus, refers to the ability of PCI bus devices to grab control of the bus and perform transfers more directly, without as much drain on the CPU's precious resources. In a process known as *bus arbitration*, PCI devices work with one another to avoid resource conflicts and to keep specific devices from being locked out when a conflict does occur.

There is also a process known as *PCI IDE bus mastering*, which allows compatible Integrated Device Electronics/Advanced Technology Attachment (IDE/ATA) hard drives to become their own bus masters. Instead of using regular Programmed Input/Output (PIO) modes, which are usually slower, to transfer data, bus mastered drives use DMA modes to move data back and forth. For bus mastering to work in this sense, you need a 32-bit operating system (such as you have with recent versions of Windows), a bus-mastering-compatible CPU chipset and motherboard (available as a standard for several years now), bus mastering drivers, and a hard drive with the additional hardware necessary for DMA transfers (again, a standard for the past several years).

Many if not most manufacturers use the following conventions for slots: ISA slots are long and black, PCI/PCIx slots are short and white (as shown in Figure 4-3), and AGP slots are shorter and dark brown (although a few manufacturers have used dark gray).

Table 4-2   System Bus Architecture Comparisons

	ISA	EISA	VLB	PCI
Data Bus Speed (MHz)	5.33/8.33	8.33	33/50	33/66
Width of Data Bus (bits)	8	8/16	32/64	32/64
Data Transfer Rates (MB/sec)	5.33/8.33	33	133/264	33/264
Bus Mastering-Capable?	No	Yes	No	Yes
Supported Slots	0–8	0–8	0–2	0–4
Support HW Auto Config?	No	Yes	Yes	Yes

Figure 4-3   Comparison between ISA and PCI expansion slots

PCIx

PCIx is an extension of the PCI bus architecture that allows a faster throughput than original PCI and has full backward compatibility. Compared to most of the types discussed in Table 4.3, PCIx supports the same 32/64 data bus bit width, operating at a clock speed of up to 533 MHz, but has a data rate of anywhere between 533.3 MB per second to 4.26 GB per second.

Today's PCIx runs about 30 times faster than the original implementation of PCI. Older PCI adapters can be installed on today's PCIx-designed motherboards, and PCIx adapters will install on older PCI motherboards (but will run at the speed of the older bus design). There is no major difference between PCI and PCIx slots.

PCIx development was deemed necessary back in the mid-1990s, when PC designs were limiting the speed of the peripherals that could be installed. Many hardware companies weren't prepared to adopt a much faster, but more expensive connection type (such as FireWire, IEEE 1394). Doing so would have driven up the price of PCs at a time when more small businesses and homes were just beginning to be able to afford a PC and to see PCs as a basic necessary appliance. Plus, as discussed in Chapter 2, an operating system must be capable of supporting the connection and its surrounding architecture. Given all that, an extension of the existing PCI design seemed an easier, cleaner, and less costly way to go.

PCI, even when extended, can go only so far. In industrial-level computing, the cPCI standard, discussed earlier, is being challenged by the development of the *switch fabric I/O architecture* (which will be explained later in this chapter), which is considered a potential replacement for the standard bus architecture of the last two decades.

You can learn more about PCI and PCIx by visiting the PCI developers' industrial group at *www.pci-sig.com*.

PROFILE: Switch Fabric I/O Architecture

When we talk about industrial-level processing power, we focus on much higher levels than what most users need for their desktop PC. Manufacturers of network and data communications equipment in particular demand an expansion range that will boost not just overall bandwidth but reliability and scalability.

Because cPCI is still tied, at least in part, to the limitations of the PCI bus architecture that has been used for about a decade, any future bandwidth and scalability is bound by these limitations. But many PCI proponents say that the bottleneck isn't in I/O but in the failure of main memory to keep pace with CPU speeds. The CPU looks to main memory, grabs both data and instructions, and looks for results. Meanwhile, the I/O communicates with main memory secondarily, delivering data in response to the operations performed.

Some in the industry are more excited about relatively newer technologies than they are in trying to get more traffic onto a traditional computer bus. Perhaps the leading alternative architecture is switch fabric, something already seen in professional networking and communications setups. It offers both the desired volume of connections as well as the transfer speed that is so badly wanted. Thus, some companies, including Rapid I/O and Infiniband, are at work on the next generation of I/O design based on switch fabric. Other manufacturers have designed bridge technology that will allow the volume of PCI devices still in use in major enterprise operations to be adapted to a switch fabric–based I/O implementation. Some research indicates that adding the slower PCI components can negatively affect the overall speed of switch fabric.

Already in use in some parts of the industry, switch fabric technology is targeting the industrial-commercial information marketplace. However, thought is being given to developing it for the typical consumer PC as a complement to PCI and PCIx I/O.

Accelerated Graphics Port (AGP)

For several years, video graphics processing has been handled either through a video chipset integrated into the motherboard or through a stand-alone video adapter installed on either the PCI bus or the Accelerated Graphics Port (AGP). Older systems might also have a video adapter installed to the ISA bus.

The AGP acts much like a PC bus, although it's more accurately a point-to-point connection. Video is also better served because it's the only thing the AGP port handles; it doesn't have to share communication with any other device. This is by design. Prior to having AGP available, many users who relied heavily upon serious graphic rendering—either for games or for work—often installed extra cards to support the slower ISA and PCI video adapters available and to enhance 3D presentation.

Video bottlenecking has been a constant concern as PC component manufacturers and game producers struggle with a way to re-create the video arcade experience on a simple PC. But AGP has direct access to the main memory, which is important because it allows AGP video to store facets such as 3D textures in main memory instead of video memory (VRAM). It also operates at 266 MB per second in 1x mode, 533 MB per second in 2x, or 1.07 GB per second in 4x mode when operating with a graphics card that is 1x, 2x, or 4x compliant on a compatible AGP 1x-, 2x-, or 4x-compliant motherboard.

AGP also offered another distinct benefit when it first appeared. Many PC users with rising hardware demands were running low on physical resources, such as IRQs, and expansion bus slots in which to add new adapters. Moving from an ISA-slot or PCI-slot video card to an AGP (pictured in Figure 4-4) one freed up at least one expansion slot. Also, some AGP cards require at least one IRQ; some require none.

Figure 4-4   AGP video adapter in AGP slot

Caches: The Bridge Between CPU and RAM

While caches are usually not something you touch unless you swap out new CPUs on an existing motherboard or assemble your own system, they play a critical role in PC system performance. If you're running a 350 MHz PII with PC66 RAM or a PIII 900 MHz system with PC133 RAM (both older machines now), you might already know that the CPU is operating at a much faster clock speed than the RAM. One way PC design tries to compensate for the difference is by using small (compared to the amount of main memory) amounts of very fast and very expensive memory (static RAM or SRAM) that sits between the CPU and the main memory and handles some of the work swiftly so that the CPU doesn't have to wait for the slower RAM.

Clock Speed, Processor Caches, and the CPU

All PCs and virtually all computers have an internal clock that provides a vital function: it sets the rate at which instructions (basic commands or requests) are executed and regulates and synchronizes all the other components directly or indirectly connected to the motherboard. *Clock speed*, also known as *clock rate*, refers to the speed at which a microprocessor, such as the CPU in your PC, carries out an instruction. Your CPU requires a set number of clock cycles (sometimes called clock ticks) to perform each instruction. For example, the equation "1 MHz = 1 million clock cycles per second" means that if you're using a system based on a 66-MHz, 100-MHz, or 133-MHz clock, it runs at 66 million, 100 million, or 133 million clock cycles per second. A 533-MHz system would operate at 533 million clock cycles per second.

Beyond that, different core components can have their own clock speeds. For instance, the CPU and the expansion bus each has its own, but the CPU's runs much faster. The CPU and your system's main memory (installed RAM) also usually operate at different speeds from one another.

Different speeds in a PC can be confusing because they are measured using different criteria. Two key examples of this are CPU or processor speed, which is reported in megahertz (MHz) and gigahertz (GHz), and the speed at which memory cycles itself, which is reported in nanoseconds (ns). These are interrelated examples, too, because you don't want your CPU waiting too long for slow memory to retrieve data, so an important relationship exists between the two speeds. Today's systems increase the likelihood of the CPU having to wait because they are superscalar, meaning the CPU is capable of performing multiple operations each clock cycle. (Some CPUs can perform as many as nine operations each clock cycle.)

L1 and L2 Caches

Two physical caches help the process: the primary or L1 cache, and the second-level or L2 cache. Both sit between the ultra-fast CPU and the slower main memory, trying to do as much work as possible before the system needs to turn to RAM and the hard disk for anything not found using these speedier means. On some systems, past and present, there is a third cache, the Level 3 (L3).

Starting with the Pentium Pro (Intel's first chipset designed with dual processors and advanced operating systems like Windows NT in mind), the L1 cache has usually been packaged in the same set with the CPU. The ultra-close proximity makes for faster communication. The position of the L2, however, varies depending on the system and the CPU. For some, it's located on the motherboard between the CPU and the main memory slots. For others, it's packaged in the processor cartridge. On some older models—and this includes some laptops—there is no L2 cache whatsoever.

How Level Caching Works

Caching works on two basic principles: layering and hit-and-miss. Layering refers to layers of recently accessed information in the cache that the system can look for before it goes to the slower main memory to retrieve it. The higher in the layer that data is found, the faster the operation will be performed. It's like your bedroom bureau. You might tend to look in the top drawer first because it's fastest to do and it's closest to your hands and eyes. To carry the analogy further, you move down through the drawers sequentially only if you can't find what you want in the top drawer.

When the CPU (or to be more exact, the chipset that controls the cache and memory) needs information or otherwise makes a request, it works its way down through the cache layers first, going from the L1 cache to the L2 cache (and on some systems, the L3 cache), and finally, to the main memory, which might have to go to the hard disk or CD-ROM to retrieve it.

This is where hit-and-miss comes in. When the CPU checks the L1 cache and finds what it needs (an event referred to as a *cache hit*), the job is done. But if it doesn't find the data in L1 (an event referred to as a *cache miss*), it sends the CPU down to L2 and continues the search. The process is repeated in L2 and on down, all the way to the slowest of all these components—the drive—if need be, until a hit is achieved. During the process, multiple millions of CPU clock cycles can be wasted.

Also, each level of caching is tied to specific devices, as shown in Table 4-4. For example, the L1 caches the L2, among other devices.

Table 4-3   **Caching Chart**

Cache	Devices Cached By It
L1	L2
	Main memory
	Hard disk/CD-ROM drive
L2	Main memory
	Hard disk/CD-ROM drive
Disk	Hard disk/CD-ROM drive

Notably, caching can be extremely reliable. By the time the processor or chipset reaches the L2 cache in its check, there's a greater than 90 percent chance it will find what it needs without having to go to the slower main memory. And this is with an L2 cache of 512 KB (which can cache up to 64 MB of main memory), which is a fraction of the amount of main memory you have installed. It's a reminder of how much raw computing power is exercised in a split second beneath the level at which our eyes and brains can detect as we sit at our keyboards.

Inside the Case

Inside the PC case are components not directly tied to the motherboard yet still integral to PC function, such as the all-important PC power supply that turns your household or office electrical current into a form usable by your system. The drive bays and drives and the adapters also reside inside the case—usually.

Components Residing Within the Case

One thing to note is that not all components listed here will necessarily exist only as internal components. Devices such as modems, network adapters, and drives might also exist externally in freestanding units specifically designed to survive outside the case.

These components are as follows:

- **Power supply**   The power supply provides power to all components of the system, with direct connections to major features such as the motherboard and drives. Its wattage ratings vary, depending on system power demands.

■ **Drive bays**   Typically measured as half-size and full-size, drive bays provide physical compartments for the installation of various internally mounted drives, including floppy disk drives, hard drives, CD/DVD drives, and removable and backup drives. Most systems have a minimum of three drive bays. (See Figure 4-5.)

Figure 4-5   A contemporary PC power supply and drive bays populated by a floppy drive, two hard drives, and a CD recorder drive

■ **Floppy disk drive**   While they were once crucial for regular storage and even for performing backups, floppy drive technology has been stagnant for many years. Floppy drives (typically just one per PC) are attached by ribbon cable to a floppy controller attached to the motherboard. They are currently used mostly for small disk storage and boot disk use.

■ **Hard disk drives**   For ATA hard drives, a ribbon cable connects the hard drive to one of the (standard) two IDE channels on the motherboard (or it might connect one drive to another drive that is connected to the IDE channel controller). For SCSI hard drives, a SCSI cable connects a series of drives (with the type of SCSI determining the number) to a SCSI host adapter installed in the expansion slots. External drives typically connect through USB and IEEE 1394 ports.

- **CD and DVD drives**   Connections for these drives are similar to those for hard drives (mentioned previously), but they typically also require a connection to the sound adapter for playing audio. This includes recordable and rewritable CD units as well as the up-and-coming DVD ROM for recording. External models are available for USB and IEEE 1394 connections.

- **Video adapter**   Also known as the graphics card, this acts as the translator between the PC and the monitor. The translation it provides allows the action from the PC to be displayed, and it determines video speed, image quality, number of colors displayed, resolution and, by association, PC performance. Video adapters can be installed to ISA or PCI slots or to the AGP port; they also are available as an integrated component on the motherboard.

- **Sound adapter (with speakers)**   Most sound cards today are actually multifunction cards, allowing for a range of playback of sound and music and the recording of audio from a microphone or other external source. They also control some of the audio quality of the speakers. They usually connect through the PCI slots, although ISA adapters still exist. There are external versions as well.

- **Network adapters and modems**   These provide external communications with other PCs on a local network, through a phone line, or through a cable or satellite connection. Both network and adapters are available in external models as well, which connect by RS-232 connector to a serial port on the back of the PC or by USB port. They can also be integrated into the motherboard.

- **Other adapters**   These include SCSI, IEEE 1394, and USB adapters that add a functionality to the PC not available directly from the motherboard. These can connect through the ISA or PCI expansion slots or, in the case of SCSI, can be integrated into the motherboard.

- **Serial/parallel ports**   Serial ports (COMs) are generally used for slower communications, such as analog modems (non-DSL/cable/satellite), digital cameras, and mice, while parallel ports (LPTs) are usually used for printers and scanners.

- **Infrared (IrDA) port**   These ports are usually seen on laptops but are available for desktop PCs. Infrared allows for connection of IrDA devices (such as a printer, mouse, or keyboard) that use infrared light waves rather than cables to communicate with the computer.

- **Universal serial bus (USB) ports**   These ports are usually for slower speed, externally connected devices such as a keyboard, mouse, printer, scanner, camera, and speakers, or for high-speed external drives. They provide a theoretical maximum capacity of 127 USB devices.

- **FireWire (IEEE 1394) ports**   These ports are for high-speed devices, including storage drives, digital video, and audio recording. They accommodate a theoretical maximum of 63 devices.

Beyond this, inside the case, you'll find various types of cables and wires as well as a battery to help store the information from complementary metal-oxide semiconductor (CMOS), and more.

Exam Tip   An excellent detailed (but slightly dated) Web-based drill-down explanation of PC components and how they both connect and operate can be found at PC Guide at *www.pcguide.com*.

Outside the Case

Now you can begin to work out from the motherboard. You'll find that all major points of attachment lead directly back to the motherboard so that the attached devices can communicate with the system proper. Wherever possible, try to follow the path the cables and such take to get there, so you can understand the points of connection.

Typical connecting devices include, but are not limited to, the following:

- **Keyboard and other input devices**   These devices allow for the connection of the (required) keyboard, the (usually required) mouse, and specialty types of input devices such as a graphics tablet, digital pen, or alternative keypad.

- **Monitor**   Connecting the monitor into the back of the PC (usually to the interface of the video adapter or sometimes the USB port) allows communication with the main system and video adapter.

- **Printer or printers**   Printers typically connect either through the parallel or printer port or the USB port (or USB) hub, which accommodates a number of different USB devices through multiple ports.

- **External drives**   These drives can be connected through a parallel port, through USB or IEEE 1394 (FireWire) ports, or by a SCSI cable to the internally connected SCSI host controller.

- **Scanner**   This device can connect either through the parallel port or USB port or an attached USB hub.

- **Hubs (network, USB, and IEEE 1394)**   Such devices provide external capability for the network or hardware connections (such as USB and IEEE 1394), and they connect directly to the PC through Ethernet ports, USB ports, and so on.

- **Speakers**   Typically 2 or 4 in number, speakers attach by means of (usually color-coded) jacks located at the back of the PC, where the rear plate of the sound adapter is positioned. (On integrated systems, speaker jacks are located at either the front or back of the PC and connect to the audio chipset onboard.)

- **Microphone**   These are available in a number of types. Microphones typically connect through a jack on the connector edge of the sound adapter, by USB port, or by a special connector built into the front of the PC.

- **Digital camera**   Depending on the age of the camera being used, it might connect through the serial or USB/IEEE 1394 ports or, in the cases of digital video cameras, directly to the video adapter.

- **Network devices**   A PC—through its network adapter or onboard network capability—is linked through cable or wireless medium to other PCs on a network. There are also devices such as network routers and hubs and wireless access points.

More About Other Hardware Connection Schemes

Beyond buses and the AGP port, there are a number of other avenues for hardware to be added to a PC. Some of these connection options are located on the motherboard and are accessible only from inside the case. Some connection options are externally accessed but connected to the motherboard or consist of connectors at the back of the PC where an adapter has been installed to a bus.

Internal Connection Points

Before you move on, you should appreciate a bit more about the comparative connections types and speeds for connecting external devices such as printers, scanners, network equipment, and so on. Today's motherboards typically include the following items:

- 1 to 2 serial/COM ports

- 1 parallel/printer port

- 1 game port

- 2 or more USB ports that support USB 2.0 or earlier

Table 4-5 lists the major PC connection types by their speed so that you can see the range of PC speeds, from very slow devices (such as typical keyboards, printers, and analog modems) to the very fast ones (high-speed USB and IEEE 1394 second-version external drives).

Table 4-4   PC Connection Types by Speed

Connection Type	When Offered	Maximum Speed
Serial port	mid-1960s	20 Kbps
Parallel port	1981	1.2 Mbps
SCSI	mid-1980s	40 Mbps
Universal serial bus (1.0)	1995	12 Mbps
FireWire/IEEE 1394	1995	400 Mbps
USB 2.0	2000	480 Mbps
1394b	2000	800–3200 Mbps

Serial/COM and Parallel/LPT Ports

These device connection schemes are the true dinosaurs, dating back to the original IBM PC design. As such, they're also the slowest in terms of communicating with the PC.

Located at the rear of the PC, serial (also called COM) ports connect serial devices such as mice, older digital cameras, modems, and telephony devices. Parallel or printer ports support devices using parallel-style connections, such as printers, scanners, and some older external drives. Both types of devices ultimately communicate through the Super I/O Controller on the motherboard.

The serial port uses DB-9 and DB-25 male connectors (meaning they accept connectors with 9 or 25 pins, respectively). The parallel port uses a 25-pin female connector. The difference between a male and female connector, as you might imagine, is determined by architecture. The female connector is a cable connector that has holes instead of pins, and a male connector has pins that fit into the female connector.

USB and IEEE 1394 (All Versions)

Universal serial bus (USB) and IEEE 1394 (called FireWire on the Macintosh line) come to the PC world from the Apple computer world and offer an important change over serial, parallel, and other external connections. The most significant change is that you can plug a USB/IEEE 1394 device directly into a port, with the PC turned on, for instant recognition. However, exactly how "instant" that recognition is can vary considerably depending on the operating system version used, whether additional drivers or software must be installed, and so on.

Yet when these options were introduced into PCs in the mid 1990s, neither attracted much attention. More recent adaptations provide far more speed even to USB and make them suitable candidates for digital video and high-speed external drives. Many of us now use this technology to connect devices we don't always need installed on the PC. For example, I have about a dozen USB 2.0 and earlier devices—ranging from a scanner and printer to cameras, a graphics tablet, microphone, drives, and even an Intel microscope—that I attach easily when I need them and then detach and shelve when I'm finished. However, you still can't find IEEE 1394 ports on many motherboards, so including IEEE 1394 devices often requires you to purchase an add-on adapter, installed to a bus expansion slot, to provide this connection.

While USB accommodates the simultaneous connection of many devices, you usually just have one or two USB ports. Additional devices can be connected through the use of hubs, which act like intelligent power strips with ports to allow multiple devices to connect through one port. Most hubs should be powered, meaning they should connect to an outlet and thus provide the electrical demands of the devices connected through them. USB and IEEE 1394 devices might or might not require an additional power connection to an outlet, depending on how much energy they draw. Each USB port gets about 0.5 amps of power delivered through the USB bus, and each has a 4-pin rectangular socket (called Type A) to receive a Type B square plug-in from a USB device. A USB cable used to connect a device to a hub has both Type A and Type B connectors. (See Figure 4-6.)

Figure 4-6   USB port, device, and hub

IEEE 1394, by comparison, uses a 6-pin socket (4-pin on laptop devices) for earlier IEEE 1394 devices, and it accepts a rectangular-shaped plug with one end coming to a point. Later IEEE 1394 uses a 9-pin socket.

Keyboard and Mouse

Today's keyboard and mouse—two of the slowest devices because we are slow in using them—typically connect to the PC through means of DIN (Deutsch Industrie Norm) connectors located at the back (or sometimes front) of a system. Mostly, this is done using a 5-pin or 6-pin connector called a Mini DIN. Its connector to the PC is often referred to as a PS/2 port or connector. DIN adapters are available to fit a different DIN connector to a different DIN connection.

Lab 4: Ride the Bus

This lab is intended to prepare you for the work you will do both in later chapters and in your technical experience to identify the PC expansion buses and their slots, and to be able to identify one adapter connection type from another.

Objectives

When you complete this lab, you will be able to address the following issues:

1. The location of the PCI bus and any expansion boards/adapters installed to it

2. The location of the ISA bus and any expansion boards/adapters installed to it

3. The location of the AGP port and whether an AGP adapter is installed to it

Necessary Equipment and Resources

The following equipment and resources are necessary for completing this lab:

1. Three PCs of varying age (at least one should be more than four years old)

2. A PCI/PCIx, an ISA adapter, and an AGP adapter

3. Your PC hardware toolkit

4. At least 30 minutes to complete this lab

Procedures to Follow

1. If possible, place the three systems you will be reviewing in close proximity to one another, and then review (as needed) the instructions for going inside the case found in Chapter 3, "Defining Your Tech Toolkit."

2. Remove the covers from each of the three systems.

3. Locate the PCI/PCIx expansion bus slots.

4. Count how many PCI/PCIx expansion slots are present and how many of them are occupied by installed adapters. Can you determine what any of the installed adapters are? In your notes, jot this information down along with the number of available slots.

5. Locate the ISA expansion bus slots, if any. If there are none present, jot this in your notes. (At least one older system should have them.)

6. If there are ISA expansion slots, is one or more occupied by an ISA adapter? Can you determine what any of the installed ISA adapters are? Record your results in the lab notes.

7. Locate the AGP port, if any. If none is present, record this in your lab notes.

8. If an AGP port is present, is an adapter installed to it?

9. Finally, look at the connection edge for each of the three adapters: PCI/PCIx, ISA, and AGP. Record in your lab notes the unique characteristics between these connections and the appearance of the slot they fit into.

Lab Notes

Record your results from the bus check in this section.

1. Record the three types of systems you reviewed. Example: PII 350 MHz, PIV 2.1 GHz, and so on.

    System #1 _____

    System #2 _____

    System #3 _____

2. Record your PCI results for each system.

    System #1 _____

    System #2 _____

    System #3 _____

3. Record your ISA results for each system.

    System #1 _____

    System #2 _____

    System #3 _____

4. Record your AGP results for each system.

    System #1 _____

    System #2 _____

    System #3 _____

5.   Record your observations about the difference between slot and con-
     nection edge types for each adapter type.

     PCI/PCIx: _____

     ISA: _____

     AGP: _____

Part II

Internal Essentials

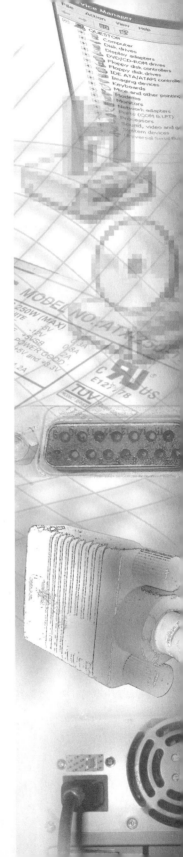

5

Motherboards

If the central processing unit (CPU) is the brain of a PC, the motherboard combines the circulatory and nervous systems. All major components either are available directly upon it or can be installed to it (either inside or outside the case). Basically all communication between the hardware and the CPU takes place along a motherboard's traffic system, such as the PCI/PCIx bus. Power to many critical components flows first from the PC power supply to the motherboard and then out to those components.

Each motherboard model can look quite different, yet all share certain similarities, even over the more than two decades of PC hardware development. While the motherboard of 1981 was nearly twice the size of today's motherboards, the level of circuitry and equipment that can be installed to modern motherboards is many times what it formerly was.

How a Motherboard Works

A motherboard isn't just any other printed circuit board—it's the chief one in a PC, and it is multilayered to pack the most capability into the smallest package possible. Different layers carry communications for different aspects of the computer, such as memory and the various buses. The motherboard is also a printed circuit board that allows other printed circuit boards—which take the form of riser cards and expansion bus adapters—to be installed to it.

Perhaps I've been working with PC hardware too long, but I can't load a game that lets you build your own model city without being reminded of a computer motherboard. The comparison seems like an apt one because a motherboard is like a city grid where there are traffic patterns, structures, organized power delivery, and virtually everything but an attacking monster and (hopefully) floods. Stare inside an open PC and you can see what I mean. The PC buses are like major traffic arteries and the CPU is a little like City Hall, with numerous other landmarks around Data City.

The motherboard you encounter in desktop systems is actually a scaled-down version of those found in mainframe computers two-plus decades ago. Further miniaturization has enabled the overall size of a motherboard to become reduced, while the capacity and feature set of a motherboard has expanded exponentially since the original IBM PC.

A motherboard engages in a booting system as soon as the power supply roars to life and supplies power to it. Then the motherboard sends this power to anything contained upon it that requires electricity and doesn't have its own direct power supply connection. For this reason, a dead or problematic motherboard (including one with an improperly installed add-on adapter or memory) should be the main suspect whenever you turn a system on and hear the power supply engage (detectable as a rising whirring sound from its fan), but the computer otherwise appears dead on arrival.

Major Types

Types of motherboards are differentiated by two major characteristics:

- The type of CPU interface built into the motherboard

- The form factor

The type of CPU interface for insertion—sockets or slots—matters a great deal because, in the majority of cases, a motherboard is designed to work with just one type of CPU. Exceptions to this rule have less to do with the motherboard and are more the result of CPUs that allow you to use an adapter to convert it from one type of insertion package to another—such as the Intel Celeron 370-pin CPU, which has an adapter that permits you to install it to a Slot 1 motherboard. Remember: this is an exception, not a rule, so you will usually have to match the CPU to the motherboard without the use of an adapter.

One critical term to understand with respect to motherboards and motherboard types is *form factor*. This refers to the overall size, shape, and design configuration. Form factor (specific examples of which are shown in Table 5-1) also determines what type of case a motherboard can fit into, as well as how other components are installed to and around the motherboard. For example, the NLX form factor motherboard is smaller in size than an ATX form factor motherboard. The NLX also uses a different power supply type, supports tall memory, and is designed to allow you to remove the motherboard from the case with little fuss or muss (often because they have no screws to remove).

If you need to replace a motherboard and want to use the same case, you usually need to obtain a new motherboard with the exact same form factor as the old one. To upgrade the motherboard to a more recent model with a different form factor, expect to buy a new case as well. Table 5-1 offers some of the PC motherboard form factors that either are still being manufactured today or remain available in older systems.

Table 5-1   PC Motherboard Form Factors

Form Factor	Size	Age	Major Design Changes
AT	12"x 11–13"	1981–1992	Is the oldest form factor
Baby AT	8.5"x 10–13"	1988–1997	Is a smaller AT design for easier motherboard installation and removal; is still seen in some systems
ATX	12"x 9.6"	1997–present	Is a larger variation of the Baby AT; avoids crowding of longer expansion boards by the CPU mounting; changes mounting of power supply
Mini ATX	11.2"x 8.2"	Late 1990s	Is basically identical to an ATX except for size
Micro ATX	9.6"x 9.6"	Early 2000	Is a smaller ATX form factor that supports Accelerated Graphics Port (AGP) and newer processors
Flex ATX	9"x 7.5"	Early 2000	Extends Micro ATX designed for custom cases; uses socket-only processors
LPX/Mini LPX	9"x 11–13"	Late 1990s	Mounts expansion boards (usually a maximum of 2 to 3) on a riser card above the main board; fits smaller case design
NLX	8-9" x 10–13.6"	Current	Supports faster AGP, tall memory sticks plus current and future processor designs; accommodates cooler thermal mounting for processor; has improved external connectivity; attaches expansion boards through add-in riser

BIOS

The basic input/output system (BIOS) is the programmable part of the motherboard, typically located on a chip mounted directly on the motherboard. As you already learned in Chapter 2, "The Operating System's Role in Hardware," the BIOS is integral to hardware detection and resource assignment and works hand-in-hand with Windows and other operating systems in the proper handling and operation of the hardware installed on a PC.

Because the BIOS is programmable, it can be updated. The term *flashing a BIOS* means to run a software utility designed to perform an update to a BIOS, which is sometimes necessary to do the following:

- Correct a BIOS corruption

- Add support for types of hardware or an operating system version not previously supported under the BIOS

- Address a design flaw in that BIOS

Sometimes, this process requires setting a jumper or switch on the motherboard to allow the BIOS chip to accept the update, but often, it's accomplished solely with the software utility. Either process makes it much easier to update a BIOS but also poses a risk. For example, the CIH virus—first seen around the time of the release of Windows 98 in June 1998—could corrupt the BIOS by exploiting the same feature that makes it easy to apply an update to that BIOS.

BIOS manufacturers often display the company name along with the BIOS identifier string—the unique identifier that dates and specifies the type of BIOS provided for a motherboard—on the boot-up screen. You can check this information against the U.S. Federal Communications Commission (FCC) database to turn the identifying string into information about the type of motherboard and BIOS in use. This information can help you to obtain the correct BIOS update. Because motherboards differ greatly, so too can the BIOS and you can rarely apply one manufacturer's BIOS update to another manufacturer's BIOS chip.

Online sites such as *www.motherboard.org* make tools such as CT BIOS and MoboCop available to help you identify your BIOS and motherboard manufacturer if that information isn't in your documentation. Other commercial sites, such as MrBIOS (*www.mrbios.com*), try to match you with a BIOS upgrade for a price.

> **Note**   BIOS updates can usually be obtained from the motherboard or PC manufacturer through a download from the manufacturer's Web site that includes complete instructions for applying the update. These are usually provided free of charge.

Upgrading

When you consider whether an upgrade is necessary, determine whether you actually need or want a new motherboard (perhaps because it offers features not supported by your current one) or whether a BIOS update itself will address the major issue at hand. Performing a BIOS update is usually much easier to accomplish, although it won't drastically alter your feature set. For example, if your motherboard has an AGP 4x slot, a BIOS update won't bump you up to AGP 8x support.

Many users choose to replace the motherboard and CPU at the same time, especially in a common upgrade situation where they want to increase the processor speed and memory speed or capacity. If the new motherboard uses a different form factor than your old one, you will also need to replace the case with one designed for the target form factor. A new power supply (sometimes available as part of a case purchase) will probably also be necessary.

A motherboard upgrade also usually means acquiring new memory because memory speeds have been jumping forward as processors get faster. Chapter 7, "Memory," discusses the topic of memory in detail.

On the Motherboard

Motherboard components and the various things that connect into the main board can differ widely, depending on the age of the motherboard and how many components are onboard (as opposed to available via a board installed into one of the expansion buses). In this section, you'll work through the main hardware connectors and components located on a PC motherboard of recent vintage, such as the one shown in Figure 5-1.

Figure 5-1 A bare motherboard with nothing installed on it yet—specifically, a Tyan Thunder K8W (S2885) designed for an AMD Opteron CPU

Before you get into the nuts and bolts, and slots and sockets, however, take a look at the circuitry available within the motherboard. Check out the array of transistors and marvel—as many of us do—at how many different elements have been brought together on an otherwise simple printed circuit board. Marvel also at the fact that simple circuit boards like this power the work done on millions of systems every day.

Many motherboards have identifying tags that appear next to each major item. These tags help you understand the layout and point of installation for components such as sticks of memory, IDE cables running to drives, and power connections coming in from the power supply. Unfortunately, these tags often appear in small print or with unusual abbreviations (often because PC components are not made in the U.S. and don't use abbreviations that we consider standard) that can make it difficult to use them as adequate landmarks.

Components

Now let's work through the main components or connectors on a motherboard that you need to know. Figure 5-2 shows the same motherboard you viewed in Figure 5-1, but this one is labeled so that you can see some of the major points of insertion.

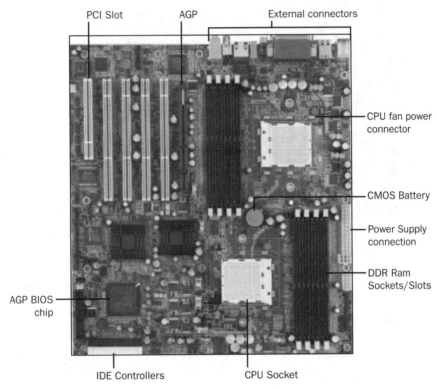

Figure 5-2   A labeled version of Figure 5-1

Then, in Figure 5-3, you see a populated, working motherboard of a recent era Celeron-based CPU system (1.4 GHz) with the Celeron CPU, memory, and related items in place.

Figure 5-3 A working Celeron-based system example with CPU, memory, and other connections in place and operational

Keep in mind that you'll learn more information about each component as you go through the chapters of this book. In Chapter 6, "Central Processing Units," for example, you'll learn about the various types of sockets and slots that permit the insertion of a CPU into the motherboard. In Chapter 7, you'll learn about the many types of memory currently in use and develop the ability to identify them.

The main components of the motherboard include the following:

- **CPU slot/socket**   Slots and sockets serve as the installation point for CPUs, where a slot allows the insertion of a printed circuit board and a socket allows the insertion of a more pin-plug-style component.

- **CPU or processor**   This is the system "brain" or center of the system's computing power. With the motherboard, it determines speed, compatible operating systems, and compatible applications.

- **Heat sink or sinks**   A piece of metal—often but not always aluminum—used to absorb the heat from a hot-running component such as the CPU or graphics processor. Attached to the component by means of either a clip or a heat-resistant, adhesive material known as *heat sink compound*, the heat sink pulls the heat from the component and displaces it gradually into the generally cooler air away from the hot component. Most but not all CPUs include a heat sink when they are installed to a PC motherboard. Over time, however, the heat sink compound might fail and loosen the tight bond necessary between the component and the heat sink itself. Reattachment can be performed by removing the heat sink and remaining heat sink compound and applying new heat sink compound.

> **Exam Tip**   Heat sink compound can be acquired almost anywhere you purchase PC hardware, especially CPUs. Don't think that because you don't have proper compound that it's all right to use any adhesive to affix the heat sink to the processor or other component. Because the CPU is one of the most integral components on your PC, you don't want to take unnecessary risks. Most general-application adhesives won't stand up to the thermal environment created and will fail (loosen) quickly; others might not be intended for use above a certain temperature and actually burn away or produce a toxic odor. The result can be damage to the CPU and possibly worse.

- **Fan or fans**   You are likely to see one or more fans. The CPU has one—often attached directly to it—to remove heat from the processor. (The power supply, located elsewhere, has a large fan directly at the rear of the PC.) Video adapters and hard-drive enclosures might also have fans, and tiny separate fans (such as Peltier fans) are sometimes installed to reduce spot heating problems, which can affect the proper operation and lifespan of components. Installation points for additional fans are usually labeled as "Aux. Fan" or something similar, although some fans will take a connection directly from the power supply.

- **System chipset or CPU chipset**   The chipset is a set of integrated circuits that provides the core functionality of the motherboard. Various chipsets are typically located on a motherboard and even on devices such as an ATA hard drive. Their job is to support the processor or processor-to-device input. But the most important of these is the CPU chipset, which oversees communications between the PC subsystems and the CPU. This chipset is actually bifurcated, splitting into the following two bridges:

  - ❏   Northbridge—Controls communication for the CPU, the PCI bus, AGP bus, memory, and the South Bridge

❑   Southbridge—Responsible for the major I/O controls, including a bridge between the older ISA bus (if it exists) and the PCI bus

■   **Caches**   A cache is a type of ultra-high-speed memory used to speed the boot-up process and store frequently used data and CPU instructions. Caches are discussed in some detail in Chapter 4, "The Workings and Connections of the PC."

■   **Voltage regulator module**   This component regulates the power or voltage supplied to the CPU. Different CPUs use varying voltage, and this should be set properly for each.

■   **BIOS**   BIOS is software built into a ROM or flash memory chip on the motherboard, usually capable of being upgraded or "flashed," that stores information on key hardware components and recalls this information on each boot. BIOS is discussed in detail in Chapter 4.

■   **CMOS battery**   CMOS retains user settings and the system date in BIOS even when the PC is turned off. It does this by means of a small battery (usually, but not always, shaped like a thick coin). This battery can become depleted, which can cause the system to have problems retaining the proper date and time or to no longer recognize attached hardware. CMOS batteries can typically be replaced at a cost of between $3 and $10 (US) by removing the current battery (which usually unclips from its retainer) and bringing it to any store that sells a variety of batteries.

■   **Super I/O controller**   This controller's job is to oversee the I/O functions of the keyboard, mouse, and similar user-input devices (including some gaming hardware) as well as the floppy disk drive.

■   **Memory**   Random access memory (RAM) is sold in various quantities (8, 16, 32, 64, 128, and 256 MB and beyond), types (SDRAM, RDRAM, DDR RAM—and some systems allow for both SDRAM and RDRAM), and speeds (66, 100, 133, 600, 800, 1600, 2100 Mhz, and beyond). Which type you use depends on the type of CPU and motherboard being used. Memory provides the working environment to run programs and, with help of the CPU, process data on the PC desktop. It's discussed in detail in Chapter 7.

■   **Memory slots**   These are physical connection slots to install RAM. All installed memory communicates to the system through the memory controller hub (MCH) located on the motherboard. Retainer clips are typically positioned on both sides of a memory slot to fully and firmly seat the individual memory sticks into place. (See Chapter 7.)

- **IDE channel controller** This provides the interface for ATA/IDE drive ribbon cables to connect to the motherboard. There are usually two present, which might be labeled IDE#0 and IDE#1 or IDE#1 and IDE#2, or primary IDE and secondary IDE, or HDD1 and HDD2.

- **Expansion bus slots** These are connection slots for the installation of peripheral expansion boards (video, audio, modem, and so on) for the ISA and PCI/PCIx bus.

- **AGP** This is a recent-generation video adapter port on a dedicated communications path (only video).

- **Any integrated components** These include functions (video, network, sound, modem, and so on) normally available in a freestanding peripheral board that have been incorporated into the motherboard itself. These are usually added to reduce equipment cost. See "The Integrated PC Motherboard" section that appears next.

The Integrated PC Motherboard

As you read in Chapter 1, "Computer Evolution," a primary way manufacturers have employed to cut the overall total cost of (PC) ownership is to provide highly integrated systems, particularly where a number of devices formerly available as separate expansion boards are included in chip form on the motherboard itself. The most commonly integrated devices include:

- Modem
- Network adapter
- Small Computer System Interface (SCSI) host controller
- Sound adapter
- Video adapter

Such highly integrated motherboards usually provide at least two expansion slots to allow you to add separate adapters to enhance or replace these built-in functions. For many users who tend to buy systems without any plans to later customize or upgrade their devices or for those who are simply budget-conscious, an integrated motherboard is fine.

However, integration usually means limitations. For example, if a motherboard has just two slots, you would have difficulty replacing three of the above integrated functions with these separate adapters. Another problem is seen with many budget PC systems where boards with integrated video might not offer an AGP port to accommodate a stand-alone adapter. Also, when a function such as video fails on an integrated motherboard, you'll probably have to replace the entire motherboard. Finally, some integrated boards offer less than robust sound and video, so the potential is high that you'll be dissatisfied with the overall sound and video capability on some ultra cheap systems.

You can see in Figure 5-4 that there is no AGP port and that there is no video adapter in place. (The only add-on board is a modem.) There is also no network adapter or sound adapter. This is an example of a low-budget, highly integrated system.

Figure 5-4   Another look at the system you saw in Figure 5-3.

> **Exam Tip**   Are you unsure which components in a system can be integrated into the motherboard? If the documentation doesn't tell you, work backwards: identify which features the system has and look for the types of adapters installed. Any discrepancy is probably explained by an integrated component. For example, if there is no AGP port and there is no PCI video adapter installed, you probably have integrated AGP video on the motherboard.

Standard Features

In the section "On the Motherboard," earlier in this chapter, you learned the key standard features available on a motherboard of recent vintage. Whenever you plan to replace your current motherboard for another, you should review the presence and location of these standard features, including:

■ CPU socket or slot

■ Memory slots or sockets

■ Super I/O controller

■ Expansion slots (The type of slots and the number available can matter if you expect to add several expansions boards.)

■ IDE channel controllers

Nice Extras

Two nice extras you can find on motherboards are onboard virus checkers (to try to protect the BIOS and beyond) and thermal probes or thermometers, which sound a warning alarm and ultimately shut down the system if an excessive temperature is reached, before permanent damage can be done to the CPU or motherboard. The latter feature is also available as an add-on product. You'll learn more about overheating and PC hardware in Chapter 8, "Power Supplies and Cooling."

A few motherboards come with an advanced diagnostic board that can perform checks during POST and through the BIOS to help determine the source of problems that might arise. An advanced diagnostic board can sometimes be purchased separately, too. This can be a very nice plus when troubleshooting a hardware issue you suspect is based on the motherboard or the BIOS.

If you need a new case to fit a change of motherboard form factors—or if you just want a new case—consider getting one that allows for easy slide-out of the chassis. These are much easier to work with than a case that requires you to remove screws, pull the cover, and then secure it again. A case with a slide-out chassis allows you easy access to the components along with better lighting conditions than the inside of a case typically permits.

Smart Shopping

You can't shop for a motherboard without considering what other components you need to use with it. The foremost consideration is which CPU to use, because the motherboard must support the type of CPU you choose. You also must think about memory (because different motherboards support different types of memory), video, the number of drives to be used, the number of expansion slots available to accept adapters as well as what components might be integrated or built right into the motherboard, the case into which you need to install it, and much more.

With motherboards, it's wise not to make saving money the dominant factor in your decision to buy. If you purchase an older motherboard that is no longer supported by the manufacturer, you might lock yourself out of both technical support and BIOS updates. If you buy a brand of motherboard no Web search engine has ever heard of, you might live to regret it. Instead, weigh the features the motherboard offers against your needs and the type of CPU it will be used with, and then try to get the best price you can for the model you want.

Considerations

In your research before you purchase a new motherboard, there are some smart questions to ask before you order or otherwise commit to a particular model. Such questions include the following:

How many expansion slots are available for use?

One rule of thumb is that you should have at least twice as many expansion slots available to use as you have currently populated by adapters. That might be unnecessary today, especially if you or the company you're working for opts to go with a highly integrated motherboard where few separate adapters are needed. Yet you definitely need at least as many slots as you plan to use, so consider what adapters you plan to install before you pick a motherboard.

What is the maximum amount of memory that can be installed?

Most motherboards support a finite amount of memory, depending on what memory types it supports. Today, 128 MB is a minimum amount of memory for virtually any setup. While the majority of users rarely ever need more than 256 MB, power users and server environments might demand 1 GB or greater. Be sure the motherboard you select gives you the option to add memory as needed.

What types of memory does the motherboard support?

A motherboard is likely to support just one type of memory format (as discussed in Chapter 7). Make certain it's the one you choose to use. If you already have RAM available to install to a new motherboard, this might determine which type of memory you want. However, you want to avoid using older and much slower memory types (such as SDRAM) with today's faster systems because they can affect overall system performance.

What do others think about this motherboard?

Check among friends, coworkers, and other colleagues to see what types or specific models of motherboard they would recommend. Sites like Tom's Hardware (*www.tomshardware.com*), ArsTechnica (*www.arstechnica.com*) and Extreme Tech (*www.extremetech.com*) frequently rate motherboard performance, quality, and expandability, and have active discussions centering around such hardware topics.

What AGP scheme does the motherboard support?

AGP 8X is available now, although most motherboards are still using AGP 4X or earlier AGP adapters and motherboards. If you want to have the maximum possible expandability of the system, you might want to be sure your motherboard supports 8X so that you can upgrade to that type of adapter at some point. Also, if you are considering a highly integrated motherboard, be sure an AGP port is present. Without one, you can't upgrade your video or replace the existing video unless you scrap the motherboard for a new one.

What is the real price of the upgrade?

All too often when pricing a major component upgrade for a motherboard, we look at the actual price of a motherboard without considering what else we might need to acquire. Other acquisitions might include a new CPU, memory, as well as a case, depending on how big a jump is being made. Some vendors will give you a price break when motherboards are bought in bulk or when you buy the CPU and motherboard at the same time. This discount might extend to memory and the case, too. Price each component individually as well as unit-wise and, where possible when multiple systems are getting an upgrade, try to package the units together to see whether you qualify for a bulk discount.

Do I need the ability to run more than one processor?

While the majority of motherboards manufactured allow for the installation of a single CPU, you can purchase models that permit more than one. Multiple processors can be useful in environments with very demanding processes. An additional CPU can share the workload so that not as much speed is sacrificed in data crunching. However, multiple processors really help only in situations where you are running applications that were written to specifically work with more than one processor—most applications are not written this way.

Installation

The first operation you want to perform as part of a new motherboard installation is to inspect the new motherboard visually. After all, whether you're replacing an existing motherboard or installing a new one into a new case, you don't want to wait until after the new motherboard is in place before you identify a problem you could have spotted sooner.

Looks for cracks or tiny fractures, warping, or anything else you think might affect your ability to install and use the board properly. If necessary, contact your dealer or motherboard manufacturer when you spot something that might be an issue.

> **Note**   Cracks happen from applying too much pressure on a board as you install it or adding a component to it. Even starting up a PC in a very cold room can produce cracks as the board heats.

Once you have satisfied yourself that the motherboard is of the right type and appears free of damage, you're ready to install it. For many of you, this means removing the old motherboard first.

However, before you remove the old board and install the new one, be sure to perform a complete backup of the system. You want to be sure your current data is protected, and you'll understand other issues once we get the new motherboard installed.

Remove the Existing Motherboard

How carefully you remove an existing motherboard depends on whether you plan to use it again, donate or sell it to someone else, or recycle it. In general, you should always exercise care. Motherboards can break, although it's far more common that they will develop cracks or fractures.

In this series of steps, you will see how to remove a motherboard from the PC. If you are installing a motherboard to an empty case, proceed to the next section.

To remove a motherboard, follow these steps:

1. Boot the PC, and enter **CMOS** (the user interface for BIOS).

2. From CMOS, look for and jot down (in your tech journal, perhaps) salient information such as drive type.

3. Exit CMOS, and shut down the PC. Once it's turned off, disconnect the main power cable (usually located at the rear of the PC).

4. Remove the case cover. Some units simply slide out; others require you to use a screwdriver or other tool to remove fasteners at the back or side of the PC before you can slide the cover off. Place any fasteners aside in an empty cup or holder.

5. Ground yourself, as discussed in Chapter 2.

6. Locate and remove connectors for the following items (also discussed in "The Quick Diagram" sidebar later in this chapter) from the motherboard:

    ❑   Power supply

    ❑   Switches leading from front of PC

    ❑   LED (light-emitting diode) displays leading from front of PC

    ❑   Drives

7. Remove the CPU and its fan (a process discussed in Chapter 6), and set them aside. (A proper case or an antistatic bag is an ideal place to put them.) This step might not be necessary if you are installing a new CPU and fan with the new motherboard and plan to donate or recycle the old CPU with the old motherboard.

8. Remove any sticks of memory you want to insert into the new motherboard or add to your in-storage collection of extra parts. Set these aside (preferably in a case or antistatic bag).

9. Locate and remove all expansion boards. For some, this means disconnecting cables or wires in the back of the PC that connect a board to your monitor, as well as speakers, microphone, USB or IEEE 1394 devices connected to hubs on an adapter, and so on. Set the expansion adapters aside in antistatic bags.

10. Remove any additional connectors at the back of the PC, such as cables for serial and parallel port devices (including mouse, camera, scanner, printer, and so on), USB and IEEE 1394 cables, network cables, keyboard and mouse, and other such items.

11. Locate the screws or retainers holding the motherboard in place, and remove them. (See Figure 5-5.)

Figure 5-5 Removing the screws holding the motherboard in place

Believe it or not, you've just completed the relatively easy part of the operation. Now let's get the new motherboard into position.

Fact How you enter CMOS Setup differs for various makes and models of PCs. Often, you see an on-screen prompt when the PC first boots telling you which keystrokes are needed to do this. Many use the Delete key.

The Quick Diagram

Until you get comfortable working with motherboard replacements and become familiar with standard connections, this might be one of your least favorite jobs. Like many, you might wish you had a quick diagram of the system so that you could match the connector to the connection later on. Sketching one yourself usually takes too much time, but if the motherboard or system you purchased came with a diagram of the motherboard, you can use that diagram to label your connections as you go. Sometimes, you can also download or print out a diagram from the motherboard manufacturer's Web site.

What I did in my early days as a technician was write a sequential number on individual pieces of tape, giving each connector and cable I removed its own number (affixed on tape), which I then wrote on the motherboard diagram from the documentation. By doing this, I was able to reconnect all the appropriate connectors and cables much more rapidly once I replaced the motherboard.

But if you don't have a diagram on hand, do you have a digital camera? If so, take a picture—or multiple pictures from different viewpoints—and label the connections on the printout once you've imported the image into a PC. A technician with a PC consulting business tells me that he takes digital images of all his clients' systems, and then refers back to the images when talking clients through a problem or an upgrade over the phone. This, he says, significantly slashed the number of times a phone call consultation turns into an on-site one.

Install the New Motherboard

Once the existing motherboard (if any) has been removed, check the system for any dust or debris deposits. Now is a good time to use a soft bristled brush to gently extract this from the chassis. You can also use a can of compressed air or a PC vacuum for this purpose.

With this done, consult your diagram again and review any accompanying documentation with the new motherboard. Then follow these steps:

1. Remove the new motherboard from its package, and install its CPU and fan (discussed in Chapter 6), any external cache (also discussed in Chapter 6), and its memory (discussed in Chapter 7).

2. Seat the new motherboard into the PC chassis, reapplying any screws or retainers (called *standoffs*) that were removed or moved in the process of extracting the old board. If your new motherboard comes with spacers, install these by following the motherboard installation instructions. This is often done before you seat the motherboard and screw it down.

3. Attach the power connector from the power supply (the same one you removed as part of extracting the old motherboard) to the appropriate place on the motherboard following your diagram. (See Figure 5-6.)

Figure 5-6   Connections running from the power supply to the motherboard

4. Again following your diagram, attach the other wire leads (to the hard-drive activity LED, to the power and reset switch, and so on) to the motherboard.

5. Locate the CPU fan connector, and attach this. (The fan usually connects either to a hard drive's power connector in a piggyback (pass-through) fashion or directly to the motherboard.)

6. Next, install priority (those absolutely needed to provide a vital function at boot-up) expansion boards only, such as an AGP or PCI video adapter to supply the video. Other expansion boards are added once the new motherboard is tested to work.

7. Connect the drive cables to either the IDE controllers on the motherboard (as shown in Figure 5-7) or the SCSI host controller (either installed as a separate adapter or integrated into the motherboard). (See Chapter 14, "Hard Drives and Drive Interfaces.")

Figure 5-7   Remember to plug in your drives as part of the reinstallation process

8. Thoroughly review your connections. Make certain they are firmly attached.

9. Connect the monitor, keyboard, and mouse to their respective connectors at the back of the PC.

10. Reconnect the power cable to the back of the PC, and turn the PC on.

11. Listen and watch.

If all goes well, you'll see a display, there will be no unusual beeps, and you can enter CMOS Setup as you did before. In CMOS Setup, you'll want to set the PC time and date, and choose either to have the BIOS try to detect your hard drives or manually enter your hard-drive information before you quit CMOS and save your changes.

If, instead, you see no display but hear a series of beeps, count the beeps and their frequency. Depending on the make and manufacturer of the motherboard and BIOS, these beeps will help you determine what is wrong. (See Chapter 1.) You'll likely need to disconnect the power, ground yourself again, and make any needed adjustments.

Once the new motherboard is recognized and working, you can shut it down again, disconnect power, ground yourself, and install your additional expansion boards or adapters, along with your other devices. When you bring your system up again under Windows 95 or later once you reconnect power, check Windows Device Manager after the Windows desktop loads.

At this point, you should also plan to reinstall your operating system. A new motherboard usually functions best when the operating system is reapplied so that it adjusts to the new BIOS and other changes. Finally, pat yourself on the back and return the bottle of your favorite headache remedy to the proper desk drawer or medicine cabinet. You've just weathered the upgrade and installation people tend to fear most.

Maintenance and Repair

Beyond keeping a motherboard clean by keeping the case cover in place, operating the PC in a reasonably clean environment where the temperature is fairly constant, and exercising care when installing or removing components to it, there is little to be done on current day motherboards in terms of maintenance and repair except for the BIOS update. Even with that, there are two schools of thought with regard to motherboard maintenance:

- Update the BIOS as often as an upgrade is available, and meticulously check the motherboard regularly for problems.

- Ignore BIOS updates until you absolutely can't live without something an update offers, and just replace the motherboard later if you have problems.

In my personal work—and this seems true for many other good technicians I know—I find it wise to be selective in BIOS updates (for example, applying them only when they're truly necessary) but somewhat vigilant in motherboard inspection.

It's smart to check your motherboard regularly—or at least whenever you go inside the case—using a good flashlight to try to spot signs of fracture, damage, undue wear, or areas that appear burned or unusually discolored. These signs might indicate a problem is afoot even before the motherboard or a component attached to that region of the motherboard misbehaves or fails. Such motherboards should be replaced as soon as possible.

In some of the figures you've seen in this book, I've shown systems where dust and debris have been allowed to accumulate. I've done this on purpose so that you understand that an internal PC might not be too pristine after a year or two of use under hard conditions. Keeping a PC clean just makes good sense. You should use compressed air to remove deposits of dust and debris that alight on the board surface and collect around expansion boards, memory, and other components and use a PC vacuum to care for the case itself. While a dear friend of mine insists that layers of smoke and grease deposits inside his PC provide a degree of thermal protection, both can reduce the lifespan of a motherboard and its components. In garage and cooking environments where PCs are being used, interior components can become so layered by grease that they either short out directly or slowly deteriorate from excessive heat. This happens because the slick coating keeps heat from dissipating off the component and into the circulating air in the case.

Also, be aware that a motherboard doesn't necessarily fail all at once. It can develop a weak spot (caused perhaps by excessive heating from an attached component being "fried") where nearby components begin to misbehave intermittently or selectively. You also might see other specific components fail permanently. For example, you might find that working memory installed to one specific memory slot will not be recognized no matter how many times you check its proper insertion, or one IDE channel controller stops working with any drives connected to it.

The solution to any of these problems invariably is to replace the motherboard. While a talented person can sometimes work wonders with a soldering iron and good instructions in performing motherboard repairs, the documentation on many motherboards is too light and unhelpful in determining what needs to be repaired or replaced.

Troubleshooting

When installing a new motherboard, the first thing you must consider when something doesn't work as it should or the motherboard seems dead is that you haven't installed connections correctly. For example, a motherboard without firm connections from the power supply to it won't get the power it needs to supply to everything else connected to that motherboard. Improperly installed RAM or adapter cards can keep the computer from booting. (You might get the series of beeps discussed in Chapter 1.) Go through the documentation and the connections you made with meticulous precision, step by step.

The possibility always exists that you might have obtained a defective motherboard. This happens, although it's a statistical rarity. It's far more likely that a connection—and almost as likely, multiple connections—have not been made correctly or firmly.

Another possible explanation many people discover—especially when they try to work quickly or attempt to force a recalcitrant motherboard into place or fit one of its components into it—is that they have killed the motherboard through improper handling or installation. I've seen new motherboards sat upon, tossed into the back of a vehicle, or thrown onto a desk with less respect than should be given a large sack of dog food. I've also seen them left on surfaces where they collect papers or bugs and have weighty items set down upon them. Printed circuit boards in general and motherboards specifically simply aren't meant to be treated haphazardly.

A motherboard also can short out if it is not properly installed. This can occur when a component or bit of circuitry on the motherboard is touched or scratched by the metal retainer clips used to mount it. Once power is supplied to the motherboard, the problem area shorts out. There might or might not be smoke or the presence of a burning smell.

Lab 5: Identify the Motherboard and BIOS, and Upgrade the BIOS

This lab is intended to help you understand the steps necessary in identifying a PC motherboard and its BIOS, and how you can accomplish the task of updating a BIOS to a later version. Before you start, there are a few things to note. Some BIOSes—in particular, Phoenix BIOSes—might not allow you to identify them through the BIOS identifier string alone. For these, you will need to check your documentation, try to identify the motherboard manufacturer, and then go online and obtain this information through the manufacturer's Web site or by calling the manufacturer's support line.

Finally, exercise care when you perform this lab. Faithfully follow all directions supplied with the accompanying BIOS update, do not cut steps out for expediency sake, and do not perform this lab when there is any question of a storm or other issue interrupting power to your work area. BIOS updates do not take well to being stopped in the process; you should complete this operation in a single, uninterrupted session.

Objectives

When you complete this lab, you will be able to address the following issues:

1. The identification of the motherboard and BIOS used in a PC

2. The procedure for locating a BIOS update for your motherboard

3. The process of "flashing" the BIOS to update it

Necessary Equipment and Resources

The following equipment and resources are necessary for completing this lab:

1. A PC (preferably one more than a year old)

2. An Internet connection

3. The documentation for your PC or motherboard

4. At least one blank floppy disk

5. Your tech journal

6. Your PC hardware toolkit

7. At least 60 minutes to complete this lab

Procedures to Follow

1. Boot the PC, enter CMOS Setup, and write down all important information, such as drive types, features enabled or disabled, and any specialty settings.

2. Exit CMOS without making changes.

3. When the PC restarts, see whether you can spot the BIOS identifier string on the boot-up screen. You might be able to pause the boot process if you press the Print Screen or Pause/Break key so that you can write down the identifier string in both your tech journal and your lab notes.

4. If you don't see the BIOS identifier string, check your documentation to see whether it specifies the type of motherboard. You might be able to locate this on the PC or motherboard manufacturer's Web site by looking under the support options for the PC model. If necessary, call the PC or motherboard manufacturer (if you can identify it) and determine the BIOS identifier string by talking to them. Write the information in your lab notes as well as in your tech journal.

5. Using the options found at *www.motherboard.org*, through the manufacturer, or by other means, try to locate a BIOS update for this motherboard. Then obtain the update (usually accomplished through downloading).

6. Once the update is located, jot into your tech journal and lab notes the following:

   ❏   Specific information about what the update is supposed to do

   ❏   Exact directions for applying the update

7. Flash the BIOS per the directions given for the BIOS update. Record your experience in your tech journal and lab notes. In particular, record any oddities seen or anything the directions failed to note.

8. Write a short procedure that outlines the steps others will need to follow to flash this motherboard BIOS.

Lab Notes

1. Record your BIOS identifier string and other notes that help identify this motherboard.

   _____

   _____

   _____

2. Detail how you determined the make and model of the motherboard.

   _____

   _____

   _____

3. Where did you locate the update for this BIOS?

   _____

   _____

   _____

4. What features does this BIOS update address? (Be as specific as possible.)

   _____

   _____

   _____

5. What are the specific instructions for applying this BIOS update?

   _____

   _____

   _____

6. Record highlights of your experience in performing the update.

   _____

   _____

   _____

7. Write a short summary of steps others should take to flash the BIOS effectively. (Don't copy this from the directions, but use your own experience to expand upon the directions.)

   _____

   _____

   _____

6

Central Processing Units

Think of the central processing unit (CPU) as the brain of the PC. The CPU is critical to the health and operation of the system in which it resides. The CPU, after all, is responsible for all the calculations that must take place in processing the data used on the computer. Its integrity and reliability are paramount.

Shortly, you'll learn more about what goes into the magnificent "brain" of that tiny chip package. It is commonly said that every CPU is made up of two distinct parts: the arithmetic logic unit (ALU), which performs the actual calculations, and logic operations and the control unit, which help manage how that data moves in and out of the chip.

How a CPU Works

Despite being one of the smallest components in a PC, the CPU acts as ground zero for almost everything that takes place during the operation of a system. Even though the CPU has become smaller over time, it can actually handle much more because of advances in chip design.

A CPU is a microprocessor composed of a number of components. These include:

- **The address bus**   Its purpose is to send specific addresses to memory, and it can be 8, 16, 32, or 64 bits wide. (Increasing the width of the bus increases the amount of data that can be transmitted simultaneously.)

- **The data bus**   This bus is responsible for communicating data to and from memory; again, this can be 8, 16, 32, or 64 bits wide and the width affects the speed.

- **A reset line** This line resets the program value to zero for execution of instructions.

- **RD and WR lines** These read (RD) and write (WR) lines specify whether an address will be retrieved or set in memory.

- **A clock line** This line is used to send a clock sequence to the processor.

The CPU and Its Multiplier

Understand that a processor's actual speed is determined by a hard-wired entity in the processor chip known as a *CPU multiplier*. Because this is hard-wired, it cannot be changed. This was not always true. Over the last decade, CPU manufacturers (with Intel leading the way) changed most of their designs so that the processor speed couldn't be tweaked as it often was in a technique known as *overclocking*. Overclocking means pushing a component's performance past its manufacturer-rated speed.

One of the most famous examples of overclocking was seen when the Intel Pentium II and Celeron processors came out in the mid-1990s. The Pentium II cost considerably more than the Celeron, so many people would buy the cheaper but less robust Celeron and boost its multiplier and system clock rate. By doing this, they could get a system faster than a Pentium II for about half the price. They did much the same with less expensive AMD processors.

But even with the processor lockdown seen in many current CPUs, overclocking is not a dead concept. Other components aside from CPU speed can be tweaked, such as the system clock and motherboard. The capabilities of a video adapter's graphics processor are sometimes overclocked, too.

If you were to write a formula to express a CPU's speed, it would look like the following:

CPU speed = CPU multiplier × system clock rate

You can't change the CPU multiplier, but as already noted, you can change the system clock rate. This is usually accomplished either by changing a setting in BIOS or by adjusting special switches located on the motherboard. (Not all motherboards support this, however.) In fact, one of your jobs when installing a new CPU (or an existing CPU to a new motherboard) is to set the system clock rate because this is usually not configured beforehand.

Major Types of Processors

The speed of the processor acts to define the type of system you're running—for example, a Pentium II 350 MHz or a Pentium IV 3.06 GHz. Each major processor class (such as Celeron, Pentium, Pentium Pro, Pentium II/III/IV, and Xeon for Intel; and K5, K6, Duron, Athlon, and Opteron for AMD) offers a range of speeds. For instance, the Pentium II operated mostly in the 200 to 500 MHz range, while the Pentium III operated up to about 1 GHz.

Figure 6-1 shows one of the most recent consumer and business processors, the AMD Athlon.

Figure 6-1   The Advanced Micro Devices (AMD) Athlon

Table 6-1 gives you a roster of major processors available in the past decade, listed by vendor.

Table 6-1   Major Processor Classes

Manufacturer	Processor Class	Speed	Major Advancements
Intel	Itanium	733 MHz	64-bit architecture; supports up to 32 processors
	Xeon	500 MHz to 1+ GHz	Server class Pentium II/III/IV; supports 2 or more processors; has up to 64 GB RAM installed
	Pentium IV	1.4 to 3.06 GHz	Introduced in 2000; has 42 million transistors; supports RDRAM and DDR SDRAM
	Pentium III	500 MHz to 1.13 GHz	Introduced in 1999; is really the Pentium II with 70 extra instructions; has from 9 million to 28 million transistors
	Celeron	266 MHz to 1.8 GHz	Is equivalent to a lower budget Pentium II through Pentium IV

Table 6-1 **Major Processor Classes**

Manufacturer	Processor Class	Speed	Major Advancements
	Pentium II	266 to 450 MHz	Equivalent to a Pentium Pro with multimedia extensions added; has 7.5 million transistors
	Pentium Pro	150 to 200 MHz	Professional Pentium class; allows for dual processors; is still used in some server setups; has 5.5 million to 62 million transistors
	Pentium	50 to 200 MHz	Has three times the number of transistors of an 80486 CPU or about 3.3 million; was introduced in 1993
AMD	Opteron	1.4 to 2 GHz	Used for servers; permits multiprocessing; has 160 million transistors
	Athlon XP (K8)	2 to 2.2 GHz	Is a 64-bit Athlon processor
	Athlon (K7)	500 to 1600MHz	Is comparable to the Pentium III
	Thunderbird	750 to 1200 MHz	Comparable to a Pentium IV
	Duron	550 to 1000 MHz	Somewhat comparable to the Intel Celeron

Note An excellent online source of detailed information about various types of processors, beyond those available at manufacturer sites such as Intel (*www.intel.com*) and Advanced Micro Devices (*www.amd.com*), is SandPile at *www.sandpile.org*.

CPU Form Factors

Just as motherboards are categorized by form factors (as discussed in Chapter 5, "Motherboards") that define the physical shape and size of the device, so too are CPUs. CPUs have just two major types of form factors:

- **Socket insertion**   The CPU package is plugged into a socket and held in place by clips.

- **Slot insertion**   The CPU package is pushed into a slot and secured by a bracket.

There are some additional differences between CPUs themselves rather than just form factor issues such as socket and slot. For instance, a slot-style CPU typically has its heat sink and fan more directly attached, while the socket-style heat sink and fan are held in place by clips. This will be discussed later in the "Cooling Issues and Fan Types" section.

When you look at the examples of common CPU sockets and slots in Table 6-2, you will see that in the Pin#/Insertion column there are various abbreviations, such as ZIF (zero insertion force), VLIF (very light insertion force), LGA (land grid array), and SECC (single-edge contact cartridge), to name a few. These abbreviations refer to the insertion method for the CPU itself.

A zero-insertion-force (ZIF) socket is the most common method of insertion and features a lever that can be moved up to release the CPU and moved down to secure the CPU into place. By comparison, a VLIF or LIF (light insertion force) has no lever and requires you to position the CPU carefully and then press it straight into place using relatively little pressure. Removal of a VLIF or LIF CPU might require a chip extractor tool—which is much like a tiny crowbar—although it's usually just as easy to gently hook the nails of your index finger and thumb around diagonally opposite corners of the CPU and pull up.

Table 6-2   Examples and Descriptions of Common CPU Sockets and Slots

CPU Type	Socket/Slot	Pin#/Insertion	Multiplier	Bus
Opteron (AMD)	Socket 940	940-pin ZIF	7.x/8.x/9.x	200(x2)
Athlon 64 (AMD)	Socket 754	754-pin ZIF	N/A	200(x2)
Itanium (Intel)	PAC611	611-pin VLIF	4.5/5.x	200(x2)
Itanium	PAC418	418-pin VLIF	5.5/6.x	133(x2)
Xeon (Intel)	Socket 603	603-pin ZIF	14.x to 22.x	100(x4) 133(x4)
	Socket604	604-pin ZIF	14.x to 22.x	166(x4)

Table 6-2 Examples and Descriptions of Common CPU Sockets and Slots

CPU Type	Socket/Slot	Pin#/Insertion	Multiplier	Bus
Pentium IV (Intel)	Socket T	775-pin LGA	N/A	200(x4)
Pentium IV and Celeron (Intel)	Socket 478	478-pin ZIF	15.x to 26.x	100(x4)
Celeron (Intel)	Socket 478	478-pin ZIF	15.x to 26.x	133(x4) 166(x4) 200(x4)
Athlon and Duron (AMD)	Socket A	462-pin ZIF	6.x-15.x	100(x2) 133(x2)
Athlon (AMD)	Slot A	242-pin SECC	5.x to 10.x	100(x2)
Pentium III, Celeron, and Cyrix III (VIA/Cyrix)	Socket 370	370-pin ZIF	4.5 to 14.x	66 100 133
Pentium II, Pentium III, and Xeon (Intel)	Slot 2	330-pin SECC	4.x to 7.x	100
Pentium Pro, Pentium II, Pentium III, Celeron	Slot 1	242-pin SECC/SEPP	3.5-11.5	60 66 68 75 83 100 112 124 133
Pentium Pro and Pentium II Over-drive (Intel)	Socket 8	387-pin ZIF/LIF	N/A	60 66 75

The Front-Side Bus

You learned about PC bus architecture as it relates to hardware expansion in Chapter 4, "The Workings and Connections of the PC." Now let's talk about the front side bus (FSB) on the motherboard, which is important when discussing the CPU because it is the bus that connects the CPU to the main memory installed in the system and can define how well a system operates for its user. The FSB goes by many names, including the system bus, the memory bus, or the local or host bus. Whatever you call it, understand that it is critical to overall PC performance.

The actual speed of the FSB is a big factor and is determined by three elements:

- The CPU being used

- The system chipset

- The system clock and how it is set

A slower speed FSB will slow down the entire system because the CPU and system memory won't be able to interact as quickly as they normally would. Conversely, a very fast FSB can boost overall system performance remarkably.

Up until recent CPU generations, the speed of the FSB was fairly fixed, meaning that an FSB sent one signal each clock cycle (as explained in Chapter 4). This signal rate was decently matched to the slower memory speeds then available. However, with the advent of the Intel Pentium IV and the AMD Athlon processors and much faster memory came an FSB that was multiplied by a factor of 2 (that is, one which had two signals per clock cycle) for the Athlon and a factor of 4 (or four signals per clock cycle) for the Pentium IV. Right now, you can purchase a motherboard with a rated FSB of 800, which is actually a 200 MHz FSB multiplied by the Pentium IV's four signals per clock cycle for a total of 800.

Cooling Issues and Fan Types

One of the byproducts of energy consumption is heat, and CPUs can run quite hot. As you learned in Chapter 4, CPUs are often installed with a heat sink and a fan to help them dissipate that heat and move it away from the sensitive chip.

Every CPU is designed with a specific normal operating temperature in mind. For example, a CPU might offer a normal temperature range of 94 to 100 degrees Fahrenheit. Pushed past that ideal operating range, the CPU might become more prone to errors and various system problems might appear (such as garbage text when you type, intermittent drive errors, and so forth). If the CPU regularly must run at sustained high temperatures, it might suffer a serious decline in lifespan. One day, it might simply fry and die, and it probably won't help your motherboard's overall health when it does (although a fried CPU does not necessarily mean a failed motherboard as well).

For the reasons just mentioned, the CPU is the most important component to keep within a normal operating temperature range. The heat sink and fan should accomplish that under normal conditions. However, these devices alone might not be sufficient in a crowded case where air does not circulate freely and pockets of hot air are allowed to build up. Even a PC case that is not jam-packed with additions might have cables, dust, and dirt accumulated around the CPU, which might prevent hot air from dispersing. Heat sinks and the default CPU fan also might not be sufficient when you are working with a system that has been pushed beyond its rated speed specifications, such as when a motherboard is overclocked.

You should check the CPU fan regularly to make certain it is not becoming clogged by dust (as is the case with the one pictured in Figure 6-2). The fan can be removed and cleaned, or you can use a can of compressed air to carefully clean the fan while it's still installed (but be sure you don't pack dust into the CPU itself as you do this).

Figure 6-2   Heavy dust on a CPU fan, a common condition when running a system in a smoky or dusty environment either with or without the cover in place

Also, not all heat sinks are designed to work with all processors. The AMD Athlon and Thunderbird, for instance, really need a heat sink manufactured specifically for them and the Socket A insertion they use. When you purchase a heat sink, be sure it's the right type for your processor. A heat sink is designed to sit flush with the CPU and should not be wedged precariously in place or set at odd angles.

Smart Shopping

The rule of thumb with CPU and motherboard upgrades is that you should get the fastest, most capable combination for the money you have to spend. If you buy an older motherboard, you're locked into older CPUs that might become less available over time. Because you don't want to perform a CPU or motherboard upgrade frequently, you should invest money in a CPU that will sustain your needs for at least six months to a year.

However, if you decide to go with an older motherboard combination (such as older Pentium IV or Athlon/Operton models), consider whether you have access to a system with a working CPU of the right type that you can harvest to use as a replacement if needed. With the speed at which some systems are retired, spare working components can sometimes be easily found. Prices for new but older vintage CPUs tend to be rock bottom, so there is no real profitability in selling these used chips. You might get a few more years of life out of an existing motherboard and case by harvesting a CPU someone else no longer wants.

When you do decide to purchase a new CPU, you should deal only with a reputable vendor who has a good customer service record with you, clients, coworkers, or other colleagues. Such a vendor might be more likely to provide bulk discounts—if needed—and replace a CPU that fails prematurely or arrives dead as the proverbial doornail (an experience that is rare but which happens).

Installation

When you obtain your new CPU, remove it from its packaging with care and examine it. A label on the back of the unit should specify at least the manufacturer's name, but it might also have information identifying the specific processor. Look at its pins and be sure nothing appears bent or misshapen; a CPU with noticeably broken pins should be replaced. Return the new CPU to its packaging (until you're ready to install it) once you have ascertained that the processor is the one you intended to purchase, is in good shape, and is ready to install.

There is one more thing you need to do in preparation, besides reading the accompanying documentation (which you should *never* throw away). Determine whether your motherboard's present BIOS is equipped to handle the new CPU. You might be able to glean this information from the motherboard or PC manufacturer's Web site under a subject heading such as "Support for Your Model." In some cases, a BIOS update (explained in Chapter 5) will be necessary to allow the CPU to be recognized for what it is. (For example, the system may report an older processor than what is actually installed until you update the BIOS.)

Removing an Old CPU

If you have purchased a new motherboard to go with the CPU, you can simply install the CPU and its fan and heat sink to the motherboard before you install the new motherboard itself. (Motherboard installation is outlined in Chapter 5.) This is usually easier than doing it before you install the motherboard to the case. If, however, you're replacing an existing CPU on an already installed motherboard, go through the steps here before you proceed.

To remove the existing CPU:

1.   Refer to the PC, motherboard, or CPU documentation to see how the existing CPU should be removed. Be sure to follow the directions.

2.   Observing proper procedures for going inside the case (outlined in Chapter 3, "Defining Your Tech Toolkit"), disconnect power from the system, remove the cover, and ground yourself.

3.   Locate and detach the power cable running from the power supply or motherboard to the CPU fan. (See Figure 6-3.)

Figure 6-3 The power cable running between the motherboard (or power supply) and the CPU fan

4. For slot-installed CPUs, disengage the CPU retention tool (such as a lever, clip, bracket, and so on).

     For socket-installed CPUs, detach and remove the heat sink/fan package first.

5. Lift the CPU from its slot or socket.

6. Place the CPU, heat sink, and fan in a safe place, preferably in their individual boxes or antistatic bags.

You are now ready to install the new CPU. However, if there is a great deal of accumulated dust in the system or in an existing CPU fan you plan to use for this CPU, first remove the debris by using a can of compressed air, let the system sit for a few minutes, and then begin the installation.

Inserting a New CPU

Look at the documentation that accompanies your new CPU. This will usually identify the retention mechanism used to secure the processor in its socket or slot, and it will provide the basic steps necessary to install your particular CPU.

Check, too, to determine whether the heat sink is already installed on the CPU and whether the fan is attached. If not, the documentation might specify whether to attach them before you install the package or afterward.

Next, look carefully at the slot or socket where you need to insert the CPU. It might be necessary or advantageous—depending on how much room you have to work with—to connect the power cable running from the CPU fan to the motherboard before you actually insert the CPU. Because the PC itself is disconnected from power, there is no danger.

You can then follow these steps:

1. Remove the new CPU from its case or antistatic bag.

2. If it has not already been done, install the CPU retention mechanism by using the steps outlined in your documentation. Align it as indicated.

3. Check for jumper settings that must be applied both for the bus speed and the CPU multiplier as well as for the voltage, and then set them accordingly. Again, you should consult the documentation while doing this. On some systems, these jumper settings are available not in jumper form but as an option in CMOS Setup for the BIOS. In those cases, you'll need to select the jumper settings when you first boot the system after finishing the installation.

4. For a slotted CPU, match the CPU's four posts to the four holes in the CPU slot on the motherboard and press the CPU into place until the retention mechanism catches and secures it.

5. For a socketed CPU, lift the ZIF lever you might see as far as it will go. Then position the CPU so that Pin 1 on the CPU—usually indicated by a mark or beveling on one of the four corners of the processor—matches the similarly marked Pin 1 on the ZIF socket. Gently but evenly press the CPU into place, and press the ZIF lever back down until it is firmly engaged.

6. If you haven't already done so (per the documentation), install your cooling mechanisms (heat sink and fan) now.

7. Be sure the power cable from the CPU fan to the motherboard is in place and firmly seated.

8.   Replace the cover and reconnect the power plug to the back of the PC. Turn the PC on.

9.   If the PC boots as it should, enter CMOS Setup, check what it reports now for a processor, and make any changes to jumper-less settings for bus speed, CPU multiplier, and voltage not performed in step 3.

Should the PC fail to boot, listen for beeps and match them to those identified in Chapter 2, "The Operating System's Role in Hardware," to determine the source of the problem. A dead CPU will seem like a dead PC with its power supply engaged, for example, but it will have no display on the screen and no apparent activity taking place except for the movement of the power supply fan. In all likelihood, the culprit will be that you have not installed the CPU properly or did not use the proper settings. Disconnect power, reground yourself, and fully check the installation.

Maintenance and Repair

The CPU tends to be a component that either works or doesn't work. There's very little middle ground, and virtually no repair is possible—unless you have a microcomputer lab available, complete with micro tools, electron microscope, and access to reams of schematics usually available only to highly trained staff at Intel and AMD. Most of us mere mortals have no way of getting hold of such things, and we wouldn't know what to do with them if we could.

Unfortunately, a common way a CPU is damaged is when one or more of its pins becomes bent during the installation or removal process. The pins are miniscule and almost impossible to straighten out even with very small tools and very steady hands. If your CPU has bent pins, you probably have to replace it.

The best way to maintain a CPU is to keep it operating within its proper temperature range, to keep it free of dust and moisture, and to check periodically that the heat sink and CPU fan are still attached and functioning properly. When a CPU fan is malfunctioning, the PC should not be operated until it is replaced or repaired. Operating a PC with a malfunctioning CPU fan will affect short-term CPU reliability and the lifespan of the CPU.

Also, when a heat sink becomes loose or misaligned, it should be reinstalled with fresh clips or thermal compound, depending on how it was affixed to start.

Troubleshooting

One of the best ways to troubleshoot a CPU that shows no sign of life in its current motherboard is to remove the CPU and test it in a compatible motherboard that you know is working and using the proper jumper or CMOS Setup settings (for the clock, CPU multiplier, and voltage) for that CPU. If the CPU works in the second motherboard, there might be a problem with the first motherboard or the slot or socket it resides in. This also usually means you need to replace the motherboard. But it's also possible the CPU was not properly installed in the first motherboard yet was in the second. You should try the CPU again in the first motherboard to see whether it was simply a transient installation issue.

Don't automatically assume that progressively worsening slowdowns of a system are necessarily the fault of an overloaded or failing CPU. Faulty or failing memory, insufficient hard disk space, a deteriorating or corrupted Microsoft Windows setup, or a computer virus are just some examples of other issues to consider in this situation.

Lab 6: Determine the CPU Upgrade Path Possible for Three Different Motherboards

This lab is intended to prepare you to identify a motherboard and the types of processors it is designed to accept. As part of this lab, you'll not only determine specifications for each motherboard listed, but you'll determine the most ambitious CPU upgrade possible on each motherboard and pricing for each of those CPU upgrades. Finally, you must determine what each CPU comes with and whether you will need to purchase a CPU fan, heat sink, and thermal compound to accomplish the upgrade.

Objectives

When you complete this lab, you will be able to address the following issues:

- The features of the three motherboards outlined

- The CPU upgrade path possible for each motherboard as is

- Whether a BIOS update will be necessary for any of the three motherboards in question

- The exact items that will be necessary to perform such an upgrade (for example, whether it needs a new fan)

- The current price for each upgrade

Necessary Equipment and Resources

The following equipment and resources are necessary for completing this lab:

1. An Internet-ready connection (preferably, a high-speed connection)

2. Knowledge of BIOS updates (obtainable from your Chapter 5 lab)

3. Online specifications for the following motherboards:

   ❏ Abit AT7-Max 2

   ❏ Soyo Socket A SYKT400DUB

   ❏ Mach Speed MZ-630TCF Socket 370

4. At least 60 minutes to complete this lab

Procedures to Follow

1. Using a Web search engine, identify the URL for the manufacturer for each of the listed motherboards and try to locate motherboard-related Web sites that offer you details in addition to what is offered on the manufacturer sites. Jot these URLs into your lab notes.

2. Use the online resources you've found to determine what the most aggressive (fastest, most powerful) CPU is that can be installed in each existing motherboard. Record this information in your lab notes.

3. Use online price search engines—such as *www.pricewatch.com*— and a mixture of merchant sites—such as *www.chipmerchant.com*, *www.tigerdirect.com*, and others—to document in your lab notes the price of each CPU for each motherboard, for a total of three prices for each.

4. Determine whether the CPU comes with the fan and heat sink. If it doesn't, determine how much each item will cost. Also record this information in your lab notes.

Lab Notes

1. Document the URLs for the manufacturer and motherboard-related sites for each specified motherboard.

   _____

   _____

   _____

2. Identify the best CPU upgrade possible for each.

   _____

   _____

   _____

3. Document prices and vendors for each CPU.

   _____

   _____

   _____

4. Does the CPU ship with a CPU fan and heat sink? If not, document availability and pricing.

   _____

   _____

   _____

7

Memory

If you consider the CPU the brain of the PC, then its installed memory is like the neurons and synapses. While the CPU juggles the instructions necessary to execute your programs, memory makes it possible to work within the programs and allows you to open and close files as part of your working desktop environment. Memory holds the operating system, applications, and files that are available while the PC is running and then discharges them again (so that you can start fresh) when the PC is shut down.

There are many types of memory in a typical system, including the caches discussed in Chapter 4, "The Workings and Connections of the PC," and the memory installed as part of the video adapter. There are even more types of memory in the peripherals, such as a digital camera or printer, attached to the PC. Some of these various memory types include:

- **Random access memory (RAM)** The dominant memory in a computer. There are two basic types: static and dynamic.

  - *Dynamic RAM (DRAM)*—This is usually the memory available for desktop work. DRAM differs from static RAM (SRAM) in that its contents are constantly refreshed by electricity. Without this constant refreshing by electricity, memory cells lose their contents.

  - *Static RAM (SRAM)*—This high-speed memory is primarily used in PC caches, such as the L1 and L2.

- **Read-only memory (ROM)** A special type of memory that is constant and does not need to be refreshed. The BIOS chip is an example of a component that uses ROM. (It's known as the ROM BIOS.)

- **CMOS RAM memory** This type of memory is used to store user-configurable BIOS settings, including hard drive specifics, time, and date.

- **Video RAM** This is the overall term for any memory installed to the video adapter or video chipset and dedicated to graphics processing. There are many types of video RAM—for example, Double Data Rate Synchronous Dynamic RAM (DDR-SDRAM), which is used by many current video adapters and is also used as main memory for motherboards.

- **Flash memory** This is a nonvolatile type of memory (because, thanks to a battery in the device, it doesn't lose its contents with the power turned off). It's commonly used in cell phones, laptop disk players, and digital cameras.

Beyond your computer, you can find different types of PC-equivalent memory installed in any number of electronic devices. Any device, for example, that is "smart" enough to retain information generally has some sort of memory installed. However, in this chapter, you'll focus on the type of memory you're most apt to work with directly in the PC, which is RAM, also referred to as the main memory or installed system memory.

How Memory Works

Managing the work of all main memory and its communication with the CPU and the rest of the system is the *memory controller*, a hardware logic circuit usually built right into the system chipset. Its primary job is to generate signals that regulate the traffic created by reading and writing data to and from the main memory. It also serves as the interface between main memory and other parts of the system that might interact with main memory. The chips making up your memory are used to build modules that go into banks that install in (or *populate*) the memory sockets on your motherboard, all of which are managed by the memory controller.

For the controller to do its work, it must see the installed memory organized in rows and columns—much like the organization you use in a spreadsheet. It uses those row and column identities to communicate with specific parts of the memory, as required.

The *front-side bus* (FSB), discussed in Chapter 6, "Central Processing Units," is actually a bus within the microprocessor charged with mediating communications between the CPU and your installed RAM. Its name helps distinguish it from a *back-side bus*, which is used as the mediator between the CPU and the L2 cache.

A good rule of thumb to remember is this: the faster the bus, the faster data is transmitted.

> **Exam Tip**   SRAM used in caches does not require regular refreshing, while DRAM needs frequent refreshing through its capacitors.

Determining Installed Memory

Before you make any decisions about upgrading or changing memory in a system, it's wise to perform an assessment of what is currently installed. The amount of main memory installed on a system can generally be determined in one of the following two ways:

■ From the boot-up screen as memory counts up during the boot process (although this option is not always available because the memory count might be turned off or otherwise unavailable).

■ From the General tab under the System icon in the Microsoft Windows Control Panel, as shown in Figure 7-1.

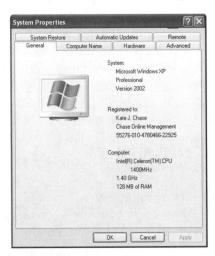

Figure 7-1   General tab from System Properties displaying the amount of installed, recognized memory

However, both of these methods depend on the system and Windows being able to determine that this memory is installed and available. A bad stick of memory, or one that is improperly installed, might not be detected. For this reason, you might find it advantageous to perform a visual inspection of the installed memory (with the power to the unit disconnected, you grounded, and the case open). Tiny labels on the memory sticks might identify the capacity of each. Any documentation you have for this memory might also specify the capacity and type.

Once you perform that visual inventory, you need to compare the amount being reported through boot-up and Windows against what you see installed. Any discrepancy between the two should be a source of concern. You might want to check the installation of all sticks as well as test each stick one by one (as outlined in the "Troubleshooting" sidebar later in this chapter) to determine which of them is not being recognized.

How Much Memory Do You Need?

Few systems today ship with less than 128 MB of memory installed, which is a decent amount for small-business and home users to handle their application and processing demands. Currently, the majority of such users still rarely need more than 128 to 256 MB, especially if they're using a consumer version of Windows such as Windows 98, Windows Millennium (Windows Me), and Windows XP Home Edition.

Others might need 256 to 512 MB to handle a fair amount of image and video processing. This requirement is often found among users who perform computer-aided design work, edit and produce digital video and audio, use heavy-duty financial applications where many large data files need to be open simultaneously, and perform other memory-intensive efforts.

Professional systems and servers, in contrast, might readily accept between 1 and 4 GB or more of memory, depending on the actual processes being run and the number of processes running simultaneously. Such systems should never have to operate with minimal amounts of available memory because both performance and processes can be negatively affected.

RAM Recommendations by Operating System

In Table 7-1, the following measures are offered:

- **Minimum**   Describes a low-requirement system on which easier tasks—such as simple word processing, record keeping, and regular net surfing (without many utilities loaded)—are conducted.

- **Recommended** Describes the range of use for a more typical user, who might have several applications open at once—including an Internet connection with two or more net-based tools loaded. This level of memory is capable of handling most functions in a timely manner.

- **Power Use** Describes users who perform serious work and lots of it, with many applications and connections in use. This level of memory is for situations requiring fast and reliable calculations and large-scale data retrieval. It's appropriate for heavy-duty efforts such as audio and video creating, editing, and production and other similar memory-intensive tasks found in a professional or demanding environment.

Table 7-1   Memory Needs by Operating System and Level of Work

Operating System	Minimum	Recommended	Power Use
Windows 95 (all types)	12 to 32 MB	32 to 64 MB	64 to 128 MB
Windows 98 and Windows 98 Second Edition	32 MB	64 MB	128 MB
Windows Me	64 MB	64 to 128 MB	128 MB
Windows XP (Home Edition)	64 MB	128 MB	128 to 256 MB
Windows XP (Professional)	128 MB	128 to 256 MB	256+ MB
Windows NT 4 (Workstation)	32 MB	64 to 128 MB	128 to 384 MB
Windows NT 4 (Server)	64 MB	96 to 256 MB	256 to 512 MB
Windows 2000 (Professional)	64 to 96 MB	128 to 256 MB	256 to 768 MB
Windows 2000 (Server)	128 MB	128 to 256 MB	512 to 768+ MB
Linux (Command Line)	32 MB	64 to 128 MB	256+ MB
Linux (Graphical Workstation)	32 to 64 MB	64 to 128 MB	256+ MB
Windows 2003 Server	128 MB	256+ MB	512 MB to 4 GB and even above

Note Not all chipsets or motherboards for Windows 95 support the use of more than 64 MB of RAM.

Memory: When More Isn't Always Better

There is a common misperception that adding more RAM will cure any problem with PC performance. It is more accurate to say that you need a sufficient amount of RAM for the work you do with your PC. Beyond adequacy, the helpfulness of the "boost" from extra RAM depends on the activities you perform, as discussed before.

Two decades ago, when our PC desktop was a command prompt and most programs were well under 256K in size, we could make do nicely with amounts of RAM measured only in kilobytes. But slowly, we became oriented to a graphical user environment, which was needed to multitask with multiple programs open and working at once. As those same programs became mammoth in size and range and as we used the Internet more and more, our minimum RAM requirements rose (in megabytes, not kilobytes) from 1 to 4 to 8 to 16 to 32 to 64 to 128.

PROFILE: Memory and Desktop or System Resources

An infrequent misunderstanding occurs among Windows users eager to increase their *system resources*, which are the fixed-capacity regions of memory that your desktop uses to work with applications. (These are sometimes also called *resource pools*.) Upset that their systems load with only 60 to 85 percent of system resources free—and that after a relatively short time that number can drop to 40 percent—they buy and install additional RAM, thinking that more resources and more RAM are synonymous. They're not—not directly, anyway.

System resources are actually hard-coded regions built into Windows that work to boost overall performance on the desktop as we work in our large, multiple applications. Because they're hard-coded segments of memory, there is no one-to-one relationship between the amount of RAM installed and the amount of system resources available to you as you work.

Yet there is something of an indirect relationship. This relationship is better seen, however, when you operate your system with an inadequate amount of RAM installed. In this situation, the entire system, to one degree or another, has to work harder to handle the demands of multiple, open applications, and you are likely to notice your available system resources drain away at a faster pace than usual. Peripheral equipment, such as a printer, is likely to seem much slower, too.

Should you suspect that a system doesn't have enough memory installed, use the System Monitor available in many versions of Windows to measure system performance issues. (You can do this in Windows XP and Windows 2003

Server by checking under Help And Support to see how to set up counters and objects.) You can measure system performance for issues such as the following:

- Percentage of CPU usage. (High, sustained usage might be indicative of an overworked CPU or memory.)

- Amount of available memory. (Low amounts might indicate too little installed RAM.)

- The peak commit charge coming close to the maximum limit (which also might indicate overtaxed memory).

You can also perform spot checks through the Task Manager's Performance tab (by pressing Ctrl+Alt+Del once, and selecting Performance), as shown in Figure 7-2.

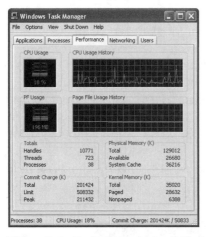

Figure 7-2   Performance tab of Windows Task Manager

Major Types of Memory

Over the more than two decades since the debut of the IBM PC, there has been an ever-changing array of memory types, which have evolved faster—in terms of both capacity and speed—than some other parts of the overall system architecture. Especially when memory was very costly, you often saw a difference between consumer systems (which often featured slower, cheaper forms of memory) and professional-level systems and servers (which tended to demand much faster, far more reliable, and more expensive memory installed in greater capacity than in consumer PCs).

In the last few years, three major types of memory have been used in most personal computers as well as professional setups and servers. The oldest of these memory types is *synchronous dynamic RAM* (also known as SDRAM and seen mostly on pre–Pentium IV systems), *Rambus dynamic RAM* (also known as RDRAM and used almost exclusively on recent-era Wintel systems), and Double Data Rate Synchronous Dynamic RAM (also known as DDR SDRAM and seen on both Intel and AMD platforms in the last four years).

Synchronous Dynamic RAM (SDRAM)

When SDRAM was introduced in the mid-1990s, it was a huge improvement over the memory types on which it was based. SDRAM matched the speed of the system bus by running first at 66 MHz, then at 100 MHz, and finally at 133 MHz, so the CPU did not have to wait for the memory to catch up to it. (That wait was referred to as a *wait state*.) SDRAM was such a significant advance because it also created an environment in which one bit of memory was accessed while the next one was being prepared to be accessed. This last part is referred to as a *burst* because it helped to keep data flowing without major slowdowns in the process as seen in earlier forms of memory. As a result, SDRAM purrs along at an average data transfer rate of about 800 Mbps on a 100 MHz bus and approximately 1 Gbps on a 133 MHz bus.

SDRAM comes in a 168-pin dual inline memory module (DIMM) stick. It's available in various sizes (32 MB, 64 MB, 128 MB, 256 MB, and up) and various bus speeds (with PC66, PC100, and PC133 being the most common), as shown in Figure 7-3.

Figure 7-3   128 MB PC100 SDRAM

Rambus Dynamic RAM

RDRAM arrived in the late 1990s with a lot of fanfare as a considerably faster memory system, but it brought with it a fair amount of controversy (discussed more in the "Double Data Synchronous Dynamic RAM" section) and concerns about overall cost and availability. While its speed difference and projected reliability made it seem like a perfect fit in highly professional environments and with servers, it was first introduced on consumer systems where the cost would be felt more acutely. Rambus uses a slightly different packaging form, typically referred to as a Rambus inline memory module (RIMM), which looks like a DIMM but must be installed into a RIMM or Rambus socket.

There is more than one type of Rambus memory, and they are used in environments other than strictly PC environments. For example, the Sony Playstation 2 came equipped with two Rambus modules. The type used in PCs is referred to as Direct Rambus/RDRAM.

Rambus memory speeds run from 600 to 800 MHz up to a dual-channel version with a 1600 MHz data-transfer rate.

Double Data Rate Synchronous Dynamic RAM

DDR SDRAM is also known by variations of its name, including DDR RAM and Double DRAM. All these terms refer to the same high-speed memory type. With a great deal of support from AMD and AMD-compatible motherboard manufacturers, DDR SDRAM evolved at least in part to compete with the then extremely costly Rambus DRAM that Intel was pushing for its Pentium IV line as well as for its servers. (Rambus DRAM also appeared early on in Intel Pentium III–based Xeon servers.)

Some system builders and users rebelled against the idea of using memory as expensive as Rambus. Rambus was also not readily available to provide data support for the faster CPUs coming out. (In fact, the first Pentium IV systems built to use Rambus shipped with SDRAM instead because of the lack of availability.) Many consumers turned for the first time to building or buying systems based on the AMD line of CPUs, which had already embraced DDR SDRAM as an alternative. Intel then backed off on its Rambus-only game plan and announced its plans to support DDR SDRAM as well.

The "double" part of its name is largely based on the fact that DDR RAM tries to double the speed of traditional SDRAM, with data-transfer speeds of 1.6 and 2.1 GBps, compared to SDRAM's 800 MBps and 1 GBps, respectively.

To the untrained eye, DDR SDRAM doesn't look remarkably different from SDRAM. If you look closely, though, you'll notice different notching (specifically, one notch for DDR SDRAM vs. two for SDRAM). Also, DDR SDRAM uses the same DIMM packaging as SDRAM, yet it offers 184 pins rather than SDRAM's 168.

PROFILE: Magnetic Memory—the Wave of the Future

Do you remember reading earlier in this book about design initiatives that would make the PC an instant-on device, always ready to work, just as our televisions have become? Magnetic RAM (or MRAM) might be one of the components needed to accomplish this because it could be used to store the information now contained in CMOS.

The chief difference between magnetic and standard dynamic memory is that the former will use magnetism rather than supplied electricity to store data. Magnetic memory will still use electricity supplied from the power supply to the motherboard, but not in the capacity currently required by DRAM, which always needs to be refreshed so as not to lose its content.

IBM has been hard at work for the past several years implementing MRAM. This technology might be available by the time you read this. Some experts believe that MRAM could replace the flash memory in cell phones and certain add-on devices, such as digital cameras (where images are also often stored in memory).

Determine the Memory Type Needed

The most important mantra to remember in acquiring new memory is, "Don't guess!" Determine the exact type of memory required by the motherboard, and get that type. You can usually determine this by doing the following:

- Checking the motherboard documentation

- Checking the PC documentation (if you bought the system as an already-assembled unit and have not made changes to the memory in the past)

- Going to the manufacturer's Web site and looking for the specifications for that PC model or motherboard

- Visiting a place that sells memory (online or in-store), and checking the PC model or motherboard information against a computerized listing (For example, if you visit a major chip merchant's site such as Kingston at *www.kingston.com*, you can use its online database to determine which type of memory you need by supplying either the PC model information or information about the motherboard.)

Notice that I didn't mention visual inspection of the motherboard as a way to determine the memory type needed. The reason I didn't is because you might not be able to determine which type is required just by looking at the motherboard. To the casual observer, RIMMs can look almost identical to regular DIMMs used for SDRAM. The notable distinguishing characteristic is that RIMM keying notches do not match those of a DIMM. Look carefully. Most motherboards made prior to the Pentium IV don't use Rambus.

Smart Shopping

Memory prices can fluctuate wildly, from the very cheap to the very expensive. Price depends on a number of things, including availability and demand. The markets can also play a factor here. When a Korean company that provides some of the coating for memory chips experienced a fire several years ago, prices for memory chips rose exponentially long before the in-stock inventory was depleted, just as oil and gas prices can take strange turns based on rumors and concerns.

Newly minted high-speed memory always tends to cost the most, but much older types of memory not much in use can be costly, too. Wherever possible, it is recommended that you do the following:

- Check the memory pricing from at least three different sources before you purchase.

- Buy from a reputable source that offers a solid return policy if the memory is the wrong type or is defective.

- Avoid buying used memory. (With prices for new memory usually low, buying used can be an unnecessary risk.)

- Avoid buying less memory than you truly need. Memory is a poor choice of components on which to economize. Also avoid buying far more than you expect to use.

- Use only the type of memory specified by the motherboard manufacturer.

- Purchase the amount of memory you need in the form of two sticks rather than one. By doing this, you'll have at least some memory available if one stick fails.

Installation

Before you start the installation, always inspect the new memory you have acquired. Most sticks will have at least some notation—either etched directly upon them or placed on a heat-resistant label—that identifies their type and capacity (usually in MBs). Don't just rely on what the invoice states or what you asked for, because mistakes happen. Also be sure the stick is not discolored, bent, or otherwise abnormal looking. Such memory sticks should be returned for a better product.

Before you begin, you should also determine how you will populate the banks with your sticks of RAM. If you're using just one stick, it's easy: it goes in the first (usually left-most) bank. In fact, wherever possible, you should always populate memory banks in sequence, starting from the lowest numbered socket or slot (usually marked 0 or 1 on the motherboard silk-screened labeling).

If you're planning to add sticks to existing memory, you need to determine which existing sticks, if any, you plan to retire so that they can be removed. In such a case, you might want to insert all the new memory in the first banks and all the older memory in later banks, which means rearranging the sticks.

Be careful about mixing sticks, however. The issue is often specific to a manufacturer; some systems, such as most of the ones made by Compaq, tend to be very susceptible to problems with mixing memory. Also, you should always avoid mixing memory metal types such as tin and gold.

With that said, let's say you're working with an older system that has a 100 MHz bus speed. You can usually add PC66, PC100, or PC133 SDRAM to such a motherboard. However, if you have sticks running at 66 MHz and sticks running at 133 MHz, they will all fall back to operating at the 66 MHz speed. You might want to replace all the PC66 memory with PC100 memory so that performance is not affected as much.

Removing Existing Memory

Because you might need to remove existing memory in a motherboard to rearrange it or replace it outright, you'll go through the steps for memory removal first. If you're populating a new motherboard or just adding memory to existing working memory, you can skip ahead to the next section.

To remove existing memory:

1.   Shut down the PC, disconnect power, remove the case, and ground yourself per the instructions in Chapter 3, "Defining Your Tech Toolkit."

2.   Locate your memory sockets or slots, as shown in Figure 7-4.

Figure 7-4   Memory sockets or slots, usually located near the CPU on the motherboard

3.   Locate the memory sticks you want to remove (if any) to populate the bank with fresh memory.

4.   Push open the retaining clips on each socket or slot, and pull the memory stick from it.

5.   Place the removed memory aside, preferably in a case or antistatic bag, and then label that case or bag with the type of memory stick inside and whether it works or not.

Nonworking memory should be properly discarded as soon as possible to lessen the chance of inadvertently adding it back into your hardware surplus inventory and rediscovering later that it doesn't work. (Even though you've labeled it, not everyone is good about reading labels.)

> **Fact** You might want to test apparent nonworking memory in another system before you decide it definitely does not work.

Installing New Sticks

New memory should remain in its case or antistatic bag except when you are directly working with it, either to inspect it or install it. Memory, like other components, is sensitive to moisture, dust, and pressure, and should be treated with great care.

If you didn't have to remove existing sticks first, you'll need to shut down the PC, disconnect its power, open the case, and ground yourself, as outlined in Chapter 3. Then follow these steps:

1. Remove any dust around the memory sockets or slots by using a can of compressed air.

2. Open the retaining clips on the sockets or slots that you'll insert memory into.

3. Remove the first stick from its case or antistatic bag, and orient it correctly (that is, put the pin side toward the motherboard).

4. Begin to push the stick evenly but firmly into its socket or slot so that each end of the stick goes into the retaining clips until those clips close around the stick (which should happen only when it's firmly and properly seated).

5. Visually check the installation.

6. Repeat steps 3 through 5 for each additional memory stick you want to install.

You should replace the cover and then reconnect the power to the PC at this point.

Maintenance and Repair

As with a CPU, there is really little maintenance to be done with actual installed memory except for keeping the sticks free of dust deposits and excessive heat. Dust can be removed using a can of compressed air; heat in the case should be monitored.

Memory sticks themselves cannot be repaired, although damaged memory sockets and slots on a motherboard can sometimes be replaced without having to replace the entire motherboard. These can typically be obtained at a nominal cost through the motherboard manufacturer, with the old socket or slot unscrewed from its position and the new socket or slot put in place and screwed down.

Also, remove sticks of RAM you believe are no longer working or not working correctly. For example, you might notice while inside the case that one stick of RAM is much hotter than the others even though it appears to be installed correctly. Rather than wait for it to fail—perhaps taking the motherboard with it—remove the RAM immediately and replace it as soon as possible.

Troubleshooting

Memory is one of the most difficult components to troubleshoot because the symptoms problematic memory can produce can be attributed to many other factors, including a faulty Windows installation, a corrupted drive, bad drivers or iffy applications, and even a malfunctioning motherboard.

Many people assume any PC problem is a virus, when this is rarely the case. Still, it's wise to perform an antivirus scan as you begin troubleshooting just to eliminate infection as a possibility.

Also, early on, determine what work was most recently done on the misbehaving system. If either hardware or software was altered (either added, removed, or reconfigured), you might want to undo that change temporarily to restore the system to the way it was before the problem developed. If the performance jumps right back to normal, the change made might have been the issue. Evaluate this before you implement the same change again. But if the problem continues once the system is restored to its previous condition, the change is more likely not related to that change.

Analyze the Symptoms

Following is a list of various issues you can see with problem memory. As you read, consider how many other things you might suspect for each issue:

- Invalid page faults in Windows
- Parity errors
- Windows Protection Fault or Fatal Exception errors

- General "slowing" of Windows operations

- Applications that won't open or don't function as they should once they're loaded

- Random device and program failures

- Corrupted data files—this can be temporary (as when the file scrambles only while in memory but is fine when saved to disk) or permanent

- Frequent "low on virtual memory" messages

- Slowed or hung boot-up

One difference between problem memory and other culprits is that many of the issues will seem far more random when you have a memory problem. For example, if one particular application always causes problems, it might be because of the program itself or a bad installation. A computer virus, by comparison, usually sets off specific failures or issues, so it's unlikely to tie itself just to the misbehavior of one application. But if different programs misbehave at different times all the time, without any sense of "when I do this, the program always crashes," you might want to consider problematic memory in addition to the possibility of a corrupted Windows installation and an overtaxed CPU.

Check the Installation

Always check the installation of memory, whether or not you installed it yourself. The sticks can be tricky to insert just right and this can lead to problems. Even experienced technicians occasionally reverse the stick, fail to seat it evenly, or don't fully secure the latch or latches retaining it in place. Sticks of memory have been known to literally spring from their enclosures if they are not secured into place. Such evicted RAM might need to be replaced—after it has been tested—because it's not meant to engage in a free fall.

Fact of life: retainers holding memory into place can fail, particularly when they are mishandled in the process of installing that memory. When they fail, the firm insertion of that memory might fail, too, and result in the system either not seeing the memory sitting in that slot or socket with broken hardware or seeing it only intermittently. Occasionally, you might also see a situation where the circuitry underlying the memory slots and sockets fails, too, which results in a dead memory bank—that is, the memory itself doesn't usually die with it, but any sticks of memory inserted into that bank will not be recognized.

Test It Stick by Stick

You might wonder how you can determine whether a stick of memory works or not. For example, say you have three sticks of memory installed in a PC. How do you know which of the three isn't working when you suddenly discover a discrepancy between the amount of installed memory and the amount Windows reports?

The time-honored approach is to try them stick by stick, one at a time, to determine which sticks work and which do not. The procedure works something like this:

1. Shut down the PC, disconnect it from power, open the case, and ground yourself as covered in Chapter 3.

2. Remove all but the first stick of memory, and set the other sticks aside in a safe place (such as into individual cases or antistatic bags).

3. Reconnect power to the PC and turn it on. If the PC boots, the first stick must work. Check Windows under the System/General tab to be sure the right amount (for that single stick) is reported. If the PC won't boot, you might not even see a display on the monitor but instead hear a beeping noise from the system. (The BIOS beep error codes are discussed in Chapter 2, "The Operating System's Role in Hardware.") Shut down the PC and disconnect power, ground yourself again, and then try a different stick.

4. Repeat this until all sticks have been tested.

As you work here, have a way to identify the sticks you've tested already from the ones you have not. Also be sure that you know which ones worked and which did not.

> **Exam Tip**   Rather than using a regular work PC to test memory this way, you'll find that some techs keep around a barebones test system (often populated by just a power supply, motherboard, CPU, memory, and perhaps a hard drive) with a display to swap out parts like memory and test them.

Verify the Memory Type

Even if you've purchased memory to install in a system that appears to fit properly, don't automatically assume it's the right type for a particular system. Some motherboards are extremely selective and occasionally won't take the exact same type of SDRAM, RDRAM, or DDR RAM used in several other motherboards.

As mentioned before, determine the type of memory recommended for your motherboard or PC model. Contact the manufacturer if you have any questions about the type.

Lab 7: Identify Memory Type and Perform a Memory Replacement or Upgrade

This lab is designed to prepare you to identify the memory currently used in each system available for this process; to identify, locate, and price the amount of memory needed to bring each system to 512 MB; and to experience the hands-on upgrade of at least one system.

Objectives

When you complete this lab, you will be able to address the following issues:

1. The identification of the major memory types used for main memory today

2. How to determine the exact type for a particular system or motherboard

3. The proper process for the successful installation or replacement of memory

Necessary Equipment and Resources

The following equipment and resources are necessary for completing this lab:

1. Two PCs (of different ages or CPU classes)

2. Any documentation for the PC or diagram of the motherboard in these systems

3. A connection to the Internet

4. Your PC hardware toolkit

5. The proper memory type to be added to one of the systems

6. At least 60 minutes to complete this lab

Procedures to Follow

1. Use instructions earlier in this chapter to identify the reported amount of memory installed on each system. Jot these down in your lab notes.

2. Following the procedure outlined in Chapter 3, shut down the PC, disconnect power to the system, remove its cover, and ground yourself.

3. Locate the memory sockets or slots, which are usually positioned near the CPU.

4. Use a flashlight if necessary and try to read any labels on the memory sticks installed on each system to identify what each stick is and what amount of memory is on the stick. Record this information for both systems in your lab notes, along with how much RAM would be needed to bring each system to 512 MB.

5. Check the documentation for the PC and motherboard and try to determine the exact memory specifications for each system. If necessary, check the support link on the Web site of the motherboard or PC manufacturer for your model and type. Note any special information in your lab notes.

6. Based on what you've learned in your documentation, go to either a physical store or an online chip seller or manufacturer and look up the type of memory needed for each system. Record this in your lab notes.

7. Determine price and best packaging (such as using three sticks of 128 MB, replacing an existing 128 MB of memory with a single 512 MB stick, and so on) for each needed type for each system. Get prices from at least three different vendors for each. Document the pricing in your lab notes.

8. Acquire a stick of working memory of the right type for one of the two systems you're working with, and then follow the process outlined in the "Installation" section earlier in this chapter to (at least temporarily) replace the existing memory in that system with the new memory stick. Record your experience in your lab notes, including any difficulties you encountered and what steps you took to troubleshoot.

Lab Notes

1.   Indicate the amount of memory currently installed.

  System #1 _____

  System #2 _____

2.   Enter the information on memory installed during physical check (step 4).

  System #1 _____

  System #2 _____

3.   List the types of memory needed for each system (with any specific requirements noted).

  System #1 _____

  System #2 _____

4.   Enter the type specified by vendor lookup (step 6).

  System #1 _____

  System #2 _____

5.   Enter the price or packaging information from three sources for each system.

  System #1 _____

  System #2 _____

6.   Enter your installation notes for one system.

  _____

  _____

  _____

8

Power Supplies and Cooling

Why combine a chapter about power supplies with one on proper cooling? The answer is simple: wherever power or energy is produced or provided, you have heat. Wherever heat is produced, you have the potential for overheating, which you already know can shorten the lifespan of sensitive electronic components or cause their quick, outright failure. Overheating can also cause very strange behavior that you might mistakenly assume is related to something else.

In this chapter, you'll learn not only about standard devices installed on your PC to provide both power and cooling, but also about devices you can add that can protect your PC from the potentially dangerous effects of power and heat. Learning about these additional devices is important because most PCs do not ship from the manufacturer with these protection devices installed. Protection devices are sometimes offered as a system option, but they are not frequently ordered, usually because people assume they can get away without one and it saves them money initially. However, while you save a bit off the initial price, you might pay a higher price later on if there is a problem.

How a Power Supply Works

First, let me define both the term *power supply* as well as the term *power source*. The power supply provides electricity to a PC in a format it can use and also tries (with varying degrees of success) to regulate the voltage distributed to the components. On the other hand, the power supply gets its power from the power source (the electricity in your home or office that is accessible through outlets and power strips and surge suppressors plugged into those outlets).

If you look at the back of your PC, you'll probably see that the power cord connecting your PC to the power source plugs in near a large, grill-covered exhaust fan like the one seen in Figure 8-1. This is the outer interface for the power supply.

Figure 8-1   The outer interface for the power supply at the rear of the PC

Press the power button on a PC and you start a chain reaction, which includes a signal that switches on the power supply. The power supply draws an electric current from a wall socket or power strip the PC is connected to, and then converts it from the typical 120-volt AC of your home or office power into the DC power—of differing voltages—needed by the PC itself. Various voltages are needed because disk drives and fan motors might demand 12 volts each, while the CPU, motherboard, and other digital circuitry often require between 3.3 and 5 volts.

Once the power supply is quickly brought to full speed and its external-venting fan is engaged, it begins to send power to the motherboard, drives, CPU, and other fans. Through the motherboard, it connects the power and reset buttons, the LED indicators, and the ports and connectors to the PC's energy flow, and it provides power to the keyboard and some of the peripherals that don't have a separate power cord.

Power from the unit to the motherboard and other components is supplied through a series of bundled wires, as shown in Figure 8-2, each of which ends in varying size connectors. These connectors have been fashioned to make it difficult to force a wrong-sized connector into a device.

Power supply   Connector bundles

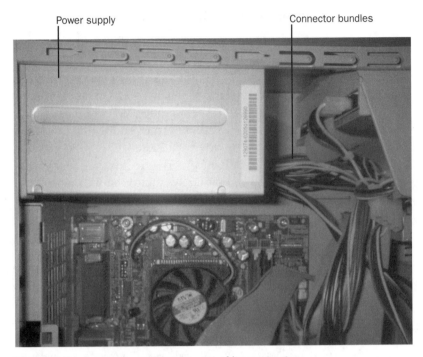

Figure 8-2   A power supply and some of its connectors

The exhaust fan on the power supply does not just remove heat from the power supply itself; it also pushes out hot air from elsewhere in the case. Unfortunately, dust and debris drawn into the case through its external vents and openings also get churned up in the fan and often begin to clog the blades as well as the grill covering the fan blades. This debris slows down the process of removing heat from the power supply and the rest of the case and can eventually block the fan's exhaust completely. Once this happens, the power supply will soon fail.

Also, like any other device with moving parts, the power supply fan blades might need lubrication to keep rotating normally. Without lubrication, the blades might stall altogether, which can also lead to the premature demise of your power supply.

Exam Tip   Throughout this book, you are told not to simply turn off the PC when you want to work with the system but to also disconnect its power. This is necessary because even though the PC is off, a small amount of electricity continues to flow through it.

Advanced Power Management and the Role of the Power Supply

For several years, the computer industry has largely followed a standard called Advanced Power Management (APM) set forth by Microsoft and Intel and adopted by manufacturers. The standard allows a PC to shift into different power modes to conserve electricity when it's not in active use. APM helps a system go into Standby or Hibernation mode, for example, or to come back to life when a key is pressed or the mouse is moved. During low-power states, the monitor might go dark and the drives will idle.

For this power state change to work effectively, every major component of the PC—from BIOS and operating system to the motherboard and installed devices right through to the power supply—needs to be APM-compliant. However, even now, a few years into this standard, you can find that enabling APM creates some conflicts in a system that affect how or whether a system actually shuts down and turns off and whether it can successfully return from Standby or Hibernate mode. Some technicians choose to disable APM at least temporarily during troubleshooting to make certain that this is not the source of a problem.

Through Microsoft Windows, you can set, modify, or disable various power management options using the Power Management or Power Options icon in Control Panel, as shown in Figure 8-3. There, you can make choices for when and if the monitor and drives power down, how long the PC is idle before it goes into Standby mode, and so on.

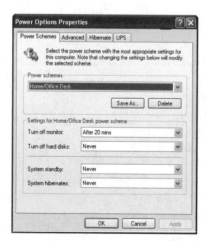

Figure 8-3 The Power Options screen available from the Windows Control Panel

Protection from the Power

The power that flows through the wiring in our homes and offices is inherently "dirty," meaning that its current is constantly affected by surges being pushed in from underground or overhead power lines, from the cycling up of other appliances on the same circuit, and from a number of other causes. If you situate a PC on the same circuit as a refrigerator in a home or office with older wiring, you'll certainly wonder how the PC is faring as you notice the room lights dim.

Any system that is regularly used and important to home and office life should have adequate protection installed between the home or office power source and the PC itself. This protection can come in different forms, in different levels—with some types, like an uninterruptible power supply (discussed later in this chapter), even offering the ability to continue working for a very short period (usually a matter of minutes) during a power outage—and at varying costs.

The protective device, at least to some small degree, acts as a barrier between common fluctuations in your home or office electrical feed and the rest of your system. This barrier won't necessarily protect a PC from a major power surge or *rocking* power (where the lights go on and off repeatedly in sequence), but it's going to take the first hit when the PC is plugged directly into a wall socket or other unprotected power source. Because this barrier takes the brunt of the beating from electrical oddities, you might see it fail more often than some other components on a system.

Power Strips as Protection

The most common form of basic power protection is a power strip. Most people buy a power strip for the number of accessible outlets it provides them. Not all power strips offer protection hardware inside them to take the hit from a power surge, but many made specifically for electronics do. These are typically labeled as surge suppressors because they try to absorb the impact of a surge without passing it along to devices connected to the strip. You pay more for them (with decent ones often starting around $15 to $20 compared to under $10 for a barebones power strip), but they provide important protection compared to having no "middle man" device at all.

As someone who used to have her office set up in a very old house that had ancient wiring and was beset by frequent, violent electrical storms, I can attest that a good power strip can save a system. (I'll spare you the tornado and ball lightning stories.) For me, power strips have saved three systems. One unit was burnt to a crisp (literally) in a power surge that also killed my refrigerator motor, but the surge did not kill the PC and peripherals attached to the power strip.

Backup Power and Protection

While a laptop or handheld computer with a charged battery can continue operating once the power goes out or becomes unsafe to use, a typical desktop has no such failsafe. At the first good power dip, the system might reboot. If the power is unstable, the PC might go on and off many times, which can possibly damage sensitive electronics. Not only is any unsaved work lost in the process, there exists a danger that data can become scrambled, drive-file integrity can be corrupted, and devices might fail.

An uninterruptible power supply (UPS) is a device that sits between the power source and PC and typically offers two separate features: surge suppression and battery backup. The battery backup is crucial for providing time to save files and to shut down the PC properly. This short window of time can make all the difference in protecting your work and the system itself from what otherwise could be a violent crash, the effects of which could ripple through both hardware and software. While it's possible to purchase a very expensive UPS with a long period (an hour or more) of battery backup, most users typically need one that provides no more than 15 minutes of power for essentials such as the PC itself and the monitor.

Major Types of Power Supply

Power supply types are based on the same form factors you learned about in Chapter 5, "Motherboards." By and large, most power supplies follow the ATX form factor, which means they are designed to work with ATX form factor motherboards and are positioned at the top rear of the PC chassis, separated by an empty space from the drive bays.

In fact, the major way in which power supplies are distinguished from one another is in terms of the wattage each uses. Most PCs operate well with a 250-watt unit or less; power systems with a large number of drives and add-ons might require a 300- or 400-watt power supply.

One thing to consider with a power supply: it's possible to overtax the unit. For instance, if you start with a two or three Advanced Technology Attachment/Integrated Device Electronics (ATA/IDE) drive system and upgrade to one using a Small Computer System Interface (SCSI) host controller connecting three or four drives, you could be operating at peak capacity on a lower wattage power supply. This isn't good: you should always have a buffer of 50 watts, and preferably more, between the wattage required by all your components and the capacity of the power supply. A power supply forced to run at or beyond capacity can result in one or more devices not receiving adequate power.

By checking a PC power-related site such as PC Power and Cooling (*www.pcpowerandcooling.com*), you can often locate tables that spell out the average wattage demand for various components. A few examples of this are offered in Table 8-1.

Table 8-1   Wattage Power Consumption by Device

Device	Average Wattage Demand
AGP adapter	20 to 30 W
ATA/IDE hard drive	5 to 15 W, depending on disk revolutions per minute (RPM)
CD/DVD drives	10 to 50 W
CPU	18 to 50 W or more, depending on speed and type
Floppy drive	4 to 8 W
Memory	Approximately 10 W per 128MB
Motherboard	20 to 35 W
Network adapter	4 to 5 W
PCI-based adapter	5 to 7 W
SCSI controller (PCI)	25 to 30 W

Shopping

Before you start to shop, know the capacity of the power supply you want to replace. This information should be contained in either your PC or power supply documentation, and it can usually be found on a label applied to the side or bottom of a unit, as shown in Figure 8-4. This knowledge will help you determine whether you want a straight replacement or one that increases the wattage capacity.

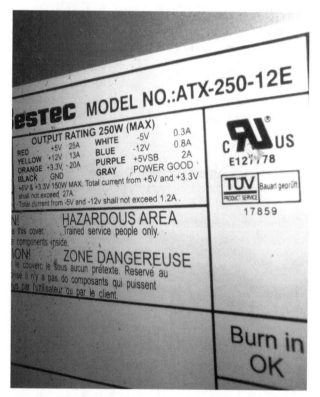

Figure 8-4   A power supply information label

Now let's discuss some important specifics in making your selection.

Power Supplies

Many different companies manufacture or distribute power supplies, and as you can imagine, not all units are created equal. For example, you might see a power supply manufacturer routinely place very short warranties on its products, which should make you wonder how long the unit will last.

While a power supply is one of the most often replaced components on a PC, it's relatively unusual for a system to require more than one or two replacements in a four- or five-year lifetime. Once you increase the replacement frequency beyond that, you have to consider several issues, including the following:

■ Whether an electrician should check the wiring in a home or office. This is especially true if you're encountering failures of devices, other than PCs, that are regularly connected to an outlet and running.

- Whether you need power protection, or simply better quality power protection, between the power source and the power supply to absorb some of the impact of fluctuations.

- Whether you're allowing the power supply fan to become hopelessly clogged or otherwise nonoperational. This can occur when operating a PC under relatively dirty, dusty, smoky, or greasy conditions.

- Whether the PC is situated in such a way as to block the external venting of the power supply fan.

- Whether you need to buy a higher capacity power supply or one from a highly regarded manufacturer.

You have several issues to consider when shopping for a power supply as well. You should consider the following guidelines:

- It's smart to buy a power supply that has sufficient wattage to cover your current needs as well as needs in the foreseeable future, such as increased power requirements from add-ons such as additional drives.

- It's also wise to have at least one spare power supply on hand because a PC cannot run without one and, depending on how close you are to a vendor, it might take up to a week to receive a replacement.

- Check the warranty. Those that offer a short coverage period (90 days or less) should be avoided.

- Avoid buying used power supplies because you don't know what the unit was subjected to before you received it.

Power Protection Devices

You can buy a cheap power strip at a supermarket, but you'll be better served by researching good surge suppression models and shopping through a vendor who specializes in electronics.

Before purchasing an uninterruptible power supply, you need to consider the level of protection you need, the amount of time you'll need a battery to provide backup power before you can safely close your work and shut down, and the number of devices you want attached to the UPS. Yes, you can buy an inexpensive UPS, but what you get for the money might not be what you want. A decent personal system UPS starts at around $75. Professional-grade UPSs featuring battery backup lives of 30 minutes, 45 minutes, and beyond along with multiple outlets with a good warranty will cost considerably more (often starting at around $250) than a consumer unit rated to last just 5 to 15 minutes without power and that connects only the PC (and not the monitor, for example). Understand that the more devices you plug into a single UPS, the greater the drain will be on the battery and the faster the battery will exhaust its power. Many well-known manufacturers of UPS devices offer a free limited liability insurance policy to cover the total replacement of equipment if their protective device fails. Check your literature to see if yours does.

Power Supply Installation

Now that you know that a power supply might have to be changed during the lifetime of a PC, you really need to know how to replace one. Thankfully, while the process takes 10 to 15 minutes, it's also relatively easy compared to other operations you might perform.

As usual, you want to begin by inspecting the new power supply. Be sure it's in pristine condition without dents or damage, that all wire bundles end in connectors and none of the wire is cut, and that the label on the unit specifies it is the wattage you wanted. Quite honestly, I've purchased more than a few power supplies that arrived looking like they had been through a battle. One or two of these were new units that had been mishandled, and another one or two were refurbished units sold improperly as new. If you buy a new power supply, it should arrive in very good condition and with no "refurbished" label attached.

Removing Existing Power Supply

Have your PC toolkit and the documentation for your new power supply handy. In the lab at the end of this chapter, you'll need additional materials to complete this exercise, which is specifically designed to help you identify components that must be reconnected to the new power supply.

Following the procedure outlined in Chapter 2, "The Operating System's Role in Hardware," to shut down and unplug the PC, remove the cover, ground yourself, and take these steps:

1. Locate each wire bundle and its connector that run from the power supply to components such as the motherboard, CPU fan, and drives. All must be unplugged.

2. Identify and remove the screws holding the power supply in place. Remember to hold your hand beneath the unit as you remove the screws so that it does not fall. (It can be heavy enough to break a few add-on boards and the processor package if it falls.) See Figure 8-5.

Figure 8-5   Removing the screws from the power supply

3.   Pull the old power supply out and set it aside.

Installing New Power Supply

First, review the documentation for your new power supply. The paperwork might indicate slight variations from the procedure shown here. After doing that, follow these steps:

1.   Position the new power supply in the case.

2.   Holding the power supply with one hand (and yes, expect to juggle), start to insert the retaining screws back into place.

3.   Use your screwdriver to tighten the screws enough to allow you to let go of the unit.

4.   Continue until all screws for installation are screwed firmly into place.

5.   Reconnect the power supply connectors to the motherboard, CPU fan, drives, and so on. Verify that you have attached everything.

6.   Replace the cover and reconnect power, and turn on the machine.

Don't be surprised, however, if there is a slight odor when the unit first powers up. This is common when a new unit heats up for the first time, and it might continue through a day or two of use. But if the smell is extremely sharp or leaves you with the distinct impression of burning, shut down the PC immediately and investigate. If you see smoke being emitted, also shut down and investigate. There is no reason for a new power supply to create smoke, so you need to verify that the power supply and not some other component in the system is creating the smoke.

Installing an Uninterruptible Power Supply

Don't begin the installation until you complete the following three important preparatory tasks:

- Completely read the instructions accompanying the UPS unit. There are enough differences in installation procedures from one product to another that a complete reading is important for the installation to be completed successfully. You might want to fill out the warranty card or log on to the manufacturer's site to register the product, too. Following the instructions is critical for more than the obvious reason: some UPS units offer replacement assistance only if your system sustains damage as a result of the unit's malfunction. However, if you fail to install the unit exactly according to the directions, you might forfeit any claim to replacement or financial reimbursement.

- Inspect the unit to be sure its housing (which is usually plastic) is free of cracks or other signs of damage and that it is the correct make and model.

- Consider again what devices will be plugged into the unit. Plug in only your most essential equipment, such as your PC and monitor. Unless you have a heavy-grade UPS, don't expect to use the printer or other peripherals that need to draw power. If you have a laser printer you absolutely must use during this process, for example, you need to get a UPS that is rated to cover that need.

Once a UPS is installed, options for using it are usually found under the Power Management or Power Options icon in Windows Control Panel. The UPS tab permits you to make changes to UPS settings. However, earlier versions of Windows normally offer no UPS tab, especially when a UPS is not installed.

Maintenance and Repair

In addition to applying power protection and trying to keep a work area as free from dust, smoke, and debris as possible, you can exercise some maintenance and repair measures. For example, you can clean, lubricate, and even replace a nonworking power supply fan without replacing the entire power supply, but considering the low cost of a power supply and issues that might crop up as a result of your repair efforts, it's usually better to simply replace the power supply.

Cleaning a Power Supply Fan

Even when used in a generally clean working area, the power supply fan is likely to need cleaning. For some, this might be a once-a-year operation; for others, it might amount to three or four times (or more) per year. The procedure isn't optional: whenever dust and debris begin to block the exhaust grill, proper removal must be done as soon as possible.

There are two different ways to clean a power supply fan. One is faster, and the other is more effective (and less likely to result in lots of dust being pushed into the unit only to come back out through the fan later).

Here's the quick method, which can be used whenever the buildup is not too extensive:

1. With the PC shut down and disconnected from power, turn your case as needed so that you have access to the rear.

2. Locate the grill covering your power supply fan and, using a stiff-bristled brush (as shown in Figure 8-6), gently begin to remove the dirt and debris, exercising caution so that none of it is pushed into the power supply itself.

Figure 8-6   Cleaning dust and debris from the grill area

While you're at it, check the vents that are strategically placed around the exterior case. Use a stiff-bristled brush to remove dirt and debris, and be sure these vents are not blocked.

The other procedure is far more involved, but it can also serve as the basis for lubricating a power supply fan as well as replacing just the fan in a power supply. However, consider whether you want to perform such a procedure.

Technically, entering the housing of the power supply might invalidate its warranty. Check the warranty if you have concerns. The procedure is as follows:

1. With the PC turned off and disconnected from power, remove the cover and ground yourself.

2. Using the same procedure for removing an existing power supply, disconnect the connectors from the power supply to other components and then remove the screws holding the power supply in place.

3. Have your power supply documentation handy, and locate the screws holding it in place in the case. Remove these screws, and set them aside with one hand while you hold the other hand beneath the power supply so that when you loosen critical screws, the power supply drops into your hand.

4. Locate the screws holding the power supply housing in place and remove these. Also set them aside.

5. With the housing removed, look for the screws or retainers holding the power supply fan in place. Remove these and set them aside as you lift the power supply fan out of its base.

6. Take the fan to the closest waste receptacle, and use a brush or compressed air to remove dust and debris. However, if you're just going to replace the fan, jump to step 8. (Be sure you have the correct type of fan for your power supply. You might want to purchase the new fan through the manufacturer to be sure you obtain the proper one.)

7. If the situation warrants, use all-purpose machine oil to lubricate the fan mechanism. (Not all fans need oil, however. Check your documentation.) With a fingertip, gently rotate the blades to make certain they move freely.

8. Replace the fan in its base, and secure it using its screws or retainers. However, if you have lubricated the fan, you might want to wait several minutes before you do this.

9. Replace the housing or put the cover on the power supply, and secure it with its screws.

10. Reinstall the power supply, and screw it into place, continuing to hold it until enough screws are secure to accept the weight.

11. Replace your cover, plug in the unit again, and turn it on.

Troubleshooting

The power supply is one of the few devices in your PC that is likely to give you an audible warning of a problem. Not all issues are detectable in this manner, but many are—for example, when the power supply is emitting a strange noise, such as a grinding or a loud vibration noise. The noise might possibly be traced to a clogged fan or one in need of lubrication. It might also signal a failing power supply. Or if you turn on the PC one day and notice that nothing happens, listen for the sound of the power supply. If the power supply is completely silent, it's noticeable even with the cover in place. Suspect that something is preventing power from getting to the power supply. This could be because the power is temporarily out, the PC is unplugged, or the power supply is dead and needs to be replaced.

A failing power supply or one with a severely compromised fan might emit a strong burning odor. Do not operate the PC until you investigate the source of the problem—which might or might not be the power supply. You'll be better able to detect it once you open the case, and then you can take steps to repair it.

Other symptoms of a failing power supply include:

- Recalcitrant starting or a straining noise as the PC starts.

- A system that repeatedly reboots spontaneously.

- Power to devices such as CD or DVD drives is intermittently unavailable.

- Frequently "fried" components. A power supply as well as a motherboard might be off enough in its wiring, perhaps because of some electrical incident, to cause other devices connected to it to fail or misbehave.

Cooling Hardware

Heat is a normal byproduct of the energy required to run a PC. You can't escape this physical fact. More than a few of us joked in the days of the IBM PS/2 and the original Pentium systems that we had these computers as much for the heat they could add to an office on a cold winter's day as for their processing power. Go inside the case of a computer that has recently been running and you might understand. The temperature difference between the interior case and the room might be more than 30 degrees Fahrenheit, and the situation in the case can get worse on a hot day if it's in a room that is not air conditioned or otherwise cooled.

Ah, you think electronics are built to withstand heat because you can think of any number of devices that can get as least as hot as the inside of a PC case. This is true, up to a point. The PC is a tool for work, communications, education, and pleasure. The integrity of data moving through it must be preserved, and it's in the best interests of everyone—from the most casual home users to the most demanding power users in a professional environment—to keep the PC in good running order and free of issues that might affect its continued strong operation.

Thus, you must be prepared to consider whether overheating is at the root of issues you see in PC performance and troubleshooting, and you must try to anticipate situations, such as adding a new device, that might cause overheating. A new device that produces a lot of heat and needs something like a heat sink or fan to direct air away from it is a prime candidate to cause heat-related issues.

Let's look at some of the issues in overheating next.

Issues in Overheating

Excessive heat is a known way to kill components or to shorten their lifespan considerably. When temperatures reach unacceptable levels, the PC's overall reliability can be affected and the PC might show a hodgepodge of symptoms, such as the following:

- Random disk errors (particularly seek, read, and write errors).
- Corruption of files saved to disk.
- Keyboard output displayed as garbage text or the keyboard becomes unavailable for use.
- Memory seems to get confused.
- The system becomes more likely to lock up or becomes intermittently unresponsive.
- The system shuts down or restarts by itself.

If you look at that symptom list, you can understand why a technician might think a computer virus or worm, a corrupted operating system, or a flat-out hardware failure might be the culprit. This is one of the truly frustrating aspects of troubleshooting issues such as overheating and bad memory—the roster of behaviors displayed can mimic those of so many other problems.

Exam Tip   A list of possible causes can make it easier for you to troubleshoot hardware problems. With a prepared list, you can eliminate one possibility at a time until you find the source of the trouble.

Short-Term Fixes

First, understand that you cannot afford to ignore certain things related to overheating. If a CPU fan isn't working, you cannot run the unit until the fan is replaced. The same is true with the power supply fan or the fan you might find on a high-capacity video adapter. But with respect to other issues that might make you suspect system overheating, you can try certain short-term remedies until you find and manage the source of the overheating problem. You can try the following short-term solutions:

- Run the PC for relatively short periods of time, such as one to two hours or less.

- Temporarily remove the cover. While most PCs were designed to operate most efficiently and safely with the cover in place, opening the case will reduce the amount of trapped warm air and increase air circulation inside the case.

- Where possible, temporarily remove the offending component (and if needed, replace it with a cooler component).

- Reduce the room temperature (by setting the thermostat a few degrees lower), while making sure that none of the PC vents are obstructed.

- Move cables and bundle them together, as much as possible, to open up airflow around hotter components.

- If you have overclocked the system in any way, restore the system to the way it was before overclocking.

Taking a long-term view, you should consider your case as well as the hardware that goes in it. Some case designs make for a very tight fit when you install several add-ons, such as adapters and drives. The more crowded the case becomes, the more restricted the air circulation is within the case. Acquiring a larger case should increase circulation by giving you more room between installed components.

Examples of Cooling Devices

In addition to having the default hardware within the PC for cooling, you might find it necessary—for example, in cases of suspected overheating—to either monitor the temperature precisely or acquire and install systemwide or spot-cooling devices to reduce the temperature around specific components.

Temperature Monitors

Some motherboards ship with a thermal monitor or probe installed that measures the interior temperature and alerts you, via an on-screen warning or audio alarm, when the temperature pushes past a recommended operating range. Check your PC or motherboard documentation to determine whether the PC you're working with has this feature, and be sure it's enabled in CMOS Setup.

You can also purchase a probe or monitor that you can install on the system to perform this task for you. Such devices usually cost from $15 up to $100 or even more. Some are meant to be mounted in one area and left in place, while others permit you to move the probe around with ease so that you can check temperature in more than one location. The latter choice is usually your best investment. Such a device can help you make a more informed analysis of the situation at hand and can better direct your cooling efforts to the appropriate regions or components.

Cooling Aids

Special cooling hardware tends to fall into two broad categories: device-specific ones, and those that try to increase overall air circulation and reduce the temperature within the case. These should be added only after you identify or strongly suspect overheating as the source of a problem you're having with a specific component or the system as a whole.

General cooling devices usually come in the form of fans you install in strategic locations within the case to draw hot air out of enclosed areas so that it can eventually be displaced outside of the case. Among the device-specific hardware you can find are these items:

- Heat sinks, which can be used with any chip package and not just the CPU

- Peltier fans (which combine a fan and a heat sink) and spot fans

- Drive and card coolers, designed specifically to remove heat from hot-running drives and adapters

The price range for these various devices can vary widely, from just a few dollars all the way up to $50 (US) or more. When you're in a situation where you believe you need one, investigate each type carefully and determine how flexible the device is in terms of installation (that is, determine whether you move it as needed) and whether the cooling hardware is suited to address the specific overheating problem you face.

Lab 8: Replace a Power Supply

This lab is intended to prepare you to identify, select, and replace a power supply in a PC, which is a necessary skill considering how often it might need to be done in a busy office environment.

Objectives

When you complete this lab, you will be able to address the following issues:

1. The overall power demands of a system

2. Informed decision-making on obtaining a suitable power supply replacement

3. The successful removal of an existing power supply and the installation of a new one

Necessary Equipment and Resources

The following equipment and resources are necessary for completing this lab:

1. An Internet-ready connection (preferably a high-speed one)

2. A PC of recent vintage

3. A replacement power supply for that unit

4. Your PC toolkit

5. Between 45 and 60 minutes to complete this lab

Procedures to Follow

1. Identify the wattage and type of the power supply currently installed on the system. Record this in your lab notes.

2. Use the information found in Table 8-1 and through online resources such as PC Power and Cooling (*www.pcpowerandcooling.com*) to perform an estimate of how much wattage is required by the type of hardware installed to the system. Jot this information into your lab notes.

3. Based on the information gleaned from steps 1 and 2, assess whether you need a power supply that matches the system's current wattage or one that exceeds it.

4. Use online price search engines such as *www.pricewatch.com* and a mixture of merchant sites found through general search engines such as Google to obtain the prices for at least three power supply models that meet your requirements. Record this in your lab notes.

5. Follow the steps outlined in the "Power Supply Installation" section of this chapter to remove and replace the existing power supply. As you disconnect each power supply connection, jot the connection type onto a piece of masking tape and attach this to the connector end. Use this as a guide when you reconnect the power supply to all the components once the new unit is in place. Document this experience in your lab notes, noting any special problems or experiences.

Lab Notes

1. Identify the current power supply wattage.

    _____

    _____

    _____

2. Identify the wattage requirements for major components in the system.

    _____

    _____

    _____

3. State whether you will replace the power supply with one of the same wattage or one that has different wattage, and offer your reasons for making this decision.

    _____

    _____

    _____

4. Document the manufacturer, make and model, and price for the three possible replacement units you researched.

_____

_____

_____

5. Record your experience of the actual replacement of the power supply.

_____

_____

_____

Part III

Working with Add-On Boards and Other Essentials

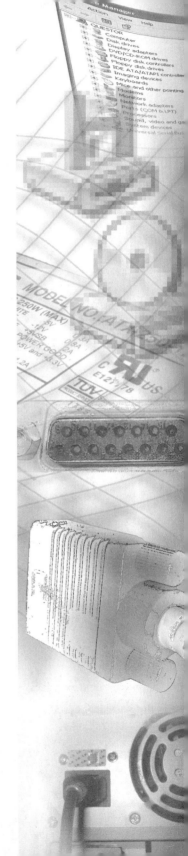

9

Video

A computer's display is something most of us take for granted as long as it works, unless we're heavy-duty gamers, computer-aided designers, or doing high-end image and video production and editing. People playing and working in those environments tend to appreciate in a way most of us do not when a color is particularly true or a line is crisply rendered. They also notice when the display fails to represent what it should, and they usually demand a better PC graphics subsystem than what the rest of us typically use for Web browsing and office file production. Thus, the video hardware industry offers a range of subsystem components, from the ultra-cheap, "looks OK, but if I stare at it too long, I get a headache" devices to the ultra-sophisticated and highly expensive "Wow" options.

The graphics subsystem of your computer is made up of two major components: the video adapter or integrated video chipset in the motherboard, and the monitor. In this chapter, you'll tackle the video component. Later, you can blend the information in this chapter with the information in Chapter 17, "Monitors."

How Video Works

As you read through this chapter, you'll find that a video adapter includes far more features than you might expect. For example, you'll find that most feature processors (also known as graphics or video hardware coprocessors), which came about as PC desktops became increasingly graphical in nature, often have a lot of onboard memory.

With the CPU busy handling all its normal work plus the additional chores of forever drawing and redrawing different windows on the display, it became mandatory and highly desirable to evolve the video adapter to take on more of the job traditionally done by the system processor. When the new hardware first appeared as add-on boards rather than being implemented directly on the video adapter itself, these were often called Microsoft Windows accelerators or just "WinAccelerators."

But as our video demands increased, our systems were already becoming too cramped with add-ons. An "onboard" graphics processor, graphics coprocessor, or accelerator was the way to go both for better speed and for conserving slots and resources. Then 3D accelerators took this a step further by taking the work of graphics animation, one of the more labor-intensive tasks, off the CPU as well.

Early video adapters provided what today is called a *frame buffer*—a place (usually in video memory) to store information in the form of a full bitmapped image from the CPU until it can be translated into analog format for the monitor. In fact, this is principally how *all* early video adapters were.

Today, the frame buffer is just one part of an adapter. Let's look at all the steps involved in taking a 3D image and placing it on your monitor. These steps will serve as an example of the work a recent-model video adapter does in conjunction with the CPU and monitor. A great deal more detail, of course, goes into this, but that amount of detail is worthy of its own book. The steps are as follows:

1. An application or game sends a request to the CPU to draw a new screen to represent a new primary window.

2. The CPU sets up the framework of the window, creating a basic model of what it should look like. At this stage, it's very much a 2D model.

3. The graphics processor or coprocessor takes that basic framework and begins to fill in all the fine detail. In recent-generation adapters such as the NVIDIA GeForce, the processor actually assumes some of the labor-intensive calculations done by the CPU in step #2.

4. Depending on the qualities of the video adapter, the amount of video memory installed, the driver used, and the demands of the application or game, a number of rendering techniques and 3D features (such as shading, texturing, anti-aliasing, and others) are applied until the full image is finished. The result is an image that is as realistic a 3D image as can be achieved.

5. This image is then sent to the random access memory digital-to-analog converter (RAMDAC) for conversion into analog and then transfer to the monitor.

When you read about standard features later in this chapter, you'll better understand the role of features such as the RAMDAC.

Fact   For the human eye to perceive full color, a palette of at least 256 colors is needed.

Fact   While many people want a range of colors extending well past 16.7 million, the normal human eye can discern only about 10 million colors. It doesn't mean that the extra colors available in most video adapters and monitors today are wasted. Humans with particularly sensitive or well-trained eyes can perceive more.

The Role of Video Card Versus the Role of the Monitor

For some, the most difficult work they ever have to do with the graphic subsystem on their PC is determine whether the adapter or the monitor is responsible for a problem they are experiencing. It's not always an easy determination to make, even for trained professionals with many years of experience. But consider this: the video adapter, in association with the CPU, does all the preliminary work regarding the display that the hardware inside a monitor tries to draw faithfully.

For example, bleeding or unusual tinting on the screen often indicates a problem with the electron guns at the back of the monitor. However, occasionally a video adapter that has taken an electrical discharge (from a power problem, lightning coming into the motherboard from an analog phone line plugged into an internal modem, and so on) might appear to act normally *except* that it also seems to scramble the information sent to the monitor, resulting in color distortion.

A quick test doesn't take great technical acumen. Try this process:

1. Try the monitor with the bad display on another PC. If the display is fine on the second system, it's less likely that the monitor has a problem. But we're not done.

2. Swap the working monitor from the second system to the first and problematic system.

3. If the known working monitor works fine on the problem system, look again at the first monitor. But if the first monitor fails, too, you need to look for a problem with the video adapter, its driver, or even the driver for the monitor.

> **Note** You can repeat this same test using a video adapter swapped into a second system with a known working adapter.

Standard Features

Whether you've ever noticed this or not, today's standard video adapter is not unlike a microcosm or miniature version of the motherboard itself, complete with its own processor, memory, and cooling features. These similarities are necessary because video has advanced widely since the days when we were happy to have a simple green or amber phosphorescent display. As our demands have grown, so too has the complexity of the video adapter. Through its own processor and memory and its connection through the fast, dedicated Accelerated Graphics Port (AGP) found on many systems, the video adapter strives to deliver clear, consistent color and motion without overburdening the CPU and the rest of the system.

Video Graphics Processor

When people choose which video adapter they want to buy, the deciding factors are usually the specifications and performance of the video graphics processor and a recognized name brand. A rule of thumb is that the more qualified and capable the graphics processor (also known as the *coprocessor*) is, the faster the overall graphics process should be because valuable CPU time isn't lost performing functions the graphics processor can handle. The processor can be relatively small and simple, assuming just some of the CPU's normal graphics processing tasks, or the processor can be quite advanced so that it can bypass the CPU early in the process to handle some of the mathematical calculations necessary in developing a 3D display.

Many video adapter manufacturers license a particular processor (or accelerator) from another chip designer or manufacturer, as is the case with the GeForce processor from NVIDIA. The manufacturers then add their own special features to the adapter and release it under their own label. Others, such as Matrox and ATI, use their own proprietary processor.

FEATURE: Graphics Processor or Graphics Processor Unit?

Usually, you'll hear the processor on a modern video adapter referred to as the graphics or video processor. Starting with the release of its GeForce256 video adapter, NVIDIA began calling their processor the first true graphics processor unit (GPU). Its reasoning was that the processor on the GeForce took over much more of the intensive work normally done by the CPU during the job of rendering a very detailed, often moving, screen and handled it quite efficiently on its own.

But this claim stirred up some controversy. Some feel that you can't yet call a graphics processor a full GPU with the credibility of a CPU because it doesn't have the full range of raw power, and developers could not routinely program the hardware of the GPU to behave in a specific fashion, as they could with a CPU. So, they said, there was not a broad base of applications available that could make use of the unique hardware features, meaning that a system running an adapter with that advanced GPU would still perform pretty normally because the game or program couldn't take advantage of it.

However, the arrival of the later GeForce series in early 2001 quieted much of this criticism: the GPU now has an instruction set to work with much as a full CPU does, and there are programmable functions that can be exploited by knowledgeable developers. These include fine functionality like key frame animation, and Vertex-based lighting and skinning (named for the on-board Vertex processor that takes care of the vast majority of 3D calculations).

FEATURE: Processor or Accelerator?

Too often, these terms are used interchangeably, but they really do mean different things. A good adapter may have one or the other, and sometimes both.

A graphics processor or coprocessor works directly in tandem with the CPU in helping with numerous processes necessary to deliver the screen information that needs to be sent in signal form to the monitor. An accelerator has a more precise job: following instructions tendered by the CPU. On a system with a graphics processor, the video adapter driver communicates directly with the graphics processor. On a system with a graphics accelerator, the driver works with the CPU, which in turn filters instructions back to the accelerator.

With that said, both processors/coprocessors and accelerators end up doing a lot of the same overall tasks, including covering important details such as anti-aliasing, shading, and texturing the screen image. The accelerator plays a particularly pivotal role in 3D animation.

Random Access Memory Digital-to-Analog Converter (RAMDAC)

A random access memory digital-to-analog converter (RAMDAC) is a single chip assembly positioned on the video adapter. RAMDAC's primary responsibility is to convert digitally encoded images into an analog signal that can be understood and then displayed by the monitor. Standard RAMDAC has four major components: static RAM (SRAM) for holding the color map used, and three different digital-to-analog converters (DACs) to handle the red, green, and blue electron guns (one DAC for each) within the monitor.

Video Memory

The following types of memory are used in the video adapter:

- **Extended data out dynamic RAM (EDO DRAM)** Almost exclusively used in older video adapters prior to the standard inclusion of SDRAM. This type should be avoided unless you're buying a replacement video adapter (or just replacement video memory) for an older system.

- **Video RAM (VRAM)** A type of DRAM developed exclusively for video adapters that requires less refreshing than some other types (including EDO). It was innovative when released because it had dual ports, meaning that it can write the next frame while the last frame is still being read. It's rarely used in modern video adapters.

- **Windows RAM (WRAM)** An extension of VRAM introduced by Matrox. It was both faster and cheaper than the original. It's rarely used in modern video adapters.

- **Synchronous Dynamic RAM (SDRAM)** Still in common use today. It operates the memory as well as the graphics processor or coprocessor at the same clock rate, improving throughput.

■ **Synchronous Graphics RAM (SGRAM)**   A specially created form of SDRAM adapted for video. It has faster access times than SDRAM but similar maximum throughput. It's used on many current video adapters.

■ **Rambus Dynamic RAM (RDRAM)**   Some newer video adapters use RDRAM to populate the graphics memory sockets.

■ **Double Data Rate SDRAM (DDR-SDRAM)**   Similar to RDRAM in that it's a newer, faster memory standard for video. Several video adapters, including models of the ATI Radeon series, use it.

Chapter 7, "Memory," discussed the fact that one reason DDR-SDRAM has become a popular standard is that video can more easily tap its resources for display. This builds on the foundation of a key AGP benefit called Direct Memory Execute (DIME), which allows the video adapter to grab untapped areas of installed main memory as if it were installed to the video adapter itself. Peripheral Component Interconnect (PCI) and earlier formats don't allow that.

> **Note**   The average amount of installed memory on a recently manufactured video adapter is often either 64 MB or 128 MB. Many, however, continue to use the 8 MB AGP adapters that were popular in 1998 and 1999.

Video Driver

From a desktop-operation as well as a troubleshooting perspective, the driver for your video adapter is just as critical as the amount and type of video memory installed or the features of the processor. Without an adequate, manufacturer-supported, up-to-date video adapter driver, you are much more likely to experience the following problems:

■ Critical errors and hangs in Windows or other (especially graphical) operating systems, including general protection faults, invalid page faults, fatal exception errors, and so on

■ Distortion or on-screen debris, as the screen might not properly redraw as you change focus from one window to another

■ Difficulty after upgrading the operating system or major Web browser (to Netscape Navigator or Microsoft Internet Explorer)

- Freezes specific to scrolling or to the mouse, particularly in the browser or long documents

- Slower overall performance, as the system might wait for the video subsystem to catch up and display or refresh the screen

- Limited number of colors available, color distortion, or both

- Increased difficulty playing games, particularly graphics-intensive ones

> **Tip**   Do you find that you can select only 16 colors for your display? This limitation is almost always a sign that a video adapter driver must be updated; a default driver that displays only 16 colors might be loading instead of the driver you want.

More Than One Monitor

Recent versions of Microsoft Windows (from Windows 98 Second Edition on) support the use of multiple monitors (referred to as multiple monitor support, where up to 10 monitors can be connected, each to a different PCI or AGP video adapter installed to the system) on a single PC. Designers, programmers, stockbrokers, and teachers often like this feature because it allows them to extend the desktop across two or more screens. However, you must have a separate adapter for each monitor to be used.

Because PCs that support AGP have just one AGP slot, you'll generally need to install the second (and third and each successive) adapter through the PCI bus. I say "generally" because you can sometimes find a motherboard with integrated video that also has an open AGP slot. In theory, you could have two monitors with this setup—one connected through the integrated video, and one connected through an adapter installed to the AGP slot. However, integrated video often automatically disables itself once it detects that a separate video adapter has been installed. Because of this behavior, you might not be able to turn the onboard video back on with an adapter installed.

External Connections

Many normal video adapters ship with just one or two external connections, as shown in Figure 9-1. One or both of these connections (the VGA and the DVI discussed earlier in this chapter) are available for connecting a monitor (standard analog or flat panel, respectively). The most common other external connection is the S-video jack, which enables you to connect the video adapter by cable to a video device such as a camcorder.

Figure 9-1   The outer interface for the video adapter, awaiting a monitor to be connected

Other Considerations

Beyond features you might seek to fulfill specific needs, several considerations come into play when selecting a new video adapter to replace an existing one. Let's briefly review some of the most common of these.

Exam Tip   Are you unsure of the type of adapter or integrated video currently in use? Go to Device Manager, click on the Display Adapters category, and check the listing provided. The listing might show AGP or PCI, for example, in the device title.

Connection Type

Before choosing a new video adapter, you need to know what type of connection your current adapter uses and what connection possibilities are available to you. While you have a few choices, connection through the AGP slot—which is possible on all but very old (pre–Pentium II) systems—is your wisest choice. The options available are as follows:

- **ISA**   While Industry Standard Architecture (ISA) hasn't been directly supported under the Wintel platform for some time, you still occasionally run into systems using an older ISA bus-connected video card. Wherever possible, these video cards should be replaced—not just because they're old, but also because you can slightly improve the overall speed of a computer if you avoid using any add-on board that connects through the ISA bus.

- **PCI**   PCI boards are less common than they used to be because AGP has been available for several years. Most video adapters that were formerly manufactured in both PCI and AGP versions now ship only with an AGP connection. Unlike AGP, PCI video adapters must share resources with anything else installed to the PCI bus, and its overall much slower performance makes it less desirable for good 3D rendering.

  Again, where possible, PCI video adapters should probably be replaced by AGP versions. There is, however, no way to upgrade a non-AGP motherboard to accept an AGP card without replacing the motherboard (and probably the CPU).

- **AGP**   The AGP slot—a single brown slot typically found between the CPU and the PCI bus slots—represents the most commonly used and fastest video connection available on a PC. An AGP slot can be of one of four speeds:

  - 1x, which supports a video data transfer speed of up to 264 MBps

  - 2x, which supports a transfer rate of up to 512 MBps

  - 4x, which supports a transfer rate up to 1 GBps

  - 8x, which supports a transfer rate up to 2 GBps

- **USB**   This form of connection is usually used only by add-on TV devices, such as a TV tuner, and not primary video adapters themselves.

Integrated vs. Add-On Video

On more and more budget systems today (and this has been true at different times throughout the evolution of PC designs), the video display is driven not by a separately installed video adapter but by a video processor included on the motherboard itself. This is often done as a cost-saving measure, but it's also done because many manufacturers are implementing newer design standards that avoid having different add-on adapters and instead adopt a more centralized approach.

One difficulty that arises is that an integrated video solution is often less robust than a full-sized video adapter. An integrated adapter typically offers fewer features and might have trouble handling graphics-intensive work environments, such as ones with fast-paced graphical games and video editing. In the past, the solution for users who required more than integrated video could offer was to disable the onboard video either through a switch on the motherboard itself or through a setting in the BIOS and then install a separate video adapter rated for the type of work or game-play a user needed.

Today, however, you can find integrated video that seems to defy disabling (or that doesn't include an AGP port for installing a separate AGP card), leaving consumers with a graphics hardware system they can't upgrade without possibly replacing the motherboard. To make matters worse, many systems that integrate video might also integrate the modem (on a hardware riser), the sound chip, or both. In those cases, replacing a motherboard could mean buying many separate devices. Thus, it's often better to avoid buying a budget or value system if you are likely to upgrade its video capability and you can't confirm that onboard video can be successfully disabled.

Some onboard adapters and their drivers automatically disable themselves when a full video adapter is installed. Your motherboard or PC manufacturer should have details on how to disable onboard video on your system. Often, this can be found under FAQs on the product Web site.

Video Resolution Capability

Resolution refers to the ability to render an image with clarity. With video, it specifically refers to the number of pixels (the dots on a screen) that make up an image. This consideration comes into play with video adapters, monitors, and digital video add-ons such as a digital camera.

Many video adapters and monitors today support various resolution levels. (These levels are listed under the Advanced or Settings tab available from the Display icon in Control Panel, as shown in Figure 9-2. This is also where the current resolution can be adjusted.)

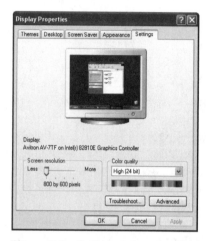

Figure 9-2   Settings tab under Display in Control Panel

The supported levels include the following:

- 640 × 480
- 800 × 600
- 1024 × 768
- 1280 × 1024
- 1600 × 1200
- 1920 × 1440
- 2048 × 1536

Game, Application, and Hardware Support

If there is a particular game or application you need to use with the video adapter, do your research prior to selecting an adapter to be sure the model you want to purchase will work with that game or application. Some games and editing software, for example, tend to run better when used with certain types of video adapters than with others. Try to get recommendations from other users.

Also, consider whether you want to add additional video hardware. For example, are you itching to add a TV tuner or do you want to connect the video adapter to high-definition televisions? If so, you need to shop with a mind toward compatibility. While looking for auxiliary video components, try to determine which video adapters are most compatible with their use and then choose accordingly.

Video Cooling

The more fully featured a video adapter is, particularly if it has a graphics processor, the hotter it tends to run. Overheating can kill your system, as you already know.

For this reason, several video adapters come equipped with either an onboard fan, a heat sink for the processor, or both. You can also obtain separate fans and card coolers that can help you dissipate high levels of heat that can build up around a hot-running video adapter.

When installing a new high-performance video adapter, carefully consider the issue of heat and monitor the system—if not the temperature itself through a thermal probe, as discussed in Chapter 8, "Power Supplies and Cooling"—for problems that might be associated with a rise in internal operating temperature. Installed cooling on the video adapter might not be enough in a crowded case, and auxiliary fans or card coolers might be necessary.

Shopping

Consider these factors when looking for a replacement video adapter for your system:

- Your specific needs for graphics.
- Compatibility with the monitor used.
- Operating system version support. The best results are typically seen with a video adapter driver written with a specific version of an operating system in mind.
- Desired resolution. Make sure it supports the range of video resolution possibilities you need.

- Connection type. Although you can find PCI adapters, you want an AGP adapter for various reasons and 4x/8x AGP if your motherboard supports it.

- Price. Depending on who you ask, the "best" video adapter of the moment usually costs between $250 and $399. For more basic use, adapters running from just below $100 to under $150 are plentiful and offer very competent 2D and 3D display.

- Reputation. Often, this is forged from two factors: the performance of a manufacturer's most recent release, and the company's history of providing both up-to-date technology support and drivers. Some have historically offered superior adapters but failed to release driver updates on a regular basis, hampering the ability of users to load new operating system versions and both load and play the latest games.

- Factors beyond the box. Go to the spec sheets, which are often available on the manufacturer's Web site, to read the detailed technical information on the adapter. Don't depend on the marketing information listed on the box in the store.

- If you plan to use a DVD drive in your system, your preference should be for a video adapter with hardware DVD support.

- If you plan to use multiple monitors, be sure you choose video adapters that support this option.

- If you plan to attach external devices such as input from a video camera or output to another device, make sure it has the S-video and other connections necessary.

Installation

Once you have your new video adapter, remove it from its packaging long enough to inspect it and be sure it's the right adapter with the proper connection and free of damage. Don't forget to review the accompanying documentation and installation instructions before you put the adapter back into its case or antistatic bag.

Before you begin the physical installation, you probably want to check for a video driver upgrade. This is especially true for an older adapter (one that's been on the market more than two to three months), which might ship with an older driver version than you'll want to use. The documentation should point you to the Web site for support of the product, where you can typically download the latest driver. Also read the online instructions for installing that driver. It might provide tips to overcome problems others have had before you.

Removing or Disabling Existing Video

Under normal conditions (for example, when you're not installing a second adapter to supplement the first one for multiple monitor support), you'll need to remove or disable your existing video to install the new one. If your current video is integrated into the motherboard, simply removing the device under Device Manager and going through the shutdown and install process for the new adapter will often effectively disable the integrated video. However, you might need to check your PC or motherboard documentation for specifics. Some motherboards require you to adjust a switch or setting on the motherboard or in CMOS Setup in addition to removing the driver.

If you're simply replacing one adapter for another, you begin by removing the driver for the current adapter. To remove the driver, follow these steps:

1. From Control Panel, double-click System and select Device Manager. (In Windows XP and Windows Server 2003, select the Hardware tab under System and then click Device Manager.)

2. From the Device Manager listing, click the plus sign (+) to expand the Display Adapters category, as shown in Figure 9-3, and select the display adapter whose driver you want to remove.

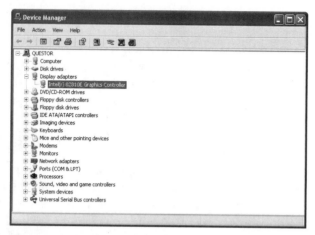

Figure 9-3 The Display Adapters listing from Device Manager

3. Click Remove, and confirm your choice. (For Windows XP and Windows Server 2003, right-click the adapter and choose Disable or Uninstall.)

Once you shut down the system to begin the physical installation, you can make any changes to the motherboard (per the documentation) that are necessary to disable onboard video.

Next, to remove the physical adapter, follow these steps:

1. Click Start, Shutdown, and when the PC turns off, disconnect it from power. Follow the instructions in Chapter 2, "The Operating System's Role in Hardware," for going inside the case (for example, remove the cover, ground yourself, and so on).

2. Locate the video adapter. If you don't immediately see it, look at the back of the PC where the monitor connects: this is the video adapter.

3. With the adapter identified, disconnect the monitor connector on the back of the PC.

4. Identify and remove the screw holding the adapter against the PC frame. Set the screw aside.

5. Pull the video adapter out in a straight, firm manner (as shown in Figure 9-4), and set it aside (preferably into an antistatic bag). Mark the bag ("working" or "nonworking").

Figure 9-4   An AGP adapter being removed from its slot, with the retaining screw removed

You are now ready to install the new video adapter.

Installing the New Adapter

Begin by again reviewing the documentation for the new adapter. Then remove the new video adapter from its packaging and follow these steps:

1. Position the adapter so that you can guide it into its slot.

2. Press the adapter into the slot. Be sure it is evenly and fully inserted and that the retaining screw hole on the adapter edge matches the hole in the chassis for that slot.

3. Reinsert the screw into the frame so that it holds the adapter in place.

4. Reattach the monitor to the monitor connection at the rear of the video adapter. (See Figure 9-5.)

Figure 9-5   The VGA connection at the back of the video adapter

5.   Replace the case cover, reconnect the power cable to the back of the PC, and turn it on.

When Windows loads, it should automatically see the new adapter and either automatically install its driver or prompt you for the driver for it.

Maintenance and Repair

A video adapter can't be repaired in most instances. Usually, a damaged or failed one needs to be replaced.

The best form of maintenance for a video adapter is to keep its driver updated. This can be especially important after upgrading your Web browser or operating system, and it can help, too, when installing the latest version of games and video-heavy applications that might require an upgrade. Some video driver updates will be available directly through Windows Update; others can be found on the video adapter manufacturer's Web site.

You should also try to keep the video adapter and its connections free of dust and debris. A carefully aimed can of compressed air is the best way to accomplish this.

Troubleshooting

Although you were just advised to keep your video adapter driver up to date, you might run into situations where installing a fresh driver can cause havoc either with just your display or your entire system. Because of this, you want to keep the previous version available in case you need to reinstall it. You can often accomplish this using Safe Mode, as outlined later in this section. Also, Windows XP and Windows Server 2003, under the Driver tab for the display adapter in Device Manager, allow you to roll back to your previous driver version.

When you suspect a problem is related to a failing or badly config-ured video adapter, try to locate a second working adapter you can try in the same system. If the second video adapter works, you might be right: the video adapter is failing. But if the second video adapter works no bet-ter, the problem might be in the monitor, which is covered in Chapter 17.

Windows Performance Settings

Windows interacts with your video adapter and its driver through its graphics subsystem. It sets aside up to 1 MB of main memory, for example, to use as a frame buffer, like the one you read about in the "How Video Works" section earlier in this chapter.

Also, through Windows, adjustments can be made to video adapter hard-ware acceleration. By default, Windows sets this acceleration rate at high (Full), but it should be adjusted when troubleshooting video and overall performance issues to see whether such modifications affect the behavior.

To check and adjust your settings, perform the following steps:

1. From Control Panel, double-click the System icon. (See the note that follows if you're using Windows XP or Windows Server 2003.)

2. Choose the Performance tab and then, under Advanced Settings, click the Graphics button.

3. Adjust the slider bar as desired between None and Full, as shown in Figure 9-6.

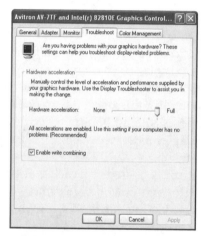

Figure 9-6 Adjusting performance settings under Windows

Note In Windows XP and Windows Server 2003, you find this same graphics hardware acceleration option by choosing Display in Control Panel. Then, from the Settings tab, click Advanced and then Troubleshooting.

Table 9-1 gives you a rundown of each of these settings available.

Table 9-1   Graphics Acceleration by Setting

Setting	None	Basic	Most	Full
Full, normal mode	No	No	No	Yes
Disabled hardware	Yes	Yes	Yes	No
Basic acceleration	No	Yes	No	No
Disabled memory	Yes	Yes	No	No
Disabled acceleration	Yes	No	No	No

Installing a Recalcitrant Video Driver

Normally, installing a new video adapter and its driver goes like clockwork. Follow the instructions and you'll likely be successful on the first try.

Unfortunately, however, there are other times when it can be very difficult to get a PC to recognize the new adapter or its driver. One of the classic, historical workarounds for this is to use Windows Safe Mode to set your display away from its current driver to a generic type, and then to install the new driver.

Here's how this is done:

1. Shut down and restart your system in Safe Mode as described in Chapter 3, "Defining Your Tech Toolkit."

2. Go into Control Panel, under Display, and choose the Settings tab. Click Advanced.

3. Choose the Adapter tab, and click Change.

4. You'll be told that Windows will look for an updated driver for your video adapter. When prompted, select the option to Display A List.

5. From the resulting list, select the option Show All Hardware.

6. Under the Manufacturers list on the left, choose Standard Display Types, and then from the right frame, under Models, choose Standard Display Adapter (VGA).

7. Complete this change, and then shut down and restart your system.

When you restart, your system is using default drivers, which might make it far easier for you to apply your new video driver as directed and give you better results.

Lab 9: Install Replacement Video Adapter and Update Its Driver

This lab is intended to prepare you to plan, prepare for, and complete a successful video adapter or device replacement. Beyond the physical operation, you'll also research any issues concerning the replacement video adapter and update for the most recent driver for that model. Knowing and performing these steps will help you perform subsequent video replacements as well as to better understand the component you're working with.

Objectives

When you complete this lab, you will be able to address the following issues:

1. The proper removal of the current video adapter display driver (which might serve to disable integrated video)

2. The successful replacement of the existing video source and the installation of a new one

3. The appropriate research and proper updating of a video driver with any troubleshooting needed

Necessary Equipment and Resources

1. An Internet-ready connection (preferably a high-speed connection)—ideally one that is available on a PC separate from the system being worked on

2. A PC of recent vintage with either integrated video or an installed video adapter, and which has an AGP slot

3. A replacement video adapter

4. Your PC toolkit

5. Between 20 and 40 minutes to complete this lab

Procedures to Follow

1. Identify the current video device in use and the connection method it uses. Record this in your lab notes.

2. Identify the video adapter replacement you'll install and the connection method it uses. Also record this information in your lab notes.

3. Using your Internet connection, visit the manufacturer's Web site and locate in its support section the following items (documenting each in your notes):

    a. Troubleshooting and installation tips for the adapter in question.

    b. A driver update, its instructions, and any special notes. Download the update, and transfer it to the network or to disk in whatever way you can to make it available to the system whose video you are replacing.

4. Using the procedure outlined in the "Installation" section of this chapter, remove the driver for your existing video device. Then follow the steps through to physical installation of the new adapter and restarting the PC to begin the hardware detection process. Document your experience and observations in your lab notes.

Lab Notes

1. Identify the current video device you are replacing or disabling. (Specify whether you're using an integrated or stand-alone adapter and how it connects.)

    _____

    _____

    _____

2. Identify the replacement video adapter and its connection.

    _____

    _____

    _____

3. Note whether anything else is connected to the back of the existing video device besides the monitor.

    _____

    _____

    _____

4. Record the manufacturer's URL for support.

_____

_____

_____

5. Document the troubleshooting and installation recommendations, the driver specifics, and instructions you located.

_____

_____

_____

6. Record your experience and observations in the actual replacement of the video adapter and driver update.

_____

_____

_____

10

Audio

Believe it or not, not long ago an audio feature was not included on most PCs—at least, not any form more harmonic than a warning bell or a beep. Although gamers wanted auditory feedback and people working with visual handicaps needed something that could "read" the text on the screen, the multimedia experience for most users didn't happen until the early 1990s.

Today, the sound coming from and going into our systems can rival all but the most sophisticated, expensive, freestanding audio setups. The quality matters because we use computer sound to alert us to new mail and messages, to confer with other workers and students, to prepare elaborate multimedia presentations, to educate children and others, to record the audio portion of instructional videos, to dictate to our word processors, to listen to Internet radio broadcasts, and so much more. We also can be quite discerning about audio quality and unhappy when that quality isn't much better than audio coming from inside a tinny little box.

In this chapter, you'll learn how computer-based audio works, what its features are, and how you can work through installations, tweaking, and troubleshooting of audio hardware.

How It Works

There are two major components of PC audio: the dynamics of human hearing, and how well the design of a sound adapter uses those dynamics to deliver audio that pleases the user.

Psychoacoustics is the study of the human perception of sound. It is used in the development of audio technology, including audio hardware and sound-compression formulas. The field of psychoacoustics tries to identify what the human ear can and can't hear, what needs "boost" to be heard, and what needs "cleaning" (the process of removing unwanted noise to achieve overall clarity) to be suppressed from normal hearing. Just as with video, the design of audio hardware on a PC or elsewhere requires a basic understanding of human physiology and how the human ear will interpret the output from an audio device. Designing audio hardware requires knowing what sound is and how it is generated, along with the physical properties of the event (the sound) itself.

Sound is produced when an object vibrates and displaces and moves air particles around it. Those air particles begin to collide with the particles around them, and this chain reaction begins to move out, away from the original vibrating object. This movement might drive that air still further by changes in the physical properties of that object (movement of its parts), in a pulse-like, waveform fashion with vibrations of its own. These vibrations disrupt the air around them as they move, creating waves of fluctuation.

Such vibrations, sent out like the ripple effect of a stone tossed in a body of water, might transmit through solids, gases, or liquids, and at frequencies ranging from 20 to 20,000 Hz. When that vibration reaches the human ear, the fluctuating change in air pressure begins to vibrate the eardrum (a slender piece of semi-transparent membrane that separates the outer ear from the middle ear). If all works properly, the human brain interprets that motion as sound and registers (consciously or unconsciously) that event.

The Job of the Sound Adapter

From a user's perspective, the following four major responsibilities are borne by the sound adapter:

- Recording audio from external devices (such as a microphone or a taped source) and then saving this in a supported audio media format

- Playing back prerecorded sound

- Processing existing sounds

- Providing sound synthesis capability

Exactly how a sound adapter works depends on what job it's performing at any particular moment. One reason so much hardware exists on even a simple sound adapter is because it must do so many different jobs—record, convert, play, and so on. Let's look at what the sound adapter does when it plays back a recorded sound:

1. When you play a recorded sound file, this file is opened from the hard disk in its digital format and sent to the CPU, which in turn delegates most of the work needed to be done to the digital signal processor on the sound adapter.

2. The digital signal processor checks to see what format the sound file has been compressed into (to reduce the storage size of the sound) and then decompresses it.

3. The uncompressed sound signal is then streamed into the digital-to-analog converter, which turns it into the analog signal typically needed to hear that sound through the speakers or headphone.

When you record a sound, this process is largely reversed. You save the file in binary format with the help of the sound adapter's onboard converter. The file is compressed with aid from the digital signal processor, to be stored on your hard drive until you want to open it.

> **Note**   Chapter 19, "Audio Externals," details the installation and troubleshooting for externally connected audio components such as the microphone, headphones, and speakers.

Standard Features

As you already know, today's typical sound adapter isn't really just one device that exists to push sound out from a signal of information generated from the CPU. Instead, it's a collection of devices (plus connections for attaching yet more devices) that bring sound into the adapter and convert it into a signal understandable by the PC, transmit sound through the speakers or headphones, or work with musical or other add-on devices such as MIDI keyboards, microphones, and gaming hardware.

The components typically seen in sound adapters are:

■ Digital signal processor (DSP) or more simplified on-board processor

■ Digital-to-analog converter (DAC)

■ Analog-to-digital converter (ADC)

■ Sample rate generator

■ Amplifier (optional, a legacy from the days when nonamplified speakers required the sound adapter to have an amplifier to push and magnify sound)

■ Memory (either ROM or Flash)

■ Musical Instrument Digital Interface (MIDI) connection

■ Jacks for various connections (speakers, line in, line out, microphone, and sometimes headphones)

■ Game port

More about the core components—DSP, converters, sample rate generator, and MIDI connectivity—follows. Before you get into the specifics, however, let's define the major sound adapter terminology, as shown in this list:

■ **3D sound**   The catch-all term for the overall depth and dimension of the sound experience. 3D sound encompasses spatialization to broaden the area of sound, and positioning to distribute the sound for both dramatic and realistic effect.

■ **8-bit audio**   Audio that is digitized using an 8-bit resolution. It's a step above AM radio–quality fidelity.

■ **16-bit audio**   Audio that is digitized using a 16-bit resolution. Because fidelity exists in direct proportion to resolution (the lower the resolution, the lower the fidelity and vice versa), a 16-bit audio sample offers noticeably higher fidelity than an 8-bit audio sample.

■ **24-bit audio**   An improvement over 16-bit audio, it offers high-definition sound capabilities.

■ **A3D**   Aureal's proprietary standard for 3D positional audio. It's supported in many sound adapters and is available in two versions: A3D1.0 (the original version) and A3D2.0 (a much better version for multiple-speaker setups and headphones).

■ **ADPCM**   Acronym for adaptive delta pulse code modulation. It's the compression and encoding formula commonly used by CD-ROM XA and CD-I formats.

■ **Audio range**   Refers to the standard operating frequency ranges (that is, 25 Hz to 20 KHz) for various multimedia devices.

■ **CD ripper**   Slang for CD software specially written to extract the raw audio data from an audio CD by sending it through the same process (through the system bus) as used for normal CD data.

■ **DAT**   Acronym for digital audio tape, a form of magnetic media usually used less for actual audio purposes and more for backing up drives.

■ **Dolby Digital**   Dolby's encoding system for digital audio, which is considered a standard for both in-theater films as well as home-theater setups. It uses a 5.1 configuration for its six channels. This term is sometimes used interchangeably with the terms *surround sound*, *3D sound*, or *AC-3* (referring to the AC-3 multichannel coder and the coding system used for Dolby).

■ **EAX**   Acronym for Environmental Audio Extensions, which is Creative Labs' proprietary and extended version of the DS3D compatibility standard for 3D positional audio.

■ **FM synthesis**   Also known as frequency modulation (FM) synthesis. It's an older form of music synthesis that tries to mimic various musical instruments. Its capabilities are surpassed in most regards by the newer WaveTable synthesis, but it is still included in many sound adapters to support features in popular older games.

■ **Full duplex**   Refers to a more fully featured sound adapter's ability to handle both recording and playback of digital sound simultaneously.

■ **Microsoft DirectSound and DirectSound3D**   The audio component of the Microsoft DirectX multimedia package. Microsoft DirectSound3D (DS3D) positional audio support is included on most modern sound adapters.

■ **MP3**   The Moving Picture Experts Group (MPEG) audio-layer-3 format file extension. The term *MP3* is used to refer to an encoding standard used for digitally transmitting music over the Internet or a file encoded using this standard.

- **Multitimbral**   Refers to a synthesizer's ability to play multiple musical instruments simultaneously.

- **PCM**   Acronym for pulse code modulation. It's a method by which an audio signal is represented by digital data. It's used by most digital audio systems, including CD, DAT, and MiniDisk. It should not be confused with the Sony F1 format, also called PCM, that allows PCM digital audio to be stored on a regular videotape.

- **Physical modeling synthesis**   The most advanced of the three types of commonly used syntheses. With this type of synthesis, software tries to approximate and emulate the sound of actual musical instruments (including their variation and pulse) by creating a virtual model of the instrument and then calculating instrument sounds based on that model.

- **Sample or sampling rate**   Refers to the frequency at which audio samples are taken and converted into a digital signal. (The frequency is normally about twice the frequency of the analog signal being converted to digital.)

- **Sampling**   Describes the initial phase of converting an analog signal into digital format. (It's also known as *digitizing*.)

- **S/PDIF**   Acronym for Sony/Philips Digital Interchange Format. It's used for connecting sound devices through a digital signal.

- **SoundBlaster-compatible**   Defines the most widely accepted (and relatively early) standards set by the Creative Labs SoundBlaster 16-bit sound adapter. While these standards have been eclipsed by more recent advances, the rating of "SoundBlaster-compatible" is still seen on currently manufactured adapters.

- **WAV**   Waveform audio files (files ending in the .wav file extension) that serve as the Microsoft Windows standard for digital audio files. When first released, WAV was notable because it offered the flexibility to alter recording sound quality based on type and situation.

- **WaveTable synthesis**   A technique that draws upon a stored collection of recorded sounds from various musical instruments (called *samples*) and devices that serve as the basis from which all other sounds can be created. (Think of it as a color palette for the ear.) Because a set of sounds exists to start with, the process of sound production is made shorter, yet it offers a far better quality than FM synthesis. It's supported by most but not all sound adapters.

Digital Signal Processor

Today's digital signal processor (DSP) is at the core of the technology that has helped sound adapters mature into far more sophisticated ranges and delivery. In many respects, the DSP behaves like the sound adapter's CPU, but it's dedicated to and optimized for audio processing, handling computations, and relieving the CPU of many demands normally placed upon it by sound functions. Plus the DSP is responsible for making any modifications to the audio, such as:

■ Chorus (a special doubling function that creates the effect of two or more instruments being played at once)

■ Delay

■ Distortion (that is, purposeful distortion)

■ Echo

■ Reverb (which is short for reverberation, or a representation of the effect you get when playing music in a concert hall)

The DSP also acts as overseer of the process of both sending and receiving signals handled directly by the DAC and the ADC (discussed later in this section), as well as the compressor of the digital signal. It is also an essential component in speech-to-text processing.

Specific jobs for the DSP depend on what mode is being used: 2D or 3D. For 2D mode, the DSP handles effects such as chorus and echo. For 3D mode, the DSP is highly involved with 3D-positional audio, such as you find with DS3D or other standards—such as Creative Labs EAX or Aureal A3D—that would usually need the computing power of a full CPU to render. For this reason, DSP allows for multiple sound streams depending on the type of support offered in the sound adapter itself.

> **Fact**   As with a video adapter and its graphics processor, the digital signal processor on a sound adapter is usually the identified core component and the one considered most important for the overall quality of the adapter. A processor with DSP or simpler technology might not be designed specifically by the manufacturer of the card, but licensed from another party for use on its adapter. A DSP can process up to approximately one million instructions per second and produce sound emulations up to a frequency of 48 KHz.

Polyphony and the Issue of Voices

Polyphony is a term you often see applied to sound adapters. In music, this refers to a composition with two or more independent melodic components blended together.

With audio technology and specifically sound adapters, polyphony refers to the maximum number of voices that the adapter's synthesizer can play at any one time. Each voice is measured as one note generated by one instrument. Sound adapters can generate voices either from hardware or software (drivers and support files), but many today combine both to offer a much larger number of voices.

Digital-to-Analog (DAC) and Analog-to-Digital (ADC) Converters

These two 16-bit (minimum) converters, along with a sample rate generator, provide the core of the digital audio component on a sound adapter. The DAC sends audio out in converted analog format through the line-out jack, while the ADC receives an analog signal and digitizes it through the line-in jack (or microphone jack).

> **Fact**   Some sound adapters have more than one DAC or ADC converter.

Sample Rate Generator

The sample rate generator's job is to clock both the converters and work with the CPU that is scheduling the samples. Most of them use discrete rather than variable or arbitrary sample rates, usually fractions of 44,100 Hz, 48,000 Hz, or both. Also, some sound adapters record and play back at differing sample rates. For instance, a sound adapter might record at only 44,100 Hz but play back audio at various rates.

Musical Instrument Digital Interface (MIDI)

The Musical Instrument Digital Interface (MIDI) is a standard, approved by the electronic music industry, for attaching music hardware devices to a computer through a sound device. The MIDI standard also dictates how these devices should be controlled and manipulated through the computer. Without such an interface, you would be left to record sound through analog devices such as a tape or cassette recorder and then find a way to convert that magnetic media-stored sound into binary format that the PC can understand. Such a conversion usually involves a loss of audio quality, and the difficulties are compounded by what is likely to be less than professional recording quality from a standard analog recording device.

Often considered the binary equivalent of ordinary sheet music, a MIDI file doesn't store the actual music but instead stores the instructions to the sound card on how to reproduce the music the composer designated. For this reason, the identical MIDI file can sound markedly different when played on sound cards of varying abilities.

There are three generally accepted MIDI standards, including:

- **General MIDI**   The original standard. It's still supported by most major sound adapters.

- **Basic MIDI**   A subset of General MIDI offered by Microsoft.

- **Extended MIDI**   Another subset of General MIDI offered by Microsoft.

A MIDI port with its standard five-pin Deutsch Industrie Norm (DIN) connector is the connection point for external audio add-on devices such as MIDI keyboards, digital instruments such as drum pads, and special effects consoles. On some sound adapters, the game port or joystick port and the MIDI port are essentially the same. The MIDI port provides the pathway to the MIDI synthesizer. The following three major synthesizer types are currently supported:

- FM synthesizer

- WaveTable synthesizer

- Physical Modeling or WaveGuide synthesizers

All three of these are defined in the listing of sound adapter terminology earlier in this chapter.

Every MIDI interface supports at least 16 channels, and each channel represents a specific instrument. Higher-end sound adapters, such as the Sound Blaster Live! Platinum adapter, have six audio channels and support for up to 48 MIDI channels allowing for three times the minimum number of channels or instruments. (Sound Blaster Live! has three audio channels and support for 16 MIDI channels.) There is no absolute direct correlation between the number of audio channels and the number of interfaces.

> **Note**   In general, you need at least 32 MIDI channels to create a realistic MIDI instrument environment.

Sound-Adapter Connections

A reasonably diverse range of devices related to sound production, recording, or transmission can be installed to the jacks and connectors on a sound adapter. Typically, these are located at the back of the PC where the sound adapter or bridge from the motherboard-integrated audio chip interface. Some devices, such as internal CD-ROM drives, connect instead with a thin connector cable running between its position in a drive bay and the expansion bus or motherboard where the sound adapter is located.

The following devices can be installed and used by the sound adapter:

- Speakers (amplified)

- Headphones (mono or stereo)

- Digital input sources (for example, CD- or DVD-ROM drive, DAT drive)

- Analog input sources (for example, microphone, CD player, tape player, joystick, or radio)

- Digital output sources (for example, CD-R, CD-RW, DVD recordable drives, and DAT drives)

Also, some recent sound adapters offer a rack or panel approach to connections. Some examples include the Creative Labs Sound Blaster Live! Platinum 5.1 adapter, which has a panel that goes into one of your PC drive bays to permit easy connections (imagine no more reaching behind the PC to blindly try to peg the correct speaker jack), and the Hercules Game Theater XP adapter, which offers a sound-console (referred to by the manufacturer as a *rack*) approach to connections and USB ports too.

Standard Connector Types

The following list indicates the connections seen on the vast majority of sufficiently equipped sound adapters:

- **Line in**   The location at which an external analog audio device (for example, a CD player) connects for input into the system and conversion by the ADC. There might be a single stereo line-out jack, two stereo jacks for multiple speakers, or two mono line-out jacks (usually labeled "Left" and "Right").

- **Line out**   The location at which the sound adapter connects outward to other devices (for example, headphones, amplified speakers, and home stereo), providing a signal converted to analog by the DAC.

- **Microphone**   A monaural jack for plugging in a standard microphone.

- **MIDI or game port**   Defined earlier in "Musical Instrument Digital Interface" section.

> **Caution**   While most sound adapters label their connectors, not all do. Check the documentation included with the adapter or the manufacturer's Web site if you have any questions. Please don't assume that it will do no harm if you accidentally plug a component into the wrong port or jack even if the receptor looks the same. The result can be fried equipment.

About the Game Port   Ever wonder why it's the sound adapter that has the game port? If you stop to think, you can see the logic of that setup.

At first, there was little demand for either sound or games with the original PCs, but this changed quickly. As the potential of using the PC as a game machine was realized, the need for sound increased. Therefore, it made perfect sense to combine the needs into a single device: the sound card with a game port.

Less Common or Special Connector Types

Considering our penchant for trying to attach more devices to perform increasingly specialized functions, it should come as no surprise that some sound adapters offer various special connectors not available on all brands and models. These include the following connectors:

- **CD Interface**   This is an Advanced Technology Attachment (ATA)–style connector for a CD-ROM and isn't usually seen on more recent sound adapters. (It comes from a time when many motherboards had just one IDE controller.) If you have one, don't use it. By using it, you'll risk introducing conflicts with your motherboard's second IDE controller as well as very slow connections.

- **Daughterboard**   This is a smaller circuit board added to the main circuit board to supply additional functionality.

- **MPC-3 Aux-In** This allows you to add auxiliary or secondary devices.

- **MPC-3 CD-In** This allows you to connect the CD/DVD cable to the sound card.

- **MPC-3 Modem-In/Out** This allows you to connect telephony modems and other modems that use the sound card for functionality.

- **S/PDIF** This acronym stands for Sony/Philips Digital Interface, and it allows you to transfer audio between the CD or DVD drive or amplifier to the sound card.

- **Speaker Out or Subwoofer Out** This connector permits the plug-in of outgoing audio for speakers or subwoofers.

Shopping

Creative Labs SoundBlaster—in its many generations, models, and revisions—remains the de facto standard in PC audio technology, but the majority of users don't need the latest, most expensive sound adapter to get the quality, features, and experience they want. Any small amount of research will show you there's an abundance of older edition PCI-connected sound adapters (some available for as little as $7 to $20) that can do an adequate job. Many of these will exceed the capabilities and quality of a cheaply implemented audio chipset integrated into the motherboard. (There are some very good onboard implementations, however.)

The following is a list of considerations you need to make in selecting a new sound adapter:

- **Purpose** This is an important determining factor. For those who rarely use sound, integrated audio will usually suffice. For those who use sound as a system notification or for casual enjoyment, a mid-range sound adapter with basic connectors and standard functionality should do. Avid gamers or PC movie-watchers, those who use sound in their work or for critical appreciation, and those who just want the most comprehensive sound adapters will want to look at high-end cards with a recognized DSP, additional connectors, and other options discussed here.

- **Operating system compatibility**   Is the sound adapter you want rated to work with the exact operating system and version you use? If not, you might lose access to valuable features or even the sound adapter itself.

- **System connection type**   How does the sound adapter connect to the PC? Where possible, the sound adapter should be PCI rather than ISA. There are also units available that connect external sound and game consoles through the USB port.

- **Synthesis type**   Most sound adapters, including older ones, will at least support FM synthesis. Better ones often use both WaveTable and WaveGuide/Physical Modeling synthesis in tandem. Look for an adapter that at least uses WaveTable.

- **Name and reputation**   With audio products, as with other industries, the presence of a brand name and a good reputation usually increases your chances for getting a product that will perform well under standard circumstances. It's usually wise to avoid a sound adapter with an unrecognizable name or one that comes from an unrecognized manufacturer.

Installation

Remove the new sound adapter from its packaging and inspect it, as always, to be sure it is the make and model you selected and that it appears free of damage or other problems. Remember to pull out the documentation, too. You'll want this handy during installation. You should also locate the URL of the manufacturer in the documentation so that you can check the Web site to see whether an updated driver is available for your new adapter.

Have your toolkit ready and your work area clear. Replacing an existing sound adapter is covered next. If you're adding a sound adapter to a PC that currently has only integrated audio, you'll want to remove the existing driver or disable the onboard sound (described in the next section); otherwise, jump to the "Installing the New Adapter" section.

Removing and Disabling Old Audio

Is your current sound supplied by a separate sound adapter or by audio integrated into the motherboard? If you don't know, you can find out either through the documentation or by physical inspection.

If the sound is supplied by onboard audio, you need to check the documentation for the PC or motherboard (or check the product support links on the manufacturer's Web sites) to determine how the onboard sound must be disabled. Sometimes, just removing the driver for the existing audio will disable onboard sound. Some products require a switch to be thrown on the motherboard itself or an option to be changed in CMOS Setup. After taking the steps necessary to disable the audio, follow these steps:

1.   From Device Manager, click the plus sign (+) to expand the category listing under Sound, Video, And Game Controllers. Select the sound adapter driver you want to remove, and click Remove (in earlier versions of Windows) or right-click and select Uninstall (in Windows 2000, Windows XP, and Windows Server 2003). (See Figure 10-1.)

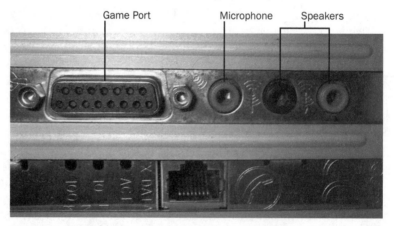

Figure 10-1   Locating sound adapter in the Sound, Video And Game Controllers in Device Manager

2.   Following the steps you learned in Chapter 2, "The Operating System's Role in Hardware," shut down the PC, disconnect it from power, remove the case cover, and ground yourself.

3. Locate the sound adapter installed in the system, and then, at the back of the PC, note the connections currently attached to the sound adapter and remove them one at a time.

4. Identify and remove the screw or retainer holding the existing sound adapter into the frame. Set this screw or retainer aside to use later. There might be a thin cable connecting the sound adapter to the CD or DVD drive. Disconnect this. If the connector is dusty, use a brush or compressed air to remove the dust.

5. Gently but firmly pull the sound adapter from the PC, and set it aside. (Placing it into an antistatic bag is best. Be sure to label the bag to indicate whether the adapter currently works or not.)

With the existing sound adapter successfully removed, you can continue the process of installing the new adapter.

Installing the New Adapter

Review the new adapter documentation, have the driver update or driver disk ready to insert into the appropriate drive, and remove the new adapter from its case or antistatic bag.

Follow these steps:

1. Identify the slot where you will install the new sound adapter, position the new adapter, and push it into place.

2. When the adapter is firmly seated into its slot, secure the adapter in place using the screw or retainer you removed from the existing adapter.

3. Reconnect the thin cable (if present) from the CD or DVD drive to the sound adapter.

4. On the back (or front) of the PC, reconnect the accessories (such as speakers, microphone, and such) into their appropriate jacks.

5. Leaving the case off until you are sure the new adapter is recognized and properly installed, replace the case cover, reconnect power to the PC, and turn it on.

Windows should see the new adapter immediately and begin its installation process. You might be prompted to supply the location of the driver or driver update. (Be sure to have the disk in the appropriate drive, if necessary.) Once the installation process is completed, test the sound adapter by playing prerecorded sounds and also by recording something. If you have a microphone attached, you can record a sampling by using Sound Recorder (under Programs/Accessories/Multimedia). Adjust the volume and other levels as needed through the Sound icon in your Windows task bar (located in the bottom right corner of the desktop screen or under Sounds in Control Panel, as shown in Figure 10-2).

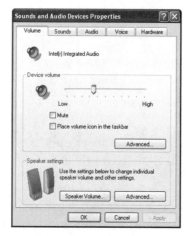

Figure 10-2   Adjusting settings for speaker volume and balance, playback methods, and more under Sounds in Control Panel

Replace the cover as soon as possible after you have completed the installation.

Maintenance and Repair

The maintenance you can perform regarding your sound adapter is relatively light. You should undertake the following tasks on a regular basis (once every month or two) and whenever you are called upon to troubleshoot a system with audio issues:

■   Check for a sound adapter driver update, and apply it as needed.

■   Inspect all connections. Be sure they are firmly seated in the proper jack or connector. Be sure that any peripherals, such as speakers, that have a power indicator are turned on and operational.

■ Remove dust from exterior connections and, when performing interior cleaning, use compressed air to clean dust deposits from the adapter itself.

The sound adapter itself does not lend itself to repair. Instead, a defective or damaged adapter needs to be replaced.

Troubleshooting

If you experience difficulty getting a new sound adapter recognized and working, be sure that you have removed the driver for the previous adapter or disabled existing integrated audio. Then check the new sound adapter's entry in Device Manager to be sure no hardware conflicts are reported.

If no listing is present in Device Manager for the new sound adapter, it's not installed—at least as far as Windows is concerned. Determine that the physical installation is firmly seated, obtain a driver update if you haven't already, and consult the documentation for the adapter. Also check again that this sound adapter is rated to work with your version of Windows, as noted in the Hardware Compatibility List (HCL).

Always suspect a loose physical connection when troubleshooting problems related to lack of sound input or output. These loose or missing connections might be on the exterior panel at the back of the PC (or front of a USB-connected console) or within the PC itself (such as the wire that connects to the CD or DVD drive for sound).

A corrupted or wrong driver can make it difficult or impossible to make changes to sound adapter volume and other settings. Replace or update the driver.

Lab 10: Installing a New Sound Adapter

This lab is intended to prepare you to plan, prepare for, and complete a successful sound adapter replacement. Beyond the physical operation, you'll also research any issues concerning the replacement sound adapter and the update for the most recent driver for that model. Knowing and performing these steps will help you perform subsequent audio replacements as well as to better understand the component you're working with.

Objectives

When you complete this lab, you will be able to address the following issues:

1. The proper removal of the current sound adapter display driver (which might serve to disable integrated sound)

2. The successful replacement of the existing audio capability, and the installation of a new one

3. The appropriate research and proper updating of a sound adapter driver, and any troubleshooting needed

Necessary Equipment and Resources

The following equipment and resources are necessary for completing this lab:

1. An Internet-ready connection—preferably a high-speed connection, and one that is available on a PC other than the one being worked on

2. A PC of recent vintage with either integrated audio or an installed sound adapter

3. A replacement sound adapter

4. Your PC toolkit

5. Between 20 and 40 minutes to complete this lab

Procedures to Follow

1. Identify the current audio device in use and what connection method it uses. Record this in your lab notes.

2. Identify the current sound adapter replacement you will install and what connection method it uses. Also record this information in your lab notes.

3. Using your Internet connection, visit the manufacturer's Web site and locate in its support section the following items (documenting each in your notes):

    a. Troubleshooting and installation tips for the adapter in question.

      b.   A driver update, its instructions, and any special notes. Download the update, and transfer it to the network or to disk in whatever way you can to make it available to the system whose audio you are replacing.

4.   Using the procedure outlined in the "Installation" section of this chapter, remove the driver for your existing audio device (or follow the procedures for proper disabling of onboard audio). Then follow the steps through to physical installation of the new adapter and restarting the PC to begin the hardware detection process. Document your experience and observations in your lab notes.

Lab Notes

1.   Identify the current audio device you are replacing or disabling. (Specify whether you're using an integrated or stand-alone adapter and how it connects.)

_____

_____

_____

2.   Identify the replacement sound adapter and its connection.

_____

_____

_____

3.   Is anything connected to the back of the existing sound adapter device? If so, please note the connected items here.

_____

_____

_____

4.   What is the manufacturer's URL for support?

_____

_____

_____

5.   Document the troubleshooting and installation recommendations, the driver specifics, and instructions you located.

_____

_____

_____

6.   Record your experience and observations in the actual replacement of the sound adapter and driver update.

_____

_____

_____

11

Modems: Analog and Broadband

Communication is an integral part of the work performed by any human with a computer. Modulator-demodulators, better known as *modems*, often play a significant role in how that communication takes place.

These communications are often differentiated—along with much else in the scientific and technical world—as analog and digital. *Analog* refers to a device in which data is represented in quantifiable measures in a continuous signal. Many rural U.S. telephone systems, as well as systems in other parts of the world, continue to rely on analog lines. The term *digital* is pretty much synonymous with computers—that is, a world where everything is transformed into the zeros (0s) and ones (1s) that a computer can understand and act upon.

In this chapter, you'll learn about modems, both the main types and the many communication services tied to them. You'll see what hardware is needed for each type of modem-based communication setup and go through the process of installing modems and troubleshooting problems associated with them.

Major Types of Modems and How They Work

Not all modems are created equal or are intended to perform the same job. First, there is a division between analog and broadband modems, as you'll read about in a moment. Essentially, you can't use a broadband modem for traditional dialup analog communications, and you can't use an analog modem to connect via satellite, cable, or high-speed phone lines as you can with broadband.

Next, these modems come in different physical styles: internal (which is any modem installed within the case) and external (which is any modem that resides as a stand-alone peripheral outside the case). An internal modem can connect through the Industry Standard Architecture (ISA) bus (which is older but still occasionally seen) or Peripheral Component Interface (PCI) bus, or it can be integrated directly into the motherboard. (This last type is not usually seen with broadband modems.) An external modem can connect via RS-232 cable to the serial port on the modem and the PC and/or via universal serial bus (USB) cable to the USB port on a PC. With some broadband services, a broadband network adapter can take the place of a broadband modem, per se, but this can differ wildly between broadband service companies. There are also PC Card modems, which fit into a PC Card (formerly PCMCIA) slot in a laptop.

Now let's look at the division of labor and various modem types in the analog and broadband categories, and learn what each of these terms mean.

Analog Modems

The job of an analog modem is to act as a smart interpreter and converter. Digital data on your PC exists separately from your analog phone line. The PC has its 0s and 1s, while the phone line uses a mechanical or electronic signal. The modem sits between them and converts data into a signal that it can then push out over your regular phone line. When a returning signal comes from another computer back to yours, it gets converted into a digital format your PC can understand.

The biggest limitation with analog modems operating over traditional phone lines is speed, which is capped at 56 Kbps. However, many users will connect at 50 Kbps or less because of a variety of factors, including the limitations of the modem and the protocols it supports, the condition of the phone lines and the distance from a phone substation, phone wiring within the home and office, and others.

Analog modems have three functional pieces:

- Direct-Access Arrangement (DAA)
- Microcontroller
- Data pump

The DAA is nothing more than the telephone line interface that connects the modem to a phone line. The DAA is responsible for converting digital data to analog and vice versa.

The microcontroller sends instructions to the data pump and acts on the information coming from the data pump. The data pump is the workhorse of the modem. Its primary responsibility is to handle the modulation and demodulation of the data stream as it arrives or departs over the phone line. This task is very processor intensive and is usually performed by a dedicated digital signal processor (DSP) chip on the modem.

> **Fact**   You might come across the acronym *UART*, which stands for universal asynchronous receiver-transmitter. The UART is a component specifically designed to handle asynchronous communication. Your motherboard has one to handle the serial (COM) ports; internal modems all have them, too. The power of UARTs is measured by their chipset. The minimum chipset you'll see in current UARTs is 16550, while the current maximum is 16950.

Analog Modem Types

Modems have other important distinctions beyond the categories of internal, external, and integrated. These distinctions are based on how much work the modem and its hardware does or how much of the burden the modem places on the computer's CPU. These types—typically referred to as modem form factors—are classified in the following sections.

Controller   Controller-based modems, also known as *hardware modems*, are prized by most users because they are the most efficient analog modems available. Because all the functional pieces are on the modem itself, the modem is capable of doing all the extensive number crunching required without putting any burden on the host computer. Having that hardware in place makes controller-based modems a more flexible fit even on older, slower computers. Other types of modems, which hand some of the work back to the system, require your system (and especially the processor) to be fast and powerful enough to handle the extra tasks without taking time away from other vital work.

Winmodem   Controllerless modems, sometimes referred to as *Winmodems* (popularized and trademarked by U.S. Robotics, one of the top names in modem manufacturing), are a popular alternative to controller-based modems because the microcontroller function is actually handled by the host computer. The corresponding parts are removed from the modem, making the modem cheaper to manufacture.

Softmodem   Softmodems take the design of Winmodems one step further. In a softmodem, the microcontroller and data-pump functions are performed by the host processor. In other words, your Pentium IV or Athlon XP chip handles a lot of the number crunching instead of the modem card. Softmodems are popular with system manufacturers because they're inexpensive (given that there's no microcontroller and data pump built in) and the computer processors are finally fast enough to handle the number crunching required by the modem. With computer systems currently shipping with a 1 GHz processor or better, they have plenty of power to run numerous applications and to handle modem functions. However, 486 and early Pentium PCs might be too slow to handle this type of modem well.

Integrated/onboard   As with the video and sound devices discussed in earlier chapters, many modems now exist not as a separate adapter but as a chipset integrated into the motherboard. When this type of modem fails, unfortunately, you must replace the motherboard, although some will work if you install a separate PCI or USB modem to replace the dead chipset.

Fact   A half-duplex modem is one that transmits data in only one direction at any given time because it generates a single tone that is used for everything. These modems were seen in the past but are rarely used today. Full-duplex modems, using two independent tones, can send and receive simultaneously.

> **Note**   *Hayes-compatibility* is a term dating back to the 1980s when Hayes, one of the biggest modem manufacturers at the time, effectively wrote the standards for a set of commands, called the AT Command Set, that told the modem what to do.

Broadband Modems and Services

Many computer communications use *baseband* technology, meaning one channel or wire carries one signal. You see this with standard networks, where a cable is used to carry messages between two PCs. You also see this with an analog modem, which simply acts as an interpreter between your PC and your voice phone line. Shortly, I'll talk about the difference between broadband and baseband, but let's first look at a broadband modem from a hardware-only perspective.

Because there are different types of broadband service, there are varying types of broadband modems. Many, however, share certain common characteristics with each other as well as some of the physical properties of an analog modem. (For example, broadband modems can be internally or externally connected.) Let's analyze the cable modem as an example.

Besides the modulator/demodulator found in all modems (and hence, the name mo-dem), a cable modem has a tuner through which the CATV cable supplying the service is connected. That tuner might also come with a splitter, to separate the Internet-based signal from the cable TV signal, as well as something called a diplexer to separate frequencies used for upstream (to the cable provider) and downstream (to the cable modem) signals.

Also in this broadband modem is a Media Access Control (MAC), also seen in any type of network device. This resides between the modulator and demodulator, and it acts as a reference desk and translator for the hardware and software protocols needed between connections.

A microprocessor is typically found on broadband modems as well to help carry the workload of the modem. Usually, it mostly takes extra work directly from the MAC. How robust a modem's microprocessor is often depends on whether the unit is designed specifically to be used with a PC or is meant as a freestanding access device (for example, a cable connection to a living room TV that provides Internet access). Finally, there is usually an Ethernet connector on such modems to allow one to connect a network cable for other computers to share a broadband connection. A DSL or satel-lite modem, as you'll read more about when we discuss broadband services, is often very similar in design to what I've just described for the cable modem.

Now let's look at the service differences. Broadband differs from base-band in a strategic way: a single wire can carry many channels, including channels of different types. This is the case with cable television as well as with Digital Subscriber Line (DSL) technology that can carry voice and data through upgraded, fiber-optic phone lines. By having this multichannel approach, the transmission speed can well exceed that of traditional phone lines and connect far more people.

A key working difference between analog and broadband is that the former is an "on demand" service, meaning that when you choose to con-nect, you dial in using a connection established in Microsoft Windows Dial-Up Networking (DUN). With broadband, the service is always avail-able and always ready for use.

There are six primary service categories within broadband modem service. These include:

- Cable

- Digital Subscriber Line (DSL)

- Satellite

- Telephone carrier lines

- Integrated Services Digital Network (ISDN)

- Wireless

Next, let's examine each of these and the equipment needed to connect them. Note, however, that unlike analog modems, where you purchase the modem and install it yourself, some broadband services require you to "rent" the hardware through the service and a few demand that they install the hardware needed and provide any servicing required.

Exam Tip   It's not unusual for a PC to have both an analog and broadband modem installed. The former is often installed and included as a fallback in case broadband service is temporarily unavailable.

Cable

Cable broadband is an interesting blend. Just as other forms of broadband blossom out of a typical telephone wire, cable Internet access can bloom from the same coaxial cable entering your home or office to provide cable TV. Cable broadband is probably also one of the more consumer-oriented categories. The idea with a cable Internet service is that it should be no more difficult to install and operate than cable TV service. Unlike other forms of broadband such as T-carrier lines and full spectrum ISDN, it was very much developed with the residential user in mind: the typical cable TV customer. Of course, cable access—along with other means of broadband access—is also being included more and more in hotel rooms, particularly those servicing business customers.

Cable access is usually available only in relatively populated areas where cable TV has been available for some time. So if you're in an area not currently served by cable TV services, you probably won't see cable modem as an access option for at least a few years, if ever. And some regions will never be wired for cable, or not before cable is replaced with some other type of distributing television signal.

If you look at just theoretical maximum throughput, cable modems appear to do pretty well for the price. Most estimate the maximum speed at about 30 Mbps, making it attractive to a person struggling to download a file at 1.5 to 3 Kbps on her dialup phone line.

In truth, just as with DSL (which we'll discuss shortly), most services don't make it possible for you to go full tilt. They put caps on the top speed the system can handle to keep data and connection integrity high for all customers. These speed caps do accomplish that. The reduction in your speed and capacity helps your provider offer the service to more people.

This leads to a related issue. Physical limitations put a real cap on how many users can be served on a cable access rollout without the whole system undergoing a real degradation of speed and performance. Many systems are straining past capacity, so their users' connections are edging downward from previous average highs. So even if the cable provider doesn't place its own caps on speed, actual circumstances might keep upstream maximum rates no higher than about 128 Kbps and downstream rates at or less than 512 Kbps. That's fast enough for most regular users but disappointing compared to the hype often associated with cable broadband (and DSL, and others as well).

Equipment Needed for Cable Internet Access   A typical cable modem has an Ethernet port located on one side that is then either connected directly to the PC or to the network. It also has a connection from the cable feed coming into its other side. The equipment you typically need for cable internet access is as follows:

- Cable modem.

- Network card (sometimes can be used in place of a cable modem); a USB port for access can also be used.

- Cable Internet account with a provider that has service in your area.

DSL

Digital Subscriber Line (DSL) access is really a hodgepodge of standards and extensions of older higher speed standards rolled into one terminology often called xDSL.

Types of DSL service include:

- **Asymmetric DSL (ADSL)**   A form of DSL that supports upstream data rates of up to 640 Kbps and downstream rates of up to 1.9 Mbps.

- **High-bit-rate DSL (HDSL)**   The oldest form of DSL and the original form of DSL available in Europe.

- **Rate-adaptive asymmetric DSL (RADSL)**   A rate-adjustable form of DSL where the provider can modify (usually throttle back) the maximum throughput in situations that demand it.

- **Symmetrical DSL (SDSL)**   A DSL type that supports the same data rates for upstream and downstream traffic and increases the distance a customer can be from a major DSL access point.

- **Very-high-speed DSL (VDSL)**   A form of DSL used over short distances but which has very high capacity. It can deliver up to five times the speed of traditional cable and DSL modems, depending on the specific conditions.

Fact   xDSL refers to the collection of all types of DSL service available.

The following equipment is needed for DSL connections:

- An upgraded DSL-capable phone line
- A DSL modem or transceiver
  and/or
- A network adapter
- Line filters (needed to ensure a clean separation between the voice and data frequencies shared on the phone line)

Let's take a moment to look at the two primary pieces of hardware, beyond a DSL-capable phone line, needed to establish a DSL connection between your DSL provider and your home and office.

DSL Access Multiplexer (DSLAM)   Even though it might be the most critical hardware component of a DSL connection, the DSLAM is one you won't see on your local DSL installation. This is because it resides at the provider's end. As its name suggests, the DSL Access Multiplexer has the job of taking the many connections coming from the provider's DSL users and combining (multiplexing) them onto the provider's single, much higher-capacity connection to the Internet (often a T-3 or multiple T-3 carrier lines). This setup—one in which a dedicated line exists between the provider's DSLAM and a DSL installation in the user's home or office—is what gives DSL access a major advantage over cable access, which operates on shared network loops rather than a dedicated line. It also makes DSL a bit more secure by default than cable modems.

The benefit of having a dedicated line is seen most clearly in the tendency of cable access to degrade as the number of subscribers increases. DSL performance, on the other hand, is unlikely to feel the impact of an increase in subscribers. Put simply, more cable customers put more PCs on one line, while DSL keeps each customer on a dedicated line. DSL has maximums, too, but there's a much higher ceiling and it's harder to reach given DSL's maximum distance limitations. Finally, this form also tends to allow static addressing, whereas many if not most cable Internet providers do not.

DSL Modem   A DSL modem isn't necessarily a modem in the traditional sense of the term. Instead, it's usually a combination receiver and transmitter rolled into one device, known as a transceiver. Like a cable modem, this unit typically connects to your PC through an Ethernet adapter or the USB port on one side, and to the DSL-capable phone line on the other side.

Satellite

Satellite is another type of broadband access available, but it's typically used by consumers and businesses in very remote locations that are not traditionally well served by other forms that require proximity to the service area. For example, my office is at the top of a rather out-of-the-way little mountain in north central Vermont where analog phone connections can be hard enough to get. Because of my geographical situation, I've been a satellite broadband user for more than three years.

Speed and consistency can be tougher to achieve with satellite connections for a number of reasons, including weather conditions (such as snow, fog, and heavy cloud cover) that can reduce signal strength between the satellites and the receiver installed to a PC. While connections tend to exceed that of dialup analog modem connections (often at least 10 times as fast), satellite access often falls short of the highest speed cable and DSL. In my experience, I can hit 700 Kbps in a good session and 30 Kbps in a bad one. There are times, because of weather conditions, when service might disappear altogether. However, my colleague, Jane Holcombe, one of the reviewers of this book, states that she gets much better throughput through her setup and it seems more tolerant of the weather, so variations do occur.

Equipment Needed for Satellite Access   The following components are typically needed for satellite access:

- Compatible satellite dish and transceiver
- Network adapter, satellite modem, or both (often USB-connected)
- Subscription to satellite Internet service (usually includes ISP)

Telephone Carrier (T-Carrier) Lines

Telephone carrier lines, known as T-carrier lines, are dedicated and usually specially leased phone connections over which high-speed data transmissions can occur and that provide a high-integrity signal. Be aware that these are professional-grade lines and are often expensive to operate and sometimes very expensive to have installed. The following are some examples of T-carrier lines:

- **T-1 carrier**   Also known as DS1 line, this is a dedicated phone connection with optimization to allow 24 different channels, each capable of a maximum throughput of 64 Kbps. This speed is slightly better than Primary ISDN (discussed later in this chapter). T-1 carrier speed tops out just above 1.5 Mbps.

- **Fractional T-1 carrier**   This is a special subset of T-1 that uses only some fraction of the 24 channels available to a T-1. Providers sometimes make this option available to smaller companies or businesses that need a quality, dedicated connection but can't afford the cost of a full T-1 line.

- **T-3 carrier**   Also known as a DS3 line, this is a dedicated phone connection with optimization to allow 672 separate channels, each capable of a maximum throughput of 64 Kbps. Its speed tops out at just over 42 Mbps.

> **Fact**   Different providers use different methods for separating service for Fractional T-1 line subscribers. They can also charge very different rates. One common formula they use is to lease a specific number of the 24 channels, with those channels running at a maximum capacity of 56 Kbps each. (Data-management needs require the other 8 Kbps.)

Equipment Needed for T- Carrier Lines   The following equipment is typically needed for communications through T-carrier lines:

- Leased T-carrier line installed by the provider.
- Router with the appropriate built-in T-Link (T-1 or T-3).

■   Channel Service Unit/Data Service Unit (CSU/DSU). The CSU both protects and diagnoses problems on the T-line as the DSU connects a terminal such as a PC to the high-speed digital line, which is required for both ends of the T-1 or T-3 connection.

> **Note**   The CSU and DSU are two different pieces of hardware typically incorporated into the same device. Does that sound a little like a modulator-demodulator (modem)? It should. It is often likened to a sophisticated, powerful, and very expensive modem.

ISDN

Integrated Services Digital Network (ISDN) by itself isn't entirely broadband in nature, as you'll read in a moment. Before broadband communications became widely available in the mid-1990s, ISDN served as an interim platform between the slowness of analog modems and the expense of telephone carrier lines for smaller companies and professionals who needed more speed. It is still in existence and use in many parts of the U.S. and the rest of the world.

There are two major platforms with ISDN:

■   **Standard ISDN**   Voice, video, and data are transmitted over a standard telephone line and can achieve speeds of up to 64 Kbps each, for a total of 128. This speed is attainable because the telephone company usually provides ISDN in two B-channels (defined in the following note), each with a total capacity of 64 Kbps. One channel is used for voice, and the other is used for data. Or both channels can be combined into 128 Kbps for data.

■   **Broadband ISDN**   This type is also referred to as B-ISDN. It's less available than standard ISDN. It allows voice, video, and data to transmit over the same fiber-optic cable, and it can achieve speeds of 1.5 Mbps.

> **Note**   B-channel stands for *bearer channel*, where *bearer* refers to data bearing. It is the main data channel in an ISDN connection.

Other recognized types of ISDN include:

- **Basic Rate Interface (BRI) ISDN**   Also known as ISDN-2. In addition to the regular two B-channels of standard ISDN, BRI ISDN also has a 16-Kbps D channel for transmitting control data.

- **Primary ISDN**   Also known as ISDN-30. Primary ISDN provides up to 23 B-channels in the U.S. and up to 30 B-channels in Europe.

Equipment Needed for ISDN Access   The following equipment is typically needed for IDSN access:

- ISDN adapter (shown in Figure 11-1). (Note that an ISDN adapter might or might not include a Network Terminator, called an NT1, used to terminate an ISDN line; however, one is needed.)

- ISDN-capable phone line.

Figure 11-1   A U.S. Robotics ISDN terminal adapter with built-in NT1 interface

Wireless Broadband

This is a burgeoning category of broadband in which high-speed access can cover—via a network of wireless broadband transmitters, receivers, and other hardware—the Internet and network communication needs of an entire building, complex, city, or geographical region. It allows users of handheld computers, using a wireless broadband network adapter, to communicate with the network without attaching phone lines or network cables. This is also referred to as *Wi-Fi*, or wireless fidelity.

Wireless broadband also extends to office and home setups, where one computer is tied directly to broadband Internet service (such as cable, DSL, or satellite) and other computers (including laptops and handheld devices) can connect to the network to share that access via wireless network adapters and a wireless access point (WAP). You'll learn more about networks and wireless computing in Chapter 12, "Network Cards and Network Hardware," and Chapter 18, "Going Wireless."

Shopping

Here are some tips that will help you when buying a modem:

- Shop where there is an adequate return policy. You might end up trying two or three modems before you find the one that works best on a particular system. (For example, you might find that two different modems rated for the same speed actually connect at different speeds, particularly on analog lines.)

- When purchasing hardware to use with broadband, be sure you get the type—or its full equivalent—required by the broadband service company. You can usually call the company or check its Web site to get details.

- Although you can still find ISA-connected modems for sale, it's better to purchase a PCI modem for performance reasons as well as compatibility with motherboards produced after January 2000.

- External modems, even though they're usually priced higher, can be easier to troubleshoot because they have indicator lights to alert you that the unit is powered up and can tell you whether the modem sees a signal or dial tone. External modems also reduce the risk of hardware address assignment conflicts.

- Consult the Windows Hardware Compatibility List to be sure the modem is supported in the version of Windows being used.

- Whenever possible, you should have a backup modem (an analog modem with an available phone line to supplement broadband, for example) when daily Internet access is needed. (As a satellite user, I always have a backup dialup modem installed, for example.)

Installation

Modems for different types of communications vary significantly in how they are installed and in what additional components are needed. In this section, you'll learn about the installation of an internally connected PCI-based analog modem, one of the most common types available. You'll be presented with steps for removing an existing modem as well as steps for installing a new one.

The installation of external modems—such as those that connect by RS-232 cable to the serial port and USB-connected modems that connect to the USB port of the PC—don't require as much detail. They can be easily installed by following the directions included with the modem. With external modems, you attach the appropriate cable (which might or might not be included with the modem) to both the modem and the serial or USB port, depending on type. You then plug in the modem's separate power adapter to a power source and let Windows detect it. The PC must be turned off when you install serial port modems, while USB modems can and should be installed with the PC up and running.

If you're establishing a DSL, cable, satellite, or T-3 connection, you'll need to do a little more than install a modem. For complete details on what steps are needed, you should refer to the explicit directions provided by your broadband service company. After reading the information provided, be sure you have everything you need to perform that installation. (The equipment you'll usually need is listed earlier under the discussions of each type of service.)

> **More Info**   Instructions for installing a network adapter can be found in Chapter 12.

To install an internal modem, begin by removing the new modem from its case or antistatic bag. Be sure there's no damage to it, and look for a label identifying it as the make and model you purchased. How you proceed next depends on whether or not you're replacing an existing internal modem. If you're installing an internal modem where none previously existed, jump to the "Installing a New Modem" section, but take the usual steps to open the case.

> **Exam Tip**   You might want to check the modem manufacturer's Web site to determine whether a driver update is available for the new modem before you install it. Modems can sit on a shelf for months before they are purchased, and one or more revisions to its driver might take place during that time.

Removing an Existing Modem

This section details instructions for removing an internal modem. If you are replacing an external modem with an internal one, perform steps 1 and 2 as described next, and then remove the cable (RS-232 or USB) from the back of the PC to disconnect the unit. Then continue with the procedure described in the "Installing a New Modem" section.

If the current modem exists as an integrated part of the motherboard, removing the driver (as detailed in step 1) might disable the modem. You should refer to the documentation for the PC and motherboard to determine the exact steps necessary to disable the onboard modem.

1. From Device Manager, click to expand the category Modems, and select the modem whose driver you want to remove. Click Remove, or in Windows 2000, Windows XP, and Windows Server 2003, right-click and select Uninstall.

2. Shut down the PC, disconnect its power, remove the cover, and ground yourself.

3. Locate the existing modem you want to replace, which is usually installed in a PCI slot on recent systems.

4. Once you locate the modem, look at the rear of the PC and disconnect the phone lines (both to the wall and to the telephone) attached to the modem. (See Figure 11-2.)

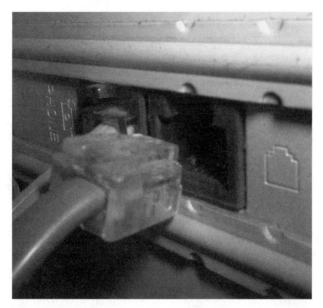

Figure 11-2   The telephone lines attached to the modem

5.   Check to see whether a screw or other retainer mechanism holds the current modem in place. If so, remove it and set it aside.

6.   Gently but firmly—and in a straight, even motion—pull the existing modem from its slot and set it aside. (Placing it in an antistatic bag is best, and be sure to mark whether or not the modem works.)

You are now ready to install the new modem adapter, which you will do in the next section.

Installing a New Modem

Review the documentation that came with your new modem for any special instructions for installation. After doing that, follow these steps:

1.   Remove the new modem from its case or antistatic bag.

2.   Install the adapter to an empty PCI slot so that it is firmly and evenly seated.

3.   Replace the screw or retainer to the slot. (See step 5 under "Removing an Existing Modem.")

4.   Reconnect the phone lines removed in step 4 in the previous instructions. Be sure to insert the correct line in the correct jack.

5.   Replace the cover, reconnect power to the PC, and turn it on.

Windows should automatically detect the newly installed modem. If you have an updated driver, you can choose to apply it at this time. Should the new modem fail to be detected, check your installation as well as recommendations provided in the "Troubleshooting" section that follows.

Troubleshooting Modem Installations

Many grizzled PC veterans will tell you there are few troubleshooting scenarios more frustrating than trying to get a modem to be detected or to work properly. This was true 15 years ago when modems were still relatively new, and it's still true today.

You should always check for the most obvious culprits first: a loose or missing connection, no dial tone, no power to the external unit, and improper installation. Where you suspect a dead modem of any type, try a second modem if you have one available. If that one works properly, the problem is indeed the first modem.

Because the problems with these modems can differ greatly between analog and broadband, let's take each separately.

Analog Modem Troubleshooting

There are always standard conditions to check when you're having a problem using a modem. Let's run through them for both newly installed and existing modems.

For newly installed modems, try the following actions:

■   Check the physical modem installation to be certain there is a firm connection.

■   If the modem is internally installed, remove and reseat it. If necessary, try it in another available slot.

■   If the modem is external, try a different cable if possible.

■   If the modem is external, be sure its power supply is plugged into a working, viable power source. If the modem has an on/off switch, be sure it is turned on. If the modem is turned on and the power is indeed available, the modem might be defective because it should at least respond with lights if it's working.

- Be sure the phone line is plugged into the Line In or Telephone In jack.

- Verify that the phone line works by using a standard telephone and listening for a dial tone while using the same line and plug you have plugged into the modem. (Remove it from the modem, insert it into the phone, and once the dial tone is verified, return it to the modem.)

- Obtain the latest driver for the specific make and model of your modem, and apply it.

- If using Windows, check under the Modem icon in Control Panel to be sure that the exact modem you just installed is listed. (Don't guess at the manufacturer make and model because different modems depend on different drivers to support their features.)

- Remove all listed modems in Device Manager, and then shut down and restart the system to see whether the proper modem is detected.

- Check for a hardware conflict.

- If possible, try the problematic modem in a different machine. If it works there, determine what is different between your machine and the machine where it does work.

For existing modems, try the following possible remedies:

- Try all the issues listed for newly installed modems.

- Shut down the PC, restart, and try again.

- Create a new connection (a DUN connection in Windows), and try dialing with that. Also be sure that DUN specifically lists the modem you're trying to use.

- Determine whether anything else is open on the desktop or in use that might be using the port.

- If necessary, remove the port in your operating system. (For Windows, go to Device Manager, locate the COM and LPT ports section, and remove the COM ports.) Windows should automatically reinstall when you restart the system.

■ Use the HyperTerminal program to check if you can dial out using
   the modem to a known modem-accessible number. To access
   HyperTerminal in Windows 98, click Start, Programs, and then
   Accessories. In Windows XP, click Start, All Programs, Accessories,
   and then Communications. If this test works, you might need to
   reinstall Dial-Up Networking (which is available under the Networks
   icon, in Control Panel for Windows 98 or the Network Connections
   icon for Windows XP).

Use Windows Diagnostics

Double-click the Modems or Phones And Modems icon in Control Panel.
Select the Properties option and you'll see the same tabs you would find if
you right-clicked or chose Properties under the Modem listing in Control
Panel. There, you'll see that you have a modem troubleshooter available from
both the General tab (which steps you through a modem troubleshooting wizard) as well as the Diagnostics tab. (See Figure 11-3.)

Figure 11-3   The Diagnostics tab, which allows you to check the
modem's responsiveness to commands

Click Query Modem to run a troubleshooting routine that checks the
modem's responsiveness. You can also click View Log to see the log for that
modem session. (See the "Check Logs" section next.)

You should also check the Resource tab to be certain that no resource
conflicts are reported between this and another installed device.

Check Logs

Many operating systems—and even programs that come with a modem you purchase—are or can be set to log your modem's operation, which can be beneficial in troubleshooting a problem. In Windows, this is called *modemlog.txt* (or modem*name*.txt in Windows 98), and it is created or appended each time you use Dial-Up Networking or whenever communications occur with a 32-bit communications program under Windows. Use the Find option from Windows Start to locate it. (It normally resides in the Windows folder.) It can be opened using any text editor, including Microsoft NotePad.

Broadband Modem Troubleshooting

When troubleshooting problems with a broadband modem, first double-check the installation if the modem is new. Be sure you followed all instructions for physical installation and configured the modem using the settings provided to you by the service provider.

If the broadband modem included diagnostic utilities to allow you to both check the modem setup as well as the availability of the service itself, run the diagnostics to see what is reported. If necessary, contact the company providing the service or, using a second Internet-accessible PC, visit the service's Web site to check FAQs and other information that might be helpful in troubleshooting your difficulty.

With existing modems, some service problems will require you to reset or power off the modem occasionally. For example, if you experience a temporary halt in cable or satellite service during an online session, the accessory software might stop responding even when the service is restored. This might lead to a full system lockup. (See your instructions for details.) Sometimes, you must fully shut down and restart the entire PC as well. If this doesn't help, check any diagnostic utility as mentioned before. Also, be sure the modem, if external, is firmly attached to both power and to the service cable or connection.

Try to determine what might have changed since the last session in which the modem operated properly. Certain utilities and upgrades have been known to interfere with broadband settings and protocols. For example, you should always upgrade your operating system with care, particularly when the operating system you're upgrading to uses different protocols or updates to protocols necessary for your broadband service. (You'll learn more about protocols in Chapter 12.) If possible, reverse any changes made since that session to see whether this restores you to proper broadband service.

FEATURE: Test Your Speed

The speed reported by a modem of any type upon connection is not always a good indication of true performance. However, a number of online sites make it easy for you to check your current connection speed and to see how it compares to other types of connection methods (from dialup to fastest broadband). A good place to check this information is at The Bandwidth Place at *http://bandwidthplace.com/speedtest.*

Don't assume, however, that your bandwidth itself provides roughly the same speed, especially in times of high traffic or when you're busy downloading several files. As with blood pressure, you might want to check it on occasion to see how it changes and determine what else might be going on at the time to influence the differences in results from test to test.

Lab 11: Install a Modem and Configure It for Use

This lab is intended to prepare you to install a modem and configure it for use, as well as to perform any necessary troubleshooting after installation. For the main example, you will work with an internally connected PCI modem for analog dialup connections, but you can also obtain the necessary information and hardware to perform this exercise for a broadband modem as well.

Objectives

When you complete this lab, you will be able to address the following issues:

1. The overall power demands of a system

2. Obtaining a suitable power supply replacement

3. The successful removal of an existing power supply, and the installation of a new one

Necessary Equipment and Resources

The following equipment and resources are necessary for completing this lab:

1. A PC of recent vintage

2. An Internet-ready second PC for reference

3. A PCI modem adapter to replace the existing modem

4.   A phone line with a modular plug that is within reach of the PC

5.   Your PC toolkit

6.   Between 30 and 60 minutes to complete this lab

Procedures to Follow

1.   Unpack the replacement modem, and review its instructions and other documentation. Record information about the modem and any special instructions for installation in your lab notes.

2.   Determine whether there is a modem in place on the lab PC that needs replacement. If so, follow the steps listed under "Removing an Existing Modem" in the "Installation" section of this chapter to remove it. Record your notes on the exercise in your lab notes.

3.   If there is no existing modem or once you have completed step 2, perform the steps outlined under "Installing a New Modem" in the "Installation" section. Document your experience in your lab notes.

4.   Reconnect power, and turn the PC back on. If the modem is detected, establish a dialup connection using Dial-Up Networking in earlier versions of Windows or Create A New Connection under Network Connections in Windows XP and Windows Server 2003. Test your connection. Add any special findings or problems to your lab notes.

5.   If troubleshooting is required, specify in your lab notes the exact nature of the problem, its symptoms, and what steps you took to try to resolve it.

Lab Notes

1.   Record the modem manufacturer model and relevant information, plus any special installation notes.

   _____

   _____

   _____

2.   Was there a modem present in the PC? Record any special infor-
      mation about its removal.

      _____

      _____

      _____

3.   Identify any special issues with installing the new modem.

      _____

      _____

      _____

4.   Was your test connection successful on the first try? If not, please
      provide details.

      _____

      _____

      _____

5.   Document any steps and measures taken in troubleshooting the
      connection and modem installation. Note the ultimate cause of the
      difficulty and the resolution, if achieved.

      _____

      _____

      _____

12

Network Cards and Network Hardware

The network of today has its foundation in the technology of the past. In the past, one large mainframe or minicomputer provided the central services and computing power, while terminals connected users throughout a facility to a room-sized and usually tremendously expensive computer system.

As PCs became more the norm, they were often stand-alone units that handled their own storage, printing, and communications. But information typically can't move speedily between each stand-alone system until the systems are connected in a way that enables them to work both in unison and alone. And that's where networks come in.

Because of the breadth of the subject matter—the number of types of networks and configurations, variations in hardware types, differences in network protocols—this chapter isn't intended to be an ultimate resource for understanding and configuring a network. Even among some packaged "quick" network solutions, a *lot* of variation can exist. What the chapter strives to offer you, however, is an overall understanding of networks as they're implemented, basic hardware that allows you to establish a connection between two or more stand-alone PCs or capable devices, and extra hardware that can be used to extend the normal geographical reach of information running along the network.

The Work of Network Hardware

A network can be defined as a means of connecting a group of stand-alone PCs (or other types of systems, including dumb terminals) into a united configuration when communication is needed between multiple systems in the same overall area. Networks are usually thought of as an equation with two unique sides: a user side, known as the *client*, and the network-handling side, known as the *server*. It's the server's job to act as host and manager, allowing (or disallowing) connections from users or clients, and to juggle any requests made by these clients. The server permits data to move back and forth either between different nodes or to storage. The client's role, on the other hand, is to make requests of the services (storage, access, and so on) offered by the server. An exception to this definition is peer-to-peer networking, which follows a different model. With peer-to-peer networks, each PC is its own client and server depending on the network function taking place. There is no central system providing a network server.

PROFILE: The OSI Model as a Foundation

We owe much of what we see in network communications today to a foundation called the International Organization for Standardization (ISO), which developed the Open System Interconnection (or OSI) Reference Model, an international standard for network data communications that implements communications across seven layers.

> **Fact**   Because "International Organization for Standardization" would have different abbreviations in different languages ("IOS" in English, "OIN" in French for *Organisation internationale de normalization*, etc.), it was decided at the outset to use a word derived from the Greek *isos*, meaning "equal." Therefore, whatever the country or language, the abbreviation of the organization's name is always ISO.

These layers are as follows:

- **Application (Layer 7)**   This layer supports application and end-user processes. Everything at this layer is application-specific. This layer provides application services for file transfers, e-mail, and other network software services. Telnet and FTP are some examples of applications that exist entirely in the application level.

- **Presentation (Layer 6)**   The presentation layer works to transform data into the form that the application layer can accept. This layer formats and encrypts data to be sent across a network, providing freedom from compatibility problems.

- **Session (Layer 5)**   This layer establishes, manages, and terminates connections between applications. The session layer sets up, coordinates, and terminates conversations, exchanges, and dialogues between the applications at each end. It deals with session and connection coordination by stopping and starting sessions as needed.

- **Transport (Layer 4)**   This layer provides transparent and complete transfer of data between end systems, or hosts, and is responsible for end-to-end error recovery and flow control.

- **Network (Layer 3)**   This layer is responsible for routing, creating logical paths for data, known as virtual circuits, and for transmitting data from node to node. Routing and forwarding are functions of this layer, as well as addressing, internetworking, error handling, congestion control, and packet sequencing between different networks and network segments.

- **Data Link (MAC) (Layer 2)**   At this layer, data packets are encoded and decoded into bits, the smallest measurable unit of data. The data link layer is divided into two sublayers: the Media Access Control (MAC) layer and the Logical Link Control (LLC) layer. The MAC sublayer controls how a computer on the network gains access to the data and permission to transmit it from node to node on the same network or network segment. The LLC layer controls frame synchronization, flow control, and error checking.

- **Physical (Layer 1)**   This layer conveys the data bit stream through the network at the electrical and mechanical level. It provides the hardware means of sending and receiving data on a carrier, including defining cables, cards, and physical aspects. Bus, ring, star, and tree network topologies (discussed later in this chapter) reside with the physical layer components.

Network Functions Explained

Networks provide the following four major functions, which differentiate them from collections of stand-alone systems:

- File management and use
- Application sharing
- Device sharing
- User or system interaction and connectivity

File Management and Use

One core principle of a network is that it allows some common means of centralizing data storage so that data can be accessed by the various nodes on the network. This common means often comes in the form of a specialized network server known as a *file server*, where files, complete directories, or both are available for relatively easy access. Networks have file servers usually in addition to storage local to each node, typically a hard disk, where private files or files in the process of being worked on can be kept.

With a centralized storage method, however, comes the risk that data held in such a repository can be accessed or used in unintended ways. For example, a user with access to this storage could also have access to a file not meant for him to see. Without some control measures, anyone with access to a node on a network could create new files, as well as view existing ones, add records, modify files, and even delete them. While that seems like a convenient arrangement, in normal business operations you usually want to restrict the access that certain categories of users have to specific files, groups of files, or even whole directories.

Restricting access helps maintain security as well as data integrity. Restrictions are often implemented through the setting of file permissions as well as system policies and help manage who has access to files and the types of access they have. For example, you could allow a file to be opened but not modified or deleted, or you could prevent a file from being opened and viewed at all by those without permission to do so.

File permissions set specific properties of access and use for the file, while system policies (such as those for Microsoft Windows NT, Windows 2000, Windows XP, and Windows Server 2003) help designate exactly how the overall system will work and what services and features are available to individual users. Access itself is managed by granting specific permissions or policies to a unique Security ID (SID) that is tied to a specific user or group account. Put more simply, a user whose ID does not match an ID that has been given either specific access to a file or permission to use the file will be kept from opening or performing other actions on it, such as deleting or altering the file.

Application Sharing

In modern offices and homes, computers can be networked to allow the sharing of an application that can be installed either just to the network itself or just to a node on the network. An application can also be installed on every machine with just the data shared between the systems.

As you can probably tell, such a method can make a lot more sense than having several people or even the same person creating data in different applications and then trying to match its format with an application on another machine. In theory and in practice, application sharing can enhance productivity, reduce the user's learning curve (because coworkers are using the same applications and can provide suggestions and peer support), and save time.

Device Sharing

Device sharing enables different nodes on a network to share devices attached to either the central network or a specific PC or node on that network. In a large office environment, device sharing makes perfect sense because most users probably won't need a dedicated printer, document imaging system, or scanner. They can share them among a group of users who also need those kinds of devices only some of the time during a work day. This saves time, valuable office space, and usually a great deal of money.

And we haven't mentioned potential reciprocal benefits that are usually, but not always, seen. These benefits include fewer service calls for maintenance and repair, fewer individual service contracts, and fewer technicians (because there are fewer pieces of hardware to support). The one caveat here is that in a large office setting, where numerous users might be using the same device, you're likely to buy a more professional-level, costlier device than an ordinary consumer might so that it will stand up under the extra workload.

For home users, device sharing is also useful. Let's say you have two or three PCs or network-capable devices but just one CD burner or one photo or other specialty printer, and you don't want to install multiple burners or printers to let all your PCs use them. The use of even a basic network would allow you to burn CDs or print files—or perform a plethora of other functions, depending on what you have installed—without a lot of extra work and without much expense (or no expense, if you already have the network hardware in place).

Another great example of how a network device can be shared for both personal and professional use is for backups and storage. Buy one adequate backup device, and let individual systems on the network back up to it.

Office Interaction and Connectivity

Can you even conceive of how much time gets wasted when you need to get up from your work area and go to a different work area to exchange information or files? Network messaging systems or even add-on messaging applications, such as ICQ (*www.icq.com*), MSN Messenger, and AOL Instant Messaging (AIM), permit users throughout the network and even the Internet to exchange messages instantly (thus the name, instant messaging) along with files and other data. This can sometimes be more useful than picking up the telephone, especially if you're working at the PC while you need to communicate.

Other applications let you and coworkers work on the same files simultaneously, where you can see changes and comments made in real time, without having to physically gather around someone's desk and lean in. Microsoft Office and other groupware packages tend to pack features that allow for greater interaction and collaboration. By using network video conferencing, as another example, people don't even have to leave their desks or at least their general office areas to attend multidepartment meetings.

Major Types of Networks

Networks typically get divided into different categories, based on the following characteristics:

- What their model of operation is (referred to as the *network model*)

- The size and scope of the network (often called the *network type*)

- How the network processes information (referred to as the *network processing strategy*), which can include:

   ❑   Central processing

   ❑   Distributed processing

   ❑   Client/server operation processing

- How the network is laid out (known as the *network topology*)

- What type of operating system the network runs on (for example, so-called Microsoft networking, Linux networking, and so on)

Types of Network Models

Let's return to a point hinted at earlier when you read about servers and clients as well as peer-to-peer networking. The point is that networks follow different organizational models depending on the goals and overall design of the type of network established. The following is a list of common network models:

- **Peer-to-peer network**   Usually consists of two or more PCs connected to share information, applications, and resources. Peer-to-peer networking usually works best when a small number of PCs (up to 10) need to be connected.

- **Server-based network**   Has most storage, administration, and other functions performed on the server end, while the client side provides the user's access to tools, applications, and data. It's very scalable and capable of supporting a large user base. Client/server-based networks require a network operating system (NOS) in addition to the standard operating system (such as Linux, UNIX, Windows, and so on).

- **Combination network** Consists of elements of both peer-to-peer and server-based networks in an environment where there might be both dedicated servers and workstations that can act as either server or client.

Network Types

General divisions of network types are split into just a few major categories, as shown in the following list:

- **Local area network (LAN)** Consists of a group of connected PCs (where the connection medium is usually cable) in a finite area, such as a large room or a building.

- **Metropolitan area network (MAN)** A network larger than a LAN but usually contained within either a single city or metropolitan region.

- **Wide area network (WAN)** A very large network that crosses countries and even continents. You could call the Internet the largest WAN available, as it combines various networks around the world into a kind of single unified platform.

> **Note** There are specialized types of networks, too, which are designed to separate a particular function or need. For example, a storage area network (SAN) can be used to keep data storage within its own dedicated network.

Types of Network Topology

Topology refers to the overall shape or configuration of a network. Several accepted topologies can be employed, including the following ones:

- **Bus topology** A low-cost and easy-to-set-up type used with Ethernet network systems. The network is laid out in a linear configuration with all separate systems connected to a central bus segment or backbone, which is usually in the form of a master cable terminated at each endpoint.

- **Ring topology** A topology used by token ring networks and Fiber Distributed Data Interface (FDDI) systems. This type is considered both more complex to configure and more expensive than bus topology, while offering better bandwidth and greater expansion. Network connectivity occurs within the closed loops of a ring created by linking each device to the two devices on either side of it.

■ **Star topology** A type in which all devices are attached to a central connection point or device—through which all data must flow—by means of dedicated links. Because the central hub is involved in the passing of all data, bottlenecks are a distinct possibility.

■ **Hybrid topology** A combination of any two or more network topologies. Instances can occur where two basic network topologies, when connected together, can still retain the basic network character, and therefore not be a hybrid network. For example, a tree network connected to a tree network is still a tree network. Therefore, a hybrid network accrues only when two basic networks are connected and the resulting network topology fails to meet one of the basic topology definitions. For example, two star networks connected together exhibit hybrid network topologies. A hybrid topology always accrues when two different basic network topologies are connected.

PROFILE: Ethernet Defined

Ethernet represents the most common type of networking standard used by both commercial concerns and consumers, and it's one of the oldest. Table 12-1 shows the recognized Ethernet standards and at what speeds each operates. Figure 12-1 shows a diagram of a simple Ethernet setup.

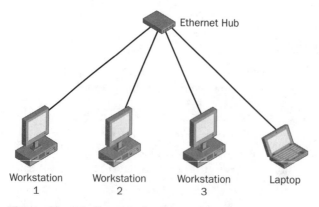

Figure 12- 1A diagram of a simple Ethernet network

Table 12-1   Ethernet Standards and Speed

Ethernet Standard	Maximum Transfer Rate
10Base-T	10 Mbps
100Base-T (also known as Fast Ethernet)	100 Mbps
Gigabit Ethernet	1000 Mbps (1 Gbps)

Basics of an Ethernet Network's Operation

An Ethernet network has at its core the cable (or some other medium) that joins all other components of the network. This medium is called a *segment*, and devices (including PCs) that attach to that segment are referred to as *nodes*.

Nodes communicate by exchanging small but concentrated bundles of data called *frames*. Instead of this bundle being just a collection of information tightly jammed together, a frame actually has a reasonably complex (or at least specific) type of construction, known as *control information*, which is established by the Ethernet protocol that's applied to it. This information determines physical characteristics of the frame, such as the frame length—both minimum and maximum length.

Just as the packets discussed elsewhere in this chapter have certain components, so too do frames. Specifically, they are organized into the following components:

- **Frame source address**   The frame source address refers to the unique ID or hardware address assigned to the system where the frame was generated.

- **Frame destination address**   This refers to the unique ID or hardware address assigned to the system where the frame needs to go.

- **Actual data**   This is the actual content of each frame.

Ethernet Frame Transmission

A chief characteristic of Ethernet operation is that every node attached to the Ethernet cable or other medium receives the same frames generated by the frame's source. Each node checks the source and destination address information and determines whether the frame is meant for it. All nodes except the source and destination address nodes ignore and discard the frame, while the destination node receives the frame and takes action. If all nodes on the network or a segment of the network receive the frame and act upon it (effectively making them all destination addresses), this is known as *broadcasting*.

Evolution of Ethernet

Most setups today use *switched Ethernet*, which has the following characteristics:

- Each node (PC) can connect to its own dedicated segment.

- Each segment connects to a switch, creating a dedicated line between the switch and the node.

- This switch has some of the same characteristics as a bridge (described later in this chapter), with the exception that many segments can be connected to a switch, not just two.

- The switch checks data coming from the nodes attached to it by segments, identifies the destination, and then intelligently directs the data only to the node identified by the destination address.

These characteristics result in reduction of unnecessary traffic on the network. Nodes don't even have to identify packets not meant for them because the switch keeps them from getting packets not addressed for that node.

Switched Ethernet also shows that we have transitioned from a time when only one node on a network segment could transmit at any given instant to a time in which all nodes are welcome to transmit at once. (With more than one node transmitting, there can be contention, described shortly, where the data from each would collide.) All nodes can now transmit at once because nodes are now connected to the switch rather than to each other, and the switch regulates the traffic. While the results still aren't perfect, this dramatically reduces the amount of problems.

Ethernet Control Through Contention

Ethernet is notable for applying contention methods to facilitate information flow throughout the network in an efficient manner. For example, Carrier Sense Multiple Access with Collision Detection (known as CSMA/CD or just *Carrier Sense*) is a contention LAN access method and is used by Ethernet for more effective and faster data transmission. CSMA/CD is a set of rules to try to govern how different network devices respond when they attempt to access a data channel at the same time. Such an event results in what is called a *collision* (where data from two or more devices crash into each other), and collisions need to be avoided as much on data channels as on roadways.

This set of rules first allows the network and devices to detect such a collision, and then the sending devices try to resubmit the message being sent. If the transmission fails the second time because another collision is detected, a short delay is added before another resend is attempted. Each time the collision recurs, additional time (at the rate of two times the previous delay) is added to the delay in an attempt to work around the point of collision. This doubling of each successive delay is known as an *exponential backoff.*

Fact   A contention protocol is one that permits two or more nodes on a network to contend for access simultaneously, and then dictates the network's behavior when this happens. CSMA/CD is the best known and most widely used network contention protocol because it's used by Ethernet.

Note   An individual segment of a cable or Ethernet medium is also called a *collision domain.* This name stems from the fact that no two devices attached to the same segment can transmit frames simultaneously without causing a collision.

Types of Ethernet Arrangements

Before you push forward into the actual hardware components involved in networking, let's examine different types of Ethernet arrangements. There are two types of arrangements:

- **Shared Ethernet**   In this type of network arrangement, all network hosts are connected to the same Ethernet bus and all contend with one another for available bandwidth. This is the typical way Ethernet is used.

- **Switched Ethernet**   Unlike shared Ethernet access, switched Ethernet doesn't allow competition or contention between hosts or devices on the same bus, which usually results in faster and more efficient network communications. It achieves this efficiency by giving hosts and network segments their own dedicated bandwidth and connecting each device to the network through the use of a switch. Such a switch replaces the repeaters used elsewhere. Just as a shared Ethernet would use a hub for connections, switched Ethernet uses a variation of this known as a *switched hub.* (Additional information on switched Ethernets appears in the "Evolution of Ethernet" section earlier in this chapter.)

PROFILE: IEEE Specifications

The Institute of Electrical and Electronics Engineers (IEEE) dates back to two earlier organizations (one founded as early as 1884) that merged in 1963. It is an organization of engineers, scientists, and students of engineering and is best known for offering technical specification standards for various electronics and computer-based technology. These specifications are typically identified as "IEEE specification *<number>*".

To learn more about the IEEE, visit its Web site at *http://www.ieee.org*. In Tables 12-2 and 12-3, you'll see examples of IEEE specifications for various hardware devices and for networking standards, respectively.

Table 12-2   Examples of IEEE Specification by Device

Specification Name	Hardware Covered
IEEE 796	Microcomputer system bus
IEEE 802.xx	LAN and MAN hardware
IEEE 1212.x	Digital memory access (DMA)
IEEE 1284	Parallel port
IEEE 1394	FireWire
IEEE 1394a (amended in 2000)	FireWire
IEEE 1596	High-bandwidth memory interface
IEEE P996	ISA bus
IEEE P1386.1	PCI bus

Table 12-3   Examples of IEEE 802 Networking Standards

Specification Name	Description
IEEE 802.1	Covers issues related to network management.
IEEE 802.2	Divides the Open System Interconnection (OSI) Reference Model data link layer into two distinct sublayers (the Media Access Control, or MAC, sublayer and the Logical Link Control, or LLC, sublayer). It also incorporates LANs and MANs.
IEEE 802.3	Is the foundation of the Ethernet standard.
IEEE 802.4	Supplies the bus network MAC layer for token-bus networks.
IEEE 802.5	Sets the MAC layer for token-ring network topology.
IEEE 802.6	Is the foundation and standard for MANs.
IEEE 802.11	Is the standard for wireless networking.

Major Types of Network Hardware

Networks can be as simple as two PCs linked by cables running between their installed network adapters and sharing the same installed protocols, or they can be as complex as encompassing tens, hundreds, and even thousands of users. You must take into consideration your operating system, specific needs, and physical work area layout when deciding on the type of network and connection you need to establish, and how you want to do that.

In general, however, just a few basic types of hardware are involved in network setup. These include

■   **Network interface cards (NICs)**   These are also referred to as *network adapters*. They're described in more detail later. Newer NICs can be external and installed through both USB and FireWire ports.

■   **Network cables**   Various types of cables are used for connecting network equipment. Frequently, Category 5 (CAT-5) unshielded twisted-pair cable or Enhanced CAT-5 cable is used.

■   **Network devices**   This includes any devices that can be added to the network, including hubs, routers, switches, and more. (See the section entitled "Other Types of Network Devices" later in this chapter.)

Network Interface Cards

NICs are the part of a network that usually installs into an available expansion bus slot in the PC or to an external port such as a USB or FireWire port. (These days, the bus slot is usually PCI, although ISA cards are still available on some systems.) In a laptop or portable system, the network card can be installed in a PC Card/PCMCIA slot (shown in Figure 12-2) or it comes preinstalled by the vendor as a mini-PCI device.

Figure 12-   2A PC Card network adapter for a laptop

You then attach to the NIC a cable that connects the NIC to the rest of the network. Wireless NICs, on the other hand, use an antenna or other external receiver/transmitter to allow for communications without the use of networking cable.

One NIC is needed for each PC connected to the network. However, NICs are often used outside of a traditional office network, such as when two users at two different PCs in the same location need to be connected. When the users want to share an Internet connection between PCs on a network, they need a NIC, a connecting medium such as a cable, and proxy software such as WinProxy or the tools available in Internet Connection Sharing in recent versions of Windows, as illustrated on the next page.

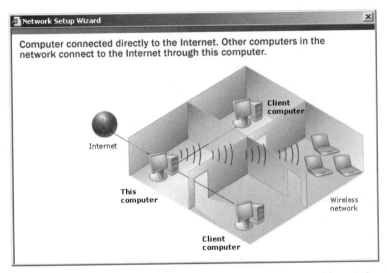

Network cards serve as the physical interface between the PC and the rest of the network. Often, they are manufactured to work with a specific type of network, although many work across different network platforms and protocols. When choosing network cards for your work, be sure to match them to the type of network you're installing as well as to the operating system you are running.

The following is a list of the general categories of network interface adapters that represent everything from simple two-node to five-node networks all the way up to networks with higher-speed, commercial-grade network transmissions:

- **Ethernet**   10 Mbps transmissions typically over coaxial copper wire.

- **Fast Ethernet**   100 Mbps transmissions over copper and fiber optic wire.

- **Gigabit Ethernet**   1000 Mbps (1 gigabit) transmissions over fiber optic wire.

- **Fiber Distributed Data Interface (FDDI)**   100 Mbps transmissions over copper and fiber optic wire, token-passing in nature, and usually used in situations where a large network serves as the backbone for a wide area network (WAN). FDDI-2, the upgrade to FDDI, permits audio and video information as well as data, and FDDT (FDDI Full Duplex Technology) bumps transmissions to 200 Mbps.

- **Fibre Channel**   A serious data transfer type where optical fiber is used in transmitting data. Specifically, it's used for devices requiring very high bandwidth or high-capacity storage devices such as network attached storage (NAS) and clustering servers. It's considered to be the ultimate replacement for SCSI in terms of fast, high-capacity storage solutions. Its best-known type is Fibre Channel–Arbitrated Loop (FC-AL).

NIC by Design   Each network adapter features a unique identity designation referred to as its *hardware address*, which is set by the manufacturer at the time the NIC is made. The hardware address uniquely distinguishes the NIC from any other hardware on a network. This is commonly referred to as the MAC address and is 6 bytes long (for example, 006B29FE43B6). Some NICs are created for use by one specific type of network, medium, and network protocol, while others can be used for several different types. MAC addresses contain specific information—for example, the first three bytes contain the unique manufacturer identification, and the last three bytes contain the unique device serial number.

Most NICs manufactured today have a transceiver—a combination receiver and transmitter—built into them that applies a signal to the network wire (transmission) and then monitors the wire for incoming signals (receiving). On Ethernet-specific networks, this transceiver is known by another name, the Media Adaptor Unit (MAU). This corresponds to the *Media Access Control layer* (also known as the *MAC layer*), which is responsible for moving data packets across the shared channel from one NIC to another and back again.

Network Cables

There is a great deal of variation in the types of cables that can be used in networking. The cable used depends on the type of network and a number of other factors.

Beyond the variation in type of cable, there is also the issue of length. One reason you have network devices such as hubs and repeaters is that the longer the cable extends between nodes or other parts of the network, the more likely the data signal is to degrade or even be lost altogether. This is known as attenuation.

Unshielded twisted pair (UTP) coaxial cable is the most commonly used cable in LANs. Several types, called *categories*, of cable are listed in Table 12-4. Category-5 (CAT-5) is by far the most widely used category because of its capacity. It's shown in Figure 12-3 as the lighter colored cable connected to a router. Fiber optic cable is increasingly being seen in even smaller workstation installations. It allows for higher speeds, but it also costs more.

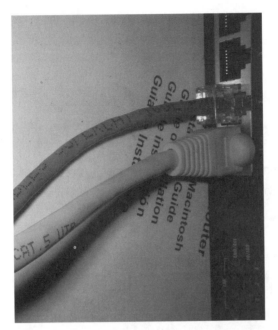

Figure 12-3   A CAT-5 Ethernet cable connected to a router

Cables can be purchased prefabricated. You can make your own by purchasing cable (available in a wide range of lengths) along with the RJ-45 connectors used to terminate cable connections and the crimper used to attach the RJ-45 connectors to the cable.

Table 12-4   UPT Category Types

Category	Properties and Usage
1	For voice communication only; not for data transmission
2	For low-speed data transmission (1 Mbps)
3	For networks with a maximum speed of 16 Mbps
4	For boosting maximum transmission rate to 20 Mbps
5	Used by Fast Ethernet; has a maximum speed of 100 Mbps

Alternatives to Cable   Of course, not all situations allow a physical cable to be used between two PCs or even two different LANs. Some systems use infrared ports for short hops between two PCs. Wireless systems might also use antennas, external transceivers, and wireless access points such as the one seen in Figure 12-4. In large, professional setups, radio frequencies or even microwaves can be used to pass information between devices.

Figure 12-   4A network wireless access point (WAP) with antenna

Other Types of Network Devices

The term *network device* can refer to a number of things. In this section, it refers specifically to equipment that can be used to extend or improve the performance of network transmissions (rather than devices such as printers that are not related to network transmissions).

Bus   A bus in networking is simply a central cable that connects the various types of devices to a LAN. The bus is sometimes referred to as the *network backbone*. While this isn't usually something you buy and add to a network, it is recognized as being part of many networks.

Bridge   A bridge is a device used to connect either two segments of one LAN or two LANs. Specifically, it's a Layer-2 device that connects LANs using the same protocol. Bridges supply a conduit that allows packets to be passed back and forth between two segments or two LANs.

By design, bridges transmit data faster than do routers (discussed in the section entitled "Routers" later in this chapter), but they don't perform the analytical and handling processes that a router does. One chief difference between a bridge and a router is that a bridge connects "similar" networks, while a router is used to connect "dissimilar" networks.

> **Note**   When working with two LANs, the LANs do not need to be of the same type to be connected by a bridge.

Hub   The role of a hub is to connect two segments of a network. But there are two types of hubs. The first type, passive, just acts to extend the network, while an active hub also provides signal amplification to be sure the signal isn't lost or too degraded as it moves along more far-reaching network segments.

A series of ports is available on a hub, as shown in Figure 12-5. Data arrives at one port during a transmission, but it's then copied to all other ports so that all nodes can see that data is there (while the node device determines whether it's addressed to them). Also, hubs are often used in Ethernet and other types of networking that use star topology. (See the section entitled "Types of Network Topology" earlier in this chapter). A shared Ethernet, in fact, is one that uses a network of hubs or hubs and repeaters.

Figure 12-5   A hub servicing a single office network

There are different types of hubs, including the following:

- **Active hub**   With this type, also called a *multiport repeater*, the hub not only amplifies the signal, it can regenerate it.

- **Intelligent or manageable hub**   This type includes normal hub functions plus features that allow administrators to monitor data flow and to control and configure the hub's ports.

- **Passive hub**   This type of hub serves merely as a data conduit and usually does not have a power source, thus is not able to produce signal amplification or regeneration.

- **Switching hub**   This type of hub also has some intelligence built in. It takes the information coming into a port, determines who the packet is addressed to, and then directs that packet only to the port channeling data to the proper destination node.

Repeater   A repeater is a special type of network device installed to either regenerate or replicate a signal (analog or digital) that has been lost during the transmission. In a network situation, the repeater performs the valuable role of message relay between parts of the network (called *subnetworks*) using different network protocols, different cables, or both. Hubs can perform this same basic function as they relay messages between nodes, and some tend to use the terms *hub* and *repeater* interchangeably. Repeaters are less intelligent than bridges, gateways, or routers.

Be aware that there are key differences between an analog repeater and a digital one. While the analog version might just amplify the signal to try to put a message out, the digital one might be sophisticated enough to do a complete reconstruction of the lost signal, making it a far more effective tool.

Router   The job of a router is to connect different LANs—for example, the broadband router connecting two office network segments shown in Figure 12-6.

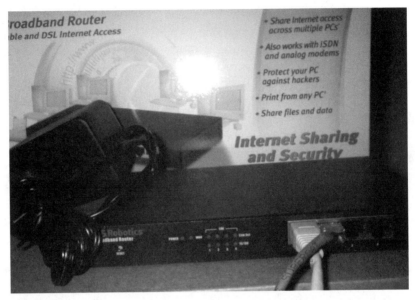

Figure 12-6   A router connecting two different office network segments

By design, routers use the following items:

- **Header**   This is a unit of information usually preceding a data transmission to help prepare for and identify that data.

- **Forwarding table**   This is used to determine where packets need to go.

- **Internet Control Message Protocol (ICMP)**   The ICMP permits the exchange of packets that bear control, error, and informational messages—that is, it makes certain that communications can occur between the different LANs and tries to optimize conditions. It also provides the foundation for ways to test for a successful Internet/network connection through the use of PING, TraceRt, and other tools.

A router uses these tools to identify where it should route a data transmission.

Switch   A switch, also known as a LAN switch or a frame switch, is a device that is responsible for both filtering and forwarding packets of information between different network segments. Specifically, it cross-connects stations or

LAN segments. Switches today frequently replace media hubs to increase the potential bandwidth. For example, while all the devices sharing a 100BaseT hub must then share the total 100 Mbps data transfer capability, each sender/receiver device pair connected through a switch get its own (unshared) 100 Mbps capacity.

Network Adapter Installation

In this section, you'll go through the removal of an existing network adapter (if one is present) and the installation of a new one. You'll finish by performing the basic steps for connecting the PC to other devices on the network.

As always, start by inspecting the new network adapter to be sure it's free of damage and is indeed the one you want to install. Replace it in its antistatic bag. Review the documentation and any accompanying disks, as well. Many network adapters ship with diagnostic utilities that help you troubleshoot their connectivity after installation. You also might want to check either the manufacturer's Web site or the Windows Update site to see whether a network driver update is needed.

Next, look at the cable you'll use to connect the PC to the network. For example, if you're using unshielded twist pair (UTP) cable, make certain the RJ-45 connector that terminates each end of the cable is firmly in place and properly oriented. The cable should not be crimped, cut, or in any other way damaged. If it is, it might not work properly as a data conduit between machines on the network.

Removal of Existing Adapter

Let's assume that you have a network adapter you need to replace as part of the installation procedure. If the existing network interface is integrated with the motherboard rather than provided through a separate adapter, check the motherboard or PC documentation (or the manufacturer's Web site) to determine how to disable the current network capability properly. As with modems, video adapters, and sound adapters you've already worked with, simply removing the driver might disable the integrated network adapter in the motherboard. With other types, you might need to make an adjustment to a motherboard switch or a change settings in CMOS Setup to use a replacement full-hardware network adapter instead.

To remove an adapter, follow these steps:

1. From Device Manager, click to expand the category Network adapters and then select the adapter you want to remove or disable. (See Figure 12-7.)

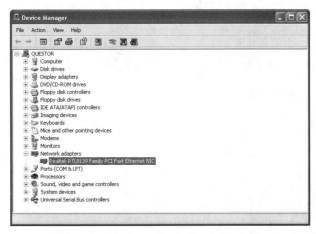

Figure 12-7   Selecting a network adapter listing in Device Manager

2. Click Remove (for Windows versions earlier than Windows 2000), or right-click the adapter and choose Uninstall.

3. Shut down the PC, disconnect it from power, remove the case cover, and ground yourself.

4. Locate the current network adapter, which is usually found in one of the short white PCI slots. If you have trouble locating it, look for the Ethernet/LAN connection on the back of the PC as shown in Figure 12-8. If there's an adapter on the other side, that's the network adapter. Disconnect the cable and set it aside.

Figure 12-8   The Ethernet/LAN connection—with cable connected—at the interface of the network adapter with the rear of the PC

5. Remove the screw or retainer holding the network adapter in place. Set the screw or retainer aside to reuse it during the installation, and place the old network adapter into an antistatic bag, which you will label with the type of modem and on which you will note whether the adapter works or not.

Installing a Network Adapter

Check the documentation packaged with your network adapter for any explicit instructions provided. After doing that, follow these steps:

1. Remove the new network adapter from its case or antistatic bag, and position it to fit firmly, straight, and securely into an empty PCI slot.

2. Replace the screw or retainer to hold the new adapter in place. (See Figure 12-9.)

Figure 12-9 Replacing the screw or retainer to hold the network adapter in place in the slot

3. Reconnect the Ethernet cable to the LAN connection at the back of the PC where the network adapter is installed.

4. Replace the cover. Reconnect power and restart the PC.

Once Windows loads, it should automatically detect the new network adapter and, if the PC was formerly connected to a network, include it again as a workstation on that network.

If instead, you are using the installation of a network adapter to start to form a basic peer-to-peer network, you would look under the Network Connections icon in Control Panel in Windows XP and Windows Server 2003 and select the "Set up a home or small office network" option. The Network Setup Wizard then steps you through the process of establishing peer-to-peer connections with one or more computers connected by a cable or wireless setup. Each computer on the network needs a network adapter, a specific address on the network, and a cable or wireless connection between each.

The Role of a Firewall

One of the time-honored ways to keep a network safe from outside intrusion is through the use of a *firewall*, defined as any implementation designed to keep network data and activity secure from those who would monitor or access it without authorization. In a professional network environment, a firewall is often hardware—such as a router or combination of routers and servers—configured to restrict access to anything lying behind it and protected by it. In simpler and consumer environments, the firewall services are often provided by software, either through third-party add-on utilities—such as ZoneAlarm or Black Ice—or through the Internet Connection Firewall in Windows 98SE and later versions.

Troubleshooting

When troubleshooting network communications, you should try your best to identify whether the problem is with the network setup or with the configuration of a workstation set up as a node on that network. Unless no computer on the network can communicate with any other, the problem is more likely to be with an individual workstation or the hardware connecting them—for example, a bad cable or a dead hub. Always have extra terminated network cable available (and be sure the cable is good) when troubleshooting because cables, which might lie exposed in some traffic areas, often sustain damage and must be replaced.

Let's examine some specific issues related to getting a network adapter recognized and a workstation configured and working on the network.

Getting a New NIC Seen

If your previous network services were installed through the motherboard itself rather than through a separate NIC, be sure to disable the onboard networking by using directions from the motherboard or PC manufacturer. When investigating why a newly installed network adapter cannot be seen by the system, you should also perform the following tasks:

■ Reinstall the drivers, and check for driver updates.

■ Thoroughly check the board's installation. Rearrange other boards, if necessary, to try the NIC in other slots.

■ Check for resource conflicts. The NIC needs an IRQ, for example. If you install the NIC on a system with no IRQs free, it might not have an opportunity to be seen initially to even bring the system into a hardware conflict.

■ If you have another NIC, try that one to see whether it's recognized. Once you can get that NIC recognized, you eliminate a set of causes that might keep the first one from being installed (and therefore know it might be a problem with the NIC or how it's configured).

NIC-Based Resource Conflicts

When these resource conflicts appear, the symptoms can mimic other problems. Resource conflicts include the following:

■ The network device, connection, or both disappear intermittently.

■ Network communications appear to hang between two systems that otherwise seem to work normally.

■ The network becomes unreliable when using a particular device (which can reside either on or off the network).

■ One or more of the systems freezes or reports various, sometimes unrelated, error messages as services are hung up.

■ General performance issues occur on both the desktop and the network.

■ Network monitoring reports a high degree of collisions.

■ The system fails to boot with the network card installed or with the cable attached to the network card.

■ The network connection disappears completely, or it is seen with a red X icon (indicating that the conflict ended up disabling the device) or yellow exclamation mark icon (indicating conflict) in Device Manager.

If you're using a Plug and Play (PnP)–enabled NIC and a PnP-supporting operating system, your operating system should work with the BIOS, the identifying information on the NIC itself, and the NIC's driver to configure the NIC automatically for use. When it doesn't, try the following possible remedies:

- Try removing the NIC and reinstalling it.

- Be sure the driver is up to date.

- Check your current resources carefully, and be aware that some devices such as sound adapters love to grab the same resources as the network adapter.

- Temporarily remove nonessential devices, get the NIC recognized, and then re-add them, juggling as necessary.

> **Note** Windows NT, early versions of Windows 95, and some other non-Windows operating systems are not PnP-capable.

What to Do When Wrong Protocols Are Installed

Installing the wrong protocols or using ones that have been corrupted because of some problem on the system or network is a fairly common source of problems. To fix such problems, follow these steps:

1. Determine exactly which protocols need to be installed.

2. Check to be sure these protocols are installed. (The protocols are available under the Network icon in Control Panel.) If necessary for troubleshooting, try removing all protocols except the ones specifically required for the communication you're trying to fix.

3. If the protocols you need are already installed, remove them, restart the system, and then reinstall the exact protocols needed. (This might overwrite a corrupted or outdated protocol.)

4. You might also want to update the network hardware driver or drivers.

Lab 12: Install a Network Adapter, and Create a Peer-to-Peer Network with a Second PC

This lab is intended to prepare you to install the network adapters and cable needed to create a peer-to-peer network connection or determine how to add both systems to an existing network. As part of this lab, you will record your observations, difficulties, and other experiences into your lab notes so that you have a record you can refer to when performing other such operations.

Objectives

When you complete this lab, you will be able to address the following issues:

1. Installing network adapters and cabling two systems together

2. Determining whether to join an existing network or create a separate peer-to-peer network

3. Determining which tools in recent Windows versions to use to join the network or set up the peer-to-peer arrangement

Necessary Equipment and Resources

The following equipment and resources are necessary for completing this lab:

1. Two PCs; both should be running Windows XP, either with a network adapter installed or without one installed. If one is installed, it will be replaced in this operation.

2. An Internet-ready third PC for reference.

3. Replacement or new PCI network adapters ready for use.

4. Your PC toolkit.

5. At least 60 minutes to complete this lab.

Procedures to Follow

1. Using Network Connections in Windows XP, determine whether either of the PCs is currently on a network. Also determine the operating system version used by each PC. Record both pieces of information in your lab notes.

2. In Control Panel, select System and click the Computer Name tab. In your lab notes, write the Computer Name of each system (which is used to identify it to other users on the network) and note whether it is currently a member of any workgroup.

3. On both systems, go to Device Manager and remove the driver for the existing network adapter, if one is present. Record specifics about the adapter being removed (as detailed in Device Manager) in your lab notes.

4. Using the steps outlined in the "Installation" section of this chapter, remove (if necessary) the existing adapter and install a new network adapter into both systems. Document any observations or difficulties in your lab notes.

5. Determine—either through personal knowledge or by asking your instructor, supervisor, or other qualified person—whether there is an existing network these systems can join (at least temporarily). If there is, connect the cables from each installed network adapter to the appropriate hub or router available for this connection. Then return to the Computer Name tab and click the Network ID button to start the Network Identification Wizard, which will help you join each system to the network. Document your experience in your lab notes.

6. If no larger network is available, connect the network cable between the network adapters on both PCs, and then run the "Set up a home or small office network" option in Network Connections. Record this experience in your lab notes.

Lab Notes

1. Record any existing network information for each system along with the operating system version used by each.

   System #1 _____

   System #2 _____

2. Record the Computer Name, and note whether each computer is part of a workgroup (and if so, what the workgroup name is).

   System #1 _____

   System #2 _____

3. For each system, enter existing network adapter information and information about the new adapters to be installed.

   System #1 _____

   System #2 _____

4. Record your experience in removing the old adapters (if necessary) and installing the new ones, noting any difficulties you had and how you overcame them.

   System #1 _____

   System #2 _____

5. Document your efforts to either join an existing network or create a peer-to-peer network, including how connections were made, any troubleshooting measures you undertook, and your final results.

   System #1 _____

   System #2 _____

13

Other Controller Cards

Before we leave this part, with its emphasis on components that can be installed on the motherboard, to jump headfirst into Part IV on drives, we'll look at adding specialty controller or functionality cards or adapters to a PC. The adapters focused on in this chapter add some level of control or functionality to your PC that the motherboard or some other feature does not already provide. Examples of this are the Small Computer System Interface (SCSI) host controller used to connect SCSI drives to the system as an alternative to IDE/ATA drives and special drive controllers that allow an older motherboard to use today's faster, high-capacity hard drives.

There are other add-on adapters as well. For example, what do you do if you want to add an IEEE 1394 (also known as FireWire) drive to a PC when there are no IEEE 1394 ports present? In that case, you need to obtain and install an IEEE 1394 adapter, which typically adds three or more ports. The same holds true for older motherboards without universal serial bus (USB) ports. (Some Pentium MMX and Pentium II models supported the use of USB ports without these ports physically present on the motherboard.) In instances where one or more of the built-in ports on a system no longer functions (depending on the motherboard, BIOS, and actual problem created), you might also need to install an IEEE 1394 or USB adapter to restore the ability to connect devices that use these ports.

Other examples of add-on adapters include but are not limited to the following items:

- Video capture boards
- TV or radio tuner cards (to enable a user to watch TV or listen to the radio on a PC)

- Diagnostic adapters to monitor and report hardware problems or assess peripheral lab equipment in a scientific setting

- Fault-tolerant drive subsystems such as RAID (discussed in Chapter 14, "Hard Drives and Drive Interfaces")

SCSI Controllers and Host Adapters

As you learned earlier in this book, drives based on Integrated Device Electronics (IDE) connect through special controller connectors directly on the motherboard. By comparison, most motherboards don't provide a way to install a SCSI drive (which is discussed in more detail in the next chapter). Instead, SCSI drives typically connect through a special controller card known as the *SCSI controller* or *SCSI host adapter*, which is installed on one of the expansion slots on the motherboard. Although you can still find Industry Standard Architecture (ISA) bus SCSI controllers, Peripheral Component Interface (PCI) SCSI controllers are far more common today. Figure 13-1 shows a PCI-connecting Ultra SCSI controller.

Figure 13-   **1**An Ultra SCSI host controller to be installed in a PCI slot

There was a time when all consumer-based systems had IDE/ATA (Advanced Technology Attachment) drives while commercial and professional systems featured only what were then far more expensive and faster SCSI drives. This was true in part because professional setups often needed to use a fault-tolerant system of connecting multiple drives known as *redundant array of independent disks* (or RAID), which were designed to work only with SCSI drives. RAID is also discussed in the next chapter.

The prices for SCSI drives today are far more comparable to IDE/ATA drives, while the speed of IDE/ATA drives has risen sharply. Additionally, RAID controllers are available now that support either IDE/ATA or SCSI. Thus, the rules for which types of drives belong in which types of systems are no longer as cut and dried.

One of the remaining major attractions of SCSI drives is that you can connect more drives with it than you can with a traditional IDE/ATA drive setup, which supports the use of up to four drives. A SCSI controller can allow the connection of 4 to 16 SCSI drives, although host adapters are also available with two controllers onboard to allow the connection of up to 30. Each device is added to the controller in a daisy-chain fashion. That is, each drive contains not just a port that connects via SCSI cable to either the controller itself or to the preceding drive in the chain, but it also contains another pass-through that connects via cable to the next drive in the chain. SCSI also allows for both internal (inside the case) chains as well as external ones.

On some motherboards, you'll find the SCSI controller integrated directly into the motherboard. If the integrated SCSI circuitry fails, you might (or might not) be able to install a separate SCSI host controller to assume the work. You also might find it preferable to disable the onboard SCSI to permit the installation of a better quality separate controller. Check your PC or motherboard documentation for specific details.

SCSI and SCSI Host Adapter Types

SCSI technology encompasses a number of specifications or types, which determine various factors, including:

- The maximum number of SCSI devices that can be connected to the daisy chain

- The length of cable that can be used (maximum bus length)

- The number of pins and types of connectors used at each point in the daisy chain

- The data bus width

Table 13-1 shows various SCSI specifications, along with the maximum number of devices each allows, their maximum data transfer rate, the maximum daisy-chain length permitted, and the number of pins used by the connector for each. (See the "SCSI Signaling Types" section later in this chapter for more details on daisy-chain lengths.)

Table 13-1 **SCSI Specifications Table**

Type	Bus Width	Max. Devices	Max. Transfer (in MBps)	Max. Length Pins (in meters)
SCSI-1	8	5	6/12/25	25
SCSI-2	8	5	6/12/25	50
Fast SCSI	8	10	3/12/25	50
Wide SCSI (Fast Wide)	16	20	3/12/25	68
Ultra SCSI	8	20	3/-/-	50
Wide Ultra	4	40	3/-/-	68
Wide Ultra	8	40	1.5/-/-	68
Wide Ultra	16	40	-/12/25	68
Ultra-2 SCSI	8	40	-/12/25	50
Wide Ultra-2	16	80	-/12/25	68
Ultra-3 SCSI/Ultra 160	16	160	-/12/-	68
Ultra-4 SCSI/Ultra 320	16	320	-/12/-	68
SCSI-1	8	5	6/12/25	25
SCSI-2	8	5	6/12/25	50
Fast SCSI	8	10	3/12/25	50
Wide SCSI/Fast Wide	16	20	3/12/25	68
Ultra SCSI	8	20	3/-/-	50
Wide Ultra	4	40	3/-/-	68
Wide Ultra	8	40	1.5/-/-	68
Wide Ultra	16	40	-/12/25	68
Ultra-2 SCSI	8	40	-/12/25	50
Wide Ultra-2	16	80	-/12/25	68
Ultra-3 SCSI/Ultra 160	16	160	-/12/-	68
Ultra-4 SCSI/Ultra 320	16	320	-/12/-	68

SCSI Signaling Types

SCSI signaling refers to the way data is transmitted through the daisy chain to the controller and beyond and then back again. Signaling plays a major role in determining the maximum length of SCSI cable that can be used. With this in mind, SCSI supports three major types of signaling:

■   Single-ended (SE)

■   High Voltage Differential (HVD), also called Differential

■   Low Voltage Differential (LVD)

Single-ended is the oldest signaling type and the most limiting. Its cable can be only 3 to 6 meters (approximately 9 to 18 feet) long. Furthermore, single-ended signaling isn't supported by any of the more recent SCSI specifications, such as Ultra-2, Ultra-3, and Ultra-4 SCSI.

High Voltage Differential is the most forgiving type because the span of SCSI devices can reach up to about 25 meters (75 feet), making it suitable for an installation spread out over a normal room size.

Low Voltage Differential doubles the best length of single-ended signaling and is about half that of High Voltage Differential, with a maximum span of 12 meters (approximately 39 feet). One major difference between this signaling type and High Voltage Differential is that LVD saves on overall power consumption.

Installation of a SCSI Controller or Host Adapter

It's best to obtain a SCSI controller of the proper specification for the drives you plan to install on it. Wherever possible, you should first decide on the drives you'll use and then, with this information, obtain the proper controller. (Specific drives might require specific controller types.) You should also check Windows Hardware and Driver Central (shown in Figure 13-2 and formerly known as the Windows Catalog and Microsoft Hardware Compatibility List) in the "Storage, Adapters and Controllers" section to find a controller that is compatible with the version of Microsoft Windows you're using. You can find this site at *http:// www.microsoft.com/whdc/hcl/default.mspx*.

Figure 13- 2 Windows Hardware and Driver Central

One significant benefit of SCSI is that there is both backward and forward compatibility in the hardware. For example, if you install an older SCSI hard drive with a later model SCSI controller, the drive should operate at its maximum transfer speed. If you install a newer specification SCSI hard drive to an older specification SCSI controller, the drive will operate at the maximum transfer speed rate for that controller.

Once you have the adapter, remove it from its packaging and be sure it's the type you ordered and is free of damage. Return the controller to its antistatic package to protect it while you review the installation instructions for the controller. After doing this, perform the following steps:

1. Shut down the PC, disconnect power, remove the cover from the PC, and ground yourself as described in Chapter 3, "Defining Your Tech Toolkit."

2. Locate a free expansion slot (or make one available by removing an adapter you either don't use or use infrequently). If a screw or retainer is present, remove it and set it aside for installing the SCSI controller.

3. Remove the SCSI controller from its antistatic bag and insert it firmly in the empty expansion slot.

4. Replace the screw or retainer to secure the controller in the slot.

5. Reconnect power to the PC, and turn it on.

When Windows loads, it should detect the new adapter and commence the installation procedure. Have available the disk that came with the drive in case a driver is needed for the device.

When Windows installs the adapter, you can at any point shut down the system again, unplug it from power, and then connect your properly configured SCSI drives using the SCSI data cable. (See Chapter 14 for details.) Why can't you just attach the drives at the same time? Because it's a good practice to ensure that the adapter is properly seen by the system and working before you add the drives themselves. Proceeding in this manner narrows the possible issues if you need to troubleshoot a problem installation.

High-Speed ATA Controllers

What happens when you install a newer, faster ATA/IDE drive designed to operate with a controller that functions at a bus speed of 100, 133, or 200 MHz to an older motherboard, such as one functioning at a bus speed of just 66 MHz (as you have with some Pentium II and earlier systems)? The answer is that the drive will transfer data at a slower bus transfer speed unless you install a special drive controller that provides an interface between the older motherboard and the faster drive. The controller acts like a motherboard bus speed upgrade, at least in terms of your drives, which are then attached by normal ATA/IDE ribbon cable to that controller. Such devices are sometimes referred to as *Promise controllers* because Promise is the name of one of the major drive adapter manufacturers.

Such adapters tend to have very specific installation instructions, based on the exact nature of the controller itself and how you need it to work. However, the instructions for installing such a controller are basically the same as the instructions provided in the previous section for installing a SCSI controller.

Add-On Functionality Cards

As mentioned at the beginning of this chapter, there are many types of adapters you can install to give added or new functionality to a system that does not otherwise provide the feature or connection. Because the range of devices is quite diverse, this section will focus on only a few of the more popular types.

Specialty Video and Sound Adapters

Before installing specialty, secondary video adapters—such as a TV tuner, video capture boards, or even radio tuner adapters—you should always research the devices. In particular, you should be sure an adapter meets the following criteria:

■   Compatibility with the software to be used with it. (For example, if you're using special video editing software, it should work with the adapter being installed.)

■   Compatibility with the version of Windows being used. (Check Microsoft Windows Hardware and Driver Central to be sure.)

■   Compatibility with the primary video adapter (or sound adapter, in the case of radio tuners or specialty music-oriented boards).

Installation of such boards is performed just like it is with other adapters you have installed to available PCI slots in the PC, but with particular attention given to specialty connections, such as cables to connect external peripherals. Because these types of devices might sit on a store or warehouse shelf for a period of time before you buy them, always check for an updated driver from the manufacturer's Web site (or in some cases, from the Windows Update site) as a possible replacement for the one which shipped on disk with the product.

USB and IEEE 1394

One of the most commonly installed "added function" adapters are those that allow you to connect external devices such as USB or IEEE 1394 drives, scanners, cameras, printers, sound mixing consoles, input devices, hubs, and more. Figure 13-3 shows a Belkin 3-port PCI IEEE 1394 adapter.

Figure 13-3   A three-port IEEE 1394 adapter from Belkin

However, when you need to add USB or IEEE 1394 devices to a system where no ports are built into the motherboard, simply adding an adapter to make these ports available might not be enough. For example, if you're working with Windows Millennium Edition (Windows Me), you can install an IEEE 1394 adapter but the operating system often won't provide IEEE 1394 support to devices.. It's coded to look for the functionality integrated into the motherboard. Windows XP and Windows Server 2003 seem best equipped to handle a range of adapters and devices. Other motherboards might require a BIOS update. (See Chapter 7, "Memory.") Still others might not work at all with these adapters, even if the adapters are detected and properly installed. In such instances, completely replacing the motherboard with one that specifically supports USB and IEEE 1394 is warranted.

It also matters which implementation of USB and IEEE 1394 you are using. Only later versions of each operate at a high data-transfer rate. Typically, to support these later versions, all of the following items must be in place:

- A supporting operating system, such as Windows XP or Windows Server 2003

- Devices rated for the higher speed, along with drivers specifically designed for the operating system being used

- A supporting motherboard and BIOS

Let's examine some related issues. Assume you install an adapter that provides three USB 1.1 ports to a system. You can usually successfully install newer, USB 2.0 devices to such ports, but they won't operate at the same speed as they would through a port that supports USB 2.0.

Now let's assume you install a USB 2.0 adapter instead. However, your motherboard BIOS and operating system are both older and don't support a USB 2.0 implementation. However, they do support USB 1.1. In such a case, your USB 2.0 devices—and the adapter ports they connect to—will function at 1.1 speed. The same principles apply to IEEE 1394 adapters. Thus, you want to be sure your operating system and BIOS can support whatever USB and IEEE 1394 adapter you install. Doing so will allow you to take advantage of the maximum possible transfer speed of the devices in question.

As with specialty video and audio boards, these adapters install just like other PCI boards you have installed on a system. You probably won't find any older ISA-based versions of these adapters because the PCI/PCIx bus was already the standard when these external connection types were added to PC architecture.

> **Note**   Some manufacturers, such as Belkin, offer combo cards that allow you to add both USB and IEEE 1394 ports in a single adapter installation, such as the one seen in Figure 13-4. Other adapters allow you to transform a USB port into a serial or parallel port adapter.

Figure 13- 4A combination IEEE 1394 and USB PCI adapter

Lab 13: Install a SCSI Controller

This lab is intended to prepare you to research SCSI controller options based on three preselected drives and then to install a SCSI controller into a system, making it ready to accept the installation of SCSI drives.

Objectives

When you complete this lab, you will be able to address the following issues:

1. The selection of the best SCSI controller to meet the needs of three specified SCSI drives

2. Installation of a SCSI controller onto a system

Necessary Equipment and Resources

The following equipment and resources are necessary for completing this lab:

1. Two PCs of recent vintage, with one or both running Windows XP or Windows Server 2003

2. Another Internet-ready PC for reference

3. A SCSI controller

4. Your PC toolkit

5. Between 30 and 60 minutes to complete this lab

Procedures to Follow

1. Based on the information available in this chapter, use online resources such as PriceWatch (*http://www.pricewatch.com*) and other resources, such as Windows Hardware and Driver Central, to determine the best SCSI adapter to work with the following three SCSI drives. Then record in your lab notes your results (including price and specifications) and the reason for your selection.

   ❏ IBM UltraStar SCSI-3/Ultra 160 with a 74.4 GB (10,000 RPM), 68-pin internal hard drive

   ❏ Seagate ST446452W SCSI-2 with a 47GB, 68-pin internal hard drive

   ❏ Panasonic LF-D291N SCSI DVD-RAM external DVD recorder

2. Record in your lab notes information about the SCSI host adapter you install for this lab.

3. Using the information found in the SCSI installation section of this book, install the SCSI adapter and check its installation through Device Manager. Document your experience in your lab notes, including any special circumstances and observations.

Lab Notes

1. Record information gathered through step 1 of the preceding procedure.

    _____

    _____

    _____

2. Document details about the SCSI controller you will install, including type, manufacturer, and so forth.

    _____

    _____

    _____

3. Record your efforts and experience in installing the SCSI controller, including any troubleshooting required so that the drive could be seen.

    _____

    _____

    _____

Part IV

All About Drives

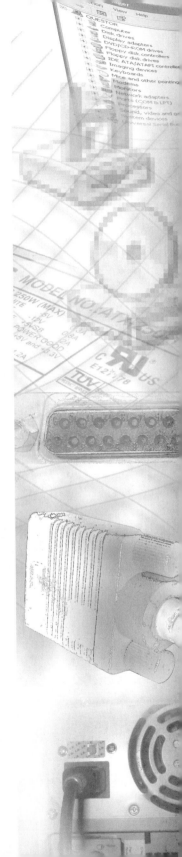

Computers have never featured more drives of different types than they do now. Knowing how to select, install, and prepare drives for use on a system is central to attaining PC technical expertise. In this part of the book, you're introduced to essential information concerning the drives commonly attached to the PC, including different types of hard drives, CD and DVD drives, floppy drives, and removable media drives for desktop PCs.

14

Hard Drives and Drive Interfaces

As users and as technicians, we've really never enjoyed cheaper per-gigabyte capacity, more total capacity, or more ways in which to connect speedy drives to a system. We need all these things, too, because much of our work occurs only on our systems rather than on paper to be relegated to large physical filing cabinets. Consider, too, how much more cheaply and swiftly we can share stored electronic files than we can paper versions.

Hard drives, also called hard or fixed disks, were first introduced in the 1950s but did not become standard issue on IBM-compatible personal computers until after the debut of the IBM PC (which originally ran from floppy only). While the systems of old were considered awesome when they included a 5-MB or 10-MB hard drive, today's systems often have more than one drive with a total capacity of anywhere from 20 GB to more than 100 GB.

In this chapter, you develop a basic understanding of the technology and physical properties within these drives; how the drives connect; and how you install, troubleshoot, and maintain them. This amounts to all the essential knowledge needed to prep them for use.

> **More Info** Laptop drives are covered in Chapter 22, "The Laptop Connection."

The Technology Within Hard Drives

If you think of the appearance of a CD or DVD, you can picture the essential physical feature contained within a hard drive: the platter or platters. Most drives today contain multiple platters. Each platter, which is made of much harder material than a CD or DVD, rotates by means of a motor. The speed of that rotation is referred to in RPM, or revolutions per minute. Typical RPM speeds include 3600, 5400, 7200, and 10,000 or more. In the center of a platter is a special hole with filters, which is designed to serve as a vent and to equalize pressure between the platters.

Platters are coated with magnetic material—the recording medium— where the actual data gets written and where it is read from. The actual process of reading from and writing to a hard drive is performed by read/write heads attached to a lightning-fast (meaning it can move across a platter up to 50 times per second), motor-driven mechanical arm with a movable mechanism. This arm resides at the side of the platters and maneuvers the heads across the spinning platters. Not only is the arm fast, it also works with incredible precision.

Sitting beneath each actual drive, within the housing, is a printed circuit board that contains the onboard electronics and controller for the drive.

Drive Organization

A hard drive's platters aren't vast open surfaces that data can be written to randomly. Instead, they are organized into a system of tracks and sectors. Tracks circumnavigate the platter working from the outer edge inward in a series, one track after another. Each track is divided into a number of sectors, each of which contains a designated number of bytes. Groups of sectors can be organized into clusters; cluster assignment is typically done through the process of installing an operating system and applying a file structure, such as FAT32 or NTFS, to it.

When a hard drive is being manufactured, it is low-level formatted— a process that organizes the disk into the tracks and sectors. This is different from the formatting (properly referred to as high-level formatting) you will do to prepare or erase a drive for use, which is the type of formatting discussed later in this chapter. Under normal circumstances, you should never attempt to perform a low-level format because you might render a drive unusable. If a situation arises where you feel low-level formatting is required, contact the manufacturer. The manufacturer might agree to do this for you or to replace the unit if you ship it back, which is a better option than risking accidental destruction of the drive.

Drive Performance

While drive capacity (the number of GB of data a drive is designed to hold) often plays a dominant role in the selection of a drive, two other major factors need to be examined. One factor is the maximum transfer speed, which determines the best rate at which the drive can deliver its data to the system. This speed is measured in megabits per second, or Mbps. The second factor is the seek time, or the time it takes for the drive to deliver the first byte of data in a file requested by the CPU. This speed is measured in milliseconds (ms). The higher the data rate and the lower the seek time, the faster and more efficiently a drive should perform.

However, all drives begin to slow over time, as they reach the upper ranges of their maximum capacity, as the system becomes cluttered with temporary files (including the temporary files left behind by Web browsing), and as the data written to the drive becomes fragmented (that is, a group of data gets written to various places on the drive, making it slower to load when requested). Maintenance tips offered near the end of this chapter should help to reduce or eliminate some effects of these issues.

About File Systems

Put simply, a PC's file system, such as FAT32 or NTFS, acts as an arbiter between the operating system that supports it and the physical hard drive in maintaining good disk file organization. Without an efficient file system, it would take far longer to locate and retrieve data stored on a drive. Just as a large print catalog of information needs an index to assist users in finding specific content, a file system expedites the location and retrieval of information on a hard drive.

The "FAT" in FAT32 refers to the file allocation table. During high-level formatting of a hard drive (which you'll learn how to perform later in this chapter), the file allocation table, like a master storage index, is written to the drive twice. This is because the table will contain a unique entry for each disk cluster. As files are written to the drive, an index of which files are stored in each cluster is kept to help the system find them later. When a file is opened or executed, the table determines which cluster to look in for the necessary data. If the file spans two or more clusters, the table also identifies each cluster and helps the operating system load information from each successive one.

Certain conditions on a PC can conspire to write files non-sequentially on a drive (an occurrence known as *disk fragmenting*) or to compromise the integrity of the file system, a result referred to as a *corrupted FAT*. Both can scramble a drive's contents, but the second can make it virtually unusable. The conditions that lead to these undesirable situations include improper shutdown of a PC, computer viruses, or a failing drive. Another possible contributing factor is using a disk utility meant for one specific file system or Microsoft Windows version on a drive that uses a different file system or operating system version.

The NTFS file system (NTFS)—available for use with versions of Windows such as Windows NT, Windows 2000, Windows XP, and Windows Server 2003—differs from the file allocation table/FAT32 file system in several important ways. It's specifically designed to work with Windows security and administrative features, it's necessary for keeping data safe in even small professional environments, and it's far more fault tolerant because it offers options to recover from a hard-drive crash (and we'll all lose a drive at one time or another).

Drive Interfaces

Hard drives are often placed into one of two major categories: internal or external. Even though external drives have always been with us in one form or another, the real boon to the external-drive market came with the introduction of universal serial bus (USB) 2.0 and both versions of Institute of Electrical and Electronics Engineers (IEEE) 1394, which permitted very high-speed data transfers. Prior to that, external drives tended to be dreadfully slower than their internally connected counterparts.

An even more important distinction between hard drives is the way in which they connect and work with the system. These interactions determine how you will install them and, to some degree, how they will be configured for use.

The following is a list of the majority of drive connection types currently (or still) available:

- ATA/IDE/EIDE
- SCSI
- USB 1.1 and 2.0
- IEEE 1394
- Parallel Port

ATA/IDE

Advanced Technology Attachment (ATA) is the specification covering all Integrated Device Electronics (IDE) drives, including Enhanced IDE (EIDE). Unlike the SCSI controller you learned about in the previous chapter and the SCSI drives you'll learn to configure and install in this chapter, current ATA/IDE drives are strictly internal and come with their controller built into the drive itself. These internal ATA/IDE drives are connected by drive ribbon cable to the two IDE/EIDE channel controller connectors on the motherboard. Each IDE/EIDE channel controller connector allows for the connection of one or two drives. Such drives represent the dominant form of hard drives used in consumer systems and account for a large percentage of drives used in professional environments.

If you check Windows Device Manager, you'll find two categories that apply to these drives: Disk Drives and IDE ATA/ATAPI Controllers (both of which are shown in Figure 14-1). The Disk Drives category lists all installed hard drives, while the IDE ATA/ATAPI Controllers category lists both the primary bus master IDE controller and the Primary IDE Channel (which refers to the first connector on the motherboard) and the Secondary IDE Channel (the second IDE connector on the motherboard).

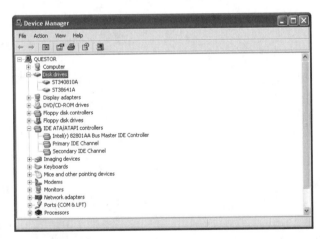

Figure 14-1   Device Manager listing for Disk Drives and IDE ATA/ATAPI Controllers

ATA/IDE Drive Specifications

Hard drives have been evolving rapidly over the last several years, both in terms of overall capacity (the 1-GB hard drive of a decade ago has morphed into a 40-, 60-, or 80-GB drive and beyond) as well as the sophisticated electronics that help it be recognized by the system and to work effectively and quickly with the system for data transfer. Table 14-1 shows a list of current ATA/IDE drive specifications, which will be followed with an explanation of the modes listed in the table.

Table 14-1 ATA/IDE Drive Specifications

Type	PIO Mode	DMA Mode	Max Transfer (Mbps)	Number of Pins in Cable
ATA	0	0	4.2	40
ATA	1	N/A	5.2	40
ATA	2	N/A	8.3	40
ATA-2,3	3	1	13.3	40
ATA-2,3	4	2	16.6	40
ATA-4, ATA-33	N/A	2	33.3	40
ATA-5	N/A	0	16.6	40
ATA-5	N/A	1	25	40
ATA-5/ATA-33	N/A	2	33.3	40
ATA-5	N/A	3	44.4	80
ATA-5/ATA-66	N/A	4	66.6	80
ATA-6/ATA-100	N/A	5	100	80
ATA-7/ATA-133	N/A	5	133	80
ATA-Serial	N/A	5	150	4

Programmed Input/Output (PIO) mode refers to the older way in which hard drives transferred data directly to registers in the CPU. PIO featured five modes (0 through 4), each offering improvements in speed over the previous one.

More recent drives use direct memory access (DMA) modes, designed to speed up data transfers by using on-disk electronics to communicate with the system memory rather than the CPU itself, which has too many other jobs to perform. This process of bypassing the need to communicate with the CPU by allowing a peripheral device to grab and maintain control of the bus over which it transfers data is known as bus mastering.

PROFILE: Serial ATA

Because it's a newcomer to the hard-drive market, Serial ATA might not be familiar to you and you might immediately think, "Oh no, who needs another molasses-speed data interface–like parallel port for connecting external drives?" But a Serial ATA (SATA) is typically internally mounted using a slender, seven-wire cable (shown in Figure 14-2) connected to the Serial ATA connector on the motherboard—not to the same old slow serial port from the ISA bus. They are appearing more frequently on motherboards being manufactured now and are expected to become commonplace within the next year or two. There are adapter kits for adding a Serial ATA connection through the motherboard, but such connections limit the bus speed compared to a motherboard with the Serial ATA connector built into it.

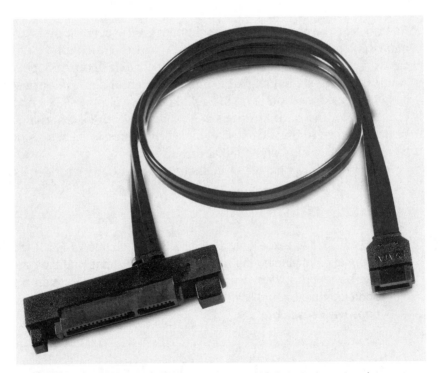

Figure 14-2   A Serial ATA drive cable, where the large connector plugs into the drive and the smaller one to the motherboard's SATA connection

Currently, the maximum data transfer rate for SATAs is 150 Mbps—or 133 Mbps if you use a Serial ATA adapter installed—but speeds of 600 Mbps or more are expected within the next few years. Recent versions of Windows (starting with Windows 98SE) support such drives.

> **Note**   Popular thinking is that a system's drives must be all ATA/IDE
> or SCSI. While this is usually the case, it doesn't have to be. ATA/IDE
> drives and SCSI drives can indeed be made to co-exist on the same
> system by adding a SCSI controller to an IDE-based system. In such
> setups, the boot-up will always be from the primary ATA/IDE drive and
> the SCSI drives will primarily be used for file storage. Check the docu-
> mentation for your SCSI drive or controller to determine the best set-
> tings for using SCSI in conjunction with the other drives.

SCSI

As you learned in the previous chapter, SCSI technology is an important
improvement over ATA/IDE technology because of the number of devices that
can be installed on a single system, in daisy chain fashion, through a single SCSI
controller or host adapter. A PC might contain either one or two controllers
allowing the connection of up to 7 or 15 devices, plus the SCSI controller which
counts as a device. SCSI drives are available both as external and internal
devices and were once exclusively used in professional setups because they
were once far faster than ATA/IDE drives.

Please refer to Chapter 13, "Other Controller Cards," for details on the various SCSI specifications.

> **Exam Tip**   An excellent, if slightly dated, source of SCSI technical
> information, including the most common questions and their answers,
> can be found at *http://www.faqs.org/faqs/scsi-faq/*. You can also find
> good information and links at the SCSI Trade Association Web site at
> *http://www.scsita.org*.

Universal Serial Bus and Both Versions of the IEEE 1394 Drives

USB and IEEE 1394 both offer platforms that allow you to connect decent-capacity, high-speed data storage drives to a system equipped to work with these devices. Originally, USB external hard drives were used as a highly portable way of sharing data between machines. However, there were good reasons to avoid using them.. Early USB drives were both far more expensive than their internal cousins and far less speedy. (Original USB drives offered a maximum transfer speed of 12 Mbps compared to the 480 Mbps offered by newer USB 2.0 drives.)

With the release of USB 2.0 and its 480-Mbps maximum data transfer rate and its increasingly attractive pricing, more and more consumers and professionals are turning to it as an option. High-capacity USB and IEEE 1394 drives provide excellent data backup and easy transfer of files between machines (even remote ones, because such drives are easy to carry).

These units connect via USB cable to a USB port on the front or rear of the PC or through a USB hub connected to such a port. (Be sure to use the proper cable for the version being installed.) External drives also often require their own power connection directly to an outlet.

> **Note**   If your BIOS and operating system support it and you have USB 2.0 ports available, always use USB 2.0 hard drives rather than USB 1.1 drives. The speed differential is significant.

IEEE 1394 external drives function much like USB drives, except that they have faster data transfer rates, particularly in the second version. (There are two versions: IEEE 1394 and 1394b.) The second version of IEEE 1394 drives have data transfer rates of 800 to 3200 Mbps, while the first version has speeds up to 400 Mbps. These are external stand-alone drives that connect through the IEEE 1394 port by means of an IEEE 1394 cable. The drives must be used with an operating system version that supports them (and all versions of Windows from Windows 2000 on do). As with USB drives, IEEE 1394 drives typically require their own connection to a power source (outlet).

IEEE 1394 drives pose slightly more of an issue than USB drives because IEEE 1394 ports are not provided on many motherboards. While you can install an IEEE 1394 adapter to give you the ports, not all adapters work exceptionally well with all IEEE 1394 drives or permit them to work at their maximum data transfer capacity.

Note that combination drives that combine the USB 2.0 and IEEE 1394 port interfaces are available from a number of manufacturers. Figure 14-3 shows such a combination drive that is available from Western Digital.

Figure 14-3   A Western Digital combo USB 2.0/IEEE 1394 external drive

Parallel Port

With a maximum data transfer speed of just 1.2 Mbps, the oldest form of PC-based external drive connections is also the slowest. Parallel port–connecting drives—drives connected by means of the same type of cable used with a parallel port printer—really aren't suitable for more than "as needed" transfers of files. Even though you can continue to find such drives, many are legacy drives, meaning that they were acquired in the relatively distant past and kept around because they still perform some service.

> **Note**   You can purchase special adapters that will allow an external SCSI drive to be connected through a parallel port. Even though the parallel port provides a much slower connection for data transfer, certain situations (usually short-term solutions) might require their use.

Working with Large or Multiple Drives

Very few computers today contain just a single drive. In fact, one of the most typical configurations involves the use of a hard drive (and many have two), an internal CD or DVD drive, and an optional external drive that is provided largely for backup or as a removable file store. Keep the concept of multiplicity of drives in mind when you go through the next two chapters, too, because they share the same drive interfaces, require the same type of configuration, but without the drive-prepping required for a new hard drive.

> **Note**   If you upgrade from a system that has two or three drives to one that has considerably more, especially if the drives are high capacity, make sure that you're using a higher capacity power supply. A 230-watt or lower power supply might need to replaced with a 300-watt or higher power supply.

Drive Limitation Issues

When you're working with slightly older machines, you might hit various limitations that affect the system's ability to see and properly prepare and work with high-capacity drives. These constraints might be the result of certain logistical limits built into either the BIOS or operating system version.

First you should understand that the issue relates to the size of a disk partition, where *partition* refers to a logical drive or segment that the hard drive's physical file space is divided into. Such partitions allow you to create more than one logical disk out of a large physical disk for the purposes of enhancing drive organization, spending less time with maintenance, and enabling you to run more than one operating system at a time. Drives are partitioned in one way or another to prepare them for use.

On very old systems—such as those using Windows 95 with the FAT16 file system—the file system limits you to disk partitions no greater than 2 GB. The only way to get around this limitation is to do one of the following:

■   Upgrade your version of Windows to one that supports FAT32 (such as Windows 95 OSR2, Windows 98 or later) or NTFS (the native file system of Windows professional and server versions) and then convert the FAT16 file system to FAT32 or NTFS.

or

■   Obtain a disk manager workaround—usually from a drive manufacturer—that tries to create an interface between the operating system and a larger drive to allow the full capacity to be used by preventing it from being carved up into tiny partitions.

Yet you can hit the virtual ceiling on newer systems, too. Some PCs in service today have a BIOS that will not properly read or prepare more than an 8-GB or 33.8-GB partition. The resulting problems are serious enough to make some systems with such a drive fail during POST, an event that results in the system not booting up.

The possible remedies for this problem are as follows:

■   Obtain a suitable BIOS update that addresses this issue.

■   Use an ATA controller rated to work with such drives (such as the controllers discussed in the previous chapter).

■   Use a third-party driver or management software, which can usually be obtained through the drive manufacturer, to try to resolve the problem.

Third-party driver or management software can also be used when you experience difficulty using and partitioning a drive that exceeds 68.7 GB, which sometimes occurs when using FDISK, the Microsoft utility for partitioning a hard drive.

ATA Hardware Settings

Before you install or work with drives, there are some set hardware configuration issues you should become familiar with. In this section, you learn about jumpers, the issue of master vs. subordinate on an IDE channel controller, why drive order can matter when dealing with different types of drives, and the cable used to connect drives.

Jumpers

Jumpers are not exclusive to hard drives or even to drives. In fact, they're one of the oldest and least expensive ways to turn a device or a feature on that device on or off. This is a good time to explore how jumpers are used in relation to both drives and other PC components because you typically need to jumper drives in the process of configuring them for use.

The process of *jumpering* involves the exact placement of a shunt, a tiny block, which can be either plastic or metal and which contains two pin-hole openings. The shunt must be placed over two parallel pins selected from two rows of pins, to make a particular selection. Figure 14-4 shows the pins on the back of a hard drive, as an example, without the shunt (also known as a *jumper*) applied. Figure 14-5 shows a drive that has been jumpered (in this case, as a subordinate drive on a Seagate IDE drive).

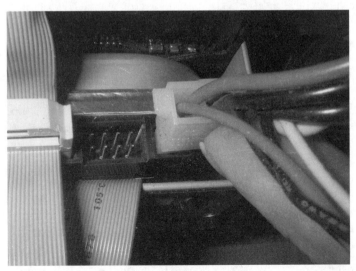

Figure 14-4   A set of drive assignment pins at the rear of an IDE drive, without the shunt in place to jumper it

Figure 14-5   The same row of pins at the rear of a hard drive, but with a shunt in place to jumper the pins needed to assign this particular drive as a subordinate

Master vs. Subordinate

A stand-alone ATA/IDE drive connects directly via ribbon cable to an IDE channel controller on the motherboard with no other devices attached to it. It is then jumpered as a solitary drive, based on the instructions provided with the drive or through the drive manufacturer's Web site.

However, when you want to connect two ATA/IDE drives to the same IDE channel controller connector on the motherboard, the first drive must be configured as the primary drive (which is also known as the *master*), while the second drive is configured as the secondary drive (which is referred to as the *subordinate*). This drive assignment is typically set through the process of jumpering the drive assignment pins at the rear of the hard drive, just as you read about in the Jumpers section. Because of the limited room available once the drive is installed and the very small nature of the pins and shunt, jumpering should be done before the drive is installed. If you need to rejumper an already installed drive, you'll usually need to remove the drive to perform the task.

Different drive manufacturers sometimes use different ways of designating the various drive assignments for jumpering, so be sure to check the documentation packaged with the drive or visit the manufacturer's Web site. When checking a manufacturer's Web site, visit the site's support area and then look up the specifications and instructions for the model of drive you are using. Once you have this information, you would jumper the first drive as the master and the second drive as the subordinate.

Deciding on Drive Order

Now that you know about designating a master and subordinate drive for ATA/ IDE connections, you need to keep in mind that the order of the drives in the assignment can matter. The fastest of the two drives to be installed to the same IDE channel controller connector should usually be assigned as the master. This configuration is best because whatever drive you connect as the subordinate can operate no more quickly than the speed of the master drive in the sequence. For this reason, a hard drive usually takes precedence in the drive order over a CD or DVD drive when both will be installed to the same IDE channel.

I say "usually" because in some circumstances you might at least temporarily use a faster drive as the subordinate. For example, assume you have a system where a slower 20-GB drive currently sits alone. You obtain a new, faster drive to which you want to copy the contents of the first drive. In such a situation, you might temporarily install the new drive as a subordinate, prepare it for use (as you'll learn to do later in this chapter), and then copy the contents of the first drive to the second. Afterward, however, you probably will want to reverse this setup to make the faster drive the master and the slower drive the subordinate. However, the physical drive order is less important than the logical drive order.

ATA/IDE Drive Ribbon Cables

ATA/IDE drives, both hard drives and other types such as CD and DVD, are connected to the IDE channel controller connectors (of which there are two) on the motherboard and to each other through the use of drive ribbon cables. Most ATA/IDE hard drives, with the exception of those using the latest ATA specifications (which you can check in the Number Of Pins In Cable column in Table 14-1), use a 40-pin drive ribbon cable. The rest, with the exception of Serial ATA drives, use an 80-pin drive ribbon cable.

Besides the number of pins used in the connectors, there is another slight differentiation in drive ribbon cables. Some cables offer just two connectors— one for the IDE channel controller connector on the motherboard and one for a drive to attach to it—while others offer connectors for two drives on the same cable, such as the one seen in Figure 14-6.

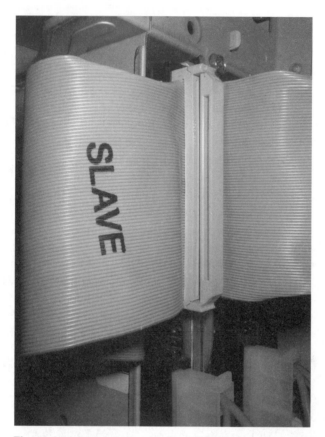

Figure 14-6 A two-drive, 40-pin ATA/IDE drive ribbon cable with a color-coded edge

Finally, look again at that figure and note that one edge of the ribbon cable is color coded (often red or blue). This color helps you orient the cable to Pin 1 on the drive during drive installation. With some cables, no specific color is used on this edge, but printing on the cable will tell you which side to orient to Pin 1 during installation.

SCSI Drives

Just as with ATA/IDE drives, you need to be aware of certain hardware details when working with SCSI drives. These details include drive ID assignment, proper SCSI termination, and the many types of SCSI cables.

SCSI Drive ID Assignment

Each SCSI drive installed to a daisy chain in a SCSI implementation needs to have a unique ID number assigned to it as a means of differentiating it from all other devices in the chain. Yet the ID serves to do more: Its number assignment also sets the priority of the drive in relationship to the other drives on the daisy chain.

In the previous chapter, you learned that different SCSI specifications allow a set number of devices to be installed, usually 7 or 15. However, the actual number of devices is truly 8 or 16, because the SCSI controller counts as a device on the chain and gets the ID assignment of 7 or 15 (the higher the ID number, the greater the priority), which is the highest priority. That leaves you with 7 or 15 other SCSI devices that can be added, each with a unique ID. The lowest priority number that can be set is 0.

How this ID is set depends on the device type itself. (Check the documentation for your device to determine how its ID is set.) The following two rules generally determine how the ID is set:

■ Internal SCSI devices have their IDs set typically through jumpers at the rear of the device.

■ External SCSI devices usually have rotary switches that can be set.

Yet some devices allow the setting of the device ID through software alone. This implementation, known as *SCSI Configured Automatically* (SCAM), is part of Plug-and-Play and makes it easier to configure hardware settings without touching the hardware itself. Often, this software, if it's available for the product, is included with the device itself; it might also be part of your SCSI controller setup utility. (Again, check your documentation because specifics vary from product to product.)

> **Exam Tip**   SCAM or software configuration of devices must be supported both by the devices and the SCSI controller in order to use this method. Check the documentation for each device, including the controller, to see whether the device supports this method.

SCSI Termination

Termination, as the name implies, allows the system to determine the last or final device connected in a chain of SCSI devices. Such termination is usually accomplished either through the positioning of a switch on the device or through the proper insertion of a resistor module into an open port on the device.

By default, a new SCSI controller typically is terminated before anything is installed on it. As SCSI devices are then added to the system, that termination moves out to the last device in the chain (and the termination on the controller itself is removed in the process). When both internal and external SCSI devices are added, the final devices in each chain must be terminated.

> **Warning**   Without proper termination, the SCSI configuration might not work properly or at all. Also, when both internal and external SCSI devices are used, termination is removed from the adapter.

SCSI Drive Cables

Don't assume just any SCSI cable is the one you need to use. If you do, the devices you're installing to SCSI either might not perform as they should or might not fit or work at all. You might also see a fast drive turned into a slow-access drive. For example, SCSI cables designed to work with older specifications won't uphold the signal integrity needed for Ultra2 and later SCSI devices.

There are different SCSI cables to work with different SCSI implementations. These implementations include:

- SCSI-1 vs. SCSI-2 vs. SCSI-3 (and so forth)

- Micro vs. regular vs. high density

- Narrow vs. wide

- Internal use vs. external use

- Regular flat vs. twisted pair that is fairly flat (sometimes called Twist-n-Flat)

- Those implementations using male Centronics (50-pin) connectors vs. those with DB-25 connectors

- The very long (120 feet or more) and the very short (3 feet)

- The preterminated and the nonterminated

When acquiring cable to perform a SCSI implementation, check the documentation for both the controller you're using as well as the devices you need to add. Then examine the length of cable required for the installation you'll perform, particularly for external SCSI devices.

Note   Special adapters exist to permit you to adapt a connector using one set number of pins to fit one that uses fewer pins (for example, an 80-pin-to-68-pin adapter).

PROFILE: RAID Essentials

Redundant array of independent disks (RAID) is a drive subsystem typically seen in commercial or professional environments where computer services need to keep working if a primary drive goes down. This methodology is referred to as fault tolerance because it allows normal operations to continue even in the event of a serious hardware failure such as a dead drive. While this technology was originally used only on servers with large file collection units, it's seen more and more in smaller operations because of the low cost of drives and the extra protection it offers.

RAID implementation spans the range from systems that have two or more drives (although four or more is most common) to stand-alone RAID units that house the drives themselves and offer uninterruptible power supplies (UPS) and copious amounts of high-speed caches. In a setup with two or more drives, each additional drive mirrors the data and services run from the primary drive. RAID can also be implemented simply through software by mirroring the contents of one or more drives to other drives, but this approach is less failsafe.

Even a basic PC can be transformed into a RAID workstation. To do this, you need the following items:

- A RAID controller installed to the motherboard (usually through a PCI slot)

- The correct number of either SCSI or ATA/IDE drives for the implementation desired (at least two)

- A good capacity UPS is also strongly advised.

USB/IEEE 1394 Drives

Because both USB and IEEE 1394 allow for multiple devices (127 and 63 devices, respectively), installing multiple drives simply requires enough ports or hubs to handle the number of devices that need to be installed at any one time, along with the proper cables needed to attach them. Part of the beauty with such drives is that you can readily swap drives—one for another—with the PC in operation. Thus, you install multiple USB/IEEE 1394 drives, but you keep only one or two plugged into their respective ports at any given time. Another grand feature is that they can be easily moved back and forth between desktop PC and mobile PC as one of the methods of sharing files between them.

Hard-Drive Installation

Installing a hard drive is not difficult work, but it can be very painstaking. This is particularly true when you're juggling other, existing drives into the mix, which is often the case. In such cases, you might need to reconfigure, through jumpering or modifying device ID assignment or recabling, the existing drives as well as install and configure the new drive.

Because the steps involved in handling each major type of drive vary, you'll examine each process one at a time, by interface. Then you'll be ready to prepare the drive for use beyond physical installation.

Proper Handling

Because of a hard drive's packaging, some people tend to treat it less carefully than they do other PC components. That is not wise because hard drives, too, can be damaged rather easily. External drives tend to be a bit more tolerant of abuse than internal drives, but all should be treated with care because what they contain—an operating system and essential data—is precious. Although the drives are relatively inexpensive to replace, their data usually is not.

To avoid damaging a drive, you should take the following precautions:

- Never drop a drive or allow it to fall.

- Do not stack drives on top of one another so that they make contact, even when in their antistatic bags.

- Do not permit an internal drive to sit on any kind of surface for any period of time.

- Where possible, do not place drives upside down or on their sides (although some PC cases do limit you to side-mounting).

■ Never install a drive that has been subjected to below normal temperatures until the drive has had several hours to acclimate (because condensation can occur, although it's rare unless you've tried to open the drive).

■ Do not attempt to open the drive housing or use hardware tools on the drive (because doing so invalidates the warranty and often damages the electronics and platters within).

■ Always properly secure the drive in its drive mounting (if it's an internal drive).

Installing ATA/IDE Drives

When you first acquire the hard drive you'll install, remove it temporarily from its packaging. Check the label to be sure it's the model you intended to install and that it's of the right type for the job. Be sure the unit does not appear to have any damage, such as dents to the housing or broken pins at the rear of the drive.

Look to see whether a cable is included with the drive. If one is not, you must obtain the proper cable—usually either a 40-pin or 80-pin ATA drive ribbon cable—to proceed (unless you're adding a second drive to an existing drive that has an available drive connector).

Return the drive to its proper packaging, and locate the instructions for drive installation. If no instructions are present, attempt to reach the drive manufacturer's Web site to locate them. They are usually found under the Product Support section, where you might be prompted to supply an exact drive model number. Specifically, look for instructions on which jumper or jumpers need to be set for the type of drive installation you are performing: a master, a subordinate, or a stand-alone drive. Also look for troubleshooting or other notes that indicate what to do if the BIOS cannot automatically detect the drive once it's installed.

Exam Tip Seagate, Maxtor, IBM, Western Digital, and virtually all the major drive manufacturers—regardless of the interface (ATA, SCSI, and so on)—have good online resources in this regard and you should avail yourself of them. You can learn an incredible amount of information and quickly advance your troubleshooting skills by taking the time to peruse Frequently Asked Questions (FAQ) lists, troubleshooting sections, and product specifications sections. Message boards or Web discussion areas can also provide you with a great deal of background information.

If you're planning to replace an operational drive with a new drive in this operation, be sure any essential or unique data that needs to be maintained from the drive you're replacing is backed up or otherwise copied to a writeable CD, DVD, or other media. When you've done that, follow these steps:

1. Shut down the PC, disconnect it from power, remove the PC cover, and ground yourself.

2. If you are replacing one drive with another, note the current connections. Then remove each of these connections by firmly but gently pulling each from the back of the drive. Then locate the drive screws (usually four or six of them) or retainers securing the existing drive in its mounting in the drive bay and remove them. (See Figure 14-7.) Pull the drive from its drive bay, and place it in its original packing or in an available antistatic bag, which you'll then label with drive information (including whether this drive is working or not).

Figure 14-7   Removing the screws or retainers holding the drive into its mounting in the drive bay

3. Remove the new drive from its packaging again, and placing it on its antistatic bag, apply the shunt to the correct two pins as outlined in the drive documentation for the type of installation (master, subordinate, or stand-alone) you are performing. Once completed, double-check the jumpering against that documentation.

4. Slide the drive into the drive bay, and secure it in place with the available screws or other retainers. The drive should sit evenly and firmly in its mounting without any slack or tilt.

5. Install the ribbon cable so that the color-coded or printed edge of the cable is aligned with Pin 1 at the right of the drive connection. Connect the other end or ends of the cable to either the IDE channel controller connection on the motherboard (as shown in Figure 14-8) or to another drive (hard drive, CD, or DVD) in place to work from this same IDE channel controller, depending on the type of setup you are performing.

Figure 14-8   Making sure the drive cable is firmly seated in one of the two IDE channel controller connectors on the motherboard

6. Locate the power connector you removed in step 2 (if you replaced an existing drive) or one of the proper fit for the power connection on the back of the drive. Plug it in. Be sure it is firmly and fully seated. (See Figure 14-9.)

Figure 14-9   Seating the power connector from the power supply into its connection at the back of the drive

7. Double-check your installation, and be sure all drives are properly connected. (See Figure 14-10.)

Figure 14-10   All connections should be made properly

8.   With the cover replaced, reconnect power to the PC and turn it on.

9.   Enter CMOS Setup, and under the Main information screen, try to determine whether the drive is seen. Select the drive letter for this drive, and select Auto Detect.

The final step might take some time as the BIOS checks the drive to try to read the information contained on the drive controller to permit it to be automatically detected and confirmed as installed by the system. If the drive is successfully detected and the appropriate information appears listed for the drive, you're ready to proceed with drive-prepping.

However, if the drive fails auto detection, refer to your documentation or the manufacturer's Web site for specific details on how to proceed. As indicated before, you might need drive management software, a drive overlay, a BIOS update, or other measures to get the drive successfully recognized. You might also be able to provide specific configuration information for the drive (such as the type of drive by number and the number of heads or cylinders) to get the drive to be recognized and operational. This information can be obtained from the drive manufacturer through an option called User Defined, which is found under the drive information in CMOS Setup.

Installing SCSI Drives

Inspect the drive or drives you'll install, and review the included documentation as indicated in the "Installing ATA/IDE Drives" section. It is especially important that you check the documentation relating to the proper setting of the device ID and termination of the final device in the chain. Specifics can vary among drive manufacturers.

Do you know whether a SCSI controller is already present in the PC where you will install the SCSI drives? This information should be available under Drive Controllers in Device Manager. If no SCSI controller is present, obtain and install one using the instructions provided in Chapter 13.

Make sure you have the appropriate SCSI cable available for the type of SCSI specification you are using or that you have adapters to fit one type of pin connector to another. Sometimes these are included with drive purchases, and sometimes they're not.

Next, determine the order of the drives as you want to install them, taking into account any existing SCSI drives that must be integrated into the SCSI setup with the new drives. Again, typically your fastest drive should be the first in the chain.

The following steps assume that you are installing an internal SCSI drive:

1. Shut down the PC, disconnect it from power, remove the cover, and ground yourself.

2. Look closely within the PC at the drive bays to see where to position the new drive, determine what SCSI devices are already present, and locate the SCSI controller in the PCI slot.

3. Determine the device ID for each of the existing SCSI devices. Depending on the way each device sets its device ID, it might be necessary to remove existing devices from their mounting (by unplugging them from the SCSI controller and cable and removing the screw or retainer holding them in their drive bays). Unless your controller and all your devices support SCAM (a software-based device ID setting), you might have to remove all the devices to modify their device ID order anyway. Do this now. Restore any drives to their bays that you want to keep in the machine.

4. Using the instructions with the drive, set the device ID for the drive you are installing. Remember to be careful that no two devices on the same chain are assigned the same ID.

5. Slide the new drive into the available drive bay, and secure it in place with the provided screw or other retainer so that it is firmly and securely mounted. Do not over-tighten the screws.

6. Reconnect the SCSI cable running from the controller to each SCSI device.

7. Using information found in the instructions for the controller or the last device in the chain, properly terminate the last device.

8. Double-check your work to be sure all connections are in place and properly made.

9. Replace the case cover, reconnect power to the PC, and turn it on. This needs to be done with a boot or startup disk or bootable disk created when you installed the SCSI host controller.

Unlike ATA/IDE drives that must be detected by the BIOS and will appear in CMOS, SCSI drives are detected and controlled through the SCSI controller. Some controllers have you create a boot disk, which then helps you install other SCSI devices, such as a hard drive or for running the SCSI controller setup utility. Please check your documentation for details.

If, instead, you're installing a chain of external SCSI devices, you need to follow the same basic process (minus the removal and insertion of drives into the PC case drive bays). This basic process includes device ID assignment and termination, and installation of the external SCSI cable to the SCSI controller inside the PC.

Installing USB/IEEE 1394 Drives

You can put your screwdriver away now because you're about to enter the usually very easy world of USB and IEEE 1394 drive installations.

Inspect the unit you're about to install and be sure it's free of obvious damage and that it's the exact model you expected. Then make sure you have the proper cable for the exact type of drive and that the cable is of a proper length to reach the port (or hub) from the location where the external drive will sit. Finally, review the instructions with the drive to ensure proper installation. There are some differences between units, and you should follow any extra steps not spelled out here.

Then with the PC on and loaded in Windows (such as Windows 95 OSR2 and later for USB, and Windows 2000 for IEEE 1394), perform the following steps:

1. Plug the drive into a power source, such as an outlet or a surge suppressor.

2. Attach the cable to the drive and then connect it to the proper port (IEEE 1394 or USB) on the PC (or USB hub).

Windows should immediately detect that a USB or IEEE 1394 drive has been installed and begin the operating system installation process. Have the drive disk software ready to load specific drivers for the device.

Unlike the other types of drives discussed, USB and IEEE 1394 drives usually provide software that you run to configure the drive and prepare it for use, such as to create or adjust drive partitions. Check your documentation and any disks provided with the product for details. Then run the setup utility and follow directions to configure it as desired.

Once installed, the drive should be visible from the listed drives under My Computer as well as from the list that appears under Disk Drives in Device Manager. A special entry might also be listed for it under USB Controllers in Device Manager.

Understand that when you remove the drive, as you can at any time, support for the device remains so that you can attach it again and use it as a recognized device without the need to reinstall the drive itself. In Windows XP and later, you can use the Safely Remove Hardware option, usually available in the System Tray, to remove the drive from use.

Drive Prepping

Hard drives fall into two other major categories: drives used to boot the PC or one of multiple operating systems on that PC, and drives used as storage only, without a bootable operating system installed. Each category is prepared for use a bit differently. Ultimately, a bootable hard drive will have an operating system installed to it while the non-bootable one will not.

But before a newly added hard drive can be used for data or have an operating system installed to it, the drive must be partitioned and formatted. For example, when an operating system is needed on the drive, a primary disk partition must be created and the drive must be formatted for use before the operating system can be used. The PC is booted for this process using a startup or boot disk.

An exception to this process, to some degree, occurs with Windows XP (although it was technically available as early as the mid-1990s with Windows NT), where you can partition and format a drive as part of the installation of the operating system from its install CD. If you're working with this version of Windows, jump right to the "Using Windows XP" section later in this chapter.

Partitioning

Earlier in this chapter, you learned that partitions are a way to divide up the capacity of a physical hard drive into smaller logical drives. You can, for example, use partitions to turn a single 74-GB drive into three (3) logical drives of nearly 25 GB each. As you learned in Chapter 2, "The Operating System's Role in Hardware," you can run multiple operating systems on the same PC if you install different operating systems on either of the different physical drives (which is often the preferred method because a drive failure can't then take out all your operating systems) or to different partitions on a single hard drive.

Partitioning can be done either through FDISK, the DOS-based utility that ships with Windows, or through a third-party utility such as PowerQuest PartitionMagic (*http://www.powerquest.com*). (You'll see references to Symantec on the site because Symantec acquired PowerQuest in 2003.) There is a large difference between FDISK and a program like PartitionMagic (which isn't true of all third-party disk partition utilities) besides the fact that FDISK is freely available to you as a Windows user. The process of partitioning a hard drive under FDISK can be a destructive process for existing partitions, meaning that any data already contained on the drive is wiped away for all normal purposes, unless you create a new partition with the intent of leaving the existing partition in place. (Drive-recovery experts might be able to retrieve it, but that's relatively hard to accomplish outside of superior expertise and special tools.) With a blank drive, such as you have with a newly acquired hard drive, this is no problem because there is nothing to lose. However, if you need to repartition or re-create a partition or resize it, you'll lose anything you haven't backed up to other media. This is one of the reasons a good backup routine is included in the comprehensive toolkit discussed in Chapter 3, "Defining Your Tech Toolkit."

PartitionMagic, by comparison, usually preserves the contents of a drive and allows you to change drive partitions after the fact, typically without the loss of the contents. It also offers a bit more flexibility in other areas.

However, because FDISK is the tool available to you as a Windows user, let's see the process for partitioning a drive using this utility. Have a boot or startup disk containing the FDISK command available. On some screens you'll work with, you'll see a number of options. Where you're instructed to accept the default, do so to use the procedure exactly as outlined.

To create a primary partition on a new drive as a master bootable drive, perform the following steps (optional steps for creating logical DOS drives with an extended DOS partition are also included):

1. With the startup or boot disk in the floppy drive, restart the PC.

2. At the command prompt, type **FDISK**.

3. You will be asked, "Do you wish to enable large disk support (Y/N)?" The default is Y; press Enter to accept it. You'll want large disk support or your partition size will be severely limited.

4. From the FDISK Options menu, press Enter to accept the default, Create DOS Partition Or Logical DOS Drive.

5. From the Create DOS Partition or Logical DOS Drive menu, press Enter to accept the default, Create Primary DOS Partition.

6. You will be asked, "Do you want to use the maximum available size for a primary DOS partition and make the partition active (Y/N)?" If you want to use the total capacity of the drive for the new primary partition, go to step 16. If you don't, press N.

7. Enter partition size in Mbytes or percent of disk space (%) to create a primary DOS partition, and then press Enter. The partition size should be at least 3 GB to accommodate the operating system and any service packs/updates. Press Esc to return to FDISK Options.

8. If you do not want to create a logical DOS drive in the extended DOS partition, go to step 14.

9. To create a logical DOS drive, you must first create an extended DOS partition. Press Enter to accept the default, Create DOS Partition Or Logical DOS Drive.

10. Press 2 to create the extended DOS partition, and then press Enter.

11. Enter partition size in Mbytes or percent of disk space (%) to create an extended DOS partition, and then press Enter. You may use any or all available disk space for the Extended DOS Partition, but keep in mind that you can only have up to one extended DOS partition per physical disk. Press Esc to continue.

12. Enter logical drive size in Mbytes or percent of disk space (%), and then press Enter. You may use any or all available disk space for the logical DOS drive. Repeat this step for each logical DOS drive you want to create (up to letter Z, or until all available disk space is used). Press Esc to return to FDISK Options.

You may have noticed a message that said, "WARNING! No partitions are set active—disk 1 is not startable unless a partition is set active." You must perform the next step to make your new primary partition active.

13. Press 2 to set the active partition.

14. Enter the number of the partition you want to make active, press Enter. Press Esc to return to FDISK Options, and skip to step 16.

15. You will be asked, "Do you want to use the maximum available size for a Primary DOS Partition and make the partition active (Y/N)?" Press Enter to accept.

16. Press Esc to exit FDISK.

Formatting

Although formatting was also touched upon earlier in this chapter, it's an important topic worthy of further discussion. Remember that there are two main types of formatting:

■ Low-level formatting, which builds the actual structure of the tracks and sectors on the drive and is typically performed by the manufacturer of the drive.

■ High-level formatting, which is a process that constructs the file structure itself into the drive tracks, including the building of the file allocation table or FAT that serves as a sort of library master card index of the data stored on the drive, sector by sector. This formatting is the type you typically perform as part of the drive-prepping procedure.

The FORMAT command, a DOS file available with Windows, is the most common way to perform high-level formatting. Without formatting, your drive won't be ready to accept files that must be installed to it.

You will find, however, that some drive management software packaged with hard drives will—usually as part of a drive overlay program that allows an older BIOS to work with a larger drive—perform both the partitioning and formatting processes for you as part of the procedure to try to get the drive up and running.

Should you encounter a situation where you find the hard drive will not properly be detected by BIOS or work at full capacity unless you install the drive management software, you might want to check the drive software publisher's Web site. You probably should acquaint yourself with the details of what the management software does before you commit to the use of such an overlay. Doing so is a good idea because if you have a problem with the drive later on, you might have more difficulty troubleshooting the issue without such knowledge.

Each partition you created needs to be formatted. Follow these steps:

1. If the system isn't already at the command prompt, restart the PC with a boot or startup disk in the proper drive. Once you are at the command prompt, do the following:

   ❑ To format a master boot disk, type **FORMAT [*drive letter*]: /s**. Then press Enter.

   ❑ To format other, nonboot drives, type **FORMAT [*drive letter*]:**.

2. When asked whether you want to proceed, verify the drive letter, type **Y**, and press Enter.

3. You are then prompted to provide a volume label for the drive. Type a label (limited to 11 characters) and press Enter, or simply press Enter to leave the volume label blank.

4. Finally, you should be asked whether you want to format another drive. If you do, select Yes and proceed to step 5. Otherwise, select No to end the procedure.

5. Type **FORMAT [*drive letter*]:** and press Enter to format any additional drives.

Your drives should now be ready to accept an operating system or to store data.

Exam Tip   The Microsoft Knowledge Base contains an excellent summary of using the FDISK and FORMAT commands to prepare drives. You can either visit the Knowledge Base at *http://search.support.microsoft.com*,   select   the   Knowledge Base, and then search for article Q255867, or visit this page: *http://support.go.microsoft.akadns.net/default.aspx?scid=http:// support.go.microsoft.akadns.net:80/support/kb/articles/Q255/ 8/67.ASP&NoWebContent=1*.

Using Windows XP

If you've installed a new hard drive and have Windows XP, the Windows XP install CD can be used to boot the system and to perform at least part of the drive preparation for you. The caveat here is that the CD can partition the drive regardless of what you intend to do with the drive, but you must install Windows XP if you want it to format the new drive as well.

To use Windows XP to handle the work, your system must be set to boot from the CD or DVD drive, whichever you'll use to run the install CD. If the system is not already configured to do this, you can enter CMOS Setup under drive or bootup specifics and set the CD or DVD drive as a boot drive. Save your changes when you exit CMOS, but remember to change this setting back later if you normally do not want the system to try to boot from the CD or DVD drive. Then complete the following steps:

1. With the Windows XP install CD present in the target CD or DVD drive that the system will boot from, restart the PC.

2. When you reach the Welcome To Setup screen, press Enter, and then press the F8 key to accept the licensing agreement (after you read it, of course).

3. If Windows XP is already installed to one of the other drives on the system, Setup will detect this and ask whether you want to repair the installation. Press Esc to refuse the repair offer.

4. A screen then appears listing all physical hard drives and both the partitioned and unpartitioned spaces available under each. Use your arrow keys to select an area to partition, and then press the C key to create a partition. (If you want to create a new partition by deleting an existing one on an already-present drive, you must delete it first.)

5. You are then prompted to provide the size in megabytes for the partition you want to create. Press Enter. (If you simply press Enter, Windows XP will create a partition of the maximum size specified.) If you need to create additional partitions, repeat step 4.

6. To install Windows XP, use your arrow keys again to select the partition on which you want to install it, and press Enter. If you do not want to install Windows XP, press the F3 key twice to exit Setup. Choosing this option means that you must use another tool, such as the FORMAT command, to format the partitions you have created on the new drive.

7.   You are next asked which file system should be applied during the formatting process. Choose the one you want to use, and press Enter.

8.   Once the formatting and installation of the file system is complete, simply follow on-screen instructions to continue the Windows XP installation.

Maintenance and Repair

You learned early in this chapter that you should not open the casing of a hard drive. That means you'll find that most of the maintenance and repair is done either through disk utility software, including System Tools in Windows, or by verifying the drive configuration (which includes jumpers, device ID assignment, device ID termination, CMOS Setup, or setup through the drive or controller's setup/configuration utility) and cable connecting a drive to the system.

Beyond that, there are overall drive maintenance measures you can take to ensure your drive has a long life and is kept relatively free of issues that would cause it to become far slower or more congested or to wear more quickly. These measures include the following:

■   Monitoring conditions so that drives do not operate beyond their normal temperature range

■   Maintaining overall good system health and using an uninterruptible power supply

■   Regularly backing up essential data on a drive to protect it in the event of a drive loss

■   Removing unneeded files from the drive

■   Optimizing the drive to reduce or eliminate disk fragmentation

■   Checking the drive for problems and addressing them before they grow larger. (Do not treat an internal hard disk like an easily removable external because internal drives can be far more sensitive to damage and were designed mostly just to be installed and sit in place.)

Now let's look at some of the Windows-included tools that can help with cleaning, optimizing, and checking a drive.

Use System Tools

While professional versions of Windows (Windows NT and Windows 2000) did not begin regularly including disk tools until the release of Windows XP Professional Edition in 2001, consumer versions since Windows 98 have regularly included a section named System Tools (under Programs, Accessories from the Start menu) designed to cover the jobs of cleaning unnecessary data (such as temporarily files, old downloads, and offline Web pages), optimizing the drive by removing file fragmentation, and disk checking. (See Figure 14-11.) These tools should be run regularly—the exact schedule of which is often best determined by how often a machine is used or abused. You can use Windows Schedule Task to perform maintenance routines once a day, once a week, or once a month, as needed.

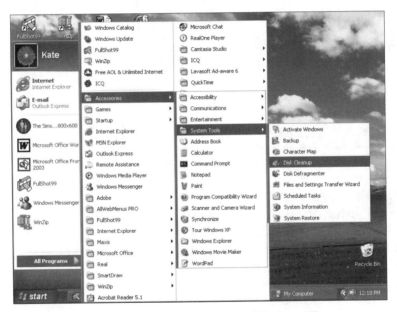

Figure 14-11   The System Tools menu under Windows XP

Disk Cleanup allows the system to remove what it judges to be unnecessary files, pending your review.

Scan Disk performs an integrity check (either surface or deep, depending on which you select) and tries to repair spot problems. Professional versions of Windows—like the one shown in Figure 14-11—do not support ScanDisk; instead, you can use a command called CHKDSK to check a drive for problems and attempt to repair them. In Windows XP, the CHKDSK command is available from Recovery Console.

Disk Defragmenter (shown in Figure 14-12) tries to better organize information that has been written to the drive in something other than a clean, consecutive fashion. Badly fragmented drives can seriously impede file access time because they increase the length of time the drive spends in finding and loading files.

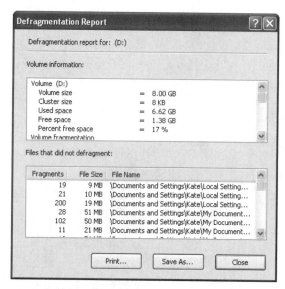

Figure 14-1 2Windows XP Disk Defragmenter utility report

Third-Party Tools

Several manufacturers and software publishers offer diagnostic and repair utilities for drives. The Symantec Norton series is the best known in the general consumer market, but you might find that your drive manufacturer ships with its drive, or makes available through its Web site, a diagnostic package that might be able to perform some repairs or at least give you a better picture of what might be wrong with the drive. Many utilities also perform regular drive maintenance, including removing old files, suggesting which infrequently used programs to uninstall, as well as performing disk scanning and optimization.

I'm not going to recommend a specific disk tool package here because I've found I'll recommend a current version only to have the next version of the same package be far less useful. It's also my experience that disk tool packages, as is the case with the music CDs we buy, often feature a few good utilities in their arsenal and many we can live without. Some utilities perform helpful services; some could destroy data if they encounter a problem they're not equipped or designed to handle. Therefore, instead of recommending a specific package, I'll provide the following list of guidelines for selecting one:

- Make sure it runs with the specific Windows version and file system you're using.

- Read the literature you can find about the package before you select it, and go through the instructions carefully once you acquire it. Disk tools should not be used without proper review.

- Ask your colleagues and friends for recommendations of utilities they prefer and ask for specific reasons (such as the exact problems the tools resolved for them) why they prefer the product.

Troubleshooting

Because drives contain a precious commodity—data—troubleshooting should be done with great care. Too many drives whose data was not irrevocably lost when the original problem developed have that data lost because of a user's steamroller approach to troubleshooting and resolution. For instance, many people race to format a drive, sometimes without backing up the data that drive contains, even when formatting will not resolve the issue (such as when the drive has bad sectors; a grinding noise; or read, seek, or write errors).

The first step in troubleshooting a problematic drive that already contains data is always to protect that data and try to remove it to a safe file location, such as to a removable drive or other backup drive, to another system, or to a file server on the network. If you can repair the drive problem and put it back into service, that's great, but everything else must take second place to protecting the data.

If the drive contains data you cannot extract or easily copy, you must determine early in the process if the data merits professional drive recovery services. These services can be expensive (sometimes costing hundreds or even thousands of dollars) and usually require that the drive has been tampered with very little from the time a problem is found until it is taken in for service. Your efforts in troubleshooting could make it less possible to recover the data on the drive.

Although some of the same issues (such as a defective drive and loose connections) can plague both newly installed drives as well as existing ones, it makes sense to divide troubleshooting into two distinct categories: troubleshooting for newly installed drives and troubleshooting for existing drives.

Troubleshooting for Newly Installed Drives

The first thing a hard drive does when the system is powered up is flash its LED indicator light. This light might go dark again for a period of time until the drive begins to fully load the operating system. If it never comes on, check the power connector at the rear of the drive. If possible, try a different connector from the power supply. Make certain it's firmly and fully seated.

When a newly installed drive fails to operate as expected, the first thing you should check was how you configured, installed, and prepared it for use. Review the appropriate sections in this chapter along with the product documentation to see whether you can discover the source of the problem. Try different cables, different drive connections from the power supply, and even different drive orders if necessary.

The drive you're trying to install might require a BIOS update or a drive overlay or management software to handle it because of the age of the BIOS. Investigate this through either the drive manufacturer or PC and motherboard manufacturer. The drive could also simply be defective, but you might want to try installing the drive to another system, properly configured, to rule this out.

If all else fails, consider removing all other drives on the controller connection so that you limit your variables to just the PC and CMOS/BIOS and the drive and its cable you're attempting to connect. Once you get the new drive detected and working, you can reconfigure it and reinstall the other drives.

You might find that with USB drives, in particular, not all drives will like being installed through a hub rather than a direct USB port on the PC itself. If you have problems installing such a drive when connected through the hub, try a direct connection instead to see if you get better results. Then you can test the drive's ability to work through another type of hub.

Exam Tip   For ATA/IDE drives, run FDISK /STATUS to verify that the system can tell there is a drive installed even if it's not automatically detected through CMOS Setup.

For Existing Drives

When troubleshooting existing drives, always start by checking connections inside the PC if the trouble appears hardware-related. A cable or connector could be loose.

Then advance in your troubleshooting by getting the answers to these key questions:

- Is the LED power indicator on? If not, the drive is either dead, not receiving power, or the LED is not connected or just not functioning.

- Is the drive spinning? Listen carefully. A spinning drive vibrates far more than an idle one. (You can still usually detect a slight vibration when a drive is idle, but that vibration is nothing compared to the vibration of a spinning one.) If the LED comes on but there is no spinning, the drive might have failed.

- Can the drive be seen through CMOS Setup or the setup utility for your SCSI controller? If not, the onboard drive electronics might have failed.

- If an ATA/IDE drive is seen in CMOS, have its settings changed? A virus or other corruption can cause this, as can a failing CMOS battery. Try to let the drive be auto-detected through CMOS again or re-enter the drive parameters under User-Defined Settings.

- If the drive runs but slowly, have you run an antivirus program along with another drive utility? If you have not, you should do so.

- Did anything change on the system—for example, something was installed or removed—since the drive last worked properly? If so, try to undo that change and re-evaluate the drive's performance.

- Is the drive making a terrible noise? If so, there is a hardware problem and the drive should be removed from service as soon as you can move the data from it.

Let's look at some other critical issues.

Corrupted File System

One of the best tell-tale signs of a corrupted file system is the presence of garbage files or directory listings on the system. These items might appear seemingly from nowhere and feature extremely long titles filled by what are typically described as "garbage" characters not normally used for file or directory names.

This situation can be caused by the use of an incompatible disk utility, certain types of computer virus infection, or a system crash in which the PC is turned off during the writing of files to disk. Even though some utilities claim to be able to repair such corruption, usually repartitioning or reformatting of the drive (or both) is required. It might or might not be possible to copy or back up files successfully from the drive to protect the data. If after reprepping the drive you see the same type of corruption reappear, this indicates one of two things: the drive itself is damaged and should be replaced, or something you've used or are using since the drive was repartitioned or formatted has reintroduced the problem.

Overheating

Once you begin to fill all the drive bays in your system, especially in a system where those drive bays are tightly packed together or where there is little circulating air around them, the likelihood increases that you'll see drive-related Read And Seek as well as other errors that come out of the blue.

If you suspect that overheating is responsible for disk-related problems, assess the internal temperature within your case, particularly around the filled drive bays. If there is an older drive you no longer use, consider removing it. Use cable ties to keep cables together and out of the way if you think they are blocking circulation. Also, although you can temporarily remove the case cover to reduce the interior temperature, you probably want to address overheating issues more proactively and permanently by installing a drive cooler or other cooling device, such as a fan, to move hot air away from the drives themselves.

Finally, if the system has been overclocked for better performance, the drives might be suffering either because of overheating or because of the configuration. Switch back to the original settings and see whether the condition improves.

Bad Sectors

Over a long period of time, many drives can develop so-called *bad sectors*, which means something has caused a problem in certain areas of the drive storage data collection and this problem has been recognized by the operating system and drive utilities. The result of bad sectors is that drive operations such as file writing or drive maintenance programs will avoid accessing those areas. Such damage can occur during serious system crashes and other cases of improper system shutdown.

A few bad sectors are no big deal. It happens, although any brand new drive reporting bad sectors should be returned and replaced. (Note, however, that some manufacturers allow up to 2 percent of the drive to contain bad sectors and pass quality assurance tests.) However, should you begin to see a drive—especially a relatively new one—develop a series of bad sectors that steadily increases, the data on that drive should be backed up or otherwise copied immediately and the drive should be replaced as quickly as possible. Drive manufacturers are actually quite good about replacing such drives, sometimes even outside the warranty period. While many drives can continue working well for even years after the development of bad sectors, bad sectors are a warning sign of drive wear and potential failure.

Losing the Master Boot Record

Viruses, disk corruption, improper installations, and other factors can create a situation where a hard drive used to boot the PC loses its master boot record (MBR). The BIOS looks for the MBR in the process of letting the system launch fully and load the operating system. If the MBR is missing or damaged, the hard drive can't boot.

The most common way to fix this situation is by using a boot or startup disk to boot the PC and then, from the command prompt, typing **FDISK /MBR**. With Windows XP, this command can be run from the Recovery Console discussed in Chapter 3. Either way it is used, this command acts to rebuild the master boot record and allow the drive to boot successfully once again.

One of our technical editors on this book raised an important point: let's say you have a large physical hard drive where two operating systems are installed, each on its own logical drive partition. If one of the operating systems is non-Windows—such as Linux—and you decide to remove it, you will not be able to boot the other (Windows) operating system until you have executed **FDISK /MBR**.

A Working Drive Is Suddenly Not Seen

Sometimes you'll find that a working drive is suddenly not seen by the BIOS or by Windows. A common and easy-to-resolve explanation for this situation is that the drive cable has either failed and needs replacement or is simply loose or disconnected. If the drive has an LED power indicator, check this. If it's not lit, be sure the connector from the power supply is firmly attached to the back of the drive. You can also try a different power supply connector.

Also consider any changes made on the system just prior to the failure. For example, if you're using a relatively low-wattage power supply and this drive seems to lose power soon after installing new equipment, the power supply might be insufficient to cover the power demands of the PC and should be replaced with one of a higher wattage. (See Chapter 9.)

Check for any drive utility that might have been packaged with the drive. Run the utility to see whether it will attempt to check the drive and report any problems it might detect.

Finally, consider that the drive might need to be replaced. Also remember that it's possible that electronics on the printed circuit board built into a drive can be replaced by the manufacturer without losing the actual data on the drive.

Increasing Drive Noise

Even very quiet hard drives make noise, but when that level of noise begins to increase, especially when it sounds as if it's grinding, you should immediately back up all data on the drive and remove the drive from service. Such noise can indicate many different things, including an impending head crash (very serious) or damaged platters or read/write heads.

Resource Conflicts

Resource conflicts can occur with drives, as well. This can result in Windows loading in Safe Mode or a drive appearing with a message that it's operating in DOS compatibility mode.

If you check Device Manager in Windows on a properly functioning ATA/IDE drive system, you should see that the primary drive controller uses IRQ 14 and the secondary controller uses IRQ 15. Is it possible you have added a new hardware device to the system that is demanding equal time on either or both of these IRQs? If so, try to determine what else is trying to use either or both of these IRQs. When you have determined what device is causing the problem, uninstall it and then reinstall it to see whether it takes a different IRQ assignment and resolves the problem.

Lab 14: Install and Configure a New Drive as a Master Boot Drive with the Operating System

This lab is intended to prepare you to configure, install, prepare, and add an operating system to a new drive. As part of this lab, you will need to make decisions on configuration based on other drives present on the system where you are performing the installation and troubleshoot any issues that arise when the installation does not go smoothly. All observations and special notes should be recorded in the lab notes following the procedure steps.

Objectives

When you complete this lab, you will be able to address the following issues:

1. Physical configuration of the drive in relation to other drives in the system

2. Installation of the drive

3. Preparing the drive for use through partitioning and formatting

4. Setting up the operating system

Necessary Equipment and Resources

The following equipment and resources are necessary for completing this lab:

1. An Internet-ready connection (preferably a high-speed connection) on a PC

2. A second PC using either all SCSI drives or all ATA/IDE drives

3. A hard drive with either a SCSI or ATA/IDE interface, with the cables and packaged software utilities needed for each and, if SCSI, a controller already installed in the system. (See the lab at the end of the previous chapter.)

4. A boot or startup disk containing FDISK and FORMAT

5. A full version of Windows (preferably Windows XP or Windows Server 2003)

6. Your PC toolkit

7. About 60 to 90 minutes to complete the lab

Procedures to Follow

1. If the system on which the new drive will be installed is up and running with Windows, check to see what the system already has installed. Start with Device Manager, and look under both Disk Drives and Drive Controllers, as well as CDs and DVDs. Document this in your lab notes.

2. Inspect the new drive, read the instructions, and record details about the new drive (such as type, manufacturer and model number, size, and interface) in your lab notes.

3. Using the information provided in this chapter, configure and install the new drive while taking into account what other drives exist. If the drive is an ATA/IDE drive, be sure to set it as a master drive. If it's a SCSI drive, be sure to set the device ID and termination. Indicate in your lab notes the exact steps you take and your results.

4. Once the new drive has been detected by the system, partition and format the drive as a boot drive. Record in your lab notes your exact actions, observations, and results.

5.   Following the instructions for the installation of the version of Windows you will use for this, run Setup from the Windows install CD and install the operating system onto the new drive. Record in your lab notes your steps, results, and any issues that arise.

Lab Notes

1.   Document the drives currently installed on the system where you will add a new drive.

_____

_____

_____

2.   Record specifics about the new drive.

_____

_____

_____

3.   Identify the steps you took to configure and install the drive, including its relation to other drives in the system.

_____

_____

_____

4.   Identify the steps, including the exact commands used, you took to partition and format the drive in preparation for use.

_____

_____

_____

5.   Record your experience, including any error messages or other issues encountered, in setting up the operating system.

_____

_____

_____

15

CD and DVD Drives

In the previous chapter, you mastered some of the tougher aspects of preparing to install a hard drive, including Integrated Device Electronics/Advanced Technology Attachment (IDE/ATA) drive jumpering and Small Computer System Interface (SCSI) device ID assignment and termination. That same information will apply here because you're working with the same interfaces as you did with hard drives.

You'll discover that there is a great deal of similarity—from the outer technical standpoint—between CD and DVD drives. Both are available as both internal and external units. They follow some of the same standards, share the same interfaces, and are installed almost identically. In addition, their overall performance, if not the details of operation, are remarkably similar. Instead, what differs is the drive's proper media and what is placed on that media.

Both are listed together under the same category of Device Manager—DVD/CD-ROM Drives. (See Figure 15-1.) They are also controlled by the interface used for attachments. This means that the ATAPI—the ATA standard for these types of drives—version will be controlled through the Primary or Secondary Controller listed under IDE ATA/ATAPI Controllers in Device Manager, the SCSI interface drives will be controlled through the installed SCSI Controller, USB and IEEE 1394 drive interfaces will be controlled through their respective bus controllers, and so on.

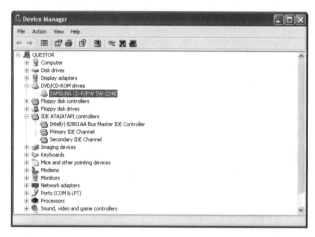

Figure 15-1   Device Manager listing for a CD-R/RW drive under DVD/
CD-ROM Drives

CD Drives

Since Sony and Phillips first offered the compact disc-read-only memory (CD-ROM) drive in 1984, it has helped provide the foundation for the evolution of both PC hardware and software. Until CDs began being widely used for distribution of software in the 1990s, we were stuck with installing from floppies; and before the price of writeable CD drives fell to mortal levels in the later 1990s, we had to write data off the main drive or drives to an assortment of floppies, tape drives, and special drives, a process that wasn't always convenient. Although advancements in DVD recording along with lowering prices make it likely that CD drives will eventually be replaced, the standard CD drive continues to play an important role in installing software and drivers, distributing formal presentations, producing recorded music CDs, and easily sharing files back and forth with others who don't have access to a network or who don't have other file transfer means.

Types

Normally, the type of CD drive you're working with is based on the format of the media used within the drive and the industry standard that applies to it. Typically, as the drive increases in features (from play to record to rewrite), it supports all the lesser standards. For example, if you buy a CD-Rewritable (RW) drive, it will not only record to rewriteable media, it will also record for one-time use only (CD-R) and will also play CD-ROMS. But not all drives always support all standards.

Table 15-1 shows the formats available.

Table 15-1   CD Drive Types

Name	Purpose
Audio CD	This is the standard format for CDs to be played in a typical consumer CD player (on computer or as part of stereo or automotive vehicle audio setup).
CD-ROM	This is the CD standard for computer-based CD play and access, although it is structurally the same as Audio CD (standard audio CDs).
CD-R	The acronym stands for CD-recordable, which means the drive can write *once* to a CD-R disc.
CD-RW	The acronym stands for CD-rewritable, which means the drive can write any number of times to CD-RW discs. This type is considered the most flexible of the CD formats because it can read standard CD-ROMs and write to CD-R discs as well.
Photo CD	This is a standard adopted by film and camera companies (and promoted by Kodak and Phillips) for the digital storage of images processed from traditional film (up to 100 35-millimeter images).
Video CD (VCD)	This is the often cheaper forerunner of DVD technology. It allows videos of up to approximately 70 to 74 minutes to be stored on CD using MPEG-1 compression format.

Interfaces

The same interfaces for connecting hard drives that were shown in the previous chapter also serve as the connections for CD and DVD drives of all types. They are also subject to the same configuration issues related to device use for ATAPI drives and device ID assignment and termination of the final device on the cable for SCSI interfaces. Such drives and their media, however, do not need to be partitioned or formatted. These interfaces include:

- IDE/ATAPI

- SCSI

- USB/IEEE 1394 (Universal Serial Bus/Institute of Electrical and Electronic Engineers)

- Parallel port

CD Drive Design

Unlike the conventional solid read heads of a hard disk or a floppy drive, a CD-ROM's read head is actually an optical lens passing from the innermost to the outermost track. The CD (or DVD) itself has one spiral track of data that encircles the disc from the innermost to the outermost circle. As the CD-ROM placed into the CD drive's tray spins, the lens reads the revolving information as it goes.

A CD-ROM itself is a polycarbonate substrate with one or more layers of metal (typically aluminum in standard CDs because it's both cheap and readily accessible, while silver and gold are often used for premium CD-R and CD-RW discs) in which the actual data are stored in binary (0s and 1s) format. Lacquer is then used to coat the surface. Different dye materials produce different colors (which is discussed later in this section).

There are two key physical differences between a CD-R and a CD. One is that a recordable CD has a dye layer where the data will be recorded that is sandwiched between the polycarbonate substrate and the reflective light layer. The other is that a recordable CD's polycarbonate substrate is manufactured with a spiral pregroove etched into it for the purpose of guiding the laser beam through the recording, which helps to measure time on the CD and control the writing process so that it produces the most accurate results.

Compared to the CD drives of more than a decade ago, today's CD-ROM drive is largely plastic. While older drives often could be repaired by a knowledgeable user, who might be able to do something like readjust or replace a nonfunctional tray, today's are often better replaced than repaired, except when the problem is a very simple issue such as a temporarily stuck tray or a dirty drive. Manufacturers might argue the point, but it's unlikely that the cheaper assembly components make for longer wearing devices. The device lifespan might matter less now, however, because advances in speed over the last few years has often made a drive obsolete before it shows signs of serious wear, and it's very possible that we'll see the CD ultimately replaced by something with more capacity. A well-cared-for CD-ROM should last far longer than its drive, in any event.

How a CD Drive Works

You already know that when you insert a CD-ROM into a drive, the drive begins to spin and the data it contains is read and made available for you to use. But let's look at a few of the specifics involved in the process:

1. The unit's infrared laser diode emits a directed beam toward the reflective mirror located in the unit's head assembly. The reflected light passes through a focusing lens to reach a specific location on the disc's surface.

2. Light is reflected back from the disc, in a measure that directly corresponds with the actual location on the disc, and that reflected light is gathered by a series of special collectors, lenses, and mirrors.

3. The light is then sent to the photodetector (PD), which is responsible for converting it into electrical energy.

When recording a CD to recordable media, the laser beam has a slightly modified responsibility: to both heat and melt the recording dye layer on the polycarbonate substrate, creating readable pits of data. A regular CD-ROM has pits, too, because some form of data has been written to it.

> **Fact**   From our perspective, the data appears as pits. From the perspective of the lens of a CD or DVD player, the data appears as bumps.

FEATURE: CD Colors

The organic dye used in a recordable CD is only one of the components making up a CD's "color." It's actually a combination of the color of the organic dye and the color of the reflective layer (gold, silver, or aluminum), which creates the typical shades of blue, green, and gold.

A great deal of debate has been waged on technical web sites and in the computing press about whether the color of CDs matters for recording purposes. In the "old" days of the technology, it might have mattered more because some CD-ROM drives had more difficulty reading CDs of a certain color. During recording itself, however, they should all behave pretty much alike, although many professionals highly recommend the use of gold-based media for best results.

But more than dye color can vary between one manufacturer's recording media and another's and ultimately affect how well they work for you and your drive. The pregroove can vary, as can the amount of dye material used and the thickness of the reflective layer. Many FAQs can be found that discuss this subject. Media Sciences offers a helpful one at *http://www.mscience.com/ faq54.html*. It discusses some of the science and debunks some of what they consider the myth of the qualitative differences in CD dye colors.

> **Note**   Materials used for the organic dye recording layer in recordable CDs include cyanine, phthalocyanine, advanced phthalocyanine, formazan, and metallized azo.

> **Fact**   Manufacturers often rate CD-R life at anywhere between 30 and 300 years.

Creating a Bootable CD

A CD that can boot the system as a boot or startup disk will require two things: a BIOS that supports the use of a CD-ROM drive as a boot drive, and a specially created CD that contains essentially the content of a boot disk stored in CD-specific format. Some CD-burning software utilities—including Adaptec Easy CD Creator, CDRWin, and Nero—have options that let you create these special CDs through their interface. Web sites such as those provided by German-based Heise Online (*http://www.heise.de/ct/Service/English.htm/99/11/206/*) and the Phoenix El-Torito Bootable CD initiative (developed by Stan Melkin and Curtis Stevens of IBM and Phoenix, respectively, and located at *http://www.phoenix.com*) spell out the manual procedure for this creation. Some Web sites even address thorny issues like what happens when Windows wants its Registry if it's not properly stored on the boot CD itself.

Drive Boot Order

There's an important detail that applies to all the drives talked about in this part of the book, and right after discussing how to create a bootable CD seems like a good time to address it. CMOS Setup allows you to designate which drive the system will look to first to try to boot the PC. In the past, this has been a floppy drive (in case you needed to boot from a boot or startup disk). Today, this might be the floppy, the primary hard drive, or a CD or DVD drive. With SCSI drives, the priority is often configured by setting the device ID, which determines drive order.

USB/IEEE 1394 by nature cannot boot drives because support for them typically loads after the operating system begins to load. You'll see this issue revisited in the discussion of input devices in Chapter 20, "Major Input Devices and Gaming Hardware," because USB-connected keyboards might not be available to allow you to press a key until the boot process is fairly well advanced.

DVD Drives

Digital versatile (or video) disc, or DVD, drives are important to PCs for two major reasons: they allow the playing of DVD movies through a PC, and they provide an incredible storage medium in the form of the discs themselves. For example, a 4.7-GB DVD general media disc is estimated to have the capacity to store the following items:

- 4700 color digital photo images

- More than a half-million standard-size documents

- Up to 14 hours of MP3 audio

- More than two hours of theatre-quality video

A disc that is double-sided and double-layered can hold more than 16 GB of data, or the equivalent of an eight-hour theatre-quality movie.

Types

DVD storage capacity, before special information and formatting take their toll, depends on the format being used. (Different drives and formats are listed in Table 15-2.) Standard DVD-ROM starts at about 4.7 GB for a single layer, single-side disc; DVD-R is 3.6 GB; and DVD-RAM is 2.66 GB.

Table 15-2 DVD Drive Types

Name	Purpose
DVD-ROM	A DVD player-only format with a standard ability to read up to a 4.7 GB disc containing video compressed using MPEG-2 high-compression, high quality format so that a full-length movie can fit in the space provided. Such drives are typically backward-compatible with CD-ROM drives, so a CD-ROM can be accessed using it.
DVD-RAM	A drive type that reads and writes in DVD format. It's randomly rewriteable up to 4.7 GB, but it's incompatible with most commercial recordings and with DVD-ROM technology.
DVD-R	A rewriteable format with storage capacity up to 4.7 GB. It's backwardly compatible with older technology, and it's compatible with some but not all commercial recordings.
DVD+RW	Rewriteable format (with a 4.7-GB maximum) that has the best compatibility with commercial recordings.
DVD-Video	Typically, this refers to the format of stand-alone home DVD players, which have more copy protection built-in than PC-based DVD-ROM players, resulting in an incompatibility between the two.

Standard DVD-ROM is available in a number of specifications, including DVD-5, DVD-9, DVD-10, and DVD–18. DVD-5 is the one just mentioned, where up to 4.7 GB of data is stored on a single layer, single-sided drive. DVD-18 represents the other end of the spectrum, offering up to 17 GB of storage on a dual-layered, double-sided disc.

Understanding DVD Regions

Both DVD drives and DVDs themselves have a region code (shown in Table 15-3) set by the manufacturer. The region code represents what part of the world (or what special venue, such as an aircraft) the drive and disc will work in. This code is included as part of the anticopying initiative to reduce pirated copying of DVD films. The theory seems to be that some areas of the world engage in far more copyright infringement by illegal copying than others, so regionalizing the globe into divisions helps prevent a bootleg copy of the movie *The Lord of the Rings: The Return of the King* that was recorded in China from being played successfully on a

DVD drive in New York City. The way this works is that a byte of data is reserved on the DVD-ROM containing the region code assignment, making it harder to defeat copy protection.

Table 15-3   DVD Regional Codes

Region Number	Area Served
1	U.S. and Canada
2	Japan and Europe
3	Southeast Asia
4	Australia and Latin America
5	Russia, Africa, and remaining parts of Asia
6	China
7	As yet undefined
8	Airplanes and other special venues

Note   If the drive manufacturer or manufacturer of the system in which the DVD drive is installed fails to set a region code, Microsoft Windows establishes one on its first boot in a system with such a drive installed.

Some hardware and software DVD decoders can be adjusted to work in various regions, while most are hard-set so that, for example, you can play only a Region 1 DVD on a Region 1 drive, decoder, and playback software. When a region of 0 is set, the DVD can be played virtually anywhere.

When you look at a DVD drive's specifications, you should see one of the following listings noted:

- **RPC Phase 1**   The region set in Windows during setup is the one used by the DVD drive, and no built-in support exists for modifying the region.

- **RPC Phase 2**   The hardware itself contains the region management support, and it allows for the region to be modified up to five times, making it more user-configurable (with limitations).

To check the region for your DVD drive, double-click the System icon in Control Panel, choose Device Manager, locate and select your DVD drive listed under CD/DVD-ROMs, choose Properties, and then click the Advanced Settings tab.

> **Note**   This information might not be available with all drives or versions of Windows. For a better understanding of how regions are established and set by manufacturers and used by Windows, you can visit the Microsoft hardware developer page for this issue at *http://www.microsoft.com/whdc/hwdev/tech/stream/DVD/DVDregion.mspx.*

> **Caution**   Reinstalling Windows does *not* reset the Registry value of your DVD region on previously installed DVD drives.

Interfaces

DVD drives use the same types of interfaces used by CD and hard drives, including:

- IDE/ATAPI
- SCSI
- USE/IEEE 1394

Because of this, they use the same types of cables as other drives using these interfaces and are subject to the same basic drive configuration, which means either jumpering for the intended purpose for ATAPI, or device ID assignment and termination for SCSI, issues discussed in detail in Chapter 14, "Hard Drives and Drive Interfaces."

How They Work

The technology and major components you learned about for CD drives basically apply again to the DVD drive. Data in the form of "bumps" (to the drive assembly) and pits (to us) is recorded into the tracks of a DVD disc, which is similar in composition to a CD with its polycarbonate substrate cover layer and metal layers below. These discs are of the same size and thickness as a CD as well.

When inserted into a DVD drive tray and the tray is closed, the disc begins to spin thanks to a drive motor that spins at roughly 200 to 500 RPM, depending on which of the concentric tracks it reads at any particular nanosecond. That reading is performed by a laser and lens assembly that zeros in on the microscopic bit of data on the layer or layers beneath the protective covering layer far more closely than does a CD player. It's able to do this because the bumps on a DVD can be much smaller. A tracking system mechanism is responsible for directing the laser beam to its precise location, moving in micron-level increments. As it directs the laser beam from the inner hub of the disc to the outer edge, the disc RPM begins to decrease to counteract the fact that the bumps are moving past the beam at increasing speed.

If the DVD drive records as well as reads and plays DVDs and CDs, it includes an even more precise but otherwise similar writing mechanism to create the bumps that contain the data and that will be read by the laser beam when played.

Issues with DVD Playing

When DVDs are to be played on a PC, it's particularly important to match the video adapter to the DVD software used for playing and the software or hardware decoder needed to decompress the MPEG-2 format that movies are stored in. A hardware decoder, such as is found with some but not all video adapters, provides more robust support than a software decoder and can make for a much more pleasing viewing experience.

Not all video adapters will play a DVD smoothly, and the result can be a badly fragmented or scrambled display. Some inexpensively implemented AGP video setups integrated into the motherboard as well as some low-powered adapters might require replacement with a video adapter that supports DVD hardware decoding for better results. Sometimes, however, the amount of problems when viewing a DVD movie can be reduced if the person watching the movie closes all other applications on the desktop, restarts the system prior to watching, or does both.

FEATURE: Recommendations for Successful CD and DVD Burning

You might find that in your work, and in the work of others you need to support, one drive or type of writeable media might not function as swiftly, flawlessly, or easily as another. The following recommendations are intended to help reduce problems when recording:

- Use proven CD/DVD writing software and drivers, avoiding betas and just-released options. Windows XP and Windows Server 2003 include the ability to write data directly to recordable drives such as these without the need to use third-party software.

- Keep the CD/DVD burner and CD/DVD media clean.

- Use the disc-at-once recording choice wherever possible, as it can minimize the chances of failure as a continuous stream of data is supplied to the CD/DVD burner's writing laser.

- Before a CD/DVD recording session, disable any utilities and background tools, including screen savers, virus scanning software (but scan your files first), disk utilities, and monitors.

- Close CPU-intensive applications.

- Use quality media, and stick with a brand you find to be reliable with your drive.

- If you typically record from contents stored on a hard disk, keep this disk clean of lost clusters and cross-linked files (by using SCANDISK or another utility) and defragmented (by using DEFRAG or Disk Defragmenter).

- For external drives, keep the unit from sustaining damage from drops, bumps, and heavy items placed on top of it.

- Where possible, avoid network connections during a burning session.

- If you live in an area prone to electrical storms or other power issues and burning CDs/DVDs is a major activity, install an uninterruptible power supply and make certain the drive, if external, is hooked into the uninterruptible power supply (UPS).

- If the system on which you typically burn CDs/DVDs is experiencing problems (such as conflicts, instability, or sluggish operation), resolve those before you try to record.

Installation

As always, inspect the new drive you're about to install and be sure it appears free of damage and is the exact type you expected to obtain. Also make certain you have the cables required to install it (which vary depending on interface type) and review the enclosed instructions in detail. For external drives, verify that you have the power connection needed because they often require a separate power source. Finally, investigate the software packaged with the drive to see what accessories you have available.

How you proceed from there depends on your interface type and whether it's external or internal. In this section, you'll learn how to install internal ATAPI and SCSI drives, as well as external USB and IEEE 1394 models. Before you do, you might find it necessary or preferable to remove an existing unit.

Removing Existing Drive

Because most such existing drives are internal, the instructions provided here are for the removal of an existing internal unit. If your drive is external, you need to perform step 1 only, and then disconnect the drive both from the USB/IEEE 1394 port and from its power supply before you move the existing drive out of place.

These are the steps:

1. In Device Manager, locate the drive you want to remove under the DVD/CD-ROM Drives category. Select it and click Remove (or for Windows XP or Windows Server 2003, right-click the drive and choose Uninstall).

2. Shut down the PC, disconnect it from power, open the case (if it is an internal drive), and ground yourself.

3. Look first at the front of the case to determine where the drive is located that you want to remove. Now follow that drive in to find the back of the correct drive, and note how it is currently connected.

4. One by one, remove the connector to the sound adapter and to the power supply, and then remove the drive cable itself.

5. Use a Phillips-head screwdriver to remove the screws holding the drive into its drive mounting. Then slide the drive out of the bay and set it aside. Later, affix a label to it indicating whether it works or not.

Installing ATAPI and SCSI Drives

Specific instructions for configuring these drives in concert with other drives of the same type used in the system are contained in Chapter 14. Please refer back to them.

Follow these steps to perform the actual physical installation:

1. Configure the new drive for use by properly setting its jumpers for IDE/ATAPI use or for device ID and termination for SCSI. (See Chapter 14 for details.)

2. Slide the drive into a free drive bay, such as the one vacated by the drive you removed. If you're using a new drive bay, you might need to take out the faceplate covering the drive bay at the front of the PC.

3. Use screws to mount the drive firmly in the drive bay. Do not overtighten.

4. Attach the CD/DVD audio connector cable (the thin wire running from the sound adapter to the proper connection (there are usually two types of audio connections) at the back of the new drive) as shown in Figure 15-2, then connect the Molex type power connector from the power supply to the drive. Next, connect the data cable to the drive. For ATAPI drives, you have two options—you can use an IDE/ATA cable for two devices if you want to daisy-chain the ATAPI drive from a master drive or you can use any IDE/ATA cable (for one or two devices) to connect directly to the IDE channel controller on the motherboard. For SCSI drives, connect the SCSI cable from the SCSI controller or from another SCSI device (if daisy-chained) to the SCSI port interface on the drive (don't forget that each device on each chain must have a unique SCSI ID).

Figure 15-2   Attached CD/DVD audio connector cable

5.   Double-check your installation, particularly with relation to other drives, and then reconnect power to the system, and turn it on.

Windows should automatically detect the new drive when it loads and finish the installation process. You might need the disk installed with the drive to complete this. If you're installing a SCSI drive, you might need to run the SCSI controller setup utility or a SCSI utility that was packed with the drive to complete this step.

Installing USB and IEEE 1394 Drives

First, be sure that USB, IEEE 1394, or both are enabled in CMOS Setup. They will already be enabled if the PC where you're installing already uses these types of devices, but they might not be enabled if this is the first USB or IEEE 1394 device you've used. Also read the instructions packed with the drive in case specific details differ from the installation steps listed here. After doing this, follow these steps:

1.   Remove the new drive from its packaging, and have any setup utility or drivers with the drive available to place in the appropriate drive.

2.   Place the drive in the location where you want it to be.

3. Plug the drive into a power source such as a wall outlet or surge suppressor. If there is a power button on the drive, turn it on.

4. With the PC up and running, connect the USB (shown in Figure 15-3) or IEEE 1394 connector from the drive to the USB or IEEE 1394 port on the PC.

Figure 15-3 Connecting the drive to the appropriate port (here, it's USB)

Windows should automatically detect the new device and begin the setup process for it. You might need to insert the driver disk for the drive at this time, or you might need to run the Setup utility for it once Windows has finished installing the foundation.

Maintenance and Repair

One of the best ways to keep a CD or DVD drive operating well is also the simplest to accomplish: don't place dirty, dusty, heavily smudged discs into the tray. Anything sitting on the surface of such a disc, including the sweat or grease from our own hands, gets introduced into the drive itself. This reduces its efficiency and causes problems reading from or, in the case of recording drives, writing to discs.

A clean, slightly damp lint-free cloth can be used to remove dust and debris. There are also specialty disc cleaners that rotate the discs while they are cleaned. Whatever method you use, be sure it is lint-free and nonabrasive or the discs will be compromised.

Clean Drive

If the lens appears dirty or you suspect it to be, you can use an applicator to gently clean the surface with CD cleaning fluid (typically sold in kits, but sometimes sold separately) or distilled water only.

Do you suspect that the moving mechanism (identifiable as a pair of guiding rails) that helps the CD be read or written to is losing its ability to move properly? The lubrication that helps it move can diminish or disappear over time and usage. Sometimes a good silicone grease can be applied (with an applicator) to the guiding rails to improve lubrication again. (This won't work in all situations, and if you use too much, you can create more problems than you solve.) Be sure to do this only after you make sure these rails are clean.

For media, most can be kept free of debris and dust if you occasionally wipe them with a soft, lint-free cloth (or special optical cleaning pads and tissues) before inserting them in the drive or returning them to a jewel case. Media not in a drive should always be encased.

Recommendations for Storing CDs and DVDs Long-Term

CD and DVD media should have a long life span, but this can happen only if they are properly cared for. The following recommendations are intended to preserve disc life and playability:

- Properly label all recorded CDs and DVDs with a waterproof marker (such as a Sharpie, which works well and is thick enough to resist fading) to reduce the chances that rewriteable media will be overwritten or that you'll toss a disc you wanted to keep.

- Store them in their proper jewel cases, and replace broken cases as soon as possible.

- Keep them away from direct sunlight.

- Keep them away from extremes of temperature (hot or cold).

- When transporting discs, observe common-sense measures such as not leaving them in a vehicle, dropping them on the floor of the vehicle, having them lie together without protective jackets, or subjecting them to other such circumstances.

- Wherever possible, make at least one additional copy of important recorded material to store in a second location. (This won't increase life span, but it gives you another copy in the event of a disaster.)

Troubleshooting by Type

If the problem is that a newly installed drive is not detected, always suspect that you've missed or misconfigured a step in installation. If you see no power light on the drive when you try to read a disc, check the power connector running from the power supply to the drive. Try another connector if one is available.

Also check for cable and device configuration. For example, if two drives on the same IDE controller channel are both configured as a slave or stand-alone drive, at least one drive won't be properly detected. The same holds true if two SCSI drives share the same device ID.

For existing drives that have been working up until this point, look in Device Manager, locate the drive, and check Properties under the General tab, as shown in Figure 15-4. Also check the IDE/ATA/ATAPI controllers to make sure they haven't been disabled or are in conflict with another device using the same interrupt requests (IRQ).

Figure 15-4   The General tab under drive Properties

If the drive begins to make excessive noise, appears to scratch more than one disc inserted into the drive, or fails to operate even when added as a test to another machine, the drive should be replaced as soon as possible.

Lab 15: Install a CD or DVD Recordable Drive and Verify Its Operation

This lab is intended to prepare you to configure, install, prepare, and add an operating system to a new drive. As part of this lab, you will need to make decisions on configuration based on other drives present on the system where you are performing the installation and troubleshoot any issues that arise when the installation does not go smoothly. All observations and special notes should be recorded in the lab notes following the procedure steps.

Objectives

When you complete this lab, you will be able to address the following issues:

1. Physical configuration of the drive, and its relation to other drives in the system

2. Installation of the drive

3. Verifying the drive's operability

4. Recording from the drive to a disc

Necessary Equipment and Resources

The following equipment and resources are necessary for completing this lab:

1. An Internet-ready connection (preferably a high-speed one) on a PC that will be used as a reference tool.

2. A second PC that either uses all SCSI drives or all ATA/IDE drives.

3. A recordable CD or DVD drive with either a SCSI or ATAPI interface (with the cables and packaged software utilities needed for each and, if SCSI, a controller already installed in the system). (See the lab at the end of Chapter 13, "Other Controller Cards.")

4. Software packaged with the recording drive. If using a DVD drive, this will be a DVD player program.

5. A blank writeable disc of the proper medium for the type of drive you install.

6. Your PC toolkit.

7. About 45 to 60 minutes to complete the lab.

Procedures to Follow

1. The system on which the new drive will be installed should be up and running with Windows. Start with Device Manager, and looking under both DVD/CD-ROM Drives (or CD/DVD Drives on some Windows versions) and IDE ATA/ATAPI Drive Controllers, as well as Disk Drives, check to see what the system already has installed. Document this in your lab notes.

2. Inspect the new drive, read the instructions, and record details about the new drive (such as type, manufacturer, and model number, size, and interface) in your lab notes.

3. Once the PC is open for the installation, recheck the presence and types of drives currently installed against what you found in Device Manager. Record this in your lab notes as an addendum to the first note you recorded for step 1.

4. Using the information provided in this chapter, configure and install the new drive while taking into account what other drives exist. If the drive is ATAPI, it will usually be jumpered as a solo device or as a slave to another drive. If the drive is a SCSI device, be sure to set the device ID and termination. Record the exact steps you took and your results in your lab notes.

5. Once the new drive has been detected by the system and appears available for use, load a compatible recorded disc into the drive and see whether it loads properly. Record your exact actions, observations, and results in your lab notes.

6. If the drive you installed is a DVD and you have a DVD movie and DVD player software available, attempt to play a movie from the DVD drive. List your results in your lab notes.

7. If you're using Windows XP or Windows Server 2003, copy some files from the My Documents or other folder and drop them in the drive letter folder for the newly installed drive to attempt to write these to disk. If you are using earlier versions of Windows, use the recording software offered with the drive you install. Record in your lab notes the steps you took, the exact software used to record (including version), and any issues that arose.

Lab Notes

1. Document the drives currently installed to the system where you will add the new drive.

_____

_____

_____

2. Record specifics about the new drive.

_____

_____

_____

3. Identify the steps you took to configure and install the drive, including its relation to other drives in the system.

    _____

    _____

    _____

4. Try to load a CD or DVD and record your results.

    _____

    _____

    _____

5. Try to play a DVD movie and record your results.

    _____

    _____

    _____

6. Record your experience—including any error messages or other issues encountered—of recording on the drive.

    _____

    _____

    _____

16

Floppy, Removable, and Backup Drives

In the final chapter of Part IV of this book, you'll learn about some other drives you might work with in a PC setup. Foremost of these drives is the venerable but outdated floppy drive, which although old and having little capacity, can still serve an important purpose beyond merely moving a few files around easily between machines.

However, there are other drives, too, including tape backup and specialty drives. These typically use the same types of interfaces you've already read about with hard drives as well as CD and DVD drives.

Floppy Drives

When personal computers were still new, floppy drives were integral to daily use because we loaded our operating system and software from them and stored our files to them. Until CD-ROM drives became commonplace in the early 1990s, floppy drives were the most common device we used for transferring files and otherwise adding files to our systems. By comparison, today you can find systems where no floppy disk drive (sometimes referred to as just FDD) is installed because it would offer so little storage space (1.44 MB before formatting).

You might wonder why this book would cover the almost-defunct floppy drive in such detail. The answer is apparent when you stop and think. How do you boot a machine when the hard drive or operating system won't load? Even though you can create a bootable CD and more recent operating systems such as Microsoft Windows XP allow you to use Recovery Console directly from the install CD, the answer is that you must boot from a floppy boot or startup disk. That's the primary reason floppy drives remain with us. Another reason they're still around is that their cost ($10 to $15 for a new floppy drive) is so low it really doesn't affect the price of a new PC.

How the Drive Works

You can understand better how a floppy disk drive works if you know about its medium: the floppy disk itself. While today's floppies are encased in plastic and feel more hard than floppy, this was not always the case. Floppies of old were very large—eight inches or more—and quite floppy.

The floppy disk itself, which is contained within the casing, is also made of plastic coated with magnetic material on either one or both sides; this serves as the recording medium. Like a hard drive, it contains tracks in the form of concentric circles with multiple sectors to each track.

When you insert a floppy disk within the floppy disk drive with the PC on, the disk it contains begins to rotate at 300 or 360 RPM, driven by a tiny motor that grabs hold of the metal hub at the disk's center assembly. The read/write heads within the drive itself begin to engage. These heads are packaged together into a single assembly and are positioned on either side of the disk itself. Another head exists to erase a sector just before data is written to it. A second motor, called a stepper motor, moves the read/write heads around the disk in precise or stepped movements. A printed circuit board at the bottom of the drive provides the drive's electronics.

Warning   Floppy disks can be damaged easily by extremes of temperature, poor handling, dirt, and being placed near a magnetic field. For example, you can erase some floppies by placing them near the speakers in a stereo setup.

How They Wear or Stop Working

Over time, floppy drives can have so much dirt and dust transferred into them that the read/write heads will no longer work. Mechanical parts within them can wear, too, making a drive unable to easily take in or eject a diskette. The cable can fail, too, or become damaged so that it no longer transfers data.

Floppies are also subject to boot sector viruses, a special type of virus that works when a diskette is left in the drive when the system is rebooted. This virus can spread to all diskettes used on that system and even affect the proper booting of the PC with or without a diskette present in the drive. Virus scans should be performed of all regularly used diskettes and any given to you by a second party for use in your machine.

PROFILE: What to Check When a Boot Disk Won't Boo tBecause the most vital job a floppy drive is usually called upon to perform is to serve as a boot drive in an emergency, in a special installation, or when partitioning and formatting a new drive, you need to know what to look for when you can't boot from a boot or startup diskette placed in the floppy drive.

First, verify the drive order established in CMOS Setup (discussed in Chapter 15, "CD and DVD Drives"). The floppy drive (drive letter A) must be on the list of bootable drives as the first drive in order to have the system automatically check for a bootable diskette in that drive when the PC starts up.

Also, you need to verify that you're using a good boot or startup diskette, as outlined in Chapter 3, "Defining Your Tech Toolkit." Having more than one boot or startup diskette copy is a smart idea. If you question the viability of the boot or startup diskette and you have another PC available to you, try the disk in that machine.

Check the physical connections to the drive as well. Both a floppy ribbon cable running from the motherboard's floppy controller to the back of the drive (and oriented so that the color-coded edge of the cable is aligned with Pin 1 on the back of drive connector) and one from the power supply to the back of the drive should be present and firmly inserted.

Finally, check the entries for both the floppy drive and the floppy drive controller in Device Manager to make certain these have not been disabled or don't show signs of conflict (indicated by a red *X* or yellow question mark).

Removable Storage Devices and Backup Drives

A *removable storage device* gets its name from the fact that the medium it writes to is easily removed from the drive device—and in some instances, the entire drive is removable—so that it can be stored at a separate location or travel with you. *Backup drive* is something of a catch-all term for any type of drive used to perform a backup of data on a primary hard drive or file storage server.

Storage devices that use Jaz and Zip media types are the two most common examples of removable storage, while many different drive devices fall under the category of backup drives, including tape drives, DVD drives (more so than CD because of their heightened storage capacity), and virtually any external drive that uses media with enough room to store data from a primary drive. A second, third, or fourth hard drive could also be pressed into service as a backup drive.

Major Categories of Removable Storage and Backup Drives

Removable storage and backup drives are defined by the type of storage recording they provide. Generally, storage recording types fall into the following three major categories (although you'll see hybrids such as magneto-optical drives):

- **Solid-state**   Storage based on various types of transistors that use no moving parts (includes FlashMemory types such as CompactFlash and SmartMedia cards). It often resembles smaller footprint, high-capacity floppy cards.

- **Magnetic**   Drives whose heads contain an electromagnet that acts by exerting magnetic influence over the iron oxide contained in the drive media (floppy disks, LS-120 SuperDisks, Zip disks, Jaz disks, tape drives, and so on). Data stored in tracks is organized into concentric rings so that the disc inside the media casing spins and the magnetic head follows this information in sequential fashion (called sequential access).

- **Optical**   A drive that uses optical technology, including an optical lens, to read the data stored on a disc (CD, CD-R, CD-RW, all types of DVDs, and MiniDisks) and that uses lasers to write data.

Fact   Sequential access technology (as opposed to random access technology, which is used by hard drives) simply means that data is written in a specific, piece-by-piece manner, and must be read the same way. For example, if you write 100 records to a sequential access drive device and you want to look at record #24, you have to go through the first 23 records to get there. Tape drives are sequential access; disk drives are random access.

Typical Interfaces Used by Removable Storage Devices and Backup Drives

Removable storage devices and backup drives use the same type of drive interfaces discussed in the previous two chapters, including:

- IDE/ATA/ATAPI
- SCSI
- USB and IEEE 1394
- Parallel

This means they'll need to be configured for use by following steps similar to the ones you've taken in the previous two chapters. They'll also need the same type of cable for each interface.

Occasionally, you'll also find specialty drives that aren't installed through one of these common interfaces. Instead, they're installed through a special adapter inserted into the expansion bus on the motherboard and are then connected by whatever cable is required for the specific type. However, not many of these types have been manufactured recently, so any you work with will likely be legacy devices from an earlier setup. Such adapter-based drives would need to be installed in the same way as any other adapter, such as the installation process for the SCSI controller discussed in Chapter 13, "Other Controller Cards."

About Specialty Drives

Over the years, a number of specialty drives with rising and waning levels of popularity have been available as well. The term *specialty drive*, as used here, refers to a drive that uses a media format that might not be readily available on most types of systems.

Probably the biggest drawback with most special drives is that they work with a proprietary medium that often can be read only by using other drives of the very same type. For example, unlike a recorded CD that should be playable on most types of CDs and DVD drives or a floppy disk that can be read in both a standard floppy drive (still included with most systems) as well as an LS-120 drive (which is like a floppy drive), a Zip disk or a Jaz disk can be read only by a Zip drive or a Jaz drive. You also can't just plug your Flash Memory card into any system: you need an interface such as a USB or IEEE 1394 port (for desktop systems) or PC Card-based reader (for laptop computers).

Thus, we differentiate between specialty drives on one hand and hard drives, floppy drives, and CD drives on the other because with specialty drives you're often using stand-alone technology. You can read and use the data you write to a specialty drive, but you might not be able to transport and read the data wherever you need to unless you take that drive with you. Portability is made easier with smaller drives and hot-swappable technology such as USB and IEEE 1394. Of course, if the same type of drive is available at the location you're traveling to, you don't need to worry about portability. The convenience of not having to carry a drive with you is a good reason to choose a specialty drive that is widely used.

But here's another related problem. When you buy a drive using a proprietary format, you have to be prepared for the potential that the drive manufacturer will strand you with a lot of unsupported product and media by either discontinuing the line or going out of business, or wholly reorganizing the company and its product.

Hybrid Drives

Hybrid drives have also become popular over the last several years. *Hybrid* means a combination of two drive types. Sometimes, the combined types are from within the same drive classification, such as drives that write to both one form of CD and at least one form of DVD media. At other times, a hybrid will combine technologies, as with magneto-optical drives.

One of the most widely available hybrid drive types today is the USB/IEEE 1394 combo drive, which uses either interface (USB or IEEE 1394) for external connection. This hybrid type is discussed briefly in Chapter 14, "Hard Drives and Drive Interfaces."

Tape Drives

Tape drives are an old but very viable standard. They've also traditionally afforded both decent capacity and economical storage. Tape drives, which are often used by many businesses and some home users, have increased in capacity over the years, edging up behind hard drives to anywhere between 4 GB and 200 GB. This isn't so bad considering that tape drives can be purchased for as little as under $100 (via discount shops both on the Web and in stores). Tape drives that can handle a network file server can rarely be found for as low as $1500, and those with even greater capacity cost more than that.

Tape drives depend on compression to fit more data into less space, and compression factors into basically all backup and storage technologies because it makes sense. If you have data you don't need to access directly on a regular basis, it's space-effective to store it in a compressed format even though doing so means it will take longer than normal to read the data (because you'll have to uncompress and restore it). Today, manufacturers offer about a two-to-one compression rate. This rate effectively doubles storage capacity and transfer rates.

Let's look at some of the common types of tape drives next.

Digital Data Storage (DDS)/Digital Audio Tape (DAT) Drives An industry standard for many people with professional backup demands who need a relatively inexpensive solution is digital data storage (DDS) tape drives. These are often referred to inaccurately as digital audio tape (DAT) drives, which represent the lower end of the technology (4-millimeter DAT as opposed to 8-millimeter DDS).

DDS and DAT drives store data to magnetic tape contained within cartridges that look like a fat card. DAT uses helical-scan cartridge technology to write data to the drive, and that means it basically uses the same write technology as videocassette recorders (VCRs). In fact, it was adapted from video recording. Old-timers will remember that in the 1980s, interface boards were sold that allowed you to back up your 10 or 20 MB (no, this is not a typo) hard disk to videotape. This concept remains with us in DDS drives.

Your old VCR doesn't use multiple passes to record a movie, and a DDS/DAT tape drive might not need more than one pass to record a full tape cartridge either. Reducing the passes means considerably less wear on the drive and medium. Some system servers and their administrators demand a storage system that uses a tape rotation scheme, and DAT works well in this situation. It might not be the fastest technology on the planet, but it works.

DDS comes in a number of formats, including the DDS-1 and DDS-2 formats meant for lower-demand customers (such as individual users, small offices, and small networks) and the DDS-4 format for professional or heavy-use environments. Each upgrade is backwardly compatible with earlier releases.

8-Millimeter Tape Alternatives Earlier in this chapter, you learned that DAT cartridges use 4-millimeter (mm) tape. But standard video cassettes, as well as another tape data type called DLT, use 8-mm tape (because video has used tape storage for far longer).

Although many of these 8-mm drives are still in use, newer technology extension has largely supplanted the 8-mm standard. These include the Exabyte Mammoth technology and the type of expanded 8-mm technology known as Advanced Intelligent Tape (AIT), which is offered by both Seagate and Sony.

Mammoth is an interesting divergence because it seeks to take some of the hardware out of the drive. Exabyte has taken this approach to prevent the hardware from wearing out and losing its calibration as a result of a large number of cartridges moving through the drive. Tape cartridges can also be coiled to different tensions after being played or rewound on other drives, and that too can affect drive performance and initiate excessive wear by preventing the hardware from operating as designed. The Mammoth also affords a special casting that helps move heat created from the moving parts away from the sensitive tape medium. (The higher the heat present, the greater the danger of medium failure and drive wear.) Indeed, Mammoth's head is rated for 35,000 hours of use, while some other manufacturers run the range from 1500 hours and up.

Mammoth-2, the second generation of Mammoth, has been available since 2000. It provides up to 60 GB of data storage (compressed from a possible maximum of 150 GB) on a single cartridge (using an improved 2.5 to 1 compression scheme known as Adaptive Lossless Data Compression, or ALDC), with a maximum transfer rate of more than 700 megabytes per minute (MBpm).

Advanced Intelligent Tape (AIT), by comparison, is more of an evolution of the 8-mm video-originated design. AIT incorporates a Memory-in-Cassette (MIC) chip, which means that flash memory is embedded in the cartridge itself. The cartridge also contains a cooling fan and a self-cleaning mechanism.

Both Mammoth-2 and AIT support and use advanced metal evaporated (AME) media, a thinner type of media that supports higher capacity storage for media that use the ALDC compression scheme noted earlier.

Digital Linear Tape (DLT) Drives   Digital linear tape (DLT)–type drives provide some of today's fastest and most expensive tape storage. These drives have a transfer rate of 2.5 megabytes per second (MBps) on the original standard 20-GB and 40-GB drives.

DLT drives underwent an overhaul as the new SuperDLT (SDLT) debuted in 2001. An ambitious but increasingly necessary initiative, SuperDLT will ultimately roll out four expected generations of expanded capacities until 2007, when it expects the technology to reach up to 1.2 terabytes (TB) on a single cartridge (or 2.4 TB before compression). It is expected to have a maximum transfer rate of over 100 MBps.

Installation

In this section, you'll learn about replacing an existing floppy drive and installing a new one. However, because the other drives discussed use the same interfaces you've dealt with in the preceding two chapters, you can refer back to those instructions for installing them. Figure 16-1 shows the back of an Integrated Device Electronics (IDE) Zip drive with its drive ribbon cable, jumpers, and connection to the power supply. This is one of the drive types I'll show you how to replace or install later in this chapter.

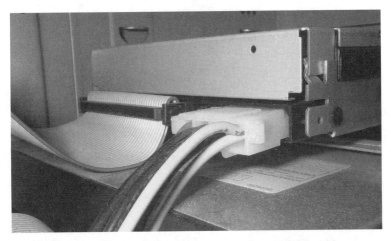

Figure 16-1   A Zip drive with connections at the rear of the drive

If you're using a proprietary adapter, install the adapter much as you have installed other components—such as a Small Computer System Interface (SCSI) controller and sound adapter—in earlier chapters, and then connect the drive as recommended in the product instructions.

Open the new drive's package, check the drive for any damage, and verify from its label that it is indeed a floppy drive. Remove the instructions and review them, and then set the new drive aside.

Removing the Existing Floppy Disk Drive

Because you'll usually need to swap one floppy drive for another, you begin by removing the existing drive to make room for its replacement. To do this, follow these steps:

1. From Device Manager, expand the category beneath Floppy Disk Drives to reveal your drive listing. Select your drive (as shown in Figure 16-2), and click Remove (or right-click Windows XP or Windows Server 2003 and choose Uninstall).

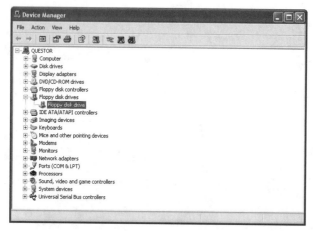

Figure 16- 2 Selecting the existing floppy drive in Device Manager

2. Shut down the PC, disconnect power, remove the cover, and ground yourself as described in Chapter 3.

3. Check the location of the floppy drive at the front of the case, and then follow it back to be sure you're working with the connections on the floppy drive itself.

4. Remove the cable connecting the motherboard to the drive and the connection from the power supply to the drive.

5. Remove the screws holding the drive in its bay, and then slide the drive out from the front of the system.

Exam Tip Replacing a floppy drive ribbon cable at the time you replace the floppy drive itself is a very smart practice. This is even smarter when the existing cable seems stiff or inflexible or appears to be showing signs of wear or damage.

Installing the Replacement Drive

Begin by reviewing the instructions that come with the new drive, and then check the existing cable running from the floppy drive controller on the motherboard that you will connect to the new drive. Replace the cable if it shows any signs of wear or damage. After doing this, follow these steps:

1. Insert the new floppy drive into the drive bay vacated by the former drive.

2. Use your Phillips-head or other appropriate screwdriver to mount the screws necessary to secure the drive in its bay and against the PC frame. (See Figure 16-3.)

Figure 16-3   Screwing the new drive into place so that it sits firmly and evenly in its mounting

3. Attach the appropriate power connector from the power supply to the back of the drive.

4. Attach the floppy drive ribbon cable to the floppy drive, and then attach the other end to the floppy drive controller on the motherboard. (See Figure 16-4 and Figure 16-5.)

Figure 16-   4 Installing the drive cable to the back of the floppy drive

Figure 16-5   Connecting the floppy drive cable to the floppy drive controller connection on the motherboard

5.   Reattach the power to the PC and turn it on. As the PC boots, check to see whether the power indicator on the drive lights up.

Maintenance and Repair

With the extremely low cost of floppy drives today, it often makes more sense to replace one than to attempt a repair. However, keeping the drive clean and making certain that diskettes inserted into it are free of dust and dirt can extend life expectancy considerably.

Other types of drives—including tape, removable and specialty drives—should be returned to the manufacturer when they fail to be recognized or fail to operate. You should also be sure to take good care of the media used in them to maintain data integrity.

Troubleshooting by Type

Because of the multitude of drives and technologies covered in this chapter, it's impossible to take you troubleshooting through all the major problems seen in each type. However, in this section, I've assembled a list of some steps to try in working with a problematic drive and some frequently encountered issues for a wide spectrum of drives.

Common Installation Problems

This troubleshooting guide addresses issues specific to drives and to the interfaces they use.

Floppy Drives

For troubleshooting floppy drives, keep in mind the following procedures:

- Check to be sure the drive has been connected properly. Have the product instructions been followed, as well as the instructions in the "Installation" section of this chapter? Double-check that this has been done.

- Try a different power connector from the power supply and a different ribbon cable.

Parallel Port–Connected Drives

For parallel port–connected drives, perform the following troubleshooting procedures:

- Check whether the drive has been properly installed to the parallel port. If it has been properly installed, try using another cable.

- If the drive has a separate power cord or power supply, check to see whether it is plugged into a viable power source.

- If the drive exists on a passthrough cable in conjunction with another parallel port device, check to see what happens when you disconnect anything other than the parallel port drive.

■   If software came with the drive to help with installation and prepare it for use, try to run it. Check any error messages you receive against the accompanying drive documentation.

■   Determine whether there is any conflict with the port in Device Manager (or under the Ports option in Control Panel).

SCSI-Connected Drives

For SCSI-connected drives, try the following troubleshooting procedures:

■   If there is no power indication, check the drive's power connection first.

■   If the drive is brand new, be sure you've removed all packing materials. (Some drives ship with special wrapping to secure the drive, and this wrapping can impede an installation if it's not removed.)

■   Check to see whether the SCSI setup terminated properly.

■   If you're using a SCSI chain, see whether you can get the drive to work in a different position in the chain.

■   Determine whether the drive is rated to work with your current SCSI host adapter. Try a different SCSI adapter, if possible.

■   Try a different cable.

■   If you have another machine you can try to install the disk to, do that. If the disk works on the second system, review your SCSI setup, including termination, cable, and power connections. Also try a different plug from the power supply.

■   See whether there is any mention of your drive or SCSI host adapter in the HARDWARE.TXT or other hardware-specific documentation related to your operating system version.

■   If software came with the drive to help with installing it and preparing it for use, be sure you run it. Check any error messages you receive against the accompanying drive documentation.

ATAPI/IDE Drives

For ATAPI/IDE drives, you can try the following troubleshooting procedures:

■   If there is no power indication, check the drive's power connection first.

■ If the drive is brand new, be sure you've removed all packing materials. (Some drives ship with special wrapping to secure the drive, and this wrapping can impede an installation if it's not removed.)

■ Be sure the drive is jumpered correctly for how it is being used (that is, as master, slave, or cable select).

■ Verify that the power connection from the power supply is firmly in place.

■ Verify that the ribbon cable is oriented correctly.

■ Consider whether your BIOS is older and in need of an update to see or work with this drive. Check with the BIOS manufacturer (or your PC manufacturer).

■ Determine whether you can force autodetection in CMOS Setup.

■ If the drive is seen in Setup but isn't usable under your operating system, check to see whether you have partitioned and formatted the disk.

■ If you have another machine you can try to install the drive to, do that. If the drive works on the second system, review the jumpering, cable, and power connections. Try using a different plug from the power supply.

■ If you can't get the drive to work as a slave off either the primary or secondary IDE controller, try installing it temporarily as the only drive on the secondary IDE controller. Once you've managed to get it recognized, you can then try to get it installed where you want.

■ If software came with the drive to help with installing it and preparing it for use, be sure to run it. Check any error messages you receive against the accompanying drive documentation.

Universal Serial Bus Drives
For universal serial bus drives, try the following troubleshooting procedures:

■ Many USB drives have an external power cord or power supply. Is yours connected to a viable outlet?

■ Check to see whether USB is enabled in your BIOS.

■ If USB is not enabled in your BIOS, check to see whether your BIOS supports the use of USB devices. Check with the manufacturer.

- Determine whether your operating system supports USB. Early Windows 95 and Windows NT 4.0 and earlier did not.

- If you have installed a USB adapter (a separate card usually installed in a PCI slot to provide USB functionality to an older motherboard), check to see whether your operating system sees the adapter.

- Check whether there are any conflicts listed in Windows Device Manager (if you're using Windows). If you don't find entries under normal drives, check to see whether they are found under the USB Controller in Device Manager.

- Check to see how many USB devices are currently in use on your system. Underpowered USB devices—or numerous devices used together—often require the addition of a powered hub. If none are in use because you have experienced problems installing USB devices before, review BIOS compatibility and determine whether your motherboard is based on the Intel LX-440 or earlier chipset, which might not have full USB implementation.

- If software came with the drive to help with installing it and preparing it for use, be sure you run it. Check any error messages you receive against the accompanying drive documentation.

- Try a different USB cable.

- If possible, try the device on another USB-capable system. If it works there, suspect the source of the problem to be the BIOS, a hardware conflict, or a USB host controller driver that might need to be updated.

IEEE 1394–Connected Drives

For IEEE 1394–connected drives, try the following troubleshooting procedures:

- If your IEEE 1394 device has a separate power cable/power supply, is it plugged into a viable power source? Is the power securely attached to the drive?

- If you're using other IEEE 1394 devices successfully, try disconnecting them and instead connecting just this drive. Do you get different results? If so, the drive isn't the problem. Instead, it's likely a cable, configuration, or power issue.

- If software came with the drive to help with installation and prepare it for use, try to run it. Check any error messages you receive against the accompanying drive documentation.

- Is your operating system IEEE 1394 compatible?

- If you're using an adapter to add IEEE 1394 capability to your system, is it recognized by your operating system and rated to work with your operating system version? Check. Are any other devices seen and used?

- If possible, try the device on another IEEE 1394–capable system. If it works there, the source of the problem is the BIOS, a hardware conflict, or an IEEE 1394 controller or software that needs to be updated.

Drives with Proprietary Adapter-Based Connections

For drives with a proprietary adapter-based connection, try the following troubleshooting procedures:

- Check to see whether the drive is rated to work with your operating system version.

- Check to see whether updated drivers are required.

- Be sure you have installed any necessary proprietary adapter according to the directions.

- If software came with the drive to help with installation and prepare it for use, try to run it. Check any error messages you receive against the accompanying drive documentation.

- Check the Device Manager for a conflict.

- Be sure your BIOS in its current form supports the use of this proprietary adapter. Check with your BIOS, motherboard, or PC manufacturer to be certain.

For Existing Drives

For a floppy drive and virtually any other type of drive listed in Device Manager, check the drive's properties under Device Manager, as shown in Figure 16-6 for the floppy drive. It's also smart to check the entry for the controller covering the drive as well.

Figure 16-6   Checking the properties of a floppy drive in Device Manager

Also consider drive behavior over a period of time: Has it been slower to write or read data or produced any noise that might indicate approaching failure? Also consider any changes made to the system just prior to the problem with the drive that might affect its ability to operate properly. If possible, try changing its connection cable and using name-brand media.

Lab 16: Replace an Existing Floppy Drive with a New One and Clean the Old Drive

This lab is intended to prepare you to clean an existing drive as well as to install and verify the installation of a new floppy drive. You will complete these tasks and verify the drive's proper operation through performance of standard disk operations, including using the drive to boot the PC as well as writing files to a blank, preformatted floppy disk. All observations and special notes should be recorded in the lab notes following the procedure steps.

Objectives

When you complete this lab, you will be able to address the following issues:

1.   Installing the drive physically

2.   Verifying the drive in CMOS Setup

3. Verifying the drive's operability

4. Cleaning a used floppy disk drive

Necessary Equipment and Resources

The following equipment and resources are necessary for completing this lab:

1. An Internet-ready connection (preferably a high-speed one) on a PC that will be used as a reference tool

2. A second PC that has a used floppy disk drive

3. A floppy drive cleaning kit (or isopropyl alcohol and long swabs with tightly wound cotton or some other material that will not stick in the drive)

4. A replacement floppy drive

5. A boot or startup disk

6. A blank formatted floppy disk

7. Your PC toolkit

8. About 30 minutes to complete the lab

Procedures to Follow

1. On the system with the existing floppy drive, prepare to clean the floppy drive by using a packaged floppy drive cleaning kit. This kit often includes a special disk that is itself treated with cleaning agents designed to clean the drive head. If necessary and no kit is available, you can take an extremely long cotton swab or applicator, apply a very small amount of isopropyl alcohol, and through the gate or opening, attempt to remove dust and debris by dragging it toward you rather than sweeping it around the drive. This operation should be performed with the PC off and disconnected from power. Let several minutes elapse before you move to step 2 if you've tried the non-kit method. Record your work and observations in your lab notes.

2. Using the instructions in the "Installation" section for replacing and installing a floppy disk drive, remove the old floppy drive and install its replacement. Document the basic steps in your lab notes.

3. Once the new drive is physically installed, restore power, turn the PC on, and check CMOS Setup to be sure it sees the new drive. Troubleshoot as needed. Note any troubleshooting measures in your lab notes.

4. When you've verified the presence of the drive under CMOS Setup, insert a boot or startup disk in the system (preferably one created for that system using its Windows version as a base), and try to boot the PC using this disk. Troubleshoot as needed, and document your results, including any troubleshooting measures, in your lab notes.

5. Restart the system normally (without the boot disk), and insert a blank, preformatted floppy disk into the drive. Attempt to copy three files to the drive to verify its full operation. Document your results in your lab notes.

Lab Notes

1. Document your cleaning process and observations.

   _____

   _____

   _____

2. Record the steps you took to replace the old drive and install the new drive.

   _____

   _____

   _____

3. What did CMOS Setup report about the new floppy drive? Document any troubleshooting measures you had to undertake.

   _____

   _____

   _____

4.   Record your results when booting from a boot or startup CD, noting any troubleshooting necessary.

_____

_____

_____

5.   Record your results when writing files to a blank floppy.

_____

_____

_____

Part V

The Peripheral Connection

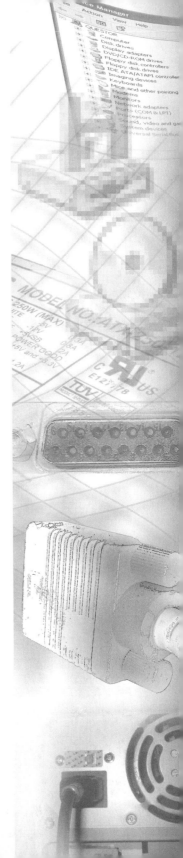

In this last major section of the book before you turn to laptop hardware and building a PC from scratch, you'll focus on the important peripherals typically attached to a desktop PC. These peripherals include the monitor; wireless setup; sound accessories such as a microphone and speakers; printers; and input devices such as keyboards, mice, scanners and cameras, and graphics tablets.

17

Monitors

Because we so often associate the word *digital* with everything connected to a PC, you might be surprised to learn that most monitors still in use today are not digital but analog. One job of the video adapter or video circuitry on the motherboard is to convert the digital PC picture into an analog form the monitor can understand and draw to the screen for us to view. However, the use of digital monitors is on the rise, with more and more people in and out of the office choosing to go with flat screens and the improved performance of digital formats as compared to analog.

Analog vs. Digital

In general, all data gets sent from one point to another (such as from a video adapter to a monitor) via electromagnetic signal, and this signal can either be analog or digital in nature. For a PC, which understands only binary code and requires all information to be transformed into such code, digital is the format. But for monitors, analog has made sense because our brains—as opposed to the brains of PCs—are designed to use the electromagnetic signal emanating from a sound or light source and perceive it properly as light and sound. We see this with standard television technology as well as with PC monitors.

Laptop and mobile displays, by comparison, are usually digital in format and much of that technology has been adapted for desktop monitor use, particularly in the form of flat-panel technology. But both monitors and televisions are on the verge of turning into all-digital equipment, where the signal that flows from the video source to the output device doesn't have to be converted into analog and can, at least ultimately, make for a more defined image and one that should be far speedier to acquire. You already see this in the form of high definition TV with all-digital tuners and in the burgeoning number of digital monitors—usually having flat-panel displays—on the market the past few years. Of course, you can have a monitor that is much less deep if you eliminate that bulky cathode-ray tube arrangement.

Major Types

In terms of technology, two basic types of monitors are in use today. These are

- Cathode-ray tube (CRT), the analog form
- Flat panel, the usually digital form, including liquid crystal display (LCD) and plasma screens

CRTs take the same basic form as televisions, while flat-panel technology comes to us from the realm of mobile devices such as laptops, which have traditionally used this method. As you'll see later under the discussions of analog and digital monitors, there are huge differences in the equipment within the two.

Another difference between the two types is that a CRT by design immediately sizes the display image from the video adapter to fix the maximum capacity of the viewing area. With flat-panel technology, this does not typically occur. Instead, the flat panel is far more precise in its strict alignment of rows and columns in the form of a matrix, and usually it fills the entire viewing area with the display only if the display resolution is set to the maximum resolution possible for that monitor. If the resolution used is smaller, the display will either appear centered in the screen or it will scale up to fit the screen, depending on the design of the monitor.

How Monitors Work

A monitor has only one function: to faithfully interpret the signal from the video adapter into the form of a display that represents whatever is taking place on the PC desktop at that moment. For all intents and purposes, all the major work in this operation is handled by the video adapter, which in turn is being fed information from the system.

Today's analog monitors are similar to a television. Both share a primary component that is the basis of an electronic screen. In the PC, this component is called a cathode-ray tube (CRT), and in a television it's known as a picture tube. Both use "guns" to regulate color distribution to the screen. Both depend on an external signal to tell them what to display.

Yet there are key differences between the two. If you try to read text on your TV set for any period of time, you should immediately see the chief difference. A monitor allows for much greater detail than today's televisions. In part, this is because a monitor allows for far more pixels and even the analog-form VGA connector splits the signals into different lines for each primary color (red, green, and blue—or RGB) and for horizontal and vertical alignment. This is one reason why if you connect your system to display through your TV instead of the monitor, it often becomes markedly more difficult to read and appreciate. Conversely, a TV signal played through a PC monitor can show a vast improvement.

The most common way to identify monitors is by their screen size. A monitor's screen size, just like a television's, is measured in inches (in the U.S.) diagonally from one top corner of the screen to its opposite lower corner. This is typically referred to as the viewable area.

Now let's review the components typically found in both analog and digital monitors. But before we do, another point should be made. Right now, a digital monitor doesn't always deliver the best picture. Users looking for high performance still often prefer the absolute crispness of an analog display to a digital one. This preference should change over time with the advancement of a new type of technology known as Organic Light-Emitting Device (OLED) for flat-panel monitors. OLED was designed to make better use of the LCD's ability to crisply display video animation.

Traditional Monitor Components

Look at a full-size analog monitor and appreciate that within that bulky case there is really no extra room. You'll see why when you explore its components. It's the presence of the CRT that requires analog monitors to be shaped so that they take up considerably more desktop space than a flat-panel screen. The CRT also requires them to consume power at between two to four times that of an LCD and about twice that of a gas-plasma display.

Cathode-Ray Tube

As the largest and most critical component of a monitor, the CRT is also the most expensive. Some have likened the CRT to a large glass jug or bottle lying on its side, in which one end (the end with the screen) is flat (or mostly flat) while the other end tapers to smaller dimensions. Air is purposely absent, for the most part, as part of the operation.

Lining the CRT is a phosphorous compound that is used because phosphor reacts to the impact of electrons (supplied by another part of the monitor) on its surface by lighting up to display a color. There is more than a small quantity of these reactions, referred to as *phosphor dots* or *stripes*. Millions are created, forming a matrix. You can see some of this with the naked eye by peering very closely at your screen. It almost looks like a fabric.

On the display, phosphor dots are grouped in quantities of three to form what is called a *pixel*. Of these three phosphors each, one will light as red, one as blue, and one as green. Red, green, and blue are primary colors. How brightly and in what combination these individual phosphors in a pixel light up determine what colors (and which of the infinite number of shades) will appear on the monitor's display. If red and blue phosphors light up in equal measure, you get a middle-of-the-road purple, for example.

Electron Guns

Most color analog monitors have three electron guns located at the back of the monitor, each charged with "shooting"—or more accurately, précising or exciting—the phosphors to create the appropriate primary color: red, green, or blue. How much they shoot and how much color will be rendered by each depends on information arriving in separate "color" streams from the video adapter supplying the data signal. The result, hopefully, will be that you have a wide range of colors, depending on what the video adapter has told the monitor to draw.

Mask

The mask is a layer of fine metal that sits between the electron guns and the phosphor layer. It is perforated in such a way as to line up with the pixels (three phosphor dots). Alternatively, it also can be a layer of minute vertical wires laid out in a striped configuration to accomplish basically the same thing. As its name implies, its job is to mask or protect the pixels from being excited by any electrons except the intended ones, with the goal of improving the image. However, the mask is a tricky matter to design and construct because you want it to be present but have to be sure it doesn't obscure too much.

Different types of masks or masklike components are implemented, depending on the manufacturer and the age of the monitor. These include the shadow mask (an older and cheaper technology) and the slotted mask (which allows better color and brightness). There is also the aperture grill, which is explained next.

Aperture Grill   The aperture grill is the Sony Trinitron standard, created as a substitute for the shadow mask. In this type of monitor, a network of minute vertical wires called *damper wires* cover the entire CRT width and are oriented around the phosphor stripes, but not as tightly as in some methods. This means that more electrons are allowed through the grill to excite the phosphors, and the result should be bright, vibrant color with less of a *pixilated* appearance. A shadowing remnant from connecting horizontal wires can sometimes be visible on the screen, however.

> **Note**   Monitors using aperture grills exhibit a behavior that can make them easy to identify. If you bump such a monitor, the image on the screen should begin to shimmer for a very short time, until the monitor can restabilize it. The aforementioned damper wires tighten the grill wires to reduce the shimmer effect.

Deflection Yoke

A deflection yoke is actually a large electromagnet positioned at the back of the monitor, situated between the electron guns and the screen. It's the mechanism of control for the electron beams shot forward to the screen. The deflection yoke helps guide the beams to the desired pixels and with the specified intensity.

Digital Monitors

Most digital monitors do away with a great deal of the heavy hardware that made old standard TVs and monitors so large. Exactly how this is done depends on the specific type of monitor and the particular technological standard it's based on.

For example, flat-panel technology has a number of standards, including digital flat panel (DFP), VESA Plug and Display, Low Voltage Differential Signal (LVDS) and its offshoot Open LDI, and Gigabit Video Interface (GVIF). All these standards are pretty much based on the Silicon Image Transition Minimized Digital Signal (TMDS) standard for signal transmission from a video source (such as an adapter) to a display device (such as a flat-panel monitor or TV). However, the Digital Video Interface (DVI) has largely replaced most earlier standards, as you'll read about in the "Video Cables and Connections" section later in this chapter.

Different types of displays are possible, too, including the plasma screen (also known as a gas-discharge display). This type was first seen on early notebooks and had an eerie orange-glowing monochrome. A plasma screen charges pixels lying along coordinates among two axis panels—one an x axis, the other a y axis—creating a glow. Field Emission Displays (FEDs) and LCDs are some of the other types of displays. Within the category of LCD, there are passive displays such as Twisted Nematic and Supertwisted Nematic and active displays, also called active matrix or TFT (thin film transistor). And finally, there are differences between the direction of the lighting source with LCD displays. For example, backlit and sidelit LCDs are best in low-light situations, while reflective displays are optimal in brightly lit rooms.

Because there is no conversion of the signal from the video adapter to the monitor (because both work with binary), there should be far less signal loss—resulting in improved video quality—between the two devices than you have with an analog monitor.

While analog monitors almost always use the Video Graphics Adapter (VGA) port to connect, digital monitors connect using any of a number of interfaces, including the following ones:

- Digital flat panel (DFP), an earlier standard that also supported USB and IEEE 1394. It's connected via 20-pin mini-D ribbon (MDR) connectors.

- Digital Video Interface (DVI), the emerging flat display standard. You'll see more about this interface in the "Video Cables and Connections" section.

- USB and IEEE 1394, the same port interface you've read about for connecting network devices and drives with many different components. A monitor with this interface type can and should be installed with the PC up and running.

- VESA Plug and Display, an early standard set by the Video Equipment Standards Association (VESA). Adapters are available to convert these connectors into ones that will connect DVI devices.

Video Cables and Connections

The cable and connector used by analog monitors is not the same as those used by digital, so you need to determine which type of monitor you're working with when installing, removing, or troubleshooting a monitor.

Analog monitors use a cable—usually referred to as the *VGA cable* because of the video standard it follows—that splits the colors red, green, and blue and both the horizontal and vertical alignment into separate lines. This 15-pin cable connects to the VGA port at the rear of the PC, as shown in Figure 17-1. With stand-alone video adapters, this cable is the connector edge of the adapter with the PC rear. On motherboards with integrated video, a VGA port is present even if the adapter is not.

Figure 17-1   The analog monitor's cable as it connects to the VGA

Digital monitors use a different cable and usually a different connector as well. The digital connection is known as the Digital Video Interface (DVI). Typically, a DVI cable is used to connect the monitor to the video adapter/VGA port at the back of the PC. DVI allows for much higher bandwidth in signal transmission and because of this, data does not have to be compressed before it is sent from the video source (adapter) to the display (monitor). However, there are three types of DVI. Which type is used between the PC and monitor matters. These types include the following:

■   DVI-A, which is used to connect analog signals

■   DVI-D, which is used for digital signals

■   DVI-I, which is an interface that blends both analog and digital

For best overall performance, a digital monitor should be connected to a DVI-D interface. This type is best because while a DVI-I interface (sometimes called a *D Sub 15*) provides support for both, it might not be a *true* DVI-D implementation. The video display might suffer as a result. However, the DVI-I interface is popular with some video adapter manufacturers because it supports the use of both analog and digital monitors. You'll find that some video adapters and video-integrated motherboards include both a VGA port and a DVI connection, rather than a DVI-I combination.

There is also something known as single-link and dual-link DVI. Single-link DVI uses just half (12) of the 24 pins available in a DVI connection, and it supports a maximum video resolution of 1920 x 1080 at 60 Hz or 1280 x 1024 at 85Hz (1 x 165 MHz). A dual-link DVI uses all 24 pins and supports a maximum video resolution of 2048 x 1536 at 60 Hz or 1920 x 1080 at 85 Hz (2 x 165 MHz). Figure 17-2 shows a representation of the different DVI interface connectors along with that for VESA Plug and Display.

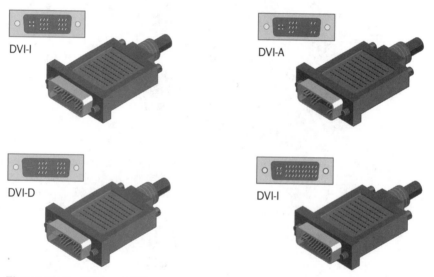

DVI-I

DVI-A

DVI-D

DVI-I

Figure 17-2   Different DVI connector types, compared with the VESA Plug and Display connector

> **Note**   For more information about digital display standards and implementation, visit the Digital Display Working Group Web site at *www.ddwg.org*.

Factors in Monitor Choice and Usage

While most monitors can be made to work with most video adapters, not all are good matches for a display you can work with. A basic monitor and basic video adapter will do the job for you if you use them primarily for Web browsing and e-mail, working on documents and office-related files, and other normal jobs. The more demanding your graphics needs (or your visual needs, if you need special options), the more apt you are to want a mid-to-higher range video adapter and a monitor with a low dot pitch, high refresh rate, and both good bandwidth and convergence (all of which are explained shortly).

The issues you should consider are the following:

- **Screen size**   The process for determining screen size was described earlier. Current systems typically come with a 17-inch screen by default. Many consumers choose to pay extra to get a 19-inch or 21-inch display. Such larger viewing areas are particularly useful for computer-aided design work, for video and image editing, and for situations where the user won't be seated directly in front of the screen.

- **Traditional vs. flat technology (also known as flat-screen technology)**   Standard monitors have a degree of curve, and with this curve, they have a tendency to reflect light. Flat technology monitors (FTM) have a flat screen, reducing reflection and glare. These monitors are not the same as *flat panel* monitors. (Flat panels are typically LCD screens that have the front-to-back width minimized.) Flat technology monitors are usually used with portable PCs and newer desktop monitors.

- **Analog vs. digital monitor**   *Analog* and *digital* refer to the type of signal the monitor accepts. (Analog is still the dominant technology—that is, more video adapters accept analog than digital.) Be sure the video adapter used supports a digital monitor. Otherwise, it might need to be replaced with one that does.

- **Resolution rate range**   *Resolution* refers to how densely the pixels are packed together, while the resolution rate range refers to the video resolutions at which a particular monitor should function well (with a compatible video card). Many of today's monitors easily start at resolutions of 1024 x 768, and go far higher (some go all the way to 2048 x 1534).

- **Dot pitch**   Dot pitch refers to the amount of room between each pixel. Greater sharpness is usually seen with a smaller dot pitch than with a larger one—for example, with a .24 dot pitch rather than a .28 dot pitch).

- **Refresh rate**   This specifies how many times per second the screen will be redrawn (also referred to as refreshed). A rate of 72 or above tends to give you a better overall display with less flickering.

- **Bandwidth**   This term refers to the range of signal frequencies the monitor is capable of handling (signifying how fast a refresh rate it displays and how much data from the system it can deal with at one time). Bandwidth is measured in Hertz (Hz) or Megahertz (MHz).

- **Convergence**   Convergence describes both the sharpness and overall clarity of each pixel displayed.

- **Interlaced vs. noninterlaced technology**   Usually, you'll want a noninterlaced monitor because interlacing is a sort of kludge to allow greater resolution to the detriment of the monitor's overall reaction speed. (It allows for less frequent refreshes, for example.)

Table 17-1   Resolution by Monitor Dimension

Resolution	15" Monitor	17" Monitor	19" Monitor	21" Monitor
640 x 480	Y	NR	N	N
800 x 600	R	Y	NR	N
1024 x 768	NR	R	Y	NR
1280 x 1024	N	NR	R	Y
1600 x 1200	N	N	Y	R
1920 x 1440	N	N	Y	R
2048 x 1536	N	N	NR	Y

Note   In Table 17-1, Y = Yes, it can be used; R = Recommended resolution; NR = Not recommended; N = No, don't use

Note   Flat technology monitors (FTMs) are a good choice in very brightly lit situations or where a user's eyes are more sensitive to reflected light. LCD displays, by comparison, are usually backlit to help sharpen the screen when viewed under low light conditions.

About Laptop Displays

While most laptop and portable PC displays use LCD technology, some also use electroluminescent display (ELD). ELD involves two plates, one coated with vertical wires and the other coated with horizontal wires. This forms a grid configuration that sits on either side of a phosphorescent film. When current passes through both a vertical and horizontal wire, the phosphorescent film layer begins to glow and is used to form a pixel.

Installation

Inspect the new monitor to determine that it is in good condition and of the desired size and model. While checking this, remove and review the instructions for installation and locate the monitor disk, which might contain monitor utilities as well as a driver for the monitor.

Also be sure that you have the correct video cable for the type of installation to be performed to the monitor connector at the back of the PC. Adapters to convert one type to another (such as a VESA Plug and Display plug to a DVI plug) are available for some products. Before you re-use an existing monitor cable, be sure it is in good shape, free of cuts, and has no bent pins.

Exam Tip   It might be necessary to obtain a driver update for the new monitor directly from the manufacturer's Web site. You should at least check this source before you begin the installation process, especially if the driver listed does not recommend your version of Microsoft Windows.

Removing an Existing Monitor

Because monitors aren't exactly optional, you'll usually need to begin the new monitor installation process by removing the existing monitor. To accomplish this, follow these steps:

1. From Device Manager, expand the Monitors section, select the monitor you intend to remove, and then click Remove or, for Windows XP or Windows Server 2003, right-click the monitor and select Uninstall. (See Figure 17-3.)

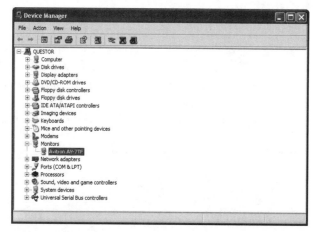

Figure 17-3   Removing the existing monitor listed under Monitors in Device Manager

2. Shut down the PC and remove the cable installed to the video connector at the back of the PC. Note, some video cables are permanently attached to a monitor and some are not.

3. Unplug the existing monitor from its power source, and move it out of the work area.

Installing a New Monitor

Unless your video adapter connection just isn't compatible with the new monitor and unless your Windows version really doesn't like the new monitor, installing a new display unit is one of the easier, faster jobs you'll perform in component replacement. To install the new monitor, follow these steps:

1. Place the replacement monitor in its new location.

2. Attach the video cable both to the monitor (if not permanently attached) and then to the video connector at the back of the PC.

3.   Plug the new monitor into a power source.

4.   Turn the PC back on.

Once Windows begins to load, it should recognize that new hardware has been installed. Windows might ask you what type of device it is and then proceed with the operating system–based installation of the new monitor. You might need to provide a disk with the proper driver if Windows doesn't automatically detect or natively support your model and type.

After Windows adds the monitor, it's important to adjust both the monitor and the Windows display settings to accommodate any changes the new monitor requires. For example, using the Advanced tab on earlier versions of Windows or the Settings tab on Windows XP and later allows you to adjust resolution and color quality. Click the Advanced button on that screen, and you see more tab options. The General tab lets you select Dots Per Inch (DPI) resolution settings, and the Monitor tab (as shown in Figure 17-4) lets you check and modify properties for the monitor. (For example, it lets you choose the Driver tab to update the monitor driver.) The Monitor tab also lets you adjust its refresh rate.

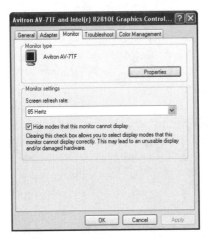

Figure 17-4   Monitor tab under Display in Control Panel

Check the front of your monitor and its instruction booklet as well. Most monitors feature a front-mounted panel or device to allow you to bring up an on-screen menu (separate from the PC) to make adjustments to alignment, appearance, and color saturation, among other features.

Maintenance and Troubleshooting

Nearly all monitor manufacturers forbid unauthorized personnel from opening the monitor case, saying that doing so will void the warranty. They have reasons for adopting such a policy.

Like a television, the monitor and all its circuitry can retain a sizable electrical charge for some time after it has been turned off. (A monitor can still be charged with as much as 10,000 volts after being disconnected from power for several weeks.) Understand that this charge is large enough to be lethal, so inside the monitor housing is really no place to go unless you're a trained professional. Yet even if you didn't have this hazard, there isn't much inside the case that most people can repair themselves. Many experienced technicians will not touch a monitor other than to check external connections and the accuracy of the controls, or to inspect it visually to diagnose a problem. Disregard any anecdotes you've heard about people repairing their monitors, and forget the "do-it-yourself" monitor repair kits you might see advertised. The bottom line: Don't even think about going inside the monitor. If your monitor is broken, just replace it.

The result is that too often today, consumers are left with two choices: sending this heavy, sensitive appliance off to the manufacturer (and not every parcel company will handle monitors) and waiting days or weeks for it to be repaired and returned, or junking it and getting another one. Once monitor prices began routinely falling below $300 (often currently at or well below $100 for a 15-inch monitor and $160 and up for a 17-inch monitor), the disposal route was chosen more often. Many consumers now buy a new monitor while sending the problematic one out for repair so that they have an extra.

If you read Chapter 1, "Computer Evolution," you understand that the disposable mentality is beginning to have a serious impact on landfills as well as on adjoining water tables, where degrading metals (including lead) work their way into water supplies. Thus, it might be smarter for you to find a recycling program that will try to reclaim materials from the monitor and other PC hardware. With all this said, there are some solutions to problems with a monitor that you can try without voiding the warranty or exposing yourself to electrical shock. These possible fixes involve the following items:

- **Monitor menu**   Most monitors today have a soft menu built into them that allows you to modify the appearance of the screen (including its color, contrast, shape, move edges, and more) and adjust settings such as refresh rate. You can familiarize yourself with these options and how modifications affect the look and performance of the monitor.

- **Video cable**   The thick cable running between the monitor and the back of the PC, where the video adapter interface is located, can become damaged both externally (where you can see it) and internally (where you can't see it). Always check to be sure the video cable is securely attached to both the monitor and the PC. Also, when troubleshooting, be sure to exchange it with a known working cable.

- **Bent pins**   Display problems can occur when the pins in the interface between the video cable and the video adapter become bent so that connections become less secure or unavailable. While you might have to replace a cable with such a connection (and this is obviously more of a problem if the cable is permanently attached to the monitor), bent pins can sometimes be gently pushed back into normal position. (I use needle-nose pliers for this while exercising extreme care.) Pushing them back into position allows the signal to be conducted properly again.

- **Items that cause external interference**   Vibrating fans, malfunctioning fluorescent lights, closely positioned radios and cordless phones, or other major appliances plugged into the same circuit as the monitor can all affect performance and display. Investigate possible sources of interference when the monitor works fine on another machine but fails when returned to its original place. In fact, multiple monitors placed too close together can interfere with one another.

- **Extreme temperatures**   Like other PC components, a monitor should not be used in extremes of temperature. Make certain the monitor's vents are exposed and not covered up with papers and other such obstructing items. When a monitor is started in a very cold room or after being brought in from a cold vehicle, condensation can form as the monitor begins to heat. This condensation has the potential to short-out the circuitry.

Issues to Check

The following is a list of issues to check or investigate when experiencing a monitor-based problem:

- Check the monitor on-board controls—something might have been changed that accounts for the problem. You also might be able to correct the situation by adjusting the controls.

- Check the Windows Display options to see whether changes have been made to resolution, refresh rate, or other factors that might account for the problem you see.

- Temporarily disable power management (under the Power Management or Power Options icon in Control Panel) to the monitor to see whether this resolves the current problem. (See Figure 17-5.)

Figure 17-5   Disabling power management settings for monitor during troubleshooting

- Update the video adapter driver and then update the monitor driver to see whether this resolves the issue. If you've just updated either one, you might want to return to a previous driver version to see whether that fixes the problem.

- Determine whether anything new has been placed in the area immediately around the monitor. Some speakers and devices—including other monitors—can cause low to medium levels of interference that might show on the display.

- Determine whether the monitor has been moved recently while still connected to the system. If so, bent pins might account for the problem you see. See whether they can be bent back into place.

Lab 17: Installing and Configuring a Monitor

This lab is intended to teach you the basic steps in replacing one monitor with another and how to adjust the video setup to work properly and optimally with the new monitor.

Objectives

When you complete this lab, you will be able to address the following issues:

1. Physical installation of the monitor

2. Interaction with the video adapter and the monitor

3. Adjustment of display settings

4. Any troubleshooting needed to complete the installation

Necessary Equipment and Resources

The following equipment and resources are necessary for completing this lab:

1. An Internet-ready connection (preferably a high-speed one) on a PC that will be used as a reference tool

2. A second PC

3. A replacement monitor and the appropriate cable to connect it

4. Instructions and accompanying disk or disks for the new monitor

5. About 30 minutes to complete the lab

Procedures to Follow

1. Review the instructions and disk or disks packaged with the new monitor to familiarize yourself with the appropriate steps for installing it and troubleshooting any problems that might arise. Record anything questionable or particularly notable in your lab notes.

2. Locate the monitor manufacturer's Web site, and look for an updated driver for your monitor model and operating system. Document in your lab notes your results, as well as the specifics about the monitor you are replacing and the monitor you are installing. Also note the type of video adapter in use in the system. (This information might be available under Display Adapters in Device Manager.)

3. Following the instructions provided in the "Installation" section of this chapter coupled with the instructions provided with the monitor itself, remove the old monitor and set up the new one in its place. Note in your lab notes the connection types for both monitors and any special observations or necessary troubleshooting.

4. Once the monitor is installed, use options available under Display in Control Panel to try different resolutions and color quality, and adjust the refresh rate for the monitor. Document in your lab notes any special observations along with the optimal settings you found.

5. Using a monitor-specific control such as the on-screen menu, experiment with different options until you think you have the best results. Record the experience in your lab notes, including any special issues you witnessed.

Lab Notes

1. Document any special instructions for installing this monitor, along with what software and drivers shipped with the monitor.

   _____

   _____

   _____

2. Record information found on the manufacturer's Web site related to tips or updated drivers. Also record the type of existing and replacement monitors used for this procedure and the type of video adapter installed in the PC.

   _____

   _____

   _____

3. What type of connections did each monitor use? Also note any special information about your installation process, including troubleshooting performed.

   _____

   _____

   _____

4. Record your Control Panel/Display options and information about results when using various resolutions, color quality, and refresh rates.

    _____

    _____

    _____

5. Record your experience in using the on-screen monitor controls.

    _____

    _____

    _____

18

Going Wireless

Throughout this book, you've heard a great deal about the cables, wires, and direct connections used to attach a device to a PC. Here, however, you're going to cut the cord, so to speak, and handle devices with no point-to-point physical connection. Instead, wireless devices transmit and receive signals without wires and cables anchoring them and the humans who use them to the desktop or laptop.

One thing to consider as you read this chapter is that some of the security and other smart measures discussed within this chapter can work well with either wired or wireless networks. This chapter offers a bit more information in this regard than did Chapter 12, "Network Cards and Network Hardware."

The Wireless Revolution

The first thing that comes to most people's minds when they think of a wireless device is a cellular telephone. Indeed, the rise in popularity of this portable phone coincided with the rise in popularity of the Internet and helped lay the groundwork for the products available today.

Also, as workers are required to become ever more productive on the job, they need the flexibility to stay connected and keep working wherever they go—around the office complex, campus, city, county, country, or even the world. Cables have been the traditional way to accommodate communications, but that standard is changing rapidly.

Web-capable cell phones and personal digital assistants (PDAs) allow you to get on the Web from wherever you happen to be, as long as you're in the virtual zone, so to speak, where you can pick up a signal. However, that isn't always possible outside of major metropolitan and large suburban areas. (See the "Remote *and* Wireless" sidebar.)

Cell phones, PDAs and mini, mobile PCs (such as the PocketPC), however, access the Web differently than other devices. Because their screens and underlying display technologies aren't as robust as those of a desktop unit or even a laptop, they depend on Web sites to furnish them with their own version of Internet information. This information is delivered not in the standard Hypertext Markup Language (HTML) of the Web but in a different format called Wireless Markup Language (WML), which makes allowances for the tiny screens and the need to make menu-based selections rather than doing much data input.

Such devices depend on one of two devices referred to as a WAP. In this case, WAP stands for *Wireless Application Protocol*. (The other device known as a WAP is a *wireless access point*, which we first talked about in Chapter 12.) WAP is the technology behind a device's ability to communicate with the Web. When you turn on a WAP device and open its miniature browser, a radio signal is emitted to try to make a connection with your wireless provider. Once that connection occurs, you choose a specific Web site to visit, and the signal goes out to look for a gateway server that uses WAP. This server, in turn, looks up the HTML for the requested Web site and encodes it in WML, which can be understood by the wireless device, and the site is then displayed in this format on your device display. However, in this chapter, the focus is on wireless networking where desktops and laptops are used predominately.

Remote *and* Wireless

As mentioned before, traditional wireless technology and cell communication often don't work outside major population areas. For example, from my remote Vermont home, I have to drive between 15 and 20 miles to receive even a poor signal on my cell phone—and forget about Web access over a Web-enabled cell phone. However, despite my remoteness, I can go virtually anywhere around the complex of buildings that includes my home, office, and studio and still be connected to the Web.

My main source for the Internet connection comes from a two-way satellite, which I receive through the same satellite dish I use for TV viewing. This feed comes into a system that acts as a gateway server, complete with firewall, and then is shared by other systems (both desktop and mobile).

When I first moved into this house, I dug a channel to run a network cable through a PVC pipe to connect the main house with the studio about 300 feet away to allow network communications between the two buildings. However, more and more of my communications are handled by wireless adapters (standard PCI adapters for the desktops and PC Card adapters for the laptops) that pick up a signal through the wireless access point (WAP), which offers transmission up to 22 megabits per second (Mbps). To get around limitations of distance, I created access points in other buildings between the main network and the network segment located in the studio. This permits me to be far more mobile, even just moving around my own property.

Wireless Networking

You learned some essentials of wireless networking in Chapter 12, but we should look at it in a bit more depth here because it's an increasingly popular way of communicating and sharing data in both offices and homes and requires a slightly different setup than traditionally wired networks. The signal in wired networks is transmitted through cables, but wireless networks depend on radio waves to transmit signals and receive them back. There are other differences, too, including the following ones:

- Wireless offers more flexibility in positioning of PCs, laptops, and mobile devices, while a wired network can cover a greater distance. (Wired networks can extend 300 feet with Ethernet cables or to about 1800 feet using fiber optic cable.)

- The speed of wireless can range from somewhat to quite a bit slower than wired communication.

- Wireless almost always costs significantly more than a wired network, although costs for wireless have slowly dropped with increased popularity and mass production.

- Wireless usually requires special conditions to make it as secure as a wired networking environment.

Issues such as speed, distance, and cost depend on the wireless networking standard being used. You'll learn more about that shortly.

> **Warning** Radio signals can be sensitive to interference, so be careful what you place between the various points of communication. Even cordless phones, microwave ovens, big radio setups, and certain building materials (such as sheetrock) can cause interference.

Standards for Wireless Networking

Making a decision to go wireless is not enough. You also need to know what type of equipment is needed and which wireless networking standard will be followed. There are presently three major standards for wireless networking (with their specifics provided in Table 18-1):

- 802.11a (also called Wireless-A)
- 802.11b (Wireless-B)
- 802.11g (Wireless-G)

Of these, 802.11b has been used for a longer period of time, with wide adoption. It is also the slowest and relatively least expensive to implement.

Table 18-1   Wireless Networking Standards and Specifics

Standard	Max Distance	Max Throughput (indoors)	Frequency	Public Access	Compatibility
802.11a	15 to 75 ft	54 Mbps	5 GHz	None	Incompatible with both other standards
802.11b	100 to 150 ft	11 Mbps	2.4 GHz	Growing	Widely adopted
802.11g	100 to 150 ft	54 Mbps	1.4 GHz	Some	Compatible with 802.11b (at 11 Mbps); incompatible with 802.11a

About Wireless Hotspots

The term *hotspots* can refer to many different things in the computer industry, but this section specifically uses *hotspot* to refer to a physical zone in which users with devices equipped with a compatible wireless adapter can sign into a wireless network, often for the purpose of sharing high-speed Internet access. Such hotspots can be either private or public, and exactly how public or private can be configured based on specific needs.

You've already learned that 802.11b is the most popular and widely adopted standard for the use of hotspots even though its maximum data transfer speed is quite a bit slower than the other two. This standard is what you usually see when Wi-Fi (or wireless fidelity), which is also discussed in Chapter 12, is implemented. This is also the most common networking standard included with small-office and home networking kits that provide you with some or all of the essentials needed to get a wireless network setup. The hardware needed to implement wireless systems is discussed later in this chapter.

But let's understand more about hotspots, their coverage, and their accessibility.

A general public hotspot can be used for any public place, such as in malls, restaurants, Internet cafes, hotels, airports, libraries, and school study areas. It's usually configured for ease of accessibility for anyone with access to the proper equipment needed to connect. Such hotspots are either free to use or commercial in nature. Free hotspots typically require the user to log on to the network using the network name or Service Set Identifier (SSID). Commercial hotspots usually require users to establish accounts, such as those secured by a credit or debit card. Some public hotspots such as libraries and airport lounges might even supply the equipment to use.

> **Note** Many organizations publish lists of the growing number of Wi-Fi hotspots available for public use. Among those is the Wi-Fi Zone at *www.wi-fizone.org*.

Other hotspots tend to be more restricted in nature. Private hotspots typically require that a person have a pre-established account (with a unique user ID and password) plus the network name (or SSID) to log in, and they include measures meant to reduce the chance that an unauthorized party can access the network.

Issues in Wireless Networking Security

A wireless network can present more security challenges than a wired one. This is because virtually anyone with access to the right equipment and who comes across the right access information (and users can be very sloppy in this regard, making a potential hacker or other opportunist's job far easier) can join the network.

There are four steps that LinkSys and other major networking hardware manufacturers typically recommend for establishing a decent level of security in a wireless networking environment—and most of these steps work for wired networks as well. The steps are as follows:

1. Change the network name, also referred to as the SSID, from the default factory name supplied by the networking equipment.

2. Disable the equipment's ability to broadcast its network name or SSID.

3. Change the default password required to access a wireless access point device, and continue to change it regularly thereafter using secured password methods, which include requiring a longer password and a combination of alphanumeric characters.

4. Enable Media Access Control (MAC) address filtering. MAC is a unique address assigned to each network adapter on a wired or wireless network (and designated at the factory). It's used as part of proper identification and authorization measures. Some access points and routers feature the ability to enable this filtering.

How you implement these security measures depends on what version of Microsoft Windows you're using. Versions earlier than Windows XP typically require this to be done through a networking client, such as one included with the networking devices you purchase and put into service. (Read the documentation accompanying your network hardware or client, or refer to the manufacturer's Web site for specifics.) However, Windows XP and later versions are designed to work with and manage wireless networks and their hardware (as long as the hardware is Windows XP–compatible and can be checked against the Windows Catalog/Hardware Compatibility List, which was covered in Chapter 2, "The Operating System's Role in Hardware"). Also, you can decide whether to let Windows XP (or later) or your network setup client handle the security settings. Here's how to configure Windows from Control Panel in Category view to manage (or not manage) your wireless networking for you:

1. Once the wireless network is set up (based upon the kit you're using or the instructions for the specific hardware used), select Network And Internet Connections, and then select Network Connections. (If you're in Classic view in Control Panel, simply select Network Connections.)

2. Select your Wireless Network Connection, right-click it, and choose Properties. (If you don't see your Wireless Network Connection, you need to troubleshoot your wireless network installation. For more information, see the section "Installation" later in this chapter.)

3. Select the Wireless Networking tab. If you want Windows to manage your wireless network, choose the Let Windows Configure Wireless Network Settings. If you want to use a client, click Add, and supply the information needed for the client to manage your wireless networking setup. (This information is usually found in the product documentation or when running the setup utility itself.)

Now let's look at another side of security: how to keep private networks and the data they make available more secure when you have to let outsiders (employees in the field, contractors and consultants, customers, and others) communicate with your network over more public connections, such as a public hotspot. This aspect of security involves setting up a special type of private network, which is discussed next.

The Use of a Virtual Private Network (VPN)

Obviously, one of the concerns created by public access to data or by people using a public network to access secured data from a private network (such as is the case when you're using an airport Wi-Fi net connection to access a private company network while waiting for your plane) is security. You don't want to make it easy for the wrong people to get private data.

Virtual private networks (VPNs) were designed to create a secure channel—sometimes referred to as a *tunnel*—between two parties (such as you and your company's system) to pass encrypted, secure data just as if you were logged in locally to the company's private network. The idea here is to lock out anyone else in a public network except the person attempting to gain access and the person or server being accessed. Without the use of a VPN, an unauthorized party on a public network could use techniques such as data sniffing (to catch user IDs and passwords) and machine address spoofing (to pretend to be an authorized party) to access the private network.

What's needed to establish a VPN? A VPN can be used whenever each side of the channel uses a VPN router or when the source (the private network) uses a VPN router with its workers, members, or other parties who are authorized to use VPN client software to communicate with it. Some types of broadband Internet access—such as my two-way satellite Internet service—use a VPN to allow subscribers to log in via a VPN client installed on their remote systems through the service network's VPN router.

VPNs and the hardware they use typically have one of the following two networking protocols for security purposes:

- **IPSec**   A highly compatible standard protocol used to secure sensitive data transmissions over an unsecured network, such as you have with the Internet. It acts like a private network layer of sorts within that unsecured network. It both encrypts data and authenticates the parties involved to create a more secure VPN. Microsoft and other sources provide excellent resources on configuring IPSec. One such reference can be found at *http://www.microsoft.com/resources/documentation/ WindowsServ/2003/standard/proddocs/en-us/Default.asp?url=/ resources/documentation/WindowsServ/2003/standard/proddocs/ en-us/IPSec_createcfgTN.asp.*

- **PPTP, or Point-to-Point Tunneling Protocol**   A protocol that allows Windows clients and servers to communicate with each other through Windows Remote Access Services (RAS), although versions to support other operating systems are also available, such as for Linux and BSD. It authorizes users by means of user ID and password only, with little or no encryption.

> **More Info**   It's important to understand that these protocols merit far more attention than can be suitably paid here, within the context of a chapter on general wireless networking. One of your best sources for more detailed information on this subject is directly from Microsoft, at the company's support page (*http://support.microsoft.com*).

For better security, IPSec is the protocol most frequently recommended— and IPSec with L2TP specifically is recommended for the best security that does not require the use of a Network Address Translation (NAT) device. This is because it both encrypts and checks the user system's Internet Protocol (IP) address beyond just an easily stolen user ID and password. Some VPN routers, however, are designed to use the PPTP protocol instead because, by not providing the same level of security, it's marginally faster. Thus, when you want to use IPSec, look for a VPN router that supports its use. VPN routers, however, typically support the use of NAT devices.

Wireless Hardware Components

Wireless networking hardware can be obtained either as separate devices or through the increasingly popular (especially among consumers) prepackaged kits, which supply some or all of the essential hardware and software needed to connect two or more systems together for wireless connectivity. Let's look, device by device, at the hardware essentials needed for establishing a wireless local area network (WLAN).

A wireless broadband router (shown in Figure 18-1) is typically connected to share Internet access from one primary system or connection to all other wireless devices. An Ethernet switch (discussed in Chapter 12) can be used to connect points of access to the network itself.

Figure 18-1   An 802.11b broadband router

Wireless access points, such as the one shown in Figure 18-2, or similar devices are used as base-station receiver-transmitters to spread the connectivity across the designated hotspots. Such devices act as a communications hub on a wireless network and are connected by standard cable back to the Ethernet switch or router. Also, a wireless print server can be added to share a printer on such a network.

Figure 18-2   A wireless 802.11b access point with its broadcast antenna

> **Note**   There are also special bridges to connect a wireless network or networks to a wired network. For example, a workgroup bridge can be used to connect a wireless network to a larger, wired network. Also, some access points allow themselves to be configured to work as a bridge, but you must use the device as either an access point or a bridge. You cannot use them as both simultaneously.

Now let's look at what each setup needs to connect to the wireless network:

■ Each desktop PC to be included on a wireless network needs either a PCI bus-installed wireless networking adapter or an externally installed USB wireless network adapter of the proper type for the standard used. (Most frequently, the standard used is 802.11b or Wireless-B.)

■   Each laptop can use either an externally installed USB wireless network adapter or PC Card (formerly PCMCIA) network adapter, which
installs to a PC Card slot available on the outside of the device. (See
Figure 18-3.)

Figure 18-3   A wireless 802.11b PC Card network adapter being
installed on a laptop

■   Each handheld mobile device, such as a PDA, can use a Compact
Flash memory card wireless adapter.

Exam Tip   Remember that VPNs, when used, require VPN-capable
routers and clients.

Fact   Wireless networks encrypt their packets using various protocol
types, including a widely used one known as Wired Equivalent Privacy
(WEP).

Installation

Exactly how you'll install and configure each component will depend on the precise nature of the intended setup and the specific directions offered with a setup kit or through a device-by-device installation you've selected. Review these directions, including any expanded ones available on the device manufacturer's Web site, before you begin. Then be sure that all the hardware you're using is compatible with the name of the wireless standard you're using.

Also, consider where you'll place your wireless access point or points in advance. To do this, you must identify where the likeliest and neediest locations around the desired area are so that you can cover them adequately. In a large house or office space, for example, more than one spot might be needed. Mounting these near a ceiling can be smart for the reasons mentioned in step 2 below.

Finally, before you start, you might want to consult the Microsoft support article on achieving good network security on an 802.11b-type wireless network at *http://support.microsoft.com/default.aspx?scid=kb;en-us;309369*. Even though it focuses on only one type of wireless network, some of the suggestions are general security precautions that can be applied to different types of wireless networking.

The basic steps for installation are as follows:

1. Install and configure compatible wireless network adapters in the desktop, laptop, or mobile devices to be included in the wireless network.

2. Install one (or more) wireless access point (or points) to distribute the signal. Wherever possible, these should be located as high as possible to counter the interference effects of furniture, equipment, building materials, and humans.

3. Connect the wireless access point (or points) to the Ethernet router or switch using a standard, properly terminated Ethernet cable. Such points might have an external power cord that must be plugged in. Run any access-point installation or configuration software, as indicated in the package instructions.

4. Run the setup software for the network, or let Windows XP or later try to detect and support the new wireless network automatically.

5. Test the network by checking for Internet and other network connectivity between devices.

Once you have everything set up so that it's working and communicating well, consider documenting your process, noting each step and configuration issue for the devices already attached. This can go into your tech journal or case notes, or wherever else you'll be able to reference this later to refresh your memory when you're doing a similar type of job or need to expand the current setup.

Troubleshooting

When troubleshooting a new installation, always consider whether you might have inadvertently connected or configured the system improperly. It might be helpful to get just two systems working on the wireless network and then add additional systems one at a time. By doing that, you can check after each addition is made that the added system is recognized and able to communicate with the others. Such testing can be done using the PING command followed by the IP address of each system connected, for example, and many network devices include a disk of utilities to check transmissions as well.

If the wireless network you install is on a Windows XP platform, be sure that the hardware you're using for the network supports Wireless Zero Configuration Service—a tool designed to allow easy operation and switching between wireless networks. Windows XP works best with this tool. With other operating systems, it might be necessary to configure and manage the devices through the networking third-party setup and drivers.

One clue that Wireless Zero Configuration Service is not supported by the hardware and drivers for the wireless network is if no Wireless Connection option is listed when you double-click Control Panel's Network And Internet Connections and then choose Network Connections. Try obtaining a compatible driver update for the device (or devices), apply it, and then recheck the listing under Windows XP.

However, at this stage with a new driver applied, you might see Wireless Connection appear under Network Connections but with no Wireless Network tab. This situation also indicates that the service isn't supported by this hardware under Windows XP. Contact the device manufacturer for support, or try using the device's own drivers and management software to establish a working connection on the wireless network without using the management support provided by Windows XP.

Windows XP and Wireless LANs

Because I've mentioned that Windows XP can handle management of a wireless network, it's also important to note something first discovered in 2002: the way Windows XP was originally designed to work can make it capable of inadvertently leaking information about SSIDs for access points and to allow data to be captured and unencrypted. This is the exact kind of information a resourceful hacker or opportunist can use to his or her advantage. Because of this early security flaw, some networking experts suggest you use software and drivers included with the hardware itself or obtained through a third-party rather than Windows XP to configure and manage your wireless network for better security. However, Microsoft has addressed the issue through Windows XP Service Pack 1, along with two utilities: the Microsoft Baseline Security Analyzer (MBSA) and the Microsoft Network Security Hotfix Checker.

If you choose to disable the Wireless Zero Configuration Service in Windows XP, do this by going to Start, My Computer, choosing Manage, and then, under Computer Management, choosing Services And Applications. Locate and right-click Wireless Zero Configuration under Services, and choose Disable.

Lab 18: Install and Configure a Wireless Network Setup Involving Two or More Systems

This lab is intended to prepare you to install and configure the hardware necessary to establish a successful wireless network implementation using two or more compatible systems. As part of this, you will record in your lab notes your observations, difficulties, and other experience as a record you can refer to when performing other such operations. Once finished, you should consider using the recommendations offered in the "Issues in Wireless Networking Security" section to try to lock down your network from unauthorized access.

Objectives

When you complete this lab, you will be able to address the following issues:

1. The basics of installing wireless network adapters and additional hardware

2. Configuration of wireless network setup

3. Successful communication between two or more machines using the wireless connectivity

Necessary Equipment and Resources

The following equipment and resources are necessary for completing this lab:

1. Two or more PCs of recent vintage (one or both should be running Windows XP)

2. An Internet-ready second PC for reference

3. Two or more wireless PCI-connected network adapters, a wireless access point or other broadcast device (which is not always required in a smaller setup), and a cable connection to an Ethernet router or switch

4. Use of all Windows XP systems, or use of the configuration setup software provided with the wireless networking hardware

5. Documentation for this hardware

6. Your PC toolkit

7. At least 60 minutes to complete this lab

Procedures to Follow

1. Check to be sure you have all equipment necessary to complete this job. Record details about the hardware in your lab notes.

2. Review the hardware documentation to determine the exact steps to take and in what order to take them. Document in your lab notes any major deviations from the steps discussed in the "Installation" section.

3. Using the documentation as a base, install the wireless network adapters into each system to be included on this wireless network following the guidelines discussed in Chapter 12. Note each system and its hardware specifics in your lab notes.

4. Still referring back to the documentation, complete the installation using the information found in the "Installation" section of this chapter. Run the configuration software or set Windows XP to manage it, as discussed in the "Issues in Wireless Networking Security" section. Document in your lab notes which type of setup and management you're using and any special issues encountered.

5. Test network connectivity by using tools that came with the wireless hardware. Be sure that at least one folder is shared on each system. (For example, right-click a folder listed on each system under a drive letter in My Computer, select Properties, Sharing, and then Share This Folder On The Network, as shown in Figure 18-4.) Record your results in your lab notes.

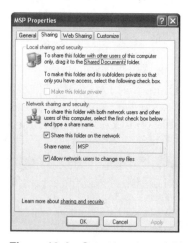

Figure 18-4   Set at least one folder on each system to be shared on the network

Lab Notes

1. List the specific hardware used for this procedure.

_____

_____

_____

2.   Note any particular steps that deviate from the procedure outlined in the "Installation" section in this chapter.

_____

_____

_____

3.   Record system-specific information and what type of wireless network adapter was installed on each system.

System #1

_____

_____

System #2

_____

_____

System #3

_____

_____

4.   Note how the wireless network is managed. Is it managed under Windows XP? If not, indicate what specific type of software it's managed under. Identify the steps necessary to configure it.

_____

_____

_____

5.   Document your troubleshooting and connectivity results.

_____

_____

_____

19

Audio Externals

You conquered the sound adapter in Chapter 10, "Audio." Now you'll work with the various external components that round out your multimedia setup, most of which can be installed either directly to the sound adapter or to jacks provided on the back or front of the PC that connect to an audio chipset integrated into the motherboard.

Major Types of Audio Externals

While Chapter 10 offered you a preview of the types of audio external devices you can routinely add to a sound adapter or audio integrated into a motherboard, you'll learn about each in more detail here, including how they connect and how they can be adjusted. Some adjustments can be done on the device itself (such as with speakers), while others might require adjustment strictly through Microsoft Windows (as with a microphone for voice recording).

The major types of audio externals include the following items:

- Speakers
- Headphones
- Microphones
- MIDI instruments
- Specialty devices, including receivers, external audio CD drives, and amplifiers

Ambient Noise

When trying to evaluate the overall quality of your sound components, you have to take into account all the ambient noise occurring in the vicinity. If you want an example, sit in a room with your sound components turned off and no other sounds in the area, while you listen closely to other detectable sounds—such as the fans and the hard disk—and feel a possible slight vibration. Then shut down your PC and listen carefully again. The older the system, the more noise you are apt to hear, generally speaking. Add in the other noncomputer noises around you and appreciate that *this* is what your sound system must compete with in delivering rich, quality audio.

Some recording devices, such as microphones, should be selected based on their ability to focus on the audio source (the person speaking into it) rather than their ability to pick up sounds throughout the room, which might reduce the overall sound quality of the file produced.

Speakers

When it came to PC audio 10 years ago, you either used the speakers that came with the PC you bought or you could purchase speakers separately at prices that could range anywhere from about $10 all the way up to a few hundred dollars. Even the best speakers in the world were not necessarily going to produce great sound, however, because sound adapters were rather lackluster compared with those available today. In fact, the situation was analogous to a child's 20-key electronic keyboard matched against a full-blown regular MIDI keyboard. Even a trained musician would only get so far using the former.

But now, in the full bloom of an era when we can watch television, news, and movies; listen to Internet radio broadcasts; and play our favorite music on the PC—and as sound adapters have become complex devices capable of rendering many instruments simultaneously—many users want more than those default $5 to $10 mystery brand speakers. And we sometimes don't just have a pair of speakers, we have four, five, or six (including the ultra-rad subwoofer, of course). In fact, impressive PC-based home theater sets—designed to provide the best audio playback for PC-based DVD and other video—sell quite well despite the fact that they are priced at $200 and up. With all this said, however, probably still a majority of PC users are fairly satisfied with those default speakers, and today's technology allows even low-end sets to offer surprising clarity and power. This level of performance is possible even though many speakers have fairly low-powered amplifiers and are quite small.

Speaker Issues

Unless you have an elaborate sound setup on your system where you battle with balancing and positional audio effects, speaker-related problems tend to be fairly few and usually center on the following issues:

- **Power**   Does the overall sound system have the capacity you need, and if it doesn't, is the fault with the sound adapter or the speakers? Try the speakers with a better sound adapter to see if the sound improves. Also try the sound card with different speakers to see if the audio improves.

- **Bad connection or cable**   Always check the connection to the proper speaker jack or connector at the back of the PC where the sound adapter is connected. With damaged wires, some speakers allow you to patch these or string new wire, while others make this harder or impractical to do.

- **Interference from other equipment**   Equipment that can cause interference includes old radios, heavy-duty machinery, and even older-style malfunctioning fluorescent lights and cordless phones. If you suspect that interference is a problem, try to isolate the PC with the speakers on a separate circuit from other appliances and remove any nearby devices that you feel could be contributing to the interference.

- **Faulty speakers**   Not all speakers are well made, even when they cost more and offer additional features. One of the drawbacks of cheap overhead pricing is often less than robust quality assurance; therefore, not all speakers are checked thoroughly—or even at all—before they leave the manufacturer. However, you can also "blow" less than robust speakers by playing music at high volumes beyond the comfortable play range of the speakers. Unless the speaker set is expensive and under warranty, most speakers should be replaced rather than repaired.

Considerations in Selecting Speakers

You should consider the following factors when selecting speakers:

- **Cost**   You shouldn't buy speakers in the $5 to $10 range unless you tend to keep all audio off except for system noises. If you have a decent mid-range to higher sound adapter, buy speakers to match (although you don't have to go much above $25 to $40 to accomplish this).

- **Number of speakers to purchase**   The usual two speakers might or might not be enough. A small cubicle, room, or office might be overpowered by anything more than a simple two-speaker standard set, while you definitely want to consider a speaker setup with four or more speakers for a larger space in which you want optimum sound and positioning you can control through adjusting speaker placement and balance.

- **Power of the amplifier**   The power capacity of the amplifier is usually listed under the specifications for each speaker set. Speaker manufacturers use two different measurements to describe output:

  - ❏   *Peak power*—This is the less valuable estimate because it refers only to how much power the amplifier delivers at maximum.

  - ❏   *Root mean square power (also known as RMS power)* —This is the more valuable estimate because it refers to the level of wattage that can be delivered continuously rather than at a theoretical peak that cannot be sustained indefinitely.

- **Frequency response**   This term refers to the frequency range the speakers can produce. Speakers are usually rated between 20 Hz and 20KHz (with 30 to 40 KHz being the top rating) at a particular decibel (dB) rate. However, the most valuable assessment here is usually not in the rated specs, which might not give a true picture of performance, but in how you appreciate the sound coming forth, noting particularly whether high treble and low bass can be heard properly.

Fact   A decibel (dB) is a logarithmic measurement of relative differences in sound intensity. To be a bit more precise, it's equal to 10 times the common algorithm of the ratio of two different electrical or acoustic levels.

- **Special connectors**   Some speakers might offer additional connectors for an additional line-in jack that could be used for an external device such as another audio source (CD player, and so on) or a subwoofer.

- **Headphones**   If you have a very confined environment, listen to sound at work that gets drowned out by office noise, or want more privacy and clarity, you should consider getting a pair of headphones. (See the "Headphones" section for more details.)

Note   One reason frequency response specifications are hard to use as a basis for speaker selection is that speakers with identical frequency response rates can sound quite different.

PROFILE: USB Speakers—Sound Without a Sound Adapter

Starting in 1998—which, not coincidentally, was the same time the first consumer version of Windows that fully supported USB 1.1 was released—USB speakers hit the PC music scene, offering one important difference over traditional PC sound hardware. USB speakers do not require a sound adapter to be present in the PC to enjoy and use them. This characteristic is useful on budget systems, where a sound adapter might not be present or, if it is present, isn't working or very good. It's also useful for enhancing the sound from a portable PC. Depending on the USB speakers being used, most of the functionality and adjustability of the speakers is done from a software window.

The downside to USB speakers is that, despite their versatility when no sound adapter is present, they don't offer the degree of control or functionality offered by their standard counterparts. (Again, this depends on the make.) For example, you might not have the degree of processing control for sound depth and quality that you have with a sound adapter and a good set of speakers. You might not be able to use a microphone or other devices in conjunction with the speakers because these devices are normally handled by sound adapter connections and features.

Many USB speakers, like standard speakers, use an external power supply. If they do not, they might need a powered USB hub to work properly.

Headphones

Headphones, as you know, are often used as a substitute for speakers or for when you want to listen to something privately. So, understandably, they share some physical sound-reproducing characteristics with speakers. Considerations for selecting headphones parallel what you've already learned about selecting speakers.

Standard headphone jacks are typically found on the sound adapter or directly on the back or front of the PC when the audio is integrated into the motherboard. Some CD and DVD drives also offer a separate headphone jack, and some speakers provide a jack on them as well as a pass-through port to allow the user to connect headphones without swapping speaker connections to the audio adapter. USB headphones, just like USB speakers, connect either directly to a USB port or through a hub that connects a series of USB ports.

The one major component besides physical design that headphones do not share with speakers is an amplifier. Almost no set of headphones has one.

Headphones with Built-In Microphones (also Known as Headsets)

More and more, largely because of the popularity of online video conferencing, you'll see headphones that also feature a built-in microphone, making it a complete headset, such as the one seen in Figure 19-1. Such microphones make it possible to record speech, provide a voice for live audio, and to use Internet telephony options. They can also be used in conjunction with voice-recognition applications and applications that support voice-recognition applications.

Figure 19- 1A headset with a mono headphone ear piece and microphone

Many times, these headsets are sufficient for normal audio output. However, some cheap, poorly designed, or poorly manufactured units won't have the quality you want. Some might offer good headphones but a bad microphone or vice versa.

But don't think you must buy a high-end unit to meet your needs. Although some high-end models offer good noise-reduction features, many lower or mid-range combination headsets do an admirable job with both major hardware functions for a price starting around $25.

Microphones and Speech Recognition

A microphone, which is not used just for recording but for Internet phone calls and videoconferencing, can be built into existing equipment (such as a monitor with speakers) or provided as a stand-alone device attached through either the microphone (MIC) or line-in jack. It connects using a 1/8-inch mini-jack. (See Figure 19-2.) Microphones most often connect through a jack located on the sound adapter at the back of the PC or through another jack made available either on the front, back, or even side of a system. Occasionally, a jack is provided on a PC monitor, usually with monitors that have speakers integrated into the frame of the monitor. There are also USB microphones that connect through the USB port.

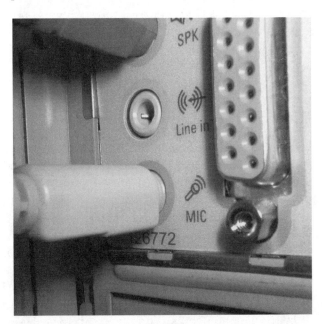

Figure 19-2   A microphone that plugs into the 1/8-inch minijack at the front or back of the PC, typically labeled "MIC"

Low-end microphones might be so lightweight that they fall over when confronted by deep breaths. Some low-end microphones can be purchased for as little as $3 to $5. Mid-level to high-end or specialty microphones (for professional recording) might allow for some adjustment, and they usually provide an on/off toggle switch.

While you can spend $100 or more for a microphone, simple voice recording can usually be accomplished on the cheapest models, too. However, low-end microphones are not recommended for recording professional presentations. Nor are they recommended for speech recognition software, such as Dragon, because the quality of the microphone can be a major factor in successfully training the software to recognize the words spoken and to have that software accurately transcribe them. Microsoft Office 2003, which has speech recognition built in, does a good job in this area. I use a $30 Altec Lansing headset for this purpose with very positive results, although I found it necessary to do extensive "training" within the software to achieve a high level of voice-recognition performance. Where possible, you should obtain a microphone or microphone headset that is specifically recommended by the speech-recognition package being used.

Increasingly, you'll find microphones combined into headsets, as manufacturers try to find products suitable for those who teleconference or use Internet telephony. But exercise care when choosing these: many of the less expensive ones tend to break easily and don't always expand or shrink properly to fit the wearer. Also with less expensive models, both the headphones and microphone components can demonstrate their inferior quality through increased static, low volume, and short lifespan.

MIDI Devices

The Musical Instrument Digital Interface (MIDI) represents a standard, approved by the electronic music industry, for music hardware to attach to the computer through a sound adapter and for these devices to be controlled and manipulated through the computer. Without such an interface, you would be left to record sound through analog devices such as a tape or cassette recorder and then find a way to convert that magnetic media–stored sound into the binary format that the PC understands. Such conversions usually involve a loss of audio quality, a loss compounded by what is likely to be less than professional recording quality from a standard analog recording device.

A MIDI port, with its standard five-pin Deutsch Industrie Norm (DIN) connector, is the connection point for external audio add-on devices such as MIDI keyboards, digital instruments (such as drumpads), and special-effects consoles. On some sound adapters, the game port or joystick port and the MIDI port are essentially the same. You'll learn more about this in Chapter 20, "Major Input Devices and Gaming Hardware." The MIDI port provides the pathway to the MIDI synthesizer. The following three major synthesizer types are currently supported (and these are defined in Chapter 10):

- FM synthesizer
- WaveTable synthesizer
- Physical Modeling or WaveGuide synthesizers

Often called the binary equivalent of ordinary sheet music, a MIDI file doesn't store the actual music but instead stores the instructions to the sound card on how to reproduce the music the composer designated. For this reason, the identical MIDI file can sound markedly different when played on sound cards of varying abilities.

There are three generally accepted MIDI standards:

- **General MIDI**   This is the original standard. It's still supported by most major sound adapters.
- **Basic MIDI**   This is a subset of General MIDI offered by Microsoft.
- **Extended MIDI**   This is a subset of General MIDI also offered by Microsoft.

Every MIDI interface supports at least 16 channels, and each channel represents a specific instrument. Higher-end sound adapters might have multiple interfaces (for example, SB Live!, which has three), allowing for multiple times the minimum number of channels and instruments.

> **Fact**   At least 32 MIDI channels are considered as necessary for creating a realistic MIDI instrument environment.

Other

While this chapter has focused on the most common audio external components to be added, there are others, including:

- External amplifiers or other devices
- Digital devices, including studio equipment, mixing boards, voice boards, and so on

- Analog devices, such as CD and tape players, external speakers, and so on

In our studio, for example, my partner uses a Roland USB-connected mixing board; along with a good-quality, ambient sound–dampening, sound adapter–connected microphone to record audio presentations; and a MIDI keyboard to play and record music.

Particularly where digital devices are concerned, be sure you are operating with the right drivers for your operating system and version. If you find that your digital device isn't supported—which sometimes occurs with some advanced or special digital sound hardware and Windows NT, Windows 2000, Windows XP Professional, and Windows Server 2003—you might want to contact the manufacturer directly and ask to beta test drivers for the device and the operating system version used with it. This can give you access to a driver—and therefore to your device—that otherwise might not be released for weeks or months. In my studio, we use several pieces of equipment that aren't natively supported by one or another version of Windows. In such cases, I've contacted the manufacturer and asked for a driver, even offering to take a "beta" driver (and sometimes, such "beta" drivers are never meant to be released to the general public but are made available as a private support channel), with about a 70 percent success rate in getting the equipment to work.

Installation and Configuration

As you work to both configure and troubleshoot audio devices you add to your system, understand that most of the basic information and control for these devices is found under the Sound or Sounds And Audio Devices icon in Control Panel. Individual devices that connect through a sound adapter, such as speakers or a microphone, are typically not displayed in Device Manager.

Fact One point you're apt to notice in the following sets of instructions is that except for USB-connected hardware, I advise you to shut down your system before plugging the components in. Yes, I realize it often works if you simply plug a microphone or speakers into a live system but the risk of damage—to the device, to the sound adapter, and in extreme cases, to the motherboard—is higher if you do so. These devices (except for USB) aren't hot swappable by design, and it's best not to treat them as such.

Installing and Configuring Speakers

Always inspect your speakers and their wires and review the enclosed documentation before you begin to install them. This can reduce troubleshooting time later if you notice a problem.

You should also think carefully about how these speakers will be placed. You need to be sure that you have enough wire to connect them to the PC from where they'll be placed and that you aren't placing speakers near devices that could cause interference. A budget set of speakers I used once would respond audibly whenever a fluorescent lamp on the same outlet began to flicker. Cordless phones, electric pencil sharpeners, and an assortment of common household and office devices can have the same effect. Once you've determined the placement of the speakers, follow these steps:

1. With the PC turned off, remove any dust or dirt around the sound adapter jacks, speaker jacks, or both.

2. Place the speakers as you want them around the workspace.

3. Review the documentation to be sure how the speakers should be connected (if necessary) and then connect them, if required.

4. Plug the speaker connector to the speaker jack on the sound card adapter.

5. Start the PC.

Once the speakers are connected, turn them on. (Most speakers include a power button.) Then adjust their volume, treble, and other settings, which are typically available through physical controls on the speaker units. It's helpful if you have a sound file playing at the time you do this to check the sound levels. You might want to keep a set volume level on the speakers themselves but adjust the Windows volume control for this. You adjust the Windows volume control by double-clicking on the Sound or Sounds And Audio Devices icon in Control Panel and making the adjustments on the Volume tab as shown in Figure 19-3. Depending on how your system is set up, you might also see a volume icon in the Windows System Tray that can be clicked on to configure volume levels.

Figure 19-3 Volume tab under Sound or Sounds And Audio Devices in Control Panel, which lets you adjust volume

Click Speaker Volume to adjust the left and right speaker balance. You can also click on Advanced and select the Speakers tab to make changes to the Speaker Setup (such as for a 5 to 1 audio play or special speaker arrangement) from the list box, as shown in Figure 19-4. Then choose the Performance tab to make modifications, as needed, to audio playback options.

Figure 19-4 Using the Advanced Audio Properties page to choose the type of speakers

Installing and Configuring a Headphone

Exactly how you install your headphone depends on whether your system has a specific headphone jack—either a jack that connects the headphones through a sound adapter or a separate jack elsewhere on the system (such as on a CD drive). You might also have a pass-through port located on a speaker to allow the connection of a set of headphones. On some systems, you'll have to disconnect the speakers and connect the headphone into the speaker jack. To do this, use the following steps:

1.   Shut down the PC.

2.   Connect the headphone jack. (Remember that you might have to disconnect the existing speakers to do this.)

3.   Restart the PC.

Some headphones have a volume control dial located on the headphones themselves or on the cable leading to the PC connection from the headphones. Otherwise, you can adjust play levels through Windows just as was done before for speakers. If the headphones include a microphone unit, see the information on installing and configuring a microphone as well as the instructions packed with the device.

Installing and Configuring a Microphone

Always check the connector at the end of the microphone cable when you first get it. Occasionally, you'll see a larger plug than can be accepted by the standard minijack on a sound adapter or back of the PC. You might need to obtain a simple microphone jack adapter to use it. Once you have everything you need to make the connection, follow these steps:

1.   With the PC turned off, remove any dust or dirt around the sound adapter jacks.

2.   Connect the connector end of the microphone in the Microphone (or "MIC") jack on the sound adapter or elsewhere on the PC.

3.   Restart the PC.

Voice recording options are available when you double-click the Sound or Sounds And Audio Devices icon in Control Panel and select the Voice tab. (See Figure 19-5.) Check to see what is listed for your Voice Recording device. (Typically, the adapter or other device providing sound is listed rather than a specific microphone itself.) Then click Volume to open a window that will allow you to adjust the volume for the device.

Figure 19-5   The Voice tab under Sounds And Audio Devices, which specifies the voice recording hardware and allows you to set or mute the volume

The simplest way to check the microphone is to open Sound Recorder in Windows (by going to Programs and then Accessories under either Multimedia or Entertainment) and attempt to record, as shown in the following screen. Sound Recorder's oscilloscope-style display should register changes in the waves during the recording. If it does not, check the settings under Sound or Sounds And Audio Devices in Control Panel to make certain the microphone is not set to Mute or that the volume has not been set too low.

Installing and Configuring a MIDI Device

MIDI devices are installed almost identically to other devices already discussed in this chapter, connecting through the MIDI or MIDI/game port. Windows volume for such devices is controlled through the standard Volume Control feature you've worked with before. Some MIDI devices might include software to provide an interface to allow you to manipulate functions on the MIDI device through it from the desktop or to configure the device for specific use.

To install a MIDI device, follow these steps:

1. Review the directions included with the device.

2. With the PC turned off, connect the MIDI connector to the MIDI port on the PC. (Usually, the connection point is at the back of the PC, at the intersection with the sound adapter or other jacks for audio integrated into the motherboard.) See Figure 19-6.

Figure 19-6   A PC with a MIDI-compatible game port

3. If necessary, plug the MIDI device into a power source such as a wall outlet and turn it on.

4. Start the PC.

You should have a MIDI-compatible sound creation and editing program, such as CakeWalk, available to test the device.

Installing and Configuring USB Audio Externals

Once again, you have to appreciate the ease with which USB devices can be installed. Installation is especially easy when the USB devices are compatible with the version of Windows being run on the PC they're being added to.

With the PC up and running, review the documentation for the device and any software included with it. Once you've done that, follow these steps:

1. Plug the external device into a power source, if needed.

2. Plug the USB connector cable running from the device into a USB port either on the PC itself or via a USB hub.

Windows should immediately see the device and install it. However, you might need to supply the floppy disk or CD that was packed with the device to install its proper driver or a utility from which you can configure and manage the USB device itself.

Maintenance and Repair

Watch the wires running from all such devices. Most audio externals have a relatively thin wire that is easily crimped and not that difficult to damage. Small nicks in a cable can sometimes be fixed by using tightly wound electrical tape, although you might find such devices then produce higher levels of static. If increased static occurs, the cable—if not the entire device—should be replaced as soon as possible.

Even a tiny amount of dust or grit on the audio component connector or on the jack can introduce sometimes high levels of static and noise into either playing or recording audio. Clean the connectors with a dry, lint-free cloth, and use a brush or can of compressed air to remove dust and dirt from jacks.

Troubleshooting

When I was doing daily technical support for many thousands of users on MSN, one of the most common complaints was related to "no sound" from audio externals such as speakers or a headset or microphone. In roughly 60 to 70 percent of these cases, the problem was the simplest to cure: no one had bothered to check the volume level on these devices, so they didn't notice the check box on the Mute option had been selected. Always be sure the Mute option is not selected. Another fairly common problem was that the audio external had been plugged into the wrong jack. Always check this, too.

Here's another situation that happens all too often. You're called upon to install a separate sound adapter to replace the function of the audio integrated into the motherboard. You disable it properly, and the new sound adapter seems to be working fine. But later, when you or someone else tries to add speakers or a microphone, you get no results. Can you guess what the problem is? You're right on the money if you thought, "They hooked the external devices up to the onboard audio ports instead of to the jacks on the new sound adapter."

Loss of Volume Control

One known "problem" with many Windows installations since Windows 95 is that the volume control tool might not be available after the operating system is installed. The word *problem* is in quotes because it's not a bug as much as a function of what hardware is detected when Windows is installed.

Windows should detect and install volume control for all normal sound adapters, with the exception of some Industry Standard Architecture (ISA) Plug and Play (PnP) sound adapters, which are seen less frequently today but are still out there. BIOS on some systems might not turn on PnP support for these ISA adapters, leaving the job to Windows when it starts up. In practice, more than ISA might do this, including some no-name PCI sound adapters with iffy drivers. This behavior is seen again when a user reinstalls Windows over the top of itself *after* installing a different sound adapter since the original Windows installation. Such a sound adapter gets seen too late in the setup detection process for Windows to consider it present, so it fails to load Volume Control because it assumes that it's not needed with an absent sound adapter.

There are two easy workarounds for this issue: one can avoid the Volume Control option from being skipped, and the other can restore it to an existing installation. The options are as follows (the first can apply to all versions of

Windows, while the next two are specific to older versions such as Windows 95 and Windows 98):

- Rerun the configuration utility for your sound adapter.

- When installing Windows, always choose the Custom setup option. When asked to select the components to install in the Multimedia section, be sure to choose Volume Control.

- From the Add/Remove Programs icon in Control Panel, choose the Windows Setup tab, select the Multimedia section, and click to check (thereby prompting to install) the Volume Control option.

> **Note** Some sound adapters, coded into the driver, install their own volume control function. With these, reinstalling the sound adapter from the Windows side should provide you with a volume tool.

Lab 19: Install, Configure, and Test Speakers and a Microphone

This lab is intended to prepare you to install and configure a basic multimedia setup employing both speakers and a PC microphone or microphone headset.

Objectives

When you complete this lab, you will be able to address the following issues:

1. The basics of installing a set of speakers

2. Installing a microphone for voice recording and conferencing

3. Successful configuration and use of both devices

Necessary Equipment and Resources

The following equipment and resources are necessary for completing this lab:

1. A PC of recent vintage

2. A set of speakers and a PC microphone or headset

3. Documentation for this hardware

4. About 20 to 30 minutes to complete this lab

Procedures to Follow

1.   Check to be sure you have all the equipment necessary to complete this job. Record details about the hardware in your lab notes.

2.   Review the hardware documentation to determine the exact steps to use and in what order to use them. Document in your lab notes any major deviations from the procedures discussed in the "Installation and Configuration" section for each device.

3.   Using the documentation as a base, install the speakers and configure them for proper use and volume following the guidelines discussed earlier in this chapter in the "Installing and Configuring Speakers" section. Record in your lab notes the exact steps you took.

4.   Test the speakers using at least two sound-based utilities (such as playing a .wav file through Sound Recorder, playing a file through Windows Media Player, and so on). Record your results in your lab notes.

5.   Reviewing the documentation for the microphone, install and configure it for use. Record your steps and the connection used in your lab notes.

6.   Test the microphone for use by using Sound Recorder to record and play back a test file. If possible, use video-conferencing software with another person to determine whether the sound quality from the microphone is adequate under these conditions. Record your results in your lab notes.

Lab Notes

1.   Specific hardware used for this procedure.

_____

_____

_____

2.   Note any particular steps deviating from the procedure outlined in the "Installation and Configuration" section earlier in this chapter.

_____

_____

_____

3. Record the steps you took when installing and configuring the speakers.

   _____

   _____

   _____

4. Document your results when testing the speakers.

   _____

   _____

   _____

5. Record the steps you took to install and configure the microphone.

   _____

   _____

   _____

6. Document your results when testing the microphone.

   _____

   _____

   _____

20

Major Input Devices and Gaming Hardware

User input is critical to PC operation, especially because it is how we communicate with the PC itself. Imagine if we could not depend on each keystroke or each minute movement of a trackball to be faithfully transmitted to the system and reproduced on our screens.

While we often take input devices for granted, most of them require extremely precise programming and control to translate the physical movement of something like a trackball or a joystick into a properly interpreted response. If you take it to another level, where you have something like a force-feed joystick that transmits feedback back to the user, it becomes truly amazing. Increasingly digital devices reduce the need for power-sapping analog-to-digital conversion of input. This reduction in power needs has truly revolutionized these devices, compared to their analog counterparts.

In this chapter, you'll get a tour of the types and connections for various input devices. One thing to consider as you read is that because peripherals such as a keyboard, mouse, trackball, or joystick can take so much daily abuse, they tend to need relatively frequent replacement. (Keep in mind that these words are written by someone who pounds her keyboard ferociously, as if she were working on the keyboard of a 1924 Olivetti manual typewriter, as she zooms through text at 110 words per minute.)

Major Types of Input Devices and How They Work

An input device is basically defined as any peripheral that allows you to communicate a signal that is received and processed by the PC itself. Obviously, this includes keyboards, mice, and trackballs, but it also covers the following items:

- MIDI devices
- Scanners
- Digital cameras
- Graphics tablets and digital drawing pads
- Gaming devices, such as joysticks and game consoles

Some people would also include card readers in this category.

Because we can type or move a mouse only so fast, most input devices are considered slow-speed technology, relegated to connecting through older standard connections, such as a PS/2 connector as well as USB 1.1. Let's look at each major type of device, starting with the keyboard and working our way through to gaming hardware and card readers.

Keyboard

Perhaps the most underrated and overlooked device on the PC, the keyboard, is one of the most important. More than any other device, it's your connection to your system as it provides the majority of user input into it. It's easy to take a keyboard for granted because you simply press a key and get a response. Yet in some ways, it's a marvel of electromechanical process and pretty representative of what input devices go through in working with the PC. Look at what happens in the process:

1. A key is pressed.

2. Step #1 results in a signal, called a *scan code*, being issued to the system, informing it that a device attached to it needs attention.

3. The keyboard controller then checks back with the keyboard to determine which key was pressed and then stores this information in memory.

4. Next, the keyboard controller signals the processor that it has a connected device—namely, a key on the keyboard—requiring the CPU's attention by means of an interrupt.

5. Because the CPU is usually busy with many other processes and it handles those interrupts in order of priority, the keyboard and its controller might have to wait for it to respond and route the key press to the operating system.

6. The operating system takes the signal and reports to the active window that a key press happened and that it was a specific key.

7. The system displays or acts upon the key press, and then alerts the operating system to send this same information to the video adapter so that it can be represented on the screen.

8. When the monitor next refreshes its display, the key (or result of a key press) will appear on the screen.

Keyboard Design

The keyboard is the entire package but let's look at what might seem to be a surprising number of features in what looks like such a simple and vital device.

Keys   What we call a key on a keyboard is actually a keycap—a plastic or special resin over-piece that sits atop the actual keyswitch. When a keycap is pressed, the keyswitch moves and, in turn, reports to the keyboard circuitry the identity of the depressed keycap. That information is then sent through the keyboard cable to the keyboard connection and into the keyboard controller.

Keycaps are sometimes removable, meaning they could potentially be replaced, by snapping off the top of the keyswitch assembly. Also, keycaps come in the following two different shapes:

- **Spherical curvature**   The surface of the keycap is concave in all directions.

- **Cylindrical curvature**   Only one dimension of the key is concave.

Which of these is better depends on your individual typing style and how you want the keyboard to feel.

Finally, keycaps are not smooth, as they might appear. Bumps are actually textured into the surface as an aid to finger traction, making it less likely your finger will slip and hit the wrong key. Over time, with wear from use, these bumps might cease to be seen or felt, just as the printing on the keycaps might fade.

Key Arrangement   Keys are laid out in a specific arrangement, and this same precision applies to the key and row spacing. Note how the first row of letters (the QWERTY line) begins farther to the left than the second row. The third row is then more indented than the second. Specific spacing is applied, usually in fractions of an inch. Certain keys and rows are always three-quarters of an inch apart, for example, while others are three-eighths of an inch or three-sixteenths of an inch apart. This precision is necessary to allow touch typists to always find their place on the keyboard.

There are variations, of course, as you see with ergonomic keyboards such as the Microsoft Natural keyboard, which divides the keys into two major sections, each angled slightly differently. Some people with many years of keyboard experience can't change to adapt to the different design, while others take to it rapidly because the QWERTY layout is preserved even though it's reshaped.

More about Keyswitches   Keyswitches come in the following two major varieties:

- **Contact**   This is the type typically used. It requires the depression of the key to initiate the process by which the keyboard circuitry sends a signal and the keypress is recognized by the system.

- **Capacitive**   This type depends on capacitors, or electronic devices capable of holding and storing an electrical charge generated when the distance between a capacitor's two or more plates is changed (as with a keystroke). This type is used in variations in many other parts of a typical PC, including power supplies and some types of RAM. Sometimes this type is considered the superior type because it can be harder to err with and it relies less on the physical motion of keypressing to initiate the signal. It might or might not be the right choice for the user looking for a high degree of physical feedback in typing.

Also, keyswitches can be made of different materials and designs, including foam-and-foil contact, carbon contact, rubber dome and membrane, and a more standard mechanical type. Different makes can affect the overall key tension (whether the keys offer resistance or depress easily) you feel.

Key Tension   The term *key tension* refers to the tactile feel of the keys as your fingertips press them down. Sometimes key tension is also referred to as *keycap travel*. A set of keys with little resistance will seem very easy to use with relatively little depression of the keycap, while another set with a much firmer touch might move the keycap a greater distance down.

Keyboard Circuitry   A standard or enhanced keyboard, as shown in Figure 20-1, requires a fair amount of circuitry to handle its many keys and functions.

Figure 20-1   A standard enhanced keyboard (not USB)

Inside, there is a tiny processor, along with a minute amount of read-only memory (ROM) to store information about which keys are pressed and what mode is enabled. For programmable keyboards, there is also erasable programmable read-only memory (EPROM) to store information about the functions or operations assigned to specific keys on the keyboard. The keyboard, along with the keyboard cable (usually four colored wires—green, white, red, and yellow—in a thick casing such as PVC) that connects it to the PC (on nonwireless and non-USB models anyway), is capable of full bidirectional communication with the system.

Typically, three LED indicators show the operating mode of the keyboard. The three modes are Num Lock, Caps Lock, and Scroll Lock. When any of these three options are lit, the option is engaged. If the LED for the mode is not lit, the mode is off. Programmable or special keyboards might have additional modes and LED indicators, and still other keyboards have the LED mounted on the key (Caps Lock, and so on) itself.

Components for the Keyboard on the Motherboard

There are two critical interfaces on a PC motherboard to support the keyboard: the keyboard connector and the keyboard controller.

Keyboard Connector   A keyboard connector is the spot where a standard keyboard connects to the PC motherboard. The two types of keyboard connectors are as follows:

- **Large**   A five-pin Deutsch Industrie Norm (DIN) dating back to early keyboard design.

- **Smaller**   A six-pin mini-DIN that is smaller in size than the DIN. It was first introduced by IBM on its PS/2 line of systems and is often referred to as the PS/2 keyboard connector. (See Figure 20-2.)

Figure 20- 2 The keyboard and mouse mini-DINs on the back of a PC

An adapter lets you switch a keyboard made for one connector to use the other connector interface. Each pin on the connector serves a specific purpose. Table 20-1 lists keyboard connector pin assigments

---

Note Bent pins on a keyboard connector can sometimes be gently but firmly pressed back into normal position. If a pin breaks off, however, you might have to replace the entire motherboard or try to go USB-only for keyboard connections.

Table 20-1 Keyboard Connector Pin Assignments

Pin #	5-pin DIN	6-pin mini-DIN
1	Keyboard clock	Keyboard data
2	Keyboard data	Unconnected
3	Unconnected	Ground wire

Table 20-1   Keyboard Connector Pin Assignments

Pin #	5-pin DIN	6-pin mini-DIN
4	Ground	Power (+5V)
5	Power (+5V)	Keyboard Clock
6	Not available	Unconnected

There are also USB keyboards, which are rising in popularity. These connect to the PC through a USB port rather than through traditional keyboard connectors. As a means to cut costs and reduce legacy attachments, some manufacturers of recent PC models have stopped including standard DIN and mini-DIN connectors, forcing their users to go with USB-only input device connections.

Exam Tip   Because USB detection occurs fairly late in the process of loading a PC, it can be smart to have a standard keyboard available in addition to a USB keyboard. Otherwise, you might not be able to use the keyboard for CMOS Setup or for any DOS-based programs that occur outside the control of Microsoft Windows.

The user base for the wireless keyboard is expanding. Wireless keyboards eliminate the need for the cord used by traditional keyboards by allowing a controller in the keyboard to communicate with a receiver station or control that is usually attached to the USB port (although some PS/2 connector models are available). While most wireless keyboards operate at a length of only between 5 and 10 feet (which still represents a nice advantage over the 2-to-3 feet of a standard corded keyboard), some newer generation wireless keyboards can successfully communicate at a distance of up to 100 feet and offer sophisticated ways to handle a situation where multiple wireless keyboards are to be in use at the same time in a work setting.

The Keyboard Clock   This is a special type of clock that regulates and synchronizes the signal (thus, making it a synchronous signal) passed to and from the keyboard and the PC. It's similar to clocks used elsewhere in the system, but it's far slower because of the nature of a keyboard and how it's used. Like other types of system clocks, this one switches back and forth between 0 and 1 with preset regularity.

Keyboard Controller   This is a chip on the motherboard that acts as the smart agent between the keyboard requesting attention and the CPU that needs to provide that attention. It's ultimately responsible for a keyboard's communication with the CPU and the desktop.

The keyboard controller uses and operates from interrupt request (IRQ1)—which is hard-wired into the system and unable to be grabbed by anything else—to communicate with the CPU.

> **Note**   Laptops and occasionally other mobile computing devices often include a keyboard connector (PS/2-style) to allow a standard-sized keyboard to be used instead of the smaller keypad on the portable device itself.

Mice and Trackballs

Pointing devices were introduced fairly early on in the use of personal computers, and they became better known in the early-to-mid 1980s. However, it took the full emergence and acceptance of the graphical user environment with Windows to make pointing devices essential PC equipment (although you can perform all major functions without a mouse if you know the required keystrokes). Note that the hand-contact surface of a mouse or trackball is textured, like the keycaps on a keyboard, to improve traction.

Mice and trackballs most frequently connect to the PC in one of two ways: by PS/2 Mouse Connector or by a USB port or hub. While they are far less common now, you might see standard serial and older bus mice, too. Serial mice connect through a serial (COM) port, while bus mice are connected through a special mouse adapter installed directly into one of the expansion bus slots on the PC motherboard. Occasionally, you see infrared mice and trackballs as well, which connect optically through the Infrared port available on usually portable computers. Chapter 18, "Going Wireless," discusses portable input devices.

Cutting the Cord

There are also optical mice and trackballs without a cord. These cordless devices, similar to cordless keyboards, communicate with a receiver or base station that is typically connected to the USB port or PS/2 mouse connector.

Yet one of the big advantages of optical input, especially with mice and trackballs, is not just the cordless nature. With fewer moving parts and a different way of operating, these units tend to wear out more slowly than their standard, corded cousins. However, interference can be an issue in some units, depending on the physical structure of other equipment housed in the area where it is being used. Consider this when installing one.

MIDI Equipment

Musical devices—including keyboards, drum pads, and electronic horns—available with a MIDI interface also qualify as input devices. You learned how to add these in Chapter 19, "Audio Externals."

Scanners

To digitize something is to convert it into a digital format that can be understood and read by the computer. Scanners of all types are used to turn printed information or images into binary format that can be stored and read by the PC. Before the advent of digital cameras, they were the standard way to get a physical image, such as a snapshot, digitized.

There are a large variety of styles and types of scanners, including handheld, flatbed, sheet readers, and bar-code scanning pens. There are also drum scanners used by the printing and publishing industries to reproduce images in digital format with amazing clarity.

Two features known as resolution and interpolation are often discussed in the issue of scanner quality. You're already familiar with the term *resolution* from discussing graphics and video. Resolution is measured in dots per inch (DPI). Most scanners allow for a minimum DPI of 300x300. Interpolation, by comparison, is more a sleight-of-hand technique used to enhance the perceived resolution by "filling in" the spaces between pixels or dots.

Another feature, bit or color depth, defines the number of different colors that a scanner can possibly capture with each pixel demanding at least 24 bits to produce true, full color. Typical scanner bit depths are 24, 30, and 36.

Scanners usually require a separate power source and connect to the computer through one of these means:

- Serial or parallel port
- USB port
- SCSI port

Many business and consumer applications build support for the acquisition of images directly into the desktop through both scanners and cameras. For example, recent Microsoft Office versions make this available, as do several graphics packages.

Digital Cameras

Digital cameras is a bit of a catch-all term for any camera with a digital interface—including Webcams, still-image digital cameras, and digital video cameras. The feature range of such devices varies from the very simple (turn it on and it does its own thing, as is the case with a Webcam) to instruments with all the complexity and capabilities of a fine 35mm analog camera.

Obviously, one of the supreme advantages of the digital camera is that it does not require film or the time-consuming, expensive, biologically unfriendly means by which film is developed. Ease of use is also a huge factor. For example, I've been known to take one of my digital cameras to an event along with two or three Flash memory cards—the standard means by which digital images are stored until transferred to a PC—and my laptop so that I can shoot and process hundreds of images in one afternoon. I know what my pictures look like almost immediately, and can reject the duds almost as quickly.

What many hand-held digital cameras do demand, however, is a lot of battery power. Often, the batteries used are easily replaced consumer batteries, such as AA batteries. When using these cameras, it makes more sense to obtain rechargeable batteries along with a recharger unit. Without these digital photographers who use their cameras frequently could fill their own landfills with exhausted batteries and undergo great expense in doing so.

Don't think of digital cameras as strictly consumer products either. More and more people use digital cameras for their work in developing Web site content, shooting product or editorial pictures for print publication, or taking employee pictures, just to name a few commercial uses.

Because cameras and scanners perform some similar functions even if their physical shape differs widely, they actually share a bit of the same hardware within. Every digital camera also features some type of processor to handle the images and store them to the storage medium being used (as mentioned, usually Flash memory).

Digital cameras can connect through a number of different means, including:

- **Serial or parallel port** Both options can be extremely slow for transferring pictures from the camera to the PC and are more often seen on older or very cheap digital cameras.

- **USB port** This method is the most commonly used today.

- **IEEE 1394 port** This method is available for digital camcorders and other higher performance non–still image cameras.

Graphics Tablets

Graphics tablets and digital drawing pads are primarily used for fine-control hand movements such as writing or drawing. These allow the user to work more naturally by using a stylus applied to a pad backed by circuitry to create their work. This method is usually far more satisfactory than doing the same work using the less precise mouse or trackball in a program such as Paint. The finished product can then be saved directly into digital format.

A graphics tablet or drawing pad is actually constructed of a carefully designed grid, which is usually invisible to the eye because of the covering that sits between the stylus and the grid. The tablet accurately tracks pressure points made along that grid's coordinates by the application of a stylus. Those pressure points are then precisely registered in whatever software is being used in association with that drawing or writing, such as computer-aided design software.

Connection methods for graphics tablets and drawing pads include:

- Serial port
- USB port

Gaming Hardware

Gaming hardware spans a rather wide range from the ubiquitous, long-available joystick to very elaborate console setups for driving games and simulations that include a steering wheel, foot pedals, and more. Yet keep in mind that not all gaming hardware is exclusively for fun and games. Lab simulations, as just one example, can use similar types of input devices to test human response, while joysticks are used in a number of industries for device manipulation and control.

Such hardware, referred to generically as a *game controller*, typically connects to the PC through the 15-pin game port (which uses a DB-15F connector), which are commonly found on sound adapters or are available as a separate external connection from an integrated motherboard. Such game ports can be either a single port or a dual port. (A single port has a simpler single connection with fewer features, while the dual port requires two connections and has more functionality.) Most game ports still available today are dual ports. Also, game ports might share the connection with MIDI devices in what is known as a MIDI-capable game port, such as the one shown in Figure 20-3. More and more, however, gaming hardware connects to a PC using a USB port or powered USB hub.

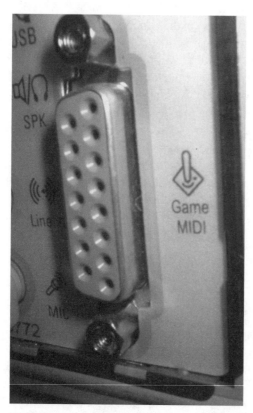

Figure 20-3   A PC with a MIDI-compatible game port to allow connection of either type of device

Today, you continue to see a mix of both analog and digital game controllers. Analog controllers typically use only a game port to connect. Digital game controllers usually can connect through the USB port, but they might still connect to a game port. For various reasons, including the fact that digital controllers tend to perform far faster and with much greater functionality than their analog cousins, try to use only digital game controllers with a recent vintage system.

> **Note**   Game ports, unlike other connections using a serial or parallel port, don't require any of the typical hardware resources such as an IRQ, DMA, or memory. Instead, standard game ports use a single I/O address and USB devices share hardware resources between all installed USB devices.

Card Readers

Card readers border the categories of both storage handling and input because they serve as an access point to retrieve data—such as digital images and stored files—from a FlashCard, Secure Digital (SD) Card, and memory stick. Today, card readers largely connect through the USB port rather than through older, slower connections, and they allow you to read (and erase) the removable memory card from a device without attaching the device itself.

These devices also tend to use the same connection interfaces as other input devices, including:

■   Serial or parallel port

■   USB port

■   A special adapter installed to the motherboard's expansion bus

Installation

As you have done in past chapters and labs, you first want to inspect your new equipment to ensure that it is free of damage, includes the proper instructions, and is of the type you expected to obtain and install.

Now let's look at how to install each type of device.

Installing a Keyboard

To install a standard keyboard, follow these steps:

1. From Device Manager, click Remove once you select the listing for the current keyboard. (In Windows XP or Windows Server 2003, right-click the device and choose Uninstall, as shown in Figure 20-4.)

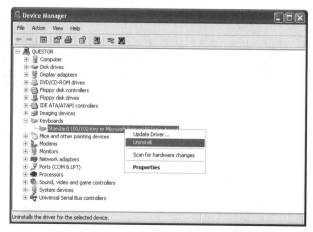

Figure 20-   4 The keyboard listing in Device Manager (Windows XP)

2. Shut down the PC. It is not necessary to disconnect it from power.

3. Pull the existing keyboard PS/2 connector from the interface (usually at the back of the PC) as shown in Figure 20-5, and set that keyboard aside.

4. Plug the new keyboard's PS/2 connector into the now-vacant keyboard PS/2 interface.

5. Turn the PC on.

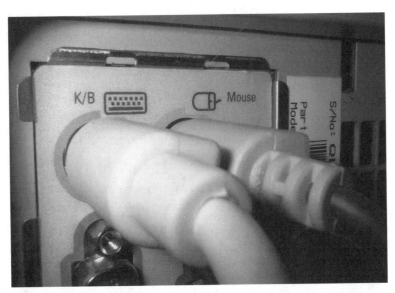

Figure 20-5   The keyboard and mouse mini-DIN PS/2 interfaces on the back of a PC

Windows should automatically detect and install support for the new keyboard, although you should have any included driver disk available just in case. It might also be necessary to configure the keyboard, especially if you want changes to the previous keyboard settings.

To make such changes, double-click the Keyboard icon in Control Panel. Here, you can set the speed (as shown in Figure 20-6) as well as select the Hardware tab to troubleshoot a keyboard installation. To modify keyboard language and other issues related to region and language, double-click the Regional and Language options in Control Panel.

Figure 20-6   Keyboard properties in Control Panel

To install a USB keyboard, you vary the process a bit. For example, a conventional keyboard is meant to be connected and uninstalled with the PC off. A USB keyboard, by comparison, expects the PC to be turned on. Always follow the explicit directions for the keyboard you're installing, although the following basic steps often can be used:

1. Leave the standard keyboard connected and the PC on.

2. Plug the USB keyboard into a USB port.

3. Once Windows detects the device, supply a driver disk if requested.

4. The next time you shut down the system, go to Device Manager and remove the existing standard keyboard listing before you do.

5. With the PC off, disconnect the standard keyboard from its PS/2 interface and move the old keyboard out of the work area.

After step 3, you can adjust the keyboard and language options from Control Panel as described previously in the instructions for installing a keyboard.

Installing a Mouse or Trackball

When you install a mouse or trackball, you follow the same basic set of instructions you did for replacing or adding a keyboard, depending on whether the device uses the PS/2 or USB interface. The only difference comes later, in configuring the mouse for use once Windows has detected and installed support for it.

Once this occurs, you can run any mouse or trackball setup utility that was packed with the device, but you'll definitely want to double-click the Mouse icon in Control Panel to set properties for speed, buttons, and pointer qualities. You should also check the Hardware tab (shown in Figure 20-7) to be sure the device is working properly. (A Troubleshoot button is also available on this tab, allowing you to run a hardware troubleshooting wizard.)

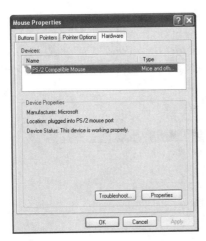

Figure 20-7   The Hardware tab for diagnostics and device properties, one of four tabs available under most mouse/trackball installations in Control Panel's Mouse option

Installing a Scanner

Windows XP and later versions make the installation and use of a scanner particularly easy, especially when the scanner is connected through the USB interface. This is accomplished through the Scanner And Camera Wizard available in Control Panel. Other versions of Windows, particularly much older Windows versions, might place a heavier demand on the use of the device manufacturer's TWAIN (which quaintly stands for "technology without an interesting name") drivers to interact with the operating system.

If the new scanner has a USB connection, simply plug the scanner into a power source, and then connect its USB cable to a USB port on the PC or through a USB hub.

If the scanner connects through the serial, parallel port or SCSI, follow these steps:

1.   With the computer turned off, attach the connector to the serial or parallel port or to the SCSI cable. (Be sure it's terminated properly, as discussed in Chapter 12, "Network Cards and Network Hardware.")

2.   Turn the PC on.

Regardless of the interface, Windows should automatically detect the new device and install it, although you might be prompted to provide the driver disk for the device. If Windows doesn't detect the device and you're using Windows XP, first be sure the scanner (if it has an on/off switch) is turned on, and then double-click the Scanners And Camera icon in Control Panel and select Add An Imaging Device. (See Figure 20-8.)

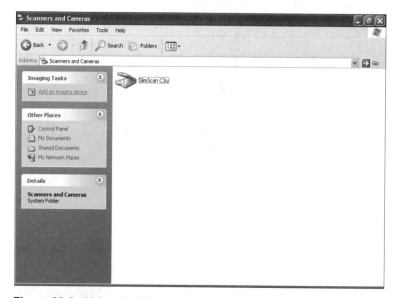

Figure 20-8   Using the Add An Imaging Device under the Scanners And Camera icon in Control Panel

Be sure to test the scanner once it's installed. This can be done through the scanner software that usually accompanies a new scanner product or directly through supported scanners in software such as recent versions of Microsoft Office (Office 2000 and later) and other packages.

Installing a Digital Camera

Exactly how you install a digital camera depends on the type used. Consult the documentation that comes with the camera for specifics, and follow them to the letter. However, let's go through the basic steps. Because most cameras today use either a USB or IEEE 1394 interface, simply follow these steps:

1.   Connect the USB or IEEE 1394 cable to the appropriate port on the PC (or through a USB hub).

2.   Turn the camera on.

3. When Windows recognizes that a new device has been attached, have your camera driver disk available in case Windows does not support the camera directly.

Once the camera is recognized and installed, you might want to test it. For Webcams and digital camcorders, this can be done through the software that typically is packaged with the camera. For digital hand-held cameras, you can either use the software with the camera or, if you're using Windows XP or later, shoot some pictures and reattach the camera to the PC. Windows should automatically detect that a removable storage device (the flash memory in the camera) is attached and prompt you with a screen like the one shown in Figure 20-9.

Figure 20-9   In Windows XP and later, the Removable Disk window greets you when you connect your camera

Installing Gaming Hardware

As with digital cameras, gaming hardware installation can vary widely depending on the type of device being installed. Always review the explicit instructions that come with the device itself, particularly as it relates to your operating system.

Follow the same basic instructions to install your gaming hardware—whether analog or digital—as you have with other such devices. But before you do, check the manufacturer's Web site to be sure you have the latest drivers and configuration software for your device.

> **Note**   It's often smart to update your drivers when you first install a new game controller. This is especially true for Microsoft DirectX support, where the machine where the device is being installed might not be updated to the latest version. This can usually be accomplished through the Windows Update site, typically available at the top of the Programs menu from Windows Start.

Maintenance and Repair

Unless you know the actual schematics of a device and happen to be particularly good with a soldering iron, there is relatively little repair you can perform on any of these devices. There are measures you can take, however, to try to keep them functioning well without getting to the point where they need a repair.

Let's review these measures device by device.

Cleaning a Keyboard

When cleaning a keyboard, you should have your system turned off and the keyboard disconnected. Some people might consider this recommendation to be overly fussy, but even if you don't run into issues with static electricity or worse, you could jam the system by pressing too many keys in a short span of time. If the keyboard is connected via a USB port, you can try to simply disconnect it from the PC while it's running, but be sure to disconnect any other devices that are connected to USB ports sometimes present on USB keyboards.

As you read the following steps, note that the first step is a wise thing to do on a regular basis to keep the area beneath the keys from getting grungy, as follows:

1. Turn the keyboard upside down (preferably over an empty carton or wastebasket), and then gently but firmly shake it back and forth to remove loose debris.

2. Use a damp cloth (just barely damp, not soaking wet) to clean the keys and the board around them. If possible, avoid using cleaning fluid. If you need to use cleaning fluid to get rid of a stubborn stain, don't use bleach and don't have the open container near the keyboard or PC.

3. Use a can of compressed air to try to force any remaining matter out from beneath the keys, or use a special keyboard vacuum to try to collect any remaining material. (A regular vacuum is not recommended and a battery-powered keyboard vacuum is better than an AC one.) If you can locate a slender applicator or ultra-thin swab (without extra amounts of cotton) that will fit, gently work down between the keys as well as you can, without applying force. (Keys on today's keyboard are likely to break off or damage can occur to the wiring beneath.)

4. If there is any residual dampness, leave the keyboard disconnected until it dries, and then reconnect it.

> **Note**   Having just mentioned vacuums, I should point out that a normal household vacuum can interfere with the operation of your computer the same way it sometimes does with your radio and television. A vacuum can pack quite a motor that can vary substantially in speed and power as the vacuum is pressed upon to concentrate on a particularly dirty area. While many systems would survive this interference fine, you should avoid plugging a household vacuum into the same outlet or power panel as the PC (or the monitor).

> **Fact**   Here's a piece of trivia you may prefer not to know. A study was just released stating that keyboards often contain more types of germs and tend to be scientifically "dirtier" than most toilets. This could make you rethink having lunch at the computer...

Cleaning a Mouse

A number of places on a mouse can become dirty and affect its movement. However, there are some variations in mouse design and between types of mice. For example, an optical mouse basically just needs to have its sensor kept clean with an optical cleaner or distilled water. Very infrequently, you can find no-name, non-standard mice that have no way to open and adequately clean them.

> **Caution** Where possible, the mouse should be disconnected from the PC before cleaning. To reduce risk, unless the mouse is optical or connected via USB port, the system should be shut down before the mouse is disconnected.

On a regular mouse, however, these are the common areas, along with cleaning methods:

■ The underside of the mouse, where one or more strips are mounted to help the mouse glide cleanly across a surface. These strips can accumulate dirt, including some dirt that should be firmly pushed off with a thumbnail.

■ Open the usually circular hatch to remove the mouse ball from its housing. Clean the ball using a lint-free cloth or a clean low-lint cloth with a tiny amount of isopropyl (rubbing) alcohol, and then set it aside.

■ Inside the open hatch, look for the rollers that control the movement of the mouse under your direction, and remove any dirt, grime, and accumulated hair, fur (your pet's, hopefully), and dust. Replace the ball and the hatch.

■ The mouse pad or other work surface is the most likely spot for dirt or moisture to be introduced into the mouse. A mouse pad should be shaken out daily and cleaned as needed. It should also be replaced when stained or no longer able to be satisfactorily cleaned.

> **Note** If you find that scrolling downward on a Web page or in a long document causes your system to freeze or crash, especially after you have recently upgraded your browser or operating system, the problem likely is not your mouse, but your video driver. Update it before you try anything else.

Other Hardware

With a flatbed scanner, it is particularly important that you keep the glass plate clean and free of dust. Also take care what types of objects you place on the glass plate. Any nicks created in the glass might show up on all subsequent scans.

Other types of scanners should be kept as completely free of dust as possible. A sheet-fed scanner, for example, runs the risk of having dust or dirt introduced into its internal housing by being transferred from the feeder tray or window or from the paper being scanned.

The lens cover on a camera should be in place at all times when it is not being used to snap a picture. The lens should be cleaned only with a very soft, very clean cloth. The same cloth, or a static free monitor wipe cloth, can be used to clean the LCD or viewfinder.

Game controllers should be kept set aside from the main work area when not in use and kept as clean as possible. A dust cover—even an improvised one made from a plastic bag—isn't a bad idea.

Watch for crimping or twisting of cables and wires on all such devices.

Troubleshooting

Information in this section is intended to help you resolve common or particularly nasty errors seen with input devices such as keyboards and mice. Trackballs and other devices work similarly, so some of the errors and problems (including dirty device, bad driver, and so on) apply to them too.

Be sure you have the most updated driver for the device and operating system version you are using. Using a driver meant for a different version of Windows can cause difficulties in getting the device recognized and working fully.

Always appreciate, too, the role you've learned overheating can play in system reliability. Keyboard errors or problems and squirrelly behavior with other input devices are not unusual in a system that is operating in excess of its recommended operating temperature. Investigate to be sure excess heat is not a factor in the trouble you are seeing.

> **Note**   USB keyboards usually *do not* function in Windows Safe Mode. This is because a reduced set of drivers is loaded in this troubleshooting mode, and USB is not one of those loaded.

> **Caution** Some USB keyboards do not respond properly to the Ctrl+Alt+Del reboot command, particularly when issued from Windows. Some automatically display this error:
>
> *"Fatal exception 06 has occurred at xxxx:xxxxxxxx. The current application will be terminated."*
>
> If this happens frequently to you, you should replace the keyboard with a non-USB type or one that handles the Ctrl+Alt+Del function appropriately.

Keyboard and Mouse Troubleshooting

Issue: Programmable keyboard no longer works as set.

Solution: The keyboard likely needs to be reprogrammed. Check the documentation for it and reprogram it.

Issue: Keyboard error at boot.

Solution: Restart the system to see if it clears. Reseat the keyboard connection. If the system is overly hot, let it cool and then retry. Try a different keyboard.

Issue: "Keyboard Bad" error.

Solution: Shut down the PC, and wait two to five minutes. Try again. Reseat the keyboard connection. Try a different keyboard. If another keyboard (that's known to work) doesn't resolve this, the problem might be the keyboard controller. Check with the motherboard manufacturer regarding replacement options.

Issue: Error: XX=ScanCode, Check Keyboard.

Solution: See "Keyboard Bad" error.

Issue: Keyboard clock line failure.

Solution: See "Keyboard Bad" error.

Issue: Problems adding PS/2 keyboard.

Solution: Reattach the old keyboard, go into Control Panel, double-click the System icon, and choose Device Manager. Locate the listing for the old keyboard, and click Remove. Then restart your system and reattach the new keyboard. See whether it is detected. Also check keyboard seating.

Issue: High-pitched whine or rapid beep when typing.

Solution: Shut down and restart the system. This alone should clear a jammed keyboard buffer. Check for stuck keys. If the problem persists, try a different keyboard.

Issue: Num Lock key on at start.

Solution: First, try turning the system off. When you restart the system, see if the Num Lock key comes on. If it does, the next time you restart your system, go into CMOS Setup, and turn off the Num Lock option.

Issue: Keyboard repeating is wrong.

Solution: Under the Keyboard icon in Control Panel, go to the Speed tab and adjust the settings for Repeat Delay or Repeat Rate, as needed. Check the responsiveness when repeating a key, and readjust as necessary.

Issue: Key responsiveness is wrong.

Solution: See "Keyboard repeating is wrong."

Issue: "Dead" LED display on keyboard.

Solution: First, check that the connection is secure between the keyboard and the back of the PC. With the PC off, disconnect it, check the DIN pins, and reconnect and retry. If this doesn't work, check for any switches on your keyboard that might have been changed. If necessary, try a different keyboard. Also, a dead LED display does not necessarily mean a dead keyboard.

Issue: Keyboard types garbage.

Solution: If it's a very hot day or the PC is operating in a very hot environment, remove the PC case cover and try to displace some of the built-up heat. After letting the PC cool for an hour, try it again to see whether the problem has been cleared up. If this problem is immediately resolved by using a different keyboard, the keyboard might be damaged. (Did it get extremely wet at any time?) It could also be a damaged keyboard controller on the motherboard or a new language might have been selected under the Keyboard icon in Control Panel.

Issue: Spilled fluid.

Solution: Immediately turn the keyboard or mouse over onto a spread-out newspaper or towel. If it connects via a USB port, disconnect it. If it's a regular keyboard, shut down the system and disconnect it. Let the keyboard fully dry and then clean it, as needed, before trying to reattach and reuse it. It might require replacement.

Issue: Suspected dead keyboard.

Solution: Shut down the system, and disconnect the keyboard. Check pins and any switches on the keyboard itself. Reattach and try to start it again. If the keyboard still shows no response, try a different keyboard. If you still get no response, the problem might be a dead or failing keyboard controller. Also try the first keyboard on another PC.

Issue: Slow/fast cursor when typing.

Solution: Go to the Keyboard icon in Control Panel. Select the Speed tab, and modify the blink rate, as desired.

Issue: Damaged PS/2 port.

Solution: Disconnect the keyboard with the PC turned off and power removed. Check the type of damage. If the problem is related to the keyboard end of the connection, replace the keyboard. If pins are bent on the PS/2 port, try to gently bend them back into position. If you can't do this, you might have to replace the port, replace the motherboard, or try to make do with a USB keyboard, if supported.

Issue: No keyboard response when starting the system.

Solution: Check the keyboard connection. If possible, try a different keyboard. Consider any other changes recently made. Check the expansion board seating.

Issue: USB keyboard fails when other USB devices are attached through its onboard USB ports.

Solution: If this is a keyboard with additional ports for other USB devices to attach, disconnect all devices first to establish that the keyboard works on its own. Add USB devices back one at a time until you encounter the problem again. Isolate the devices that are causing the problem, and attach them to the PC not through the keyboard but through a powered USB hub.

Issue: Can't add keyboard language.

Solution: Make sure you have Multi-Language Support installed under the Windows Setup tab under Add/Remove Programs in Control Panel. Also check Regional Settings in Control Panel for the language selected. Reapply additional languages as needed.

Issue: Rapid failure of keyboards.

Solution: Check the type of keyboard being used, and try a different brand. It could be a problem emanating from the system itself—either a bad or erratic keyboard controller—that is contributing to the short lifespan.

Issue: Device Manager lists two keyboards.

Solution: If you are not actually using two keyboards (a USB type and a PS/2-type, for example), remove the additional keyboard entry.

Issue: USB keyboard not detected.

Solution: Check to be sure USB is enabled in the BIOS. Check the "Keyboard" section in this chapter.

Issue: USB keyboard disappears.

Solution: This can happen occasionally and doesn't necessarily indicate a problem. If it happens frequently, check the USB host controller in Device Manager for a conflict or other problem. If you're plugging other devices into such a keyboard, try removing these to see whether the keyboard is seen more reliably without the extra load. Make certain the mouse is firmly connected to the USB port. Check the earlier discussion of USB keyboards in this chapter.

Issue: Stuck keys.

Solution: Clean the keys per the instructions given earlier in this chapter.

Issue: Mouse cursor doesn't move.

Solution: Is the system hung up? Try keyboard input. If necessary, restart the system. Is the mouse dirty? Clean the mouse per the instructions given earlier in this chapter. Is the mouse properly connected? Do you see any problem with the mouse's connection (serial, PS/2, or USB) in Device Manager or Control

Panel? You might also want to remove the mouse in Device Manager and let the system redetect and reinstall it on restart.

Issue: Cursor or mouse jerks.

Solution: Clean the mouse if you haven't recently. Make certain the surface the mouse is working on is also clean and dry. Check Device Manager for conflicts. This problem is also sometimes caused by an outdated or corrupt video driver.

Issue: Mouse buttons wrong.

Solution: Double-click the Mouse icon in Control Panel, and adjust the buttons.

Issue: Mouse responsiveness wrong.

Solution: Double-click the Mouse icon in Control Panel, adjust Double-Click Speed on the Buttons tab, and modify the settings as needed on the Motion tab.

Issue: USB mouse not seen.

Solution: If this is your first USB device, be sure USB is enabled in the BIOS and that the device is firmly plugged into the USB port. Check the USB Host Controller in Device Manager for a conflict or other problem. Try a different mouse.

Issue: Need to customize pointers.

Solution: Double-click the Mouse icon in Control Panel, and modify the settings under Pointers as needed.

Issue: Scrolling mouse locks PC.

Solution: If you've just upgraded your operating system and use a special mouse (for example, IntelliMouse), reinstall your mouse software (but check for an update for the new operating system version). Clean the mouse if you haven't recently. Make certain the surface the mouse is working on is also clean and dry. Check Device Manager for conflicts. This problem is also sometimes caused by an outdated or corrupt video driver.

Issue: Optical mouse movement jerky.

Solution: Check the optical mouse's accompanying documentation to see whether this addresses the specific problem you're seeing. Be sure that nothing is blocking the optical window. Check your installation: uninstall the mouse and then reinstall it. Make sure nothing within close range of the desktop surface is causing interference. Contact the manufacturer.

Issue: Mouse doesn't work in DOS.

Solution: A driver for the mouse must be loaded in either the CONFIG.SYS or AUTOEXEC.BAT files or the WinStart.BAT for Windows 9x (except when the operating system is Windows Millennium Edition, which would need a driver loaded on the Windows Me Startup disk) to work in full DOS mode.

Troubleshooting Scanners and Digital Cameras

As you know now, if you didn't before, scanners and digital cameras share much of the same technology, including many of the same hardware components. They're also alike in that there is not a lot of repair that can be done on them. Digital cameras have almost no moving parts, and any inside-the-casing attempt to fix them invalidates the warranty.

Scanners are much the same, except that you can repair and reattach a broken cover, replace a bad external power supply, or mend a damaged cable on a hand-held scanner.

So your best defense in keeping these devices working is a good offense, meaning keep them clean and free of cable-wire twisting. In the case of the camera, you also have to keep it from incurring physical damage from being dropped or accidentally hit against a desk, door frame, or other hard surface.

Again, for those who have much older scanners connected through an ISA SCSI host adapter, think about replacing it with a newer scanner. This is especially relevant if you begin to experience problems having your scanner supported by your current operating system, or if you want to upgrade to a motherboard that has no ISA slots.

But one problem that often happens with both scanners and cameras involves their shared TWAIN drivers. The problem occurs when these drivers become damaged or outdated, or are accidentally deleted.

TWAIN Drivers

To have a digital input device such as a scanner or camera communicate with the PC requires a TWAIN driver. Sometimes, when uninstalling and removing software, when reformatting a hard drive, or when some problem occurs, you'll lose the functions that the TWAIN driver provides. This loss of service can be because a file is missing, corrupted in some way, or is viewed to be too old or not of the right type to work with your operating system version. Often, uninstalling and reinstalling the software that came with the camera or scanner will restore the TWAIN driver, along with the device's functionality.

However, sometimes files get left behind in the process, ones that could prevent a full removal and reinstallation of the scanner or camera and its software. So while a key TWAIN file may be gone, others may remain and need to be removed.

To do this in Windows, for example, you would use the following steps:

1. Use Windows Explorer or My Computer, and search for the following files:

   ❑   TWAIN.DLL

   ❑   TWAIN_32.DLL

   ❑   TWUNK_16.EXE

   ❑   TWUNK_32.EXE

2. Delete each of the files listed in step 1.

3. Also look for a folder labeled Windows\TWAIN. If you find it, delete it and any files it contains.

4. Reinstall the scanner or camera software.

Troubleshooting Gaming Hardware

There are two primary points you need to consider when you're trying to troubleshoot problems with gaming hardware. First, this is a type of device where it really pays to follow the Microsoft Hardware Compatibility List (HCL) or Windows Catalog to verify the compatibility of the specific model with the operating system being used. Otherwise, you might spend a significant amount of time on the manufacturer's tech support line or Web site trying to get it recognized and working with full functionality. Often, such hardware should also be compared against the type of software (such as games) these devices will be operated with, because not all games like or work well with all types of gaming hardware. Do some research.

Second, you should realize that even when the connector fits, not all game controllers are compatible with all game ports. Occasionally, you might need to obtain and install an expansion board to give you a compatible game port for some controllers.

Lab 20: Install and Configure a Keyboard and Mouse

This lab is intended to prepare you to install and configure an input setup, including both a mouse and keyboard of any type. It will also prepare you to configure input devices for use and to troubleshoot them as the situation requires.

Objectives

When you complete this lab, you will be able to address the following issues:

1. The basics of installing and configuring a keyboard

2. The essentials of installing and configuring a mouse

3. Performing troubleshooting procedures as needed for either or both devices

Necessary Equipment and Resources

1. A PC of recent vintage

2. A replacement keyboard and mouse

3. Documentation for this hardware

4. About 20 to 30 minutes to complete this lab

Procedures to Follow

1. Check to be sure you have all equipment necessary to complete this job. Record in your lab notes details about the hardware (such as the type of existing keyboard and mouse, the type of new keyboard and mouse, and the operating system version you're using on the target PC).

2. Review the hardware documentation to determine the exact steps to use and in what order to use them. Document in your lab notes any major deviations from the procedures discussed in the "Installation" section for each device.

3. Using the documentation as a base, install the keyboard first. Configure it for use, test it, and troubleshoot it. Then follow the same instructions for installing the mouse. Note the exact steps you took in your lab notes.

Lab Notes

1. Note the specific hardware used for this procedure.

    _____

    _____

    _____

2. Note any particular steps that deviated from the procedure outlined in the section entitled "Installation" earlier in this chapter.

    _____

    _____

    _____

3. Record your steps in installing and configuring the keyboard and the mouse. Note any troubleshooting measures that you take.

    _____

    _____

    _____

21

Printers

For years, people have talked about how computers would help achieve a paperless office, where every form, every report, and every transaction occurs without using endless reams of paper. Yet the reality is that we probably consume as much if not more paper now than we did before. And much of that paper consumption is generated by our printers because of our tireless need for hard copies of what we do. A system without a working printer these days is not a pleasant concept. In a large office environment where a number of people at different workstations share a single printer, a nonworking printer is even more of an issue. For this reason, you need to know the basic types of printers, how they work, how to install them, and how to troubleshoot them. These topics are the focus of this chapter.

About Printing

Before you jump into the actual mechanics of printers and the printing process itself, you should have some background information that applies to virtually all print operations performed on a PC that uses Microsoft Windows as its operating system. Toward that end, let's look at both the Windows printing subsystem and the phenomenon of "in the background" printing, along with the reasons why both are important.

The Windows Printing Subsystem

The Windows printing subsystem is responsible for both coordinating and operating all print-based functions that occur anywhere in Windows, regardless of what application is open. After all, that's one of the hallmarks of an integrated operating system: install a device once, and you have it available just about everywhere. However, there are those who still use DOS applications—some of which might not run from a Windows session—and these might need special installation and drivers.

It's the printing subsystem that communicates with the printer driver and, in turn, with the print device itself. It reports to applications when the printer isn't available or when a page exceeds the normally possible print margins.

Background Printing

Even though it's something we take for granted these days, the ability to let print jobs run in the background while we continue working on other material has been a simple yet critical advance in how we work. In the slow old days, we not only had to install a printer driver for every application from which we printed, our desktops were essentially frozen while we waited for our current print jobs to chug their way along with very slow impact printers until they finished. But several advances in technology have helped bring us to where we are today, able to work as we print. These advances include the following:

- A powerful computer of a fast speed and with large amounts of RAM installed

- A multitasking and integrated operating system, such as you have with Windows

- A printer with installed memory and a solid driver

Major Printer Types

For PCs, there are different types of standard printers, most of which fall into two major mechanical types:

- **Impact**   With this type, some key part of the printer touches the paper in the process of printing. Included in this category are ball-type printers, daisy-wheel printers, dot-matrix printers, and line printers. Dot-matrix and line printers are used for high-volume printing.

- **Nonimpact**   With this type, no major component touches the paper. Included in this category are ink-jet printers, laser printers, and several forms of commercial-grade printing systems.

Nonimpact printers were an important addition to the PC because, as the name implies, less raw physical effort is required by the unit. Nonimpact printers are less likely to exhibit the accelerated wear that impact printers often develop from having part of the mechanism driving against the "ink" source and thus onto the paper. Also, nonimpact printers have fewer moving parts, which translates to less wear. They also tend to have better letter and graphics quality than some impact printers from previous years. In the early 1990s, you had the following questions to answer when purchasing a printer:

- Do you want high-speed or letter-quality printing?

- Do you need to print graphics?

- Do you want to print in color?

Depending upon the answers to these questions, one might be purchasing a high-speed dot-matrix printer, an ink-jet printer, or a laser printer, to name just a few. There were trade-offs for each of them. It was customary to sacrifice speed for higher print quality and vice-versa. But with advancing printer technologies, speed and quality have improved for both nonimpact and impact printers alike.

Before you learn about the most common types of printers in use today, let's take a quick look at some less common printers that fall into the category of nonimpact printers. Many of them have specific industrial or commercial uses and are priced accordingly. These include the following types:

- **Dye sublimation**   Here, solid dyes are introduced into transparent film that serves as the printer's "ink" source. A heating element located in the print head then heats and vaporizes the transparent film onto glossy paper, where it attaches and dries. The heating element's temperature is determined by the color and depth of color it is directed to apply by the demands of the print job.

- **Solid ink**   Some printers use a solid ink source. That solid almost always is wax, which is melted onto the paper.

- **Thermal autochrome**   This type of printer, used for some professional publications, is unique in that the ink is located in the paper introduced into the printer. The paper is manufactured with three different layers of color (cyan, magenta, and yellow) within. A heated print head passes over the paper three different times (once for each color), heating the colors in the paper until they appear on the surface of the page. How much heat is applied depends on the color and the depth of the color called for by the print job.

- **Thermal wax**   Thermal wax printers use a ribbon with alternating bands of the four basic colors of printing. A print head containing very small pins waits for the ribbon to pass before it. The pins, which are mechanically heated, direct the "ink" on the ribbon to melt onto the paper, causing print to appear. Just as it sounds from this description, thermal wax is something of a technological hybrid of both the dye sublimation and solid ink print schemes described earlier in this list.

Exam Tip   The four basic colors of printing are cyan (C), magenta (M), yellow (Y), and black (B).

Laser Printers

Originally priced well into the thousands of dollars, laser printers were formerly available only to professional offices and companies depending on their printed product. Today's typical laser printers are much less expensive (especially monochrome lasers, which are significantly cheaper than color units that use up to four different toners), have greater capacity than their forebears, and are frequently bought as an upgrade to or as a better-looking adjunct to an ink-jet or other cheaper printer technology. Print speed can vary considerably between different models, depending on how much RAM is installed and the resolution at which you print. A low-end speed of four to six pages per minute (PPM) is still seen in many laser printers—especially cheap or older ones—while newer, higher-capacity units can print 24 PPM or more in monochrome.

Enhanced resolution and a virtually unlimited array of font possibilities is the hallmark of the laser printer's success. Besides the printer's resident fonts, additional font types can often be added through a cartridge or soft fonts often can be added by increasing the amount of RAM installed on the printer.

Tip   High-resolution printing demands higher amounts of RAM than more typical printing. For example, a minimum of 4 MB of RAM installed on the printer is needed to print at 600 dots per inch (DPI).

Laser Printer Programming Support

To support the quality of their output, laser printers typically use one of two different programming language standards:

■   PostScript (For more information, see the section entitled "PROFILE: PostScript Printers" later in this chapter.)

■   Printer Command Language (PCL). Developed by Hewlett-Packard, PCL allows for fonts to be added by adding an HP font cartridge to the printer or through options directly available within supporting applications.

Laser Printer Components and Operation

Frequently, you are warned about avoiding static electricity in components of a PC, but if you use a laser printer, you depend on static electricity for it to work. The typical revolving *cylinder*, or *drum*, in a laser printer's drum assembly acts as a photoreceptor to pull light to it. In fact, the entire assembly is made of exceptionally photoconductive material. When a laser print job is started, the *corona wires* or the *charged roller* (depending on type and model) administer a positive charge to the cylinder or drum. As the cylinder begins to turn, a light beam hits specific points on it. Those points are the images of the letters, numbers, or figures the printer has been directed to print. But these images are unique in that they are electrostatic images created by a series of electrical charges.

Once the images are drawn, the print toner is applied (from its reserve in the toner cartridge) to coat the cylinder. The toner itself is positively charged, so it affixes itself to the area where the electrostatic charges created images. Because any area of the cylinder that was not "written to" still has a positive charge of its own, the toner leaves it alone, and this serves as the background of the printed document. Why? Remember, opposites attract in natural science.

Paper located in the paper tray is then fed by a roller or rollers along the path to meet the cylinder. Just before the paper is fed against the cylinder, a negative charge is applied to it by the corona wire or charged roller. Because the charge applied to the paper is stronger than the charge applied in creating the electrostatic images on the cylinder, the paper, as it moves against the cylinder, picks up the toner ink that rests against the electrostatic images (the printing). Once that transfer is complete, the surface of the cylinder is subjected to a discharge lamp, which helps clean off the remaining toner to prepare the cylinder for the next page.

At this point, you have a page with toner lying on it, and that toner might come off if the process ended here. So the paper then passes through a pair of heated rollers, usually referred to as the *fuser*, that fuse the toner particles to the paper. Both the fuser's heat and pressure is needed to accomplish this. The paper then slides out into the tray.

> **Note**   If you don't know why most pages feel quite warm coming out of either a laser printer or copier, the fusion process with its heated rollers is the answer.

> **Fact**   Toner is a powdery substance (although it might also appear suspended in liquid) that has been electrically charged to adhere in a situation, as you have with either a laser printer or photocopier, where a drum or paper has been given a negative charge. Laser printers and photocopiers are very similar in applied technology.

> **Caution**   Never attempt to pick up spilled toner powder with a vacuum cleaner. The material is so fine that it goes right through many bags and filtration systems and has the potential to burn out the motor on your first attempt.

PROFILE: PostScript Printers   Although the technology has begun to age a bit (with the last major release occurring in 1997), PostScript printers are still used and purchased. They are still predominantly used by Macintosh systems and systems devoted to desktop publishing.

PostScript differs from standard printers in several ways, a few of which are key to its continued use. First, understand that when Adobe developed the technology more than 10 years ago, our usual printer hookup (if we had one) was a not-very-evolved dot-matrix.

Adobe Page Description Language (PDL), a programming language created just to force better control over the printer and its output in the way it works with documents, serves as the core of PostScript. While specifically written for documents to be printed on a laser printer, it was later adapted to other types of devices.

PDL is also an object-oriented programming (OOP) language, and it was unique in that it treated all images, including the fonts used in a document, as geometrical objects rather than bit-mapped images. (More standard printers see fonts as bitmaps.) It was also unique in that it permitted the use of well-defined, scalable fonts. A PostScript printer, for a time, allowed for far more fonts than its contemporary counterparts. Postscript/PDL was also able to make much fuller use out of high-resolution printing systems than bitmapped-based ones. Regardless of a bitmapped font's size, it looks the same at just about any resolution, while PostScript fonts improve in quality the greater the resolution used. Having this kind of control over fonts and such has made PostScript a standard many publishers and commercial print firms use to derive the best quality from what they print.

Every PostScript-compatible printer has an integrated interpreter for handling PostScript programming commands. Some laser printers today might not be PostScript-capable by default, but they allow you to add an optional cartridge to add PostScript capabilities or—more commonly today—they allow you to download and install PostScript drivers to use all the fonts they need.

There are three different levels of PostScript (called Level 1, Level 2, and Level 3). The last two—Level 2 and Level 3—developed and added features and functionality beyond the foundation of Level 1. PostScript printers today usually support the most recent level (which is Level 3, released in 1997).

Inkjet Printers

Among the many brands and models of inkjet printers available today, there are two major types seen. One type differs from the other largely in the manner in which the ink is applied to the page. One type involves the use of vibration, while the other needs heat. These types are as follows:

- **Piezoelectric technology**   With these, a special crystal called a *piezo* is positioned at the rear of each nozzle's ink reservoir. When a slight charge is applied to these crystals, they vibrate and the resulting motion forces ink from the nozzles onto the page while also pulling another shot of ink from the cartridge or cartridges into the reservoirs.

- **Thermal bubble technology** In this type, a heating element comprised of mini-resistors lies parallel with the ink reservoir. As the resistors warm, the resulting heat begins to vaporize the ink and a bubble forms and grows, pushing ink from the nozzle onto the page. The bubble continues to expand until it pops, and the vacuum left by this action acts to draw more ink up from the cartridge.

Inkjet Print Components and Operation

Inkjet printers all contain a small circuit card on which is mounted both a small processor and some amount of memory (often 512K or more) to help handle print jobs effectively. However, this isn't the core of an inkjet printer, as it is commonly perceived. Instead, the core is considered to be the print head, which bears a set of miniature nozzles through which ink drawn from the print cartridges is shot into a reservoir. This is what makes the inkjet stand out in printer functionality as a reasonably inexpensive technology. The inexpensive nature of the technology has helped make inkjets the most widely sold consumer printer type.

> **Fact** The dots of ink applied by an inkjet printer are smaller than the diameter of a human hair. Inkjet dots are about 40 to 60 microns in size, while a normal human hair measures about 70 microns.

Other Major Inkjet Components

The following list defines other major inkjet components:

- **Print head stepper motor** A stepper motor is a special type of motor that moves in calculated, stepped revolutions. In this case, it moves the whole print head assembly across the page and back as the print process proceeds.

- **Stabilizing bar** This component is provided to help control the smooth and precise motion of the print head assembly.

- **Belt** The belt provides the attachment between the print head assembly and its stepper motor.

■   **Ink cartridges**   Often at least one different ink cartridge is needed for black and for color, but these might be combined into one cartridge serving both. Some printers also have one black and then more than one cartridge to handle the other colors. (See Figure 21-1.)

Figure 21-1   An ink cartridge inserted into an Epson Stylus inkjet printer

■   **Paper-feed assembly**   A paper-feed assembly is usually made of the following parts:

❏   A blank paper tray (or perhaps a feeder instead). There is also a finish tray for depositing the printed page.

❏   Rollers, for helping control movement of the paper from its tray or feeder to the print head and to reposition the paper during the print process.

❑ A paper-feed stepper motor controls the precise movement of the paper through the print process. It's aided by the rollers, making for a smoother motion with less friction and less ability to jam.

■ **Power supply** A power supply is usually built into the printer rather than built as an external source. It does not draw power from the PC.

■ **Computer interface** The interface (which is a parallel port or USB port) is for the cable connecting the printer to the PC for communication.

InkJet Operation

Using the inkjet printer as our example, let's see what exactly transpires when you choose to print a file:

1. You choose to print a document, and select that option from an application.

2. The application then signals the printer driver of a pending print job and begins to transmit the data.

3. The driver has to translate the data contained in the print job into a printer-friendly format.

4. The driver also queries the printer to make sure it is both turned on and available to receive work. Once the driver establishes that the printer is on and ready, data begins transmitting over the printer cable connecting the printer to the PC.

5. As the data comes into the printer, it's temporarily stored in the print buffer (which usually has a capacity equal to the amount of memory installed on the printer).

6. Meanwhile, the printer is busy initializing itself for use. (This might not happen if a print job has just completed.) It might go through something called a *cleaning cycle*, where it moves rollers and restores hardware positions to make sure its mechanical self is clean and ready to print.

7. Circuitry located within the printer turns on the stepper motor that controls the feed from the paper tray so that the first sheet of paper is drawn into the printer properly.

8. Once the paper is correctly positioned, the print head stepper motor begins moving the print head assembly smoothly back and forth across the page, with pauses to allow the print head nozzles to spray the ink that forms the letters, which happens almost imperceptibly.

9. Once a pass is complete, the paper is advanced ever so slightly by the paper-feed stepper motor and the print head continues its work, either returning to the original side of the page to print again or simply changing direction and moving back the other way.

10. When the print job or page is complete, the print head assembly might be parked (although this isn't true of all models) or returned to a specific position.

11. The paper-feed stepper motor finishes its job by pushing the finished page into the output tray for retrieval.

Installation

Most printers connect to a PC through one of several interfaces: the parallel or printer port (also called an LPT) or through a USB port. However, you can still find those that connect via the serial port as well as those that use infrared and a PC or laptop's IrDa port. While USB-interface printers are increasing in popularity, parallel port connections remain the most common. In a network situation, a printer might be installed on a single PC and then shared with other workstations on the network or attached to the network by means of a print server and then made available to others. Figure 21-2 shows the printer and USB ports (among others) at the back of a PC.

Figure 21-2   The parallel (printer) port and USB ports for connection of a standard or USB printer

Before you begin the installation, review the documentation for the new printer and be sure you have the cartridges, paper, and other accessories that the documentation indicates must be installed to the printer as part of the process of setting it up. Some printers include the cartridges and have them already inserted in the printer. For other printers, you'll need to install them.

To replace an existing parallel port printer with a new one, follow these steps:

1.   Double-click the Printer (or Printers And Faxes) icon in Control Panel, select the existing printer you want to remove (as shown in Figure 21-3), and click Delete or Delete This Printer.

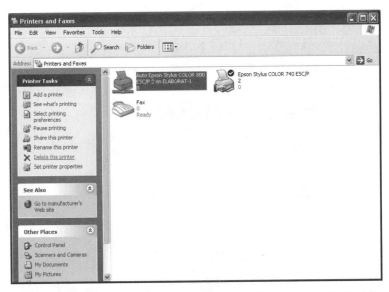

Figure 21-3   Selecting printer to manage from Printers And Faxes view

2. Shut down the system, and disconnect the existing printer from the parallel (printer) port. Then disconnect the existing printer from power, and move the printer to another location.

3. Position the new printer, plug it in to a power source, attach its cable to the parallel (printer) port, and then turn the printer on.

4. Restart the PC. You might need to provide the printer driver when Windows detects the new printer and begins to install support for it.

Now let's look at a USB printer installation. If you plan to remove an existing parallel (printer) port printer as part of this procedure, follow the first two steps under the previous set of instructions and then turn the PC back on. Once you have done that, follow these steps:

1. With the PC on, insert the USB plug from the USB cable connected to the printer to the USB port on the PC unless otherwise directed by the manufacturer's instructions.

2. Plug the new printer in, and turn it on.

3. When prompted to do so during the installation procedure, provide the printer driver disk, as needed.

To share a printer on a network:

1. Double-click the Printers or Printers And Faxes icon in Control Panel.

2. Right-click on the printer you want to share, and select Sharing. Doing this will open the Sharing tab (shown in Figure 21-4).

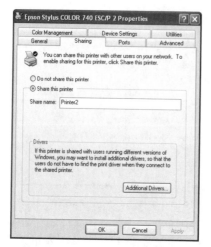

Figure 21-   4 Sharing and Drivers options from the Sharing tab

3. Select Share This Printer, and provide a name for the printer on the network. Click OK to finish.

Maintenance and Repair

If you compare the price of cartridges and toners to the cost of most printers (even laser) used in smaller offices and homes, you'll notice a considerable discrepancy. This is because most of the cost of printer production is recovered not by the price of the printer at the time of sale but by the money paid for the products to support that printer's use. Even with some laser printers, it can be more expensive to replace the toner and other accessories than it is to purchase a new printer.

When it comes to repair and replacement of actual hardware within a printer, the manufacturer—if the product is still covered by warranty—frequently will just ship a new or reconditioned printer rather than exhaust a great deal of time trying to repair a unit. Thus, most printers today are considered disposable hardware.

To keep a printer in good working condition, follow these guidelines:

- Keep the unit clean, clear of bits of paper and smeared ink, and free from dust.

- Update the printer driver as needed.

- Use only recommended accessories (papers, cartridges, toner, and so on) for the printer model in use.

Troubleshooting

When working on a troublesome printer issue, you might want to try any of these actions to localize the problem:

- Verify the connections between the printer port or USB port and the power source.

- Remove and reinstall the printer driver.

- Remove and reinstall the printer port itself, and then reinstall the printer.

- Check to see whether the cartridge is empty. (An empty cartridge is one of the leading causes of problems.)

- Check the printer utility installed on your system. Run any diagnostics tests provided in it. (You can also find this utility under Properties by right-clicking on the printer under Printers in Control Panel, as shown in Figure 21-5.)

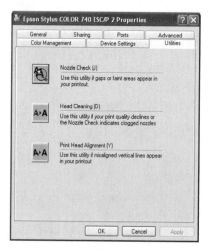

Figure 21- 5The Utilities tab under printer properties

■ Check the front panel of the printer for any error codes or flashing lights, and check these against the printer manual. (See Figure 21-6.)

Figure 21-6 The front panel of an inkjet printer showing lights detecting a cartridge problem

- Attempt to print a test page. (If the test page prints fine, the odds are that the problem is PC or PC-to-printer based. If a test page won't print, the problem is likely with the physical printer itself.)

- Restart the system. Low system resources, stalled applications, and previously failed print jobs can affect the start of a print job.

- If the printer is sharing a parallel port with another device—such as a scanner or Zip drive—using a pass-through setup, try removing anything else and plugging only the printer into the parallel port. If printing is restored, the problem is with the pass-through (cable or configuration) setup. Some (if not most) pass-through devices don't recommend the use of a printer as part of the pass-through.

- If the printer is one of two or more installed on a switch box (allowing you to mechanically switch back and forth between different printers), remove the printer from the switchbox and install it directly into the parallel port. If this provides the remedy, the problem is with the switchbox or its connections or configuration.

- If the printer is USB and installed on a keyboard or powered hub, remove the printer connection from it and install it directly on a USB port on the PC. If this fixes it, the problem is with the original device the printer was plugged into or with the printer being too high demand for that device. Wherever possible, print device ports should not be shared with other devices.

- Fully test access to either a shared printer or print server, if applicable.

- Update your printer driver.

- Remove any extra connections, such as those for network print availability, as you troubleshoot.

- Adjust spool settings—including both printer port and timeout settings—as needed.

- To rule out a problem with the application you're trying to print from, or the file itself, attempt to print the same file from another PC with another printer (preferably, not one attached through the network to the PC with the current printer failure).

- Temporarily remove a network client or network protocol in use and try the printer again.

> **Caution** Always look very carefully at a cartridge when you check it for fullness. Even with transparent-walled cartridges, ink can build up on the sides and make it appear as if the cartridge contains far more ink than it does.

Don't forget to refer both to the printer manual as well as the manufacturer's Web site (usually in the product support pages). Many printers have a label inside the cover that details the steps for cartridge or toner replacement as well as definitions of common error codes. Figure 21-7 shows a label stating how to replace cartridges and align them afterward.

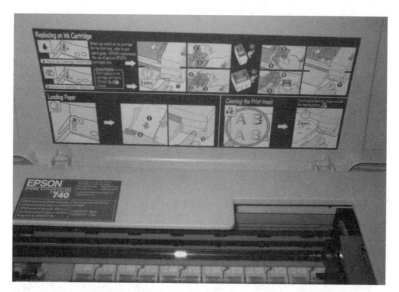

Figure 21-7 An example of a printer label indicating how to perform common operations

Print Manager Software and Self-Test

Most printers today are packaged with management software that works with the printer and your operating system to perform basic diagnostics (such as tools for determining whether there is bidirectional communication between the printer and the PC or whether the system is reporting that the printer is out of ink) as well as maintenance functions (such as procedures for cleaning and realigning cartridges). When a problem develops with the PC, refer to your printer's documentation as well as the print manager software that you installed with your printer or through the Windows Print Manager. These sources might offer either important clues or outright fixes for the identified issue at hand.

The printer self-test function, on the other hand, is built into the programmable part of the printer itself and doesn't require proper communication with the PC to perform. Your printer manual will tell you how to perform a self test if the option is not clearly identified on your printer's control console.

Table 21-1 lists common printing problems and likely solutions.

Table 21-1   Common Printing Issues and What to Do

Problem	What to Check
No printer power light	Check the connection to the power source, and make certain other devices work from the same source. Check for a firm connection of the power cable. If possible, temporarily swap out the power cable for a different one.
Printer light is on, but there's no responsiveness	Check all connections running from the printer (such as to the PC, to the power source, and so on) to be sure all are firmly connected. Check documentation, and run a printer self-test. (This doesn't depend on the connection with the PC at all; it just tests the printer's ability to work.) If the self-test works fine, shut down and restart the system and then try to print again. (A problem during a previous print job can keep the printer in "wait" mode and unavailable to you.) Also check the "print manager" software that comes with the printer to see what it reports in diagnostics.
No printer action after a new cartridge is installed	Check to see if the cartridge is installed properly. Check cable and power connections. Check print manager software. Remove and reinstall the printer driver if necessary. Contact the manufacturer.
Print job starts, but no print appears on the page	Check Print Manager to see whether a problem has been reported. If you recently changed cartridges, check the cartridge seating and reinstall it. Then align the cartridge or cartridges using print manager software. Check to be sure any tape or cover on the head of the cartridge has been removed. If possible, swap in a fresh print cartridge to rule out a bad one. Check Print Properties for the current print job as well, and adjust the features (such as changing from optimum to fast draft).

Table 21-1   Common Printing Issues and What to Do

Problem	What to Check
Paper repeatedly jams	Make sure you're using clean, dry paper of the proper type for your printer. Also, check to see if the printer is clean: rollers, in particular, might have a buildup of dust and debris that could cause this problem. If necessary, remove the paper tray and clean it. Check inside printer for anything (such as paper) that might be stuck in the rollers.
Printer malfunctions during big print jobs	Turn off the printer, and let it thoroughly cool. Open printer cover to allow this to happen more effectively. Check documentation to see if a maximum print job for continuous operation is given and that you are not exceeding it. Larger print jobs should always be done using paper specific to the type of printer. Try again to print. On jobs far exceeding the printer's normal capacity, try printing in batches of a set amount rather than attempting to do it all at once.
Can print in DOS and Linux but not in Windows	Go to Windows Device Manager, and locate the printer in question. Remove it and restart the system. Windows should redetect the printer and begin installation. Be sure you have the latest printer driver for your operating system.
Can print in DOS and Linux, but a problem is reported in Windows only	The solution is similar to the one just described, but on your second attempt, find and remove the LPT port in question in Device Manager as well. Windows should redetect the port on the next install, and then reinstall the printer.
Printer keeps losing the PC signal	Check printer connections. If possible, temporarily swap out the cable between the printer and the PC. Remove and reinstall the printer driver.
Printer won't work after a move	Check the power light. If it's on, perform a printer self-test. If the test works, remove and reinstall the printer driver in the operating system.

Lab 21: Install a Printer

This lab is intended to prepare you to install and configure a printer as well as configure it for use. It also prepares you to troubleshoot printer problems as the situation requires.

Objectives

When you complete this lab, you will be able to address the following issues:

1. The basics of installing and configuring a printer

2. The essentials of installing and configuring a mouse

3. Performing troubleshooting procedures as needed for either or both devices

Necessary Equipment and Resources

The following equipment and resources are necessary for completing this lab:

1. A PC of recent vintage

2. A new or replacement printer

3. Documentation for this hardware

4. About 15 to 20 minutes to complete this lab

Procedures to Follow

1. Check to be sure you have all equipment necessary to complete this job. Record in your lab notes details about the hardware (including the existing and new printer, plus the operating system version you're using on the target PC).

2. Review the hardware documentation to determine the exact steps to use and in what order to use them. Document in your lab notes any major deviations from the procedures discussed in the "Installation" section for each device.

3. Using the documentation as a base, install the printer and then perform a test by printing documents from it (preferably, one in black and white and one in color, if the printer you've installed prints color). Note the exact steps you took in your lab notes.

4. If the PC you have installed the printer on is part of a network, share this printer.

Lab Notes

1. Note the specific hardware used for this procedure.

    _____

    _____

    _____

2. Note any particular steps that deviated from the procedure outlined in the "Installation" section in this chapter.

    _____

    _____

    _____

3. Record your steps for installing and configuring the printer for use. Note any troubleshooting measures taken.

    _____

    _____

    _____

4. Note your results for sharing the printer on the network, if applicable.

    _____

    _____

    _____

Part VI

Taking It to Another Level

You're very close to wrapping up, but there's one more tier to go. Now it's time to take our study to a different level: to the realm of mobile computers. We'll explore the similarities and differences between a portable PC and a desktop PC. We'll also go beyond that and use all you've learned thus far to assemble a complete PC from the motherboard on up, all the way to successful boot-up and operation.

22

The Laptop Connection

Now we enter the world of mobile computing. When portable computers first appeared on the market in the early 1980s, they were almost invariably less powerful, less proficient, and less productive than a desktop PC. The emphasis was on trying to keep the unit from weighing too much to carry while still providing people with a means to have computer capability—albeit more limited—wherever they were.

Today, portable computers are thinner, fairly lightweight, and pack every bit as much power as their desktop counterparts. This is necessary because more and more people work outside the standard office workplace, whether they're in a plane, train, or automobile or somewhere else hundreds or thousands of miles from the home office. Portable computers are used on the battlefield, too, although they're usually packaged in a much more rugged case. (Some specialty manufacturers produce units capable of sustaining the weight of a military vehicle being rolled over it—but you shouldn't need anything that tough.)

Finally, we have reached the point where we can address laptops—their hardware, their connection interfaces, and their troubleshooting—as more than just an alternative to the standard PC desktop. You'll see their similarities to a desktop PC, as well as their differences. Understanding these differences will be necessary if you have to support them and work with their hardware.

Different Types, All Mobile

There are different types of portable computers, with a portable computer defined as one that is 15 pounds or less and meant for at least partially mobile use. For example, while the terms *laptop* and *notebook computer* are often used interchangeably, a notebook is a subset of a laptop category (with laptops weighing between 4 and 8 pounds). Notebooks are particularly slender, usually weigh between 4 and 6 pounds, and are easily transported within a standard briefcase or portfolio.

A sub-notebook, by comparison, is typically slimmer than a notebook, with a weight of between 2 and 4 pounds. Finally, a pocket-sized computer usually weighs about 1 pound.

Major Laptop Architecture

My first glimpse of a truly portable computer was some 20 years ago, when a fellow journalist brought one to a meeting we were both covering for our respective newspapers. *Portable* seemed to be the wrong word because it looked—and felt by its weight—about as portable as one of those really old Singer sewing machines, back when they used real steel. It was massive and extremely heavy (more than 20 pounds). As this poor fellow tried to balance it on his lap, I watched in both wonder and horror. He mentioned its price—well in excess of $10,000—and when I pestered him for details, he admitted it was not really compatible with the PC back at the office because it used a different operating system and the floppy drive was proprietary.

Sure, the potential of a portable computer was terribly exciting, especially because even fax transmissions would not become a standard office communication technique for some time. But the price and the weight were out of the range of all but the most dedicated, and its incompatibility with desktops made absolutely no sense to me.

Thankfully, the industry has changed the architecture and pricing considerably in the intervening two decades, making the configuration tighter, the components smaller and far lighter, and the price much more competitive with a desktop system. Today, there are many who rarely if ever use a desktop PC; all their work gets done on laptops and hand-helds. In most regards, when you work with a laptop, you're working with the same basic system as a desktop, although you'll find that there is no Peripheral Component Interconnect (PCI) expansion bus (because CardBus and PC Cards replace this in laptops), more of the components are integrated into the motherboard to save space, and maintenance and repair can be a bit harder to perform. A laptop has many of the same issues related to hardware resource assignment (IRQs, DMA channels, and all that jazz, so to speak), although you'll find that expansion of the system often occurs outside the housing proper.

In this section, we'll explore the major components either contained within or available to a portable computer. Before we do, let's look at some important issues related to working with hardware on laptops.

> **Exam Tip** Expansion tends to be more limited with laptops. Three of the most common ways to expand a laptop's performance capabilities are to increase the RAM, increase the hard disk space, or to do both at once.

Special Issues in Working with Laptops

Many laptops are simply not as serviceable as desktop systems. Indeed, laptops vary widely in terms of how much can be replaced by a knowledgeable user or field service technician and what needs to be replaced or repaired by the manufacturer or its authorized service agent. For example, you'll see that some laptops make it easy to add or replace memory, while with others you would literally almost need to break the housing to reach the memory. The same can be true of laptop drives and other components.

It's smart to familiarize yourself with the overall anatomy of a particular system before you try to work with it for repair or replacement. Often, this type of detail is not found within the user documentation, but it might be available in the support area of the manufacturer's Web site or obtainable by calling the manufacturer and requesting it.

Here's an example. If I look in the user manual for my Dell laptop, I won't necessarily glean from it what I need to know to add memory or change a drive installed to it. So when I need that kind of detail, I go to the Dell Web site (*http://support.dell.com*) and begin to browse through the support options until I reach *http://support.dell.com/systemdocumentation/index.aspx*, which gives me options to explore user guides for case assemblies, devices, and so on.

You also must consider warranty and service contracts when working with a laptop. For some portable computers, doing anything except attaching or removing a device accessible from the outside of the case will invalidate the warranty, which could mean you'll lose all future support that would be covered under the agreement. Do your research here, too, to be sure you're not invalidating the warranty or service contract with the measures you perform.

Another big difference between desktops and laptops is that instead of installing adapters to an expansion bus within the laptop, you typically add new devices either through the external ports and jacks or through the use of PC Card (formerly known as PCMCIA) devices—such as the PC Card modem shown in Figure 22-1—which install to the PC Card slots available. Think of PC Card devices as the functional equivalent of the desktop's bus expansion adapter, although they're easier to install and remove.

Figure 22-1   A PC Card modem being inserted into a Type II/III PC Card slot on a laptop

PC Card devices come in a number of types, with Type II and Type III being the most prevalent right now. For instance, you can add needed memory to some units simply by inserting a compatible memory PC Card. You'll learn more about this in the section entitled "Cardbus and PC Card Components" later in this chapter.

Operating System

Laptops don't require a special operating system; the same Windows versions compatible with your desktop system should also be compatible with your laptop. This differs from hand-held devices that tend to use proprietary operating systems such as Windows XP Tablet Edition for Tablet PCs or Windows Compact Edition (CE) for hand-held units.

You should be aware that there can be more concerns with upgrading an operating system on a laptop simply because a laptop might use more proprietary or specialty hardware than a desktop. For this reason, it's smart to check the laptop manufacturer's Web site for specific information about updating the operating system before you perform the upgrade itself to be sure the BIOS and other components won't present any nasty surprises.

Motherboard and BIOS

A laptop motherboard is smaller and far more concentrated in structure than a desktop motherboard. It's also more integrated, with more of the components needed installed directly into the motherboard circuitry rather than available as separate options.

A motherboard might be very specific and proprietary to the unique layout of a particular type of laptop design. For example, a laptop motherboard might fit only one or a small number of models of laptop because of the way the rest of the unit is built around it within the overall unit's housing. This often translates into the need to replace one type of motherboard with the exact same type of motherboard. Keep this in mind when you face a situation where you might need to replace a mobile motherboard.

With this point comes another issue: it can be virtually impossible for you to replace a motherboard on a laptop. There are two reasons for this: you might not be able to gain physical access to the motherboard itself, and even if you could, few manufacturers will sell such a component to anyone but an authorized service technician (one specifically trained to work on those laptops). Also, the laptop's motherboard must be compatible with the type of CPU used. This is similar to a desktop system.

Remember the BIOS update process performed in Chapter 5, "Motherboards"? The same procedure can be necessary for a laptop—and is achieved in the same manner—particularly when performing an operating system upgrade or adding a new device not currently supported by the motherboard BIOS.

Processor

Just as with desktops, the processor in a laptop rules its domain. But the processors used in laptops typically are designed specifically for use in mobile units (often classified as *Processor M* or *mobile processors*), such as the Intel Centrino platform, although they follow the same conventions (Celeron, Pentium III, Pentium IV, and AMD style) as desktop systems. Thus, you can't exchange a standard CPU for a dead mobile CPU.

Memory

A laptop, because it often runs the same applications and same operating system as a desktop, requires the same amount of the proper type of RAM to be installed. Anyone using a laptop today with 64 MB of RAM or less is apt to feel the pinch when working with graphics or other large files and with multiple programs open at the same time.

Finding the physical memory installed on a laptop can be a bit of an issue, unless you have the documentation or check the manufacturer's Web site for specifics. Different units and even different models from the same manufacturer might provide access to the memory in varying physical locations. For example, on some systems, you'll have a mechanism that allows you to remove the keypad to gain access to memory positioned beneath it. On others, memory will be located behind a panel on the back or bottom of a laptop where you might need to remove a screw or two to access it. There are even some laptop models—hopefully fairly rare—that make it almost impossible to access the memory. They're made this way, perhaps, with the expectation that they'll be returned to the manufacturer or authorized dealer to perform such upgrades. Try to establish the memory location through online or print documentation before you proceed.

Also look for the exact type of memory used in the laptop. Often, when you go to obtain new laptop memory, you need to match it to the exact type recommended by the manufacturer of the laptop for that model.

The most commonly used type of laptop memory is called a SODIMM, or small outline dual inline memory module. SODIMM is a smaller, thinner type of memory than the DIMMs used in some desktops. These are typically part of a thin small outline package (TSOP) plastic rectangular memory chip mounting with gull-wing pins on either of its short sides.

Depending on the specifications of the laptop, SODIMMs can be installed alone or in pairs. If a laptop requires pairs, you must install two SODIMMs; if you install just one, the laptop will not recognize the memory or work. Also, some laptops have just a single SODIMM slot, while others have two (which is necessary when pairs are required but might even be the case when SODIMMs can be installed individually).

To install or replace memory in a laptop, follow these steps:

1.   With the laptop and anything attached to it turned off and disconnected from power, remove whatever panel or mechanism is necessary to reach the memory. (See Figure 22-2.)

Figure 22-2   The memory access panel, with the screw removed, at the bottom of a laptop

2.   Ground yourself as discussed in Chapter 3, "Defining Your Tech Toolkit."

3.   Remove any existing SODIMM you want to replace by lifting the clamps that usually hold a laptop memory module in place. Then carefully lift the edge of the memory to about a 45-degree angle before you pull the module from its slot.

4.   Gently holding the new memory module, also place it at a 45-degree angle before you connect it into the slot and restore the clamps to hold it in place.

5.   Replace the panel or mechanism that covers the memory area, restore power, and check the system to be sure it boots up and recognizes the new memory.

Please note that in step 3, you might actually have to push down, rather than lift up, the clamps holding the memory module. It depends on the architecture of the system you have. Consult your laptop documentation or manufacturer's Web site for details.

Power Supplies and Cooling

This area is one where laptops and desktops can differ by a fair amount. Unlike a desktop system, which you want to pack with far more power than you would normally use and with options ranging from simple to elaborate hardware schemes to cool components within, most laptops are built to provide a power supply offering just enough power to cover the hardware attached to it and usually have no major ventilation system.

Figure 22-3 shows the access panel at the bottom of a laptop to reach the power supply, while Figure 22-4 shows the power supply fan. Like desktop power supply fans, a laptop power supply fan can become clogged with dust and should be routinely cleaned to keep it in proper operation.

Figure 22-   3 Laptop access panel for the power supply

Figure 22-4   The power supply fan beneath the access panel

The limited power and cooling capabilities of a laptop make sense. A laptop would be much heavier and consume more battery life if it required a more robust power supply. Also, because special cooling devices take up space, a laptop would need to be larger overall to contain them. So cooling is often limited to the fan on the laptop power supply and one or more vents in the housing. Thus, a laptop operates with a thinner margin of error than a desktop for both power and cooling. For this reason, a laptop is not a good candidate for the sort of system overclocking that some people perform to push desktop computers past their normal performance ratings.

A laptop user, however, isn't stuck with the power and cooling limitations imposed by the manufacturer. There are external cooling devices, such as cooling trays and pads, designed to move hot air trapped beneath the laptop away from the unit. There are also uninterruptible power supplies (UPSs) designed specifically for laptop use, as well as portable surge protectors that can be carried within the laptop case.

Batteries and AC Adapters

Laptops come with both a battery pack to allow the machine to be used when not plugged into a wall socket as well as an AC adapter. Some batteries feature separate recharging units, while others will come back to full charge as the laptop is plugged back into power.

Lithium ion, nickel cadmium, and nickel metal halide are the three most commonly used battery types found in laptops. Of these, lithium usually offers the longest usage life in terms of how long you can operate it before you must revert back to AC power or install a spare battery while you wait for the first to be recharged. (The recharging process can take almost as long, depending on battery type, as the battery operates without AC power assistance.) Nickel cadmium tends to offer the lowest level of sustainable power. Many experts recommend that you regularly allow a battery to be drained through service and then recharged so that a battery can be conditioned to recharge fully. Otherwise, you might find that a battery develops a shorter life between recharges.

Standard laptop battery life between recharges is usually limited to two or three hours or less, depending on the type of activity performed. Almost any operation involving frequent disk activity, including playing a DVD, can shorten this span significantly.

To extend battery life, most laptops are preconfigured to go into sleep or hibernation modes, which are low-power modes used when the laptop isn't in active use. These modes are similar but usually a bit more aggressive than the power management used on a desktop system. This design can sometimes cause problems when trying to "wake" the unit from sleep, as you'll see later in the "Troubleshooting" section of this chapter.

You might also discover that AC adapters (shown in Figure 22-5) and batteries are often specific to the unit. The result is that when you need to replace an adapter or battery—or purchase a spare battery—you need to look for one specifically designed for use with that type and perhaps exact model of laptop.

Figure 22-5   An AC adapter for a laptop with its connector for attachment to the laptop

Beyond standard batteries, there are a growing number of accessory products for laptops. One option is power pads with an external battery that can maintain a laptop running for between 10 and 20 hours.

> **Note**   Here's an interesting point. If you pick up the AC adapter on several laptops, you'll notice a large difference in the weight. Some weigh in excess of 1 or 2 pounds. However, when a laptop computer's weight is computed, the weight of the adapter is not factored in.

Video Display

The job of a standard video adapter is usually integrated directly by chipset into the motherboard on a laptop, obviously as a space-saving consideration. The problem with this setup is that a damaged or problematic video chipset means you must replace the laptop motherboard if not the laptop itself. (The latter option might be necessary only if there is no way to achieve the video results you want with the integrated motherboard you need to use as a replacement.)

The overall quality of video display on a laptop computer can vary widely, from amazingly crisp and clear to displays you must look at dead-on to view the screen. Poor quality can be the fault of the video chipset itself, the display technology backing the screen, or both. See Chapter 10, "Audio," and Chapter 18, "Going Wireless," for specifics on video and monitor displays. Further details appear in these chapters because many laptops now share the same type of digital video formats for display as digital monitors.

Active matrix, or thin film transistor (TFT), flat-panel displays are probably the most common type of laptop display in recent years. These tend to offer a crisper display than passive matrix or dual-scan flat-panel options, although these are still used on some budget laptops.

A video monitor port (shown in Figure 22-6), which is available on many laptops, allows the connection of a standard VGA monitor. This is also available through docking stations, which are discussed later in this chapter. You can also have a dual display if you use both an external monitor and a hookup to a data projector that projects the laptop display onto an overhead screen or wall along with the laptop's flat panel display.

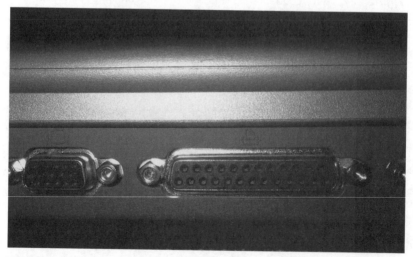

Figure 22-6   The monitor port, along with the printer port, at the back of a laptop

Devices are available, too, that allow you to install a separate video adapter through the PC Card slot. This is usually done to supplement a less-than-robust onboard video chipset or for special-use applications.

Audio

Like the video chipset on a laptop, a desktop system's sound adapter is typically integrated directly into a laptop motherboard. A speaker system is built in as well. (You wouldn't normally want to carry around separate speakers, after all.) Replacement of integrated audio usually means the replacement of the entire motherboard.

The same jacks seen on a desktop system for adding external audio components are usually seen on a laptop, as shown in Figure 22-7. These include connectors for external speakers, headphones, and a microphone (although a microphone can be integrated into the motherboard as well). The same external audio devices are compatible with either desktop or laptop systems.

Figure 22-7   External audio component jacks on a laptop

CardBus and PC Card Components

PC Card components are one of the most common ways to add new functionality or capacity to a laptop, and using them is much easier than going inside the case to install something. Let's discuss them now in more detail.

CardBus is the laptop's PC Card expansion bus, which is very similar in functionality to the PCI bus in a desktop system. It works with the system to identify and communicate with installed PC Card devices and permits a maximum data transfer rate of 132 Mbps using a 33MHz, 32-bit data transmission path. Very old laptops, such as those manufactured before 1995 and 1996, predate CardBus.

Support for PC Card devices—called Card Services and Socket Services—is loaded automatically at system startup. These services are usually loaded by the manufacturer and are often included in new PC Card devices through a software or driver installation bundle. The job of Card Services is to directly work with hardware resources—such as interrupt requests (IRQs), direct memory access (DMA), and so on—that are needed for the PC Cards installed. Socket Services, with support often integrated directly into the system BIOS, directly communicate with the controller chips used to manage the PC Card devices installed.

PC Card devices are Plug-and-Play compliant. Although many PC Card devices can be inserted and recognized with the laptop on, others won't be recognized. Check the PC Card documentation for each PC Card device.

By standard, all PC Card devices and the slots that contain them fit specific size requirements (85.6 millimeters in length by 55 millimeters wide) and connect through a 68-pin interface to the slot. Where they vary is in thickness, and this brings us to different types of PC Cards.

There are three major types of PC Card adapters and the slots which house them, including the following:

- **Type I**   With an original thickness of 3.3 millimeters (mm), this type is most frequently used for memory.

- **Type II**   These types are thicker (5.0 mm) and are used for PC Card modems, network adapters, memory, and other additions.

- **Type III**   These types are thicker still, at 10.5 mm. They're used for special adapters, some card readers, PC Card hard drives, wireless networking transmitter-receiver, and other devices. Two Type II PC Card devices can fit into one Type III slot.

Almost any functionality you can add through a PCI adapter or other means installed on a desktop PCI is available as a PC Card device, including hard drives, memory, modems and network adapters, receivers, and special-use devices. Jacks are available on PC Card devices, such as a modem or network card, to accommodate the cable connections required.

> **Note**   You might sometimes see Type IV PC Card devices and slots as well. Developed by Toshiba, these are the thickest type at 16 mm and have not yet been formally rolled into the PC Card standards. Type IV slots will accommodate the smaller types as well.

Modems and Network Adapters

Both modems and network adapters can either be integrated directly into the motherboard or added through a Type II or Type III PC Card adapter. Jacks either in the laptop housing itself can be used, or they can be connected through the PC Card adapter supply connections for either a telephone or digital Internet connection or for an Ethernet cable. See Figure 22-8 for a PC Card network adapter and connector for the network.

Figure 22-8   A LinkSys PC Card network adapter and cable connector

Wireless network adapters can also be installed through PC Card slots to communicate with a wireless network. Additionally, some laptops connect to a network through the use of the infrared port. (See the "Other Interfaces and Connections" section later in the chapter.)

Memory Card Readers

Many of today's laptops come with a multiple card reader (discussed in Chapter 20, "Major Input Devices and Gaming Hardware") that is available in PC Card format. The multiple card reader permits the easy reading of other types of removable media, such as Flash memory, by inserting it into one of the PC Card device's slots.

Drives

Most laptops ship with at least three types of drives: one floppy drive, one hard drive, and some form of CD/DVD drive.

Laptops use the same overall drive devices—hard drive, floppy, various formats of CD and DVD, and others—that desktops do. However, older laptops generally need very specific, smaller footprint hard drives, while newer laptops can sometimes accommodate the same overall size drive as a desktop. Check your documentation or manufacturer's Web site to see what a specific system has by default and your options for upgrading and replacement.

You can also connect external drives, such as universal serial bus (USB) and Institute of Electrical and Electronics Engineers (IEEE) 1394 interface drives, through their respective ports on the laptop or into a docking station (discussed in the "Docking Station" section later in this chapter) to which the laptop is then inserted. There are also PC Card controller cards that allow you to work with other types of external drives that you install directly through a Type II or Type III PC Card slot.

Before we go through the steps to replace a laptop hard drive as an example of one of the drives you can work with, understand that most laptops do not accommodate the internal installation of more than one physical hard drive. However, the external and PC Card drives mentioned before will allow you to add space as needed. What this tells you is that when you perform a laptop hard-drive upgrade, you really want to select a model capacious enough to handle the main work of the system; you can run into problems if you low-ball a system with a low-capacity drive. Doing this could force you into the addition of extra drives you'd prefer to avoid.

To replace an internal laptop hard drive, follow these steps:

1. Back up any data from the existing hard drive as needed or as possible.

2. Consult your manufacturer documentation for the laptop, and obtain the correct type of drive for the laptop.

3. Turn off the PC, disconnect it from power, and disconnect anything attached to it from power. Then locate and remove the panel covering the currently installed hard drive. Often, this access panel is located on the bottom of the PC, where one or more screws (and possibly also a slider switch to actually remove the panel) must be removed.

4. Using the method outlined in the laptop documentation, disconnect the drive and gently slide or lift the existing hard drive out of the system. Some drives will be attached to a small rack that must be separated from the hard drive (with the rack staying with the laptop itself).

5. Orienting the replacement drive, connect it the same way the existing drive was before removal and seat it firmly into place. *Do not* force it into place.

6. Replace the access panel cover.

7. Prep the drive by partitioning and formatting the same way you learned in Chapter 14, "Hard Drives and Drive Interfaces," for desktop systems, with an available boot or startup disk. Then install the operating system.

Interchangeable Drives

Some laptops allow you to exchange drives. For example, you can trade a floppy drive for a CD-ROM drive. These drives are not typically hot swappable, which means the exchange should be performed with the PC turned off. If you try to swap them while the PC is on and operating, you'll usually send the laptop into a crash or into Microsoft Windows safe mode or compatibility mode— either of which will operate more slowly and with limited services available. Check the documentation for the exchangeable drives to see whether they support hot-swapping.

With laptops that allow the exchange of drives, you typically slide a slide switch to unlock the drive, pull the current drive out of the laptop, and insert its exchange partner in its place, locking it into position. Figure 22-9 shows a CD-ROM drive being removed from a laptop with a slider mechanism present to assist.

Figure 22-9   A CD-ROM drive being slid out of its bay on a laptop, with the slider switch at the bottom right

Input

In addition to coming with a keypad, laptops typically come with at least one pointer mechanism in one (or more) of the following forms:

- **Touchpad**   This mechanism has you move your finger across a pad to simulate mouse motion. (See Figure 22-10.)

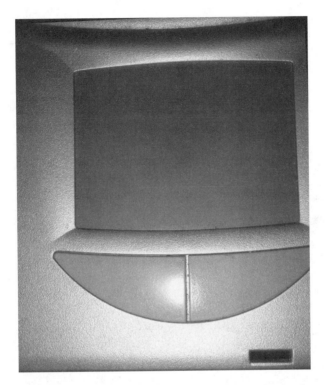

Figure 22-10   A touchpad on a recent-model notebook computer

■   **Trackball**   This is a smaller version of the trackball discussed in Chapter 20.

■   **Trackpoint**   This mechanism has you move a small point to move the cursor. This device is sometimes also called a *track stick* or a *track pointer.*

However, most laptops come with at least one method of adding full-size input devices—such as a PS/2 port, USB port (see Figure 22-11), or both—to allow the attachment of a keyboard or mouse. These devices can be used to temporarily replace or at least augment the laptop's own input mechanisms. Some docking stations and port replicators (discussed later in this section under "Docking Stations") also supply input ports and can support wireless input devices as well.

Figure 22-11 A laptop's rear with a USB port, video signal jack, and PS/2 connector for keyboard and mouse attachments

Cameras, scanners, game hardware, and other input devices can be added through standard ports (such as a serial, parallel, USB/IEEE 1394, or game port), providing the laptop has them available. Sometimes these devices also can be implemented through a specific PC Card adapter.

Printers

The same printer used for a desktop system can be connected to a laptop either through the laptop's external parallel port or USB port, depending on the printer's interface. There are also infrared capable printers that can communicate through a laptop's infrared port. (For more information, see the section "Other Interfaces and Connections" later in this chapter.)

Docking stations, discussed next in this chapter, allow you to connect a printer directly to the station so that you can simply connect the printer into the station and have your necessary peripherals immediately available. Laptops can also be attached to a network and share a network printer.

You'll also see special printers on the market that were designed for portability. These printers are lightweight enough to be carried in a large laptop case.

Docking Station

A docking station is a device that serves as a platform to allow a laptop to be used in a desktop setting without much rearrangement. For example, you can connect a desktop PC monitor, printer, and keyboard to the docking station and leave them in place so that the laptop can then be plugged into the station itself to allow easy transfer of services to the full-sized desktop devices attached. Many, if not all, docking stations also allow you to charge a laptop's battery while it's connected to the station, thus preparing it for mobile use once the laptop is detached.

This capability is particularly useful to people who use the same laptop at the office or at home as they do on the road and who want an easy way to transform the portable unit into a more desktop-oriented setting.

A docking station might also provide a wireless transceiver to permit the use of a wireless keyboard and mouse along with other services, depending on the type of station. Some also offer expansion slots and drive bays to allow you to install desktop-type adapters and drives.

Finally, you'll also see other types of docking stations, including those specifically for digital cameras and for hand-held computers, among other devices.

Port Replicator

A port replicator can serve much the same function as the newer-implemented docking station, permitting you to install desktop-style hardware to a laptop by providing common interfaces such as serial, parallel, and USB ports.

The major difference between a port replicator and a docking station is that a docking station typically offers more features, such as expansion slots and drive bays, while a port replicator usually does not. However, either can be used as a desktop station for a laptop that is moved from home to office and beyond and then back again. Some advanced port replicators come close in capabilities to a full docking station, and some docking stations advertise themselves as also being a port replicator. You can also find network port replicators as well.

Most laptops do not come with a port replicator as standard equipment. Port replicators are usually purchased separately, but you should check with the manufacturer to be sure the port replicator you want to use is fully compatible with the system it will be used to support. For manufacturers that do not make port replicators for their own laptops, you most likely can use a universal port replicator that connects through the USB or IEEE 1394 ports on the laptop.

Other Interfaces and Connections

Worth noting at this stage is the fact that while most laptops made in the last several years contain at least one USB port—which supports either version 1.1 or both 1.1 and 2.0 and is required for Windows design compatibility—many do not have 1394 ports. You can, however, obtain and install a PC Card adapter that provides ports for either or both USB and 1394. This might or might not be feasible on older laptops, especially those using earlier versions of Windows that don't support either or both of these types. Windows NT 4 supports neither USB nor IEEE 1394, Windows 98 supports USB 1.1, Windows Millennium supports both versions of USB, and Windows XP and Windows Server 2003 support both USB and IEEE 1394. Even with a compatible operating system, a slightly older laptop's BIOS might still need to be upgraded to support USB 2 or IEEE 1394.

There is one additional method of connection we've barely mentioned thus far. This method is available via the infrared or IrDA (for Infrared Data Association) port on a laptop or other mobile device. Introduced in 1993 and appearing in devices around two years later, infrared ports—which serve as both a transmitter and receiver for infrared signals—are one of the earliest and still-working forms of wireless communications between computer devices, requiring no cable to connect a laptop to a printer, desktop PC, or network. Each device must have an infrared port, however, and this must be enabled, usually in the BIOS/CMOS Setup. Many hand-held units also offer an IrDA port.

In the usual implementation, data-transfer communication is limited to roughly 115 Kbps, although there is also Fast Infrared, which permits up to 4 Mbps. The first implementation uses a universal asynchronous receiver-transmitter (UART)–based chip; the second one does not.

Infrared is different from some other forms of wireless communications because it requires strictly line-of-sight data transfer; nothing can be interposed between the two devices if the communication is to be successful. This technology is similar to a TV/video remote control, which also uses infrared communications.

Maintenance and Repair

The single most common cause of damage to a laptop is dropping the unit or banging it, unprotected, against a solid object such as a door frame or a wall. The display screen is one of the most frequently injured parts as a result. A busted display usually means you have to purchase a new laptop because the repair job involved, which must be performed by the manufacturer or an authorized service agent, will often cost more than a new laptop. An associate of mine just ran into this problem with a new unit that cost $1300. The estimate for replacing the display, which was broken when it was accidentally pushed off his lap tray on an airplane, was about $1350.

Thus, one of the best, proactive forms of maintenance you can offer a laptop is to try to promote measures that will keep it from sustaining a significant physical shock. This means encouraging the use of cases with good, shock-absorbent padding (or, for less than ideal cases, fitting them with custom-cut foam to achieve the same effect), as well as emphasizing the importance of returning the unit to its case whenever it's not in active use and under the complete control of its user. One incidental note to make here, however, is that with airport security being what it is today, a very well-padded case is apt to undergo a bit more scrutiny by security screeners and you'll usually be asked to remove a laptop from its case. Still, a well-padded bag is worth the inconvenience of waiting a couple of moments while someone checks the case.

Beyond this, a laptop is subject to the same needs as a desktop unit. Using it in a clean, dry environment is essential because laptops do not fare well with moisture. Even though you frequently see ads where someone is freed from their desktop to sit beside the ocean to type away on a laptop, the sand and salt water are not conducive to great laptop health and, practically speaking, most laptop displays aren't designed to be used in the bright sunshine anyway.

You'll also need to keep the drivers updated, the disk regularly freed of unnecessary files and applications, and the disk scanned and defragmented on a regular basis. Regular backup should be performed, although this is often achieved more easily when the unit is docked either into a station or a port replicator and an external backup drive (unless the unit has an onboard CD-R or DVD-R).

Many laptops come with diagnostic utilities specifically for the unit, and they should be run as needed to detect existing or potential problems. The battery should be monitored for signs that it no longer holds a full charge (and thus, exhausts too quickly). A backup battery for each laptop is strongly recommended.

One situation that's often overlooked with laptops is overheating. If you look at any laptop, you'll notice one, two, or more vents that are designed to transfer the heat from within the case out into the room. However, the different ways a laptop can be used might block these vents and prevent that cooling from occurring. For example, many people use a laptop while seated on a sofa or in a chair, using a cushion, a coat, or even a lap blanket as the "stand" for the laptop, any of which can cover the vents or at least partially block them. Operating a laptop for a few minutes this way is no problem, but repeating this again and again for long periods of time can have an effect on the overall life of the laptop and its internal components. However, you can find accessories designed specifically to give the laptop enough clearance from the surface to permit good venting.

Troubleshooting

Troubleshooting issues with a laptop take much the same form as troubleshooting issues with a desktop system. However, you should make use of diagnostic utilities, mentioned in the previous section, which come packaged with the laptop and consider whether overheating or physical damage (from a drop or bump) factors into the misbehavior being experienced.

A common issue with laptops occurs when the system goes into sleep or low-power mode and won't wake up. You might find that you can neither turn the unit off nor get it to fully awaken. The quickest solution I've found—and the one that works most often on a wide number of portables—is to temporarily remove the battery (not just the power cord) from the unit, wait 60 seconds or more, and then reinstall the battery. You should then be able to turn the unit on. If the situation recurs frequently, however, you should investigate the problem further to see whether a driver or an application being used does not permit the proper shift in operational modes. Temporarily, you can disable power management on the system (under the Power icon in Control Panel) until you find the proper fix, to prevent the need to "wrench" it from sleep.

Lab 22: Set Up a Laptop as a Desk-Based Network Workstation

This lab is intended to prepare you to install and configure a laptop as a desktop workstation available on and to an established network, which represents a common situation in a work environment.

Objectives

When you complete this lab, you will be able to address the following issues:

1.   The basics of installing and configuring a keyboard for use on a laptop

2.   The essentials of installing and using a standard monitor with a laptop

3. Installing a PC Card network adapter, and getting the laptop recognized on the network

4. Troubleshooting, as needed

Necessary Equipment and Resources

The following equipment and resources are necessary for completing this lab:

1. A laptop of recent vintage with a keyboard port (PS/2 or USB) and monitor port using Windows XP or later. If ports are unavailable, you will need to install a port replicator or use a docking station.

2. A keyboard and standard monitor.

3. A PC Card network adapter with a LAN cable or wireless network setup available for access.

4. Access to a network.

5. Documentation for this hardware.

6. About 30 to 60 minutes to complete this lab.

Procedures to Follow

1. Check to be sure you have all equipment necessary to complete this job. Record in your lab notes details about the hardware (the laptop, keyboard, monitor, and PC Card network adapter employed) and the operating system version you're using on the target PC.

2. Review the hardware documentation for the devices for any special recommendations on how to proceed with the attachment of the hardware to a laptop. Document in your lab notes any major deviations from the procedures discussed in the "Installation" section for each device.

3. Using the documentation as a base and with the laptop turned off, install the keyboard, monitor, and PC Card network adapter. Then turn the laptop on and let Windows detect the attached hardware. Be prepared with drivers in case they are needed. Note in your lab notes the exact steps you took.

4. From Network Connections in Windows XP or later, use the Create A New Connection option to connect the laptop to the existing net-

work, being sure to have available specific information about the network to which you will connect it. Record details in your lab notes.

5. Test the keyboard, monitor, and network access. Document this in your notes, along with any troubleshooting you needed to perform.

Lab Notes

1. Note the specific hardware and operating system used for this procedure.

    _____

    _____

    _____

2. Note any unusual steps necessary for installing the designated components.

    _____

    _____

    _____

3. Record your steps for installing and configuring the hardware for use. Note any troubleshooting measures taken.

    _____

    _____

    _____

4. Note your results in getting the laptop to communicate with the designated network.

    _____

    _____

    _____

5. Record any troubleshooting measures taken, along with the results of your work.

    _____

    _____

    _____

23

Building Your PC

Already we have reached this final chapter, bringing us to the time when you take the information from all the earlier chapters and roll it into some practical experience by assembling a system from the empty case onward. This chapter not only provides a highly valuable hands-on lab, but it also cements some fine details that are easy to miss when working with major hardware components as you have throughout this book.

A PC can be assembled very quickly. I've seen it done very well in less than 10 minutes by technicians who build systems on the fly for buyers at PC shows. However, some smart advance work needs to be done that can take far longer than the assembly itself. You have to know what the system will be called upon to do and what you need to obtain, and then you usually have to compare the prices of the necessary components before you order or purchase them so that the cost of the build stays within reasonable limits. Intelligent research always takes time at the beginning but can often save you time, expense, and nasty surprises further along in the process.

The Work Before You Build

As you were forewarned in the introduction, a substantial amount of work needs to be done before you ever order a part or pick up a screwdriver. While you'll likely one day have the experience of building a basic system from scrap and spare parts, you should also know how to act as a system architect. Acting as a system architect involves deciding among the dozens of video adapters, motherboards, CPUs, and other components to use according to the unique set of circumstances and demands for the PC you need to build.

Yet any good architect must keep in mind compatibility and the expenses or risk that might be driving the overall cost of the project—in parts, labor, and troubleshooting—outside the realm of practicality. So the advance work often involves being a good project manager, too—someone who can compare features and compatibility against need and make the job stay within a reasonable budget and time frame.

In this section, you'll tackle some of these advanced steps to help plan and secure a successful outcome: the creation of the exact PC you want or need to assemble.

The Jobs the PC Will Perform

Before you go to the time and effort to build a PC, you have to ask the following question: what are the primary jobs you'll need the PC to perform? If it's simply word processing and Web browsing, almost any bargain PC off the shelf will do. If it's a serious gaming machine, one that requires top-quality graphics for professional design work or video editing, a system that will act more as a server, or one that demands a multiprocessor setup, not every PC off the shelf will suffice and customizing the unit specifically to meet those demands might be worth the effort. Factors such as video adapter and monitor capability, the capacity and roles of the drive or drives, the amount of memory needed, and what processor-motherboard to use can play major roles in the decision-making process.

Cost Considerations

Way back in Chapter 1, "Computer Evolution," I told you that building a PC isn't the cost-saver it once was when assembling a system from scratch was almost always far cheaper than getting one with a logo and a nice printed manual. Yet determining the total cost of ownership for a self-assembled PC will usually require an analysis of costs. In most situations, we don't get to operate under the "money is no object" philosophy. For example, if it costs you twice as much to build a PC with only 10 to 15 percent more power or functionality than one you buy in the store, it makes little sense to build it yourself.

If you simply need far better video, you'll want to weigh the costs of upgrading an off-the-shelf PC with a higher quality video adapter and monitor and adding more memory as needed against the cost of building the system from the motherboard up. You'll find that several manufacturers and dealers are happy to build a system to your specifications, within reason, and they might be able to deliver it at a price that's the same or better than doing it yourself.

Once you decide to build from scratch, you need to assemble a list of needed components, compare prices for each, and put this information into something like a spreadsheet so that you can track costs. When I do this, for example, I usually create a spreadsheet that has at least three possible choices for each major category (motherboard, CPU, monitor, drives, and so on) and prices for each, along with supplier information so that I can analyze it all before I buy. You'll see a sample component list in Table 23-1 in the section entitled "Assembling Your Parts."

You can use Web sites such as BizRate.com and PriceWatch.com to see what the going prices are for each component. Once you've assembled your list with prices, it's smart to compare it against a similar premanufactured system from a major manufacturer. If there's a substantial price difference in the manufacturer's favor without sacrificing functionality, it might be smarter to buy the pre-assembled system.

Issues of Warranty

Some aspects of designing and assembling a PC can be quite fun. Others are just pesky.

One of the peskiest issues is that rather than getting a neat little one-page document stating what the PC manufacturer will cover on a new system under what circumstances and for how long a period, you must document and track the warranties for each component—or at least for the components you don't want to replace at your own cost if you don't have to.

There is no single blanket policy for warranties and components. One motherboard might have a one-year warranty, while a very similar model has a two-year warranty or longer—unless you decide the best way to clean dust and grime off a motherboard is to place it in the dishwasher, that is. (Don't laugh; it has happened.) Standard warranties will not cover every dumb or misguided thing we do to our equipment in the name of upgrading or building a PC. So be prepared to distinguish between normal use and extraordinary abuse because the manufacturer might hold you to that standard if you call with a complaint.

Sometimes, you can find a warranty that will indeed cover almost anything you can possibly do to a component or the entire system. But these are usually optional warranties you pay for over and above the regular warranty terms and coverage.

You'll also notice a large range of warranty periods among different components. Your super new CPU might be covered for one or two years, while the high-quality, seems-like-such-a-deal, refurbished flat wide-screen monitor might offer a warranty good for only between 30 and 90 days. Read each warranty carefully.

Appreciate, too, that some manufacturers can use the term "refurbished" quite differently from others. While for most, "refurbished" means a unit that has essentially been restored to a "like new" state, you can find some refurbished equipment that has had little or no repair to it before it was sold again.

Document Your Warranties

Here's a suggestion to make your life easier, particularly if it's your system or you are building it for someone who will expect you to support the unit. Once you assemble your parts, create a database or spreadsheet that contains, among other details, the warranty period and any special terms for each component used. Then place all the written warranties together into a single file folder, or scan them into your PC into a single master warranty document, so that you have both the warranty periods and the warranties themselves if you need them for later reference.

Assembling Your Parts

With the lists of parts you need, it's time to begin getting the components and checking them off on your master list. Table 23-1 shows a basic checklist, along with options for noting the price of three possibilities for each component.

As you obtain each, inspect the part to be sure it's what you wanted and is a good match with the other components you're assembling. If there's a problem, you should replace it immediately rather than wait until you begin the assembly process. Then check them off on your list, noting the final price paid for each. Keep these components together in a safe place, out of the way from usual traffic in your home and office.

Table 23-1   A PC Component List

Component	Option #1	Price	Option #2	Price	Option #3	Price
Case						
Power Supply						
Case Coolers						
Motherboard						

Table 23-1 **A PC Component List**

Component	Option #1	Price	Option #2	Price	Option #3	Price
CPU/Chipset						
CPU Fan						
Heat Sink/Thermal Compound						
Other Cooler(s)						
Memory						
Drives:						
Floppy						
Hard Drive #1						
Hard Drive #2						
CD/DVD #1						
CD/DVD #2						
Other						
Drive Cables:						
SCSI						
IDE/ATA						
Adapters:						
Video						
Sound						
Network						
Modem						
SCSI Host						
Other #1						
Other #2						
Keyboard						
Mouse/Trackball						
Monitor						
Speakers						
Printer						
UPS						
Surge Protector						
Operating System						

Compatibility

If you plan to run this as a Microsoft Windows–based system, be sure to use the Microsoft Hardware Compatibility List (HCL) or Windows Catalog (*http://www.microsoft.com/whdc/hcl/search.mspx?*) to check component compatibility for the version of Windows you plan to use. Remember, too, the concept of compatibility with other components. Review all the documentation that comes with each of your components. Also be sure you have the latest drivers for each major device on hand. Your motherboard needs to be of the correct type to accept the CPU and memory you choose to use. The motherboard must also fit the case you select. The video adapter and the monitor should be a good match for one another.

Don't fail to review earlier chapters to refresh your knowledge of such topics as motherboard and CPU compatibility. You'll also find recommendations on motherboard manufacturers' Web sites for good CPU matches, and motherboard recommendations on some of the CPU manufacturers' Web sites. There is a wealth of useful information out there.

Inspection and Inventory

As you begin to obtain the necessary components for your system, you want both to inspect them to be sure they are in good shape (without obvious defects) and are of the type you wanted and to check them off on your master parts inventory. If you decide to keep something like the spreadsheet or database of warranty information I recommended, this is a great time to enter that data. If you wait until you're done, you might never get around to the task. (I say that with an overflowing tray of documents on my desk to be entered and filed.)

Assembling the PC

Once you have your components and case, your PC repair kit, a full version of Windows, and a boot or startup disk, you're ready to begin the assembly. Remember what you learned in Chapter 2, "The Operating System's Role in Hardware," about using a suitable work area that is free from distractions but accessible to a telephone as well as a second Internet-ready system that can be used to research additional information as needed.

One consideration to take into account is that depending on how you purchased your components, some of the work might already be done for you. For example, your case might already have a power supply installed or you might have purchased a motherboard with the CPU and fan already mounted and the configuration already in place.

Examine the Case

Too often, a case gets overlooked until the last moment before building a system. That's a mistake because only when you have the case can you begin to fully assess the job ahead and any particular obstacles you might face.

Once you have a case (shown in Figure 23-1), remove the cover, look the case over well, and try to picture how you'll arrange the components and how much flexibility you'll have in regard to placement. If you're actually reusing a case rather than purchasing a new one, clean the case with a lint-free cloth and remove any dust and debris.

Power Supply

5.25" Drive Bays

3.5" Drive Bays

Expansion
Slots

Figure 23-1   An open case that allows you to examine the layout carefully and visualize the assembly process

Consider which drives should go in which drive bays, for example, and think about where your adapters will be placed in their slots. If you have an adapter that requires a bit more clearance room, take this into account. Some adapters have components that are so tall they barely fit under another adapter when the two are installed side by side in the usually horizontal PCI slots.

Also, before you start, you might want to take the time to remove the holder plates that are typically found on empty PCI slots (shown in Figure 23-2) and the face plates for empty drive bays you plan to use. Also examine the motherboard and visualize how you need to place and mount it within the case frame. As you do this, determine whether you need to remove retainer screws or move *standoffs*, which are the small devices used to hold the motherboard above the mounting plate so that it doesn't come into direct contact with the frame. You must remember the provisos from Chapter 6, "Central Processing Units," about taking care in the mounting process. This is also the time to be completely sure the motherboard you have acquired will indeed fit the case you've purchased because the motherboard is not something you can modify. You'll need to obtain a different case if it won't fit.

Figure 23- 2 Removing holders such as slot faces and drive face plates

Review your case documentation, too, because not all cases arrive completely ready to be populated with parts. You might need to attach feet to the case, for example, to make it sit high enough above the surface of the table or floor.

Also look for extremely sharp edges. Some cases have such razor sharp edges (usually because the case is less expensive and has not been finished off properly) that you can easily lacerate yourself. It's no joke—people have been rushed to the hospital to staunch the bleeding from a deep cut incurred this way. I sometimes take a simple file (nail or other type) to reduce the sharpness of the edges before I begin to install components. Doing this reduces the risk of injury to myself and to slender cables.

With the case ready, you can proceed with the assembly at your own pace. However, you should do the total assembly in one progressive, continuous operation, if possible. This lessens the risk you'll forget to perform some aspect of the assembly that you left undone in a previous session. You probably want to keep a running notebook as you work, or at least use a checklist like the one in Table 23-1 earlier in this chapter.

Another Approach

It often makes sense to do a very basic installation first and then test to see whether this works before you begin adding everything else, such as PC bus adapters, into the system. A basic installation typically includes the motherboard (and connecting the power switch and any additional cables from the case to the motherboard), power supply (and its connections to the motherboard), CPU and cache, and memory. You can add a video adapter and monitor if you want, but you won't get very far in the boot process until drives are added anyway. The point is to determine whether the power supply engages and the PC tries to power up without onboard beeps (which can be present even without a sound adapter or speakers installed because there might be a very basic onboard speaker) indicating a problem during startup.

Prepping the Motherboard

In Chapter 5, you learned about the essentials of installing and replacing a motherboard as well as its major components. Please review that chapter, especially if it's been awhile since you read it, before you get to work. Also remember to exercise extreme care because a motherboard and the items you install on it can be damaged or can break without much force applied.

With that said, understand that some of the work involved here can be done before you install the motherboard into the case. In many respects, this is desirable because it can be more difficult to work with smaller components—such as positioning the shunt properly on a jumper—once the motherboard is installed. It's critical that you consult your motherboard manual as you do this because you want to get your settings right the first time and then double-check and triple-check them before you mount the motherboard.

Begin by removing the motherboard from its antistatic bag or box. Rather than laying it flat on a tabletop, consider placing it on top of the bag or box from which you removed it. Don't leave this unattended for any period of time. (I'll spare you a particularly nasty story about a cat with an upset stomach that snuck into my work area while I was assembling a system.)

As you consult the manual, locate the specific parts of the motherboard, such as jumpers, which must be set as part of the process. If the motherboard manual isn't great, check the manufacturer's Web site. Keep this site up and available on another system, hopefully within easy consulting distance of the system you're assembling. This is a bad time to employ guesswork.

To configure the motherboard, you need to do the following:

■ Set the voltage.

■ Configure the motherboard for the speed of the processor used.

■ Establish the cache size and type.

■ Set the asynchronous memory speed.

Let's look at these tasks one at a time, because you might not need to do all of them.

Setting the Voltage

Depending on the type of processor used in the system you're building, you need to set either a single voltage or a dual voltage for the CPU. Older CPUs use a single voltage; newer CPUs use dual voltage to establish both core voltage as well as input-output (I/O) voltage. Voltage should be set to match the requirements of the CPU being installed. (Check the CPU documentation.)

Voltage is usually set through the use of jumpers (discussed in detail in Chapter 14, "Hard Drives and Drive Interfaces"), which are related to drives but typically used on motherboards as well. On some newer designs, proper voltage is detected and set automatically, requiring no physical settings change on your part.

Configuring the Motherboard for Processor Speed

Here, again, you need to check the motherboard and CPU documentation to determine the appropriate settings for system bus speed as well as the proper multiplier needed. Processor speed is often set through two different jumpers (one for bus speed and one for the multiplier)—the location for each should be indicated in the motherboard documentation or in CMOS Setup.

Setting the Cache Size and Type

Although setting the cache size and type isn't always required (especially if the cache is internal in nature, which most are today), a jumper is sometimes present on the motherboard to configure for the cache size and type. Check your documentation and set this if needed.

Setting the Memory Bus Speed

This is another option not necessary for all setups, but a jumper might be present for setting memory bus speed if the motherboard supports the use of asynchronous SDRAM. (Via chipsets might use this.) You might also have to set this if you want the memory speed to operate at a different clock rate from the system as a whole. As with other options, this option might not be set through a physical jumper but through CMOS Setup.

Other Jumper Settings

Review the motherboard documentation along with the motherboard itself to see what other jumper settings are available and what the factory has set them to by default. These settings can include a jumper set to On to allow you to make changes to the system through CMOS Setup, as well as a jumper that lets you configure whether or not the BIOS can be automatically updated through *flashing*. To prevent a BIOS-targeting virus from making changes to your system, the BIOS flashing jumper should be set to Off and then switched to On only when you are actually performing a BIOS update.

Now let's move forward to install the CPU itself.

Installing the CPU and CPU Fan

With your motherboard now configured, it's time to remove the CPU from its antistatic bag or case to install it on the motherboard. Remember that this process is covered in Chapter 6 and exact steps will depend on the type of processor and the type of insertion method used by it.

For example, if the CPU uses some version of the zero insertion force (ZIF) insertion type, you would move the lever to open it for insertion. Then you orient the CPU so that the mark on the CPU package indicating Pin 1 corresponds to Pin 1 on the socket or slot. Press it gently into place and then lower the lever to secure it into its position. If you're working with a slot rather than a socket, you need to line up the CPU with the socket.

However, you want to hold off just a moment. Following the instructions in the documentation, you might need to install the CPU fan either just before you install the CPU or immediately thereafter. Then connect the CPU fan connector to its proper place on the motherboard, as defined in the instructions. (See Figure 23-3.)

Figure 23-3   Connecting the CPU fan to its connector on the mother-board to provide power to it

There is also the issue of the heat sink. On a slotted CPU, the heat sink is applied to the processor before the CPU is installed, while on a socket-type CPU, this is done after installation. To install the heat sink, apply a thin but full layer of thermal compound to the area where the heat sink will be attached, and then press the heat sink itself into place following any advisories in the motherboard or CPU installation instructions. Clips might be present to help hold the heat sink in place. Remove any extra thermal compound before you proceed by using a small, lint-free cloth. Do not let this ooze out and create a mess.

Installing the Cache

Unless you're constructing a system that uses a much older CPU type, the cache will be internally mounted and you will not have to install it yourself. However, if you're working with an older CPU, follow the instructions for installing the cache to its appropriate slot by lining it up with the module and pressing it into place.

Installing Memory

Remove the sticks of memory you'll add to the system from their antistatic bag or case, and install them on the motherboard (as shown in Figure 23-4), starting with the socket with the lowest number and moving forward. Refer to Chapter 7, "Memory," for specifics. Be sure these are firmly and fully seated and that the clips on either end were secured around them as they were pushed into place.

Figure 23-4   Installing the memory into the memory sockets on the motherboard

Before you finish this part and install the motherboard into the case, review your work along with the instructions to assure yourself that everything is jumpered and installed as it should be. Again, it's usually far easier to work with jumpers and such before the motherboard is actually mounted than after.

Installing the Motherboard into the Case

Begin by looking back and forth between the motherboard and the case chassis to which the motherboard will be installed to mentally line up the screw holes and how to apply the spaces and stand-offs. It's better to do this now than to juggle the motherboard around a lot once you begin the mounting process.

Locate the plastic stand-offs that should be present either with the case or motherboard. Insert one in each eyelet hole in the motherboard where another hole is available corresponding to the motherboard on the case.

Next, slide the motherboard into place, being sure it rests on the plastic spacers so that it doesn't come into direct contact with the chassis. Now push the stand-offs from the motherboard into the eyelet holes in the case itself.

Apply the screws to the proper locations (usually through the spacers) on the motherboard and begin to screw them down using a screwdriver. (See Figure 23-5.) You do *not* want to overtighten, but you do want to secure the motherboard into place, leaving no extra room that allows the motherboard to shift about.

Figure 23- 5 Screwing the motherboard into place

Finally, carefully review your work before you proceed. The motherboard should not touch the chassis or the mounting plate and should be firmly mounted without leaving any real ability to bend it. Also be sure that a battery is installed in the CMOS battery slot, as shown in Figure 23-6. If not, you must obtain one (usually for between $3 and $10 at any store that sells a variety of batteries). There are several types of battery used for CMOS, from the very common ("AA" or "AAA") to the harder-to-find.

Figure 23-6   Verifying the CMOS battery installed on the motherboard

Installing the Power Supply

Exactly when you install the power supply can be a matter of preference. Some prefer to do it as one of the last steps in the build process, while others perform that step even before doing the work with the motherboard. Others, like me, prefer to install it at this stage, once the motherboard is mounted.

Consulting both the case and power supply directions as well as the steps offered in Chapter 8, "Power Supplies and Cooling," install the power supply and apply the necessary connections between the power supply and the motherboard. The power supply connections are usually a 20-wire bundle with a connector keyed specifically for insertion into the motherboard.

At this time, you also might want to install the cables running from the front of the computer (covering the power button, the LED light, and so on) to the motherboard. (See Figure 23-7.) This step can also be performed later in the process if you prefer, but it must get done at some time.

Figure 23-7   Plugging the LED and power connector from the front of the case to the motherboard

Here's another point you should know if you're building a system with older components. Non-ATX-style motherboards often supply the I/O ports—the connector pins from the motherboard to multifunction I/O ports—but you must actually install and connect them. Do so following the directions provided. If you're using an ATX or later motherboard, this work is already taken care of for you. It's likely the vast majority of you will have a motherboard with these already installed.

Drives

Some technicians would take steps at this point to begin to populate the motherboard with any additional adapters they want. However, I suggest you install the drives at this point simply because, in some cases, you need more room to work than the case structure allows and you don't want to bump your hands or the drives against delicate printed circuit boards.

Review Chapter 13, "Other Controller Cards," Chapter 14, "Drive Interfaces and Hard Drives," and Chapter 15, "CD and DVD Drives," for instructions for installing your drives and the cables connecting them to other drives, to the motherboard, or to the SCSI host adapter. (See Figure 23-8.) If you're using a SCSI configuration, you'll install the SCSI host adapter when you install additional components on the motherboard. You need to configure Integrated Device Electronics/Advanced Technology Attachment (IDE/ATA) drives ahead of time for whether they are a primary, a secondary, or the only drive on an IDE controller, while SCSI drives need to be chained through the SCSI cable, which must end in proper termination.

Figure 23-8   An ATA cable being installed to the IDE channel controller on the motherboard

Remember for later that IDE/ATA drives should be autodetected through CMOS Setup, while SCSI drives usually will need to be assessed through the setup utility for the SCSI host adapter installed.

Installing Components on the Motherboard

Taking them one at a time, remove your adapters from their packaging and install them on the PC, using the documentation and information from the appropriate chapters (that is, those dealing with video, audio, network hardware, and the SCSI host adapter) as guidelines. Be certain each is fully and firmly seated and that raised components from one adapter do not come into contact with another adapter. Also double-check to make sure you have all your bases covered. If the motherboard you obtained does not contain onboard video, audio, networking, or a SCSI host adapter, you need to install them as adapters.

Are you installing any additional cooling devices, such as a fan or a drive cooler? These items can be installed at this time.

Externals

First, don't replace the cover now that you're done with installing internal components on the system. You'll want the cover to remain off until you have the system up and running properly so that you don't have to remove the cover to troubleshoot or adjust anything.

Pull together the externals that must be installed on your system, including the following items:

- Monitor
- Keyboard
- Mouse
- Printer
- Audio speakers
- Other externals, such as a scanner, graphics tablet, gaming hardware, and so on

You might want to start by just installing absolutely necessary externals such as the keyboard, mouse, and monitor. In this way, you can reduce the variables if you experience a problem that requires troubleshooting. Be sure that any equipment, such as a monitor, that must be connected to a separate power source as well as the PC itself is both plugged in and turned on. Look for the power indicator light on each of these devices.

If any of these external devices are to be connected through universal serial bus (USB) or Institute of Electrical and Electronics Engineers (IEEE) 1394 ports, wait until you have the system running with your operating system in place to install them. If you are planning to install a USB keyboard as your primary keyboard, you'll want to install a standard keyboard temporarily simply for feasibility at this stage. You can always replace it with the new USB keyboard later. Attach each device to its necessary connection using both the instructions provided with each piece of equipment and what you've learned in this book.

With this step complete, it's time to test your work. We'll do this next.

Testing

At this point, your system doesn't have drives prepared or an operating system installed, so your ability to test is a bit limited. Plug the power cord in. Turn the system on, and see whether you get an error message. You should get an error message that reads something like "no operating system" or "non-system disk." The point of this testing is to be sure the system will indeed turn on.

If it does, you can then enter CMOS Setup (through whatever key combination is required to do so), enter the time and date, and see whether the drives are automatically detected, at the very least. You want to check and perhaps modify any motherboard configuration settings that need to be assigned through CMOS Setup rather than through jumpers on the motherboard. Remember to save your changes when you exit.

Once you've ascertained that things are as they should be, you can use a boot or startup disk to see whether the system will boot. If it does, hurray! Put away the headache remedy and celebrate. If you have SCSI drives installed, it's time to run the SCSI setup utility. (See Chapter 13.)

If the system doesn't turn on, it's time to troubleshoot and that's best done by trying to determine where in the process the system is not responding. If you can't even get the system to turn on, connections might be wrong or loose. Recheck everything to verify the connections are OK. If the power supply doesn't power up, it might be bad.

Finishing Up

Once the PC appears to be working, it's time to prepare the drives and install the operating system, both of which provide additional tests of the system you've built. Follow the instructions in Chapter 14 for preparing a new master boot drive (including partitioning and formatting) for use as well as installing the operating system. This requires you to run Setup from the Windows installation CD, but remember that you need a full or nonupgrade version as your base.

You might have heard the term *benchmark testing*. Benchmarks refer to specific markers recognized—if not always by the industry as a whole, then by a large group of hardware gurus—as being appropriate standards for measuring the performance of a system or a particular aspect of a system (such as video, CPU, drive speed, and other factors) against the performance of a same or similar system or component. This process essentially involves gauging how your hardware stacks up against the competition.

These tests can be worthwhile to be sure a system or a component therein is functioning within reasonable performance levels. The downloadable SiSoft Sandra, PC Magazine benchmarks, and WinBench are among some of the most commonly used benchmark tests, and there are add-ons available to specifically test audio, video, CPU, and drive capacity among different types of drives.

Unfortunately, achieving great benchmark results is sometimes treated as a whole pursuit unto itself. People can become so zealous about outdoing the results others get with the same hardware that their efforts are detrimental to using their systems for normal work—that is, they don't want to reduce their benchmark rating by tweaking their system for optimum workload performance rather than optimum benchmark performance. My recommendation is to use benchmark tests as a troubleshooting and testing tool and don't concern yourself with performance egotism. The PC is, at its foundation, a tool and should be treated as such.

Finally, there is one more issue related to benchmarks you should understand. The use of non-brand-name hardware can cause you to have to work hard to get the device recognized by the system and can sometimes result in the device not being identified properly and rated by a benchmark study. For example, the video adapter on one of my systems is a name-brand component, but it's not directly supported by my version of Windows. As a result, it's frequently misidentified and the ratings for it vary widely. Take this into account if you're using non-standard equipment on your system.

Troubleshooting

If there is a problem, try to examine the symptoms (such as no power, inappropriate sound or vibration, or some functionality is available but not all) and determine the most likely causes. Don't guess and don't assume that there is just one problem afoot. It's possible to make two or more mistakes in the process that might prevent the system or a specific component within from starting up or operating properly.

Should you get frustrated and find it hard to troubleshoot, walk away for a short period of time. When you return, your eyes and thought processes should be refreshed and ready to tackle the problem again.

Also, don't hesitate to review the "Troubleshooting" section for the installation of individual components. Something as simple as one bad cable, such as for a SCSI or IDE/ATA hard drive, can be a big deal. Expect that drivers will need to be updated for many devices, and perform these updates as soon as possible.

Even when it seems as if everything in the new system is purring along, you should try to monitor the system carefully, especially during the first 72 hours. This is best done with the cover off so that you can listen, smell, and see better what is happening inside the case. Listen for odd or grinding sounds, which can indicate a problem. Smell to be sure the initial aroma of new electronics "burning in" is beginning to fade and that no smoke is present. New equipment usually produces a smell only for a short period before it begins to fade. Look to see whether fans aren't turning or whether something appears precariously seated. Also verify that lights that should be on are. Watch for error messages that need to be investigated. At the end of this trial period with everything operating properly, you can replace the case cover and assume the assembly is a success.

The trial period, however, is an excellent time to load the most aggressive, demanding applications you have and see how the new system performs with them. Hardware-intensive games, video production and editing software, and working with large data files are some examples of this. Doing this can help you identify deficits with the system or one of its components that should be corrected or replaced as soon as possible.

Congratulations. With this final lab, our work together is done. Yet with that said, I encourage you to think of this as the foundation for a lifetime of learning. Even though you have tackled a great deal in this book, the industry and the systems we use are changing daily. Today's hot new procedure and device is tomorrow's dim memory. Spending even a short time away from PC technical work can mean a great deal of missed news and new detail.

Don't miss an opportunity to roll up your sleeves and learn with your eyes and hands. Read all you can, and try to hook up with a good online technical message forum, one in which you can see real questions and problems being presented along with information to help them get resolved.

Lab 23: Develop a Plan for Building a PC, and Then Assemble a PC from Scratch

This lab is intended to prepare you to both plan and assemble a system. Although the PC you build might not be the same as the PC you design through planning, it gives you the breadth of the total experience, along with the necessary steps for success.

Objectives

When you complete this lab, you will be able to address the following issues:

1.   The components needed to build a system

2.   Compatibility and pricing of those components as part of a build plan

3.   Assembling a PC from basic parts

4.   Troubleshooting, as needed, in the building and successful booting of the PC you assemble

Necessary Equipment and Resources

The following equipment and resources are necessary for completing this lab:

1.   Access to the Internet for the purpose of researching components, compatibility, and price

2.   The case and all components needed to assemble a basic PC, plus a boot disk and a full version of Windows to install

3.   Documentation for this hardware

4.   About 2 to 3 hours to complete this lab

Procedures to Follow

1.   Using the checklist in Table 23-1 and the knowledge you have gleaned along the way in this book, come up with a master component list for building a PC from the case through external necessities such as a printer, keyboard, mouse, and monitor. Note the compatibility with the operating system version you intend to use, along with price for each component. Come up with a final price for the assembled system. Record details about the hardware and pricing in your lab notes, and compare them to a pre-assembled model from a major manufacturer such as Dell, Gateway, Hewlett-Packard, or IBM.

2.   Review the hardware documentation, do your advance planning through examination of the case, and build a PC from the available components for this lab. Document your process in your lab notes along with any troubleshooting necessary.

3.   Once the PC appears to be operating, use your boot or startup disk and begin installing the operating system. Record your results, along

with any necessary troubleshooting, in your lab notes. Also document any surprises you found along the way. Then perform a full system review, through Device Manager and any diagnostic utilities you have on hand, and record special information in your lab notes.

Lab Notes

1. Using as many separate sheets of paper as you need (or an electronic spreadsheet), document the hardware you want to use to build your PC, along with the specific role or jobs this PC will be used to perform. How does the PC you intend to build compare in price and functionality against a target pre-assembled manufacturer system?

    _____

    _____

    _____

2. Document your process of building a PC from components, including specifics about the hardware used.

    _____

    _____

    _____

3. Record your results in getting the system up and running with an operating system, and add any special notes about any problems discovered in Device Manager.

    _____

    _____

    _____

Index

Kate J. Chase

Kate J. Chase is the author or editor of almost 20 technical books, an experienced journalist and columnist, and has operated highly successful online support communities on America Online and MSN for more than a decade. While she specializes in PC hardware and operating systems, she also writes and prepares training programs for those striving to learn popular applications such as the products found within the Microsoft Office System and has written extensively about help desk issues and customer relationship management. Kate resides in northern Vermont, where she also runs her business, Chase Online Management.

The manuscript for this book was prepared and submitted to Microsoft Press in electronic form. Text files were prepared using Microsoft Word 2000 for Windows. Pages were composed by nSight, Inc., using Adobe FrameMaker for Windows, with text in Garamond Book and display type in Helvetica Condensed. Composed pages were delivered to the printer as electronic prepress files.

Cover Designer:	Patricia Bradbury
Copywriter:	Julia Stasio
Interior Book Designer:	James D. Kramer
Layout Artists:	Peter Amirault and Joanna Zito
Electronic Artist:	Joel Panchot
Project Manager:	Susan H. McClung
Technical Editor:	James Robertson
Copyeditor:	Roger LeBlanc
Proofreaders:	Charlotte Maurer and Robert Saley
Indexer:	Rebecca Plunkett